Sustaining the Cherokee Family

To Arthew —— ——

for — celebration —
of — family history!

Rose — Stremfar

Top section:
- Myrtle L Winget — 21853 (Sections 8)
- Nelson Crittenden — 20793 (Section 9)
- Lydia A Crittenden
- Henry D Holland — 1376
- Thomas R Holland — 1376
- James B Holland — 1373, 203
- Infant Crittenden — 20801, 30655, 20801 (Section 10)
- Hummingbird Crittenden — 20769
- Stoll Jackson — 20800
- Susan Crittenden
- Walter Jackson — 25909
- Coo... Critte... — 305...

Middle section:
- ...nget — 15245 (Section 17)
- Johnson Mannon — 15245
- Thomas Mounce — 25110, 25314, 23314
- Ned Hatlin — 30599
- Rosanna Mounce — 20800, 25109, 15646 (Section 18)
- Wyly Beavers — 15646
- John Heller — 15646
- Watt Crittenden — 20301 (Section 15)
- 20782
- Martin Foreman — 20802
- Betsy Burd — 20782
- James Mulkey — 576

Lower middle:
- Mary E Washington — 15239, 15235
- Elizabeth Washington — 15235
- Daniel B Frog — 25855 (Section 20)
- John Sand — 49631, 20363
- Noah Sand — 20363
- George Hughes — 20363 (Section 21)
- Eliza Siwaie — 16573
- Linnie Hughes
- Johnson Mannon
- Susan Burd (Section 22)
- Betsy Burd

Bottom section:
- ...m Chewey — 26060 (Sections 29)
- Samuel Chewey — 25853
- Mose Crittenden — 1331
- John Pierce
- Eliza Siwaie — 16573 (Section 28)
- Susan Burd — 30638
- Susan Burd — 30638
- Elizabeth Washington — 15235
- Edward C Gordon — 1113 (Section 27)
- White... (Section 33, 34)

Sustaining the Cherokee Family

Kinship and the Allotment of an Indigenous Nation

ROSE STREMLAU

First Peoples
New Directions in Indigenous Studies

THE UNIVERSITY OF NORTH CAROLINA PRESS

CHAPEL HILL

*Publication of this book was made possible, in part,
with a grant from the Andrew W. Mellon Foundation.*

The paper in this book meets the guidelines for permanence and
durability of the Committee on Production Guidelines for Book Longevity
of the Council on Library Resources.

The University of North Carolina Press has been a member of the
Green Press Initiative since 2003.

Library of Congress Cataloging-in-Publication Data
Stremlau, Rose.
Sustaining the Cherokee family : kinship and the allotment of an indigenous nation /
Rose Stremlau.
p. cm. — (New directions in indigenous studies)
Includes bibliographical references and index.
ISBN 978-0-8078-3499-2 (cloth : alk. paper)
ISBN 978-0-8078-7204-8 (pbk : alk. paper)
1. Cherokee Indians—Land tenure. 2. Cherokee Indians—Cultural assimilation.
3. Cherokee Indians—Kinship. 4. Allotment of land—Government policy—
Cherokee Nation, Oklahoma. 5. Cherokee Nation, Oklahoma—History.
6. Cherokee Nation, Oklahoma—Social conditions. 7. United States—Social policy.
8. United States—Race relations. I. Title.
E99.C5S8665 2011
976.6004'97557—dc22
2011008427

Portions of this book were published, in somewhat different form, as
"In Defense of 'This Great Family Government and Estate': Cherokee Masculinity
and the Opposition to Allotment," in *Southern Masculinities*, ed. Craig T. Friend
(Athens: University of Georgia Press, 2009), 65–82; and "'To Domesticate and
Civilize Wild Indians': Allotment and the Campaign to Reform Indian Families,
1875–1887," *Journal of Family History* 30.3 (July 2005): 265–86.
Used by permission.

For Jack

Contents

Illustrations and Map

Acknowledgments

The staffs at the following libraries and archives guided me while I researched this project: the Hampton University Archives in Hampton, Virginia; the Oklahoma History Society in Oklahoma City, Oklahoma; the Western History Collection at Oklahoma University in Norman, Oklahoma; the Davis Library at the University of North Carolina in Chapel Hill, North Carolina; the Livermore Library at the University of North Carolina in Pembroke, North Carolina; and the southwestern branch of the National Archives and Records Administration (NARA) in Fort Worth, Texas. Staff at the Red Cross Hazel Braugh Records Center and Archives and the Cherokee Nation GeoData Center shared materials and answered my questions. Many librarians and archivists have been generous with their time and knowledge, and they have made my research more efficient and enjoyable. In particular, I thank Kent Carter, Meg Hacker, Ridley Kessler, Mary Jane Warde, Bill Welge, and Chad Williams.

Others have supported me financially through the stages of this project: the University of North Carolina at Chapel Hill, particularly the Royster Society of Fellows; the American Philosophical Society; the University of North Carolina at Pembroke; the American Association of University Women; and the First Peoples Initiative. The generosity of those I have never met has made this achievement possible, and I am grateful to these donors.

I am humbled by the enthusiasm for my research shown by colleagues over the years. Vernon Burton has mentored me since I was a college student, and he inspired me to become a scholar. Since the beginning of my academic career, Mike Green and Theda Perdue have struck the balance between "the carrot" and "the stick," and I know they will be proud to read this book. The historians at the University of North Carolina at Chapel

Hill nurtured me intellectually when this project was in its infancy, and then my colleagues in the Departments of History and American Indian Studies at the University of North Carolina at Pembroke encouraged my bringing it to completion. Over the years, respondents at many conferences have improved my analysis. Several special women have gone out of their way to support me and this project in unexpected ways at important times; thanks are due to Janet Gentes, Kathleen Hilton, Sandra Hoeflich, and Susan West.

Before I knew I could do this, Mark Simpson-Vos, my editor, believed that I could. I am glad that he was right and that I benefited from his direction and encouragement. The readers, Katherine Osburn and Margaret Jacobs, provided suggestions that enabled me to dramatically improve my work, and I hope the final product does right by their thoughtful reports. Catherine Cox worked with me to improve the manuscript, and through her feedback, I first saw this project as whole.

Before I began researching allotment in the Cherokee Nation, I had never been to Oklahoma. A friend from there told me that Oklahomans are the most down-to-earth, hospitable people I could ever know. Over the years, I have found this to be true. Many improved this manuscript with their enthusiasm, and I am deeply appreciative. Bill Welge, a living encyclopedia of Oklahoma history, read an entire draft of this book. I appreciate his feedback and support. Special thanks go to members of the Goingsnake District Historical Association who shared information and stories about their ancestors. Several years ago, Gail Crittenden sent me copies of photographs from her collection. When I opened her package, I saw the faces of the people about whom I was writing for the first time. I am grateful for that kind gesture. Several Cherokee scholars—especially Julia Coates, Wyman Kirk, and Benny Smith—provided feedback and insight. Jack D. Baker deserves special thanks. Many years ago, he suggested to Perdue and Green that someone should write about allotment among Cherokees. When that someone became me, he encouraged and supported my research, which included telling me what I got wrong. I would not have started this project without Jack, and, without question, I could not have finished it without him. Likewise, Richard Allen thoughtfully critiqued the manuscript. I am honored that he took the time and effort to share his honest thoughts, and I am glad that he delivered them with humor and kindness.

I could not have finished this project without a circle of supportive scholars who have become dear friends. My early writing group mates,

Pam Lach and Barb Hahn, celebrated each small accomplishment with me over sangria swirls at Los Pos in Chapel Hill, and their feedback and counsel enabled me to rediscover pleasure in a process that had become a struggle. Jaime Martinez and Ryan Anderson have continued in this tradition of combining feedback and fellowship with good results. The friendship of Charles Beem, Jane Haladay, Mary Ann Jacobs, Malinda Maynor Lowery, and Cary Miller has been one of the best rewards of my chosen profession. My dearest "old" friend, Angie Oliver, regularly reminded me that I had a life before this project and that I would have one again after I completed it. She and my parents have weathered the highs and lows of this whole process no less than I have done. For the last dozen years, Leon and Rosemary Stremlau have encouraged me with their cheer, a line from a favorite old movie. I love the irony of my northerner parents motivating their daughter, who has made her home in the South and who is writing a book on American Indian history, by shouting out a line from a John Wayne movie in which he played an angst-ridden Union general: "Get 'er done, Johnny Reb! Get 'er done!" And so I did.

In the middle of this process, I met and married the best man I know, Stephen Herbster. He never complained about the evenings and weekends I have spent working on this book rather than enjoying time with him. He picked up take-out whenever I asked for it, and he surprised me with comic books when I met deadlines along the way. I have benefited from a million hugs and back rubs and have been refreshed by miles of long walks with him and our dogs. Through him, I have learned the meaning of devotion and have come to appreciate that it is the richest, deepest love that champions the dream of another.

Sustaining the Cherokee Family

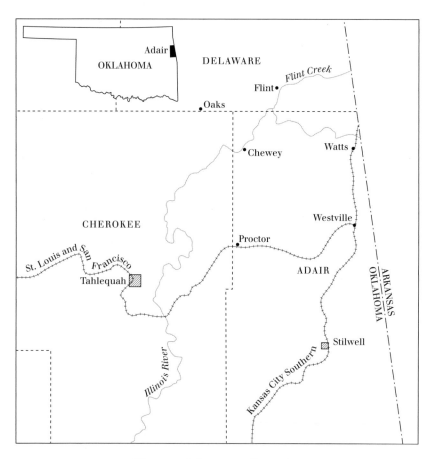

Chewey and the surrounding region

Introduction

In the early months of 1920, Nannie Wolfe lost the farm in Chewey, Adair County, Oklahoma, that had been her home for thirty-four years. She was then sixty-eight years old. Nannie had done nothing wrong; the decisions leading to this outcome were not hers. This process began in 1905 when the Dawes Commission allotted the farm that she shared with her husband, Tom, to him because they believed adult men to be the rightful heads-of-households, a notion common among Anglo-Americans but inconsistent with gender roles among Cherokees. They assigned her land to the northeast in what became the boundary between Delaware and Cherokee Counties. Like others categorized as "full bloods," the Wolfes' homestead was tax exempt, but that protection ended with the death of its legal owner.[1] On June 7, 1914, Lewis Sourjohn, a twenty-five-year-old Cherokee man visiting his maternal relatives in the area, killed Tom Wolfe. Sourjohn subsequently pled guilty to manslaughter in the first degree and was sentenced to ten years in McAlester, the Oklahoma penitentiary.[2]

At first, Nannie stayed in the home she had made with Tom for twenty-eight years, even though her husband's son from a prior marriage, John Wolfe, had inherited half of it and was actively searching for a buyer for the farm. Sam Chewey, her grown son from a previous relationship, lived with her. They had twenty acres under cultivation. When Sam joined the American Expeditionary Force and was stationed in France during World War I, Nannie kept up the farm. John may have helped her with the heavy labor; he certainly remained familiar with the condition of the homestead on which he had grown to adulthood while he was trying to sell it. After the armistice, Sam returned home and presumably would have resumed working on his family's farm, but by then, John had found a buyer for his father's allotment.[3] John and his wife, Dora, were

Tom and Nannie Wolfe and some of their children. Seated from left to right:
Tom Wolfe; Sam Chewey; Nannie Wolfe, Sam's mother. Standing from left to right:
Jesse Wolfe, Tom's son; Louella Sunday, Nannie's daughter; John Wolfe, Tom's son.
Photo courtesy of Jack D. Baker.

expecting their seventh child, and the sale would bring much needed cash into their large household. The couple's finances were particularly precarious because they rented land on nearby Spring Creek. They could not live on either of their allotments, which were not well suited for farming and were located too far from the school their children attended. More important, the land that they rented kept them close to kin; their neighbors were Dora's sisters, Sissa and Tinna.[4]

The buyer had served the war effort in another capacity. David Watkins was a young white man from Missouri who had moved to Oklahoma to work in the lead and zinc mines in Picher, Ottawa County. A return to peace had reduced the demand for the metals, but Watkins had saved $1,000 with which to purchase a farm.[5] That money would be split evenly by Tom Wolfe's heirs, his son and his widow. Nannie did not want to sell her home, but she did not have the money to buy out John or pay the taxes on it. As a subsistence farmer, her only source of cash was her allotment, which was unimproved land of poor quality. At most, it was worth $500 *if* she could find a buyer. And so Nannie Wolfe lost the farm that she had

John and Dora Wolfe and their children. From left to right, their children are Janie, Agnes, Jessie, and Reece. Photo courtesy of Jack D. Baker.

built with her late husband.[6] Sam briefly attended a mechanic school in Kansas City, Missouri, before returning to Adair County to marry, raise a family, and farm.[7] Nannie never left the community. She moved into the home of her neighbors Jim and Bettie Wilson. Bettie was her maternal niece, her sister's daughter. There, she died in 1922.[8]

Plainly told, the story of allotment is about the loss of land, and yet the reasons why Nannie Wolfe's farm became that of David Watkins are anything but simple. The determinations of the lawmakers who designed allotment policy and the clerks who implemented it shaped her life, but so did the needs and expectations of the relatives and neighbors among whom she lived. Allotment created a predatory system that legally robbed Cherokees of the land promised to them in perpetuity in treaties, and this process particularly discriminated against women, but those facts do not explain why and how Cherokees believed and acted as they did in response to allotment. Kinship does. It was this extended network of relationships and the obligations and hospitality associated with it that brought Lewis Sourjohn to the Chewey area, that account for John and Dora Wolfe's decisions, and that enabled Nannie to survive the loss of her husband and her farm without ever being destitute or homeless. That Cherokees responded to the policy and used their allotments in ways consistent with their culture and the values and behaviors common among them is not surprising, in retrospect, but to the advocates of allotment, this came as a shock because the policy was intended to sever these fundamental relationships by preventing Cherokees from sustaining them and convincing them that doing so was wrong.

This book examines this effort by the federal government to make Cherokees indistinguishable from other Americans by closely focusing on the families and family structures that had differentiated Native Americans from European Americans and their descendants since contact. By the late nineteenth century, the U.S. government had conquered and contained American Indian people by relocating them onto reservations and into Indian Territory, and it next concentrated on assimilating them into American society. Its approach was multifaceted. By suppressing indigenous spirituality and celebration, language, subsistence activities, socialization and parenting, healing, and self-rule, the federal government sought to compel American Indian people to accept Christianity, the English language, market-oriented agriculture conducted through nuclear family units, Anglo-American social organization, and, eventually, American citizenship. Toward this end, the government staffed reservations with agricultural instructors and field matrons; removed (often forcibly) American Indian children for reeducation in military-style boarding schools; made the distribution of annuities, including food and other resources, contingent on compliance with reservation officials; and privatized the communal land that had sustained tribal societies and their cultures. This last initiative was called allotment.[9]

Between 1887 and 1934, allotment—the subdivision of common land into smaller, individually owned tracts—was a central component of federal-Indian relations. Reformers advocated the program as a means to assimilate Indian people into the margins of American society because they reasoned that private property ownership would undermine the communalism characteristic of most indigenous societies that thus far had enabled resistance to wholesale cultural change. The General Allotment Act of 1887, commonly referred to as the Dawes Act, provided for the allotment of reservations, which were held in trust for Indian people by the federal government. Because the tribal republics of Indian Territory owned their land in fee with a patent, however, a committee—the Dawes Commission, established through the Department of the Interior—negotiated separate terms with and subsequently allotted the Cherokee Nation under the Curtis Act of 1898 and the Cherokee Agreement of 1902. This process entailed the federal assumption of decisions over citizenship and the creation of a tribal roll; the surveying of tribal property, including the identification of minerals and other exploitable resources; the issuing of homesteads to individuals; and the severe restriction and ultimate disbanding of the tribal government, which left the administration of Cherokee allottees to Indian Service personnel and, eventually, state and local officials.

Allotment resulted in impoverishment and marginalization, and if desperation was reason to assimilate, then it sometimes caused that, too, although to a much smaller extent than its champions had predicted. American Indian communities survived, but non-Indians gained title to much of their land through outright fraud and, more often, the legal but ethically questionable ways in which Indian estates were managed, taxed, and probated. Advocates for Indian rights and scholars have documented and measured the losses. In the long term, the policy was universally devastating to every community in which it was applied. Across the United States, total tribal land holdings declined from 138 million to 55 million acres before the policy was repealed in 1934.[10] Indian communities did not experience dispossession evenly, however; those that had owned valuable land in more desirable areas suffered the most. This is particularly true for the Cherokee Nation, located in what is today northeastern Oklahoma. Before allotment, the Cherokee Nation held title to approximately 7 million acres of land. By 1971, individual Cherokees retained ownership of only 146,598 acres of it.[11] In 2003, Chadwick Smith, the principal chief of the Cherokee Nation, estimated that Cherokees lost over 90 percent of their pre-allotment acreage by 1920 and have since struggled to keep what remains in their families.[12]

The dismemberment of tribal land bases has created an enormous range of obstacles to economic development in tribal communities, including those within the Cherokee Nation, and has squandered human potential and caused suffering on an immeasurable level. But that is not the whole story, at least not for Cherokees. A close examination of their experiences during the allotment years suggests that they responded to the policy as they had to other enormous disruptions to their way of life: they adapted and survived within the basic unit of social organization in Cherokee society, their extended families. Throughout the nineteenth century, Cherokee families had proven remarkably able to incorporate elements of non-Indian culture into their way of life and yet remain committed to core values that shaped the way they interacted with one another: they remained egalitarian, particularly regarding gender roles; flexible in size and geographic orientation, expanding and contracting and relocating to adapt to changing circumstances; inclusive of elders, especially grandmothers, and other kin beyond spouses and children; and decentralized, particularly concerning their ownership of property and means of providing for the needs of the group.

At the beginning of the twentieth century, Cherokees responded to allotment rationally and made decisions intended to perpetuate their familial well-being. By this I mean that Cherokees did not succumb to powerlessness and victimization but made informed, deliberate, and conscious decisions intended to maintain the style and quality of life they had known prior to allotment. For this reason, Cherokee existence in the first decades following allotment was remarkably similar to that prior to allotment. By the mid-1920s, however, the outcomes of the policy exacerbated the regional environmental and international economic problems that would characterize the Great Depression of the 1930s. In other words, it was not that Cherokees could not or did not adapt to private landownership. Rather, the removal of restrictions against the sale of Indian land rapidly increased settlement and caused overuse of soil and the mismanagement of other natural resources. As a result, their homeland became a difficult one in which to make a living for anyone, not just Cherokees. Many non-Indian migrants to the area left. Some Cherokees may have moved west to California on what Smith calls the "economic Trail of Tears." Many more Cherokees stayed. They depended on the networks of hospitality and reciprocity rooted in their extended families that had enabled their survival for so many generations to once again enable them to endure hardship.

Over a century after the passage of allotment laws, the story of the policy remains unfinished. In 1996, Elouise Cobell, a citizen of the Blackfeet Nation, initiated a class-action lawsuit against the U.S. government on behalf of half a million American Indian trust-holders and their heirs. She and her co-plaintiffs charged the Department of the Interior with mismanaging Indian trust funds set up under the allotment laws.[13] They estimated the loss of fiscal resources from Indian land in the hundreds of billions because of the department's negligence in collecting, managing, and accounting for these monies. The federal government countered that the actual amount unaccounted for totaled in the millions. Both sides agreed, however, that compensation was due to the holders of Indian trust accounts, by now mostly descendants of original allottees. In early 2010, they reached an agreement that will provide $4 billion for both payments to individuals and funds for targeted economic development. As communities repair the damage done by allotment, it is important to acknowledge this adaptiveness. The past can provide insight for tribal communities devastated by the policy as they use funds made available through this settlement to rebuild land bases and enrich local economies.

For this infusion of cash to be effective, it is important to understand how allotment policy created a predatory system that isolated individual property owners in order to undermine effective collective responses. Any initiative intended to revitalize impoverished areas must be flexible enough to allow Indian people to access and manage resources within groups of their choosing. Likewise, this resolution must not share the historical amnesia and cultural blinders that characterized allotment laws and the bureaucracies that enforced them. For this reason, understanding of the history of the pre-allotment and allotment eras is essential for creating post-allotment recovery. The particular story is different for each allotted community, and the challenge for those implementing this settlement is to enable as many specific positive outcomes as possible within a system that by necessity groups American Indian peoples together into a generic whole. A century from now, the success of the Cobell settlement will be judged by whether or not it empowered Indian nations to reinvigorate the most valuable and relevant aspects of their traditional economies, diversify their range of usable resources in sustainable ways, and reestablish their self-sufficiency and autonomy. This is an enormous challenge to which I hope all parties involved are able to rise.

MY TASK IS FAR more modest, and my goal in writing this book is to humanize the impersonal process of allotment. For this reason, the narrative is based on the stories of specific Cherokee allottees who lived in one particular area. My partner in selecting these families was Jack D. Baker, a citizen of the Cherokee Nation, member of the tribal council, and expert on Cherokee genealogy, who grew up in the community of Chewey. No single area within the Cherokee Nation was a microcosm of the whole, but this community was a particularly attractive one for this research project. Few non-Indian intruders lived there, and the Cherokees who did reacted to allotment in a variety of ways along a spectrum of compliance and resistance. With Baker's help, I selected a random sample of three dozen families that he knew to have a thorough documentary record throughout the allotment era. These families include about two hundred people who hail from Chewey and the surrounding area. The community existed before the allotment era. It still exists today. Other towns in the region, such as Chance, were established later and have since declined. This area was once the northernmost part of Goingsnake District, one of the political subdivisions within the Cherokee Nation. It is now northern Adair County, specifically townships 19 North and 24 and 25 East. Adair County shares a boundary with Arkansas to the east, Sequoyah County to the south, Cherokee County to the west, and Delaware County to the north. Located in the western end of the Ozarks, it is a landscape defined by rock and water. The resulting valleys offer small patches of good farmland within a larger panorama of hills and cliffs.

I do not claim that these families represent the experiences of all allottees or even of all Cherokee allottees, although I am fascinated by the diversity of experience within my sample. A comprehensive study analyzing the whole nation was never my intention because the strength of this study is its intimacy, and there are important stories from the allotment era, including that of the freedmen and freedwomen, that remain beyond the scope of this study.[14] My purpose was to write this story from the ground up in order to enable readers to understand allotment through the complicated experiences of human beings. The particular stories of allottees offer a trenchant response to a policy that reduced Cherokees to their number on a census roll and grouped them by their presumed percentage of Indian ancestry. I have tried to write about each person as unique and fully human. Doing so enables the dismantling of colonial structures that necessitated bureaucratic anonymity and misrepresentative categorization in order to chew up Indian communities and spit out people separated from valuable resources thus opened to non-Indian exploitation.[15] Such familiarity with specific cases illuminates the range of common responses within a community undergoing such a transition and reminds us that we should measure cultural persistence not by consistency but rather by adaptability.

At the same time, rooting the stories of the people whose experiences compose this narrative in a thick description of Cherokee culture makes them intelligible as evidence of resilience.[16] Toward this end, I have used ethnohistorical methodology. Ethnohistory is a disciplinary hybrid, a fusion of historical and anthropological approaches enabling scholars to study American Indian history despite gaps in the documentary record and misrepresentations of indigenous people in written information authored by non-Indians. Instead of giving preference to such written documents, ethnohistorians evaluate them by cross-checking them against additional sources of evidence that provide other interpretations by and of Native people, including oral tradition, ethnography, and archaeology.[17] Because Cherokees have been a literate people for nearly two centuries, an ethnohistorian writing about them benefits from an abundance of material documenting their views and sharing their expressions. I have incorporated these sources whenever possible.

Ethnohistorical techniques must be used deliberately in order to be effective. Historians commonly "downstream," which means explaining cause and effect beginning with distant time and working toward that which is more recent. Anthropologists, on the other hand, "upstream," which refers to using contemporary observations to theorize about that which occurred before. Both "sidestream," or look to related and comparable groups for models and explanations of behavior.[18] All are valuable techniques, but without mindful application, downstreaming can tend toward relegating Indian people to the role of passive, powerless victims of relentless change; upstreaming can read as presentist; and sidestreaming can sanitize societies of their uniqueness. As historian Frederick E. Hoxie has commented, at its best, ethnohistory should "explore cultural differences through time. . . . The outgrowth of this exploration should be self-critical narratives that question their insights even as they make them. These narratives also resist the desire to compress, essentialize, and manipulate the people who lie at the heart of their inquiries."[19] That has been my goal.

What this also means is that the practice of ethnohistory extends beyond what Patricia Galloway has called "trying to wring blood from the stones of European incomprehension and representation of Native behavior and testimony."[20] As a way of interacting with sources and, more important, with the people depicted in them and their descendants, ethnohistory has evolved to require that scholars be aware of their own roles, particularly when they are outsiders to the community whose past they are interpreting. That ethnohistorians increasingly reflect upon the process of doing research and writing and think about ethics and the outcomes of their work is the result of the demands of indigenous leaders and scholars for accountability and fairness.[21] It is right. I am aware that I have made countless decisions in writing this book. That I have tried to be comprehensive in my search for evidence, accurate in my interpretation, and sensitive in my explanation does not change that what follows is one scholar's account. I am not Cherokee, and I do not speak for the Cherokee Nation or the United Keetoowah Band, the two federally recognized Cherokee groups in Oklahoma whose members include the descendants of those included in this study. Although I have shared drafts with and sought feedback from individuals affiliated with the Cherokee Nation, the final product is my own, and I take responsibility for my conclusions.

I also found inspiration in community studies, an approach that uses ethnography to understand social processes and group cohesion. Originally associated with sociologists who conducted research in urban, ethnic neighborhoods, practitioners of community studies most commonly use direct observation and interviews to determine how collectives function to sustain their members. This approach demonstrates how to focus on the local level to investigate who belongs, how people interact and why, and whether or not this changes and how, making it a logical complement for ethnohistory. In fact, I am not the first scholar of Indians to use such methods. In his study of the Creek *talwa*, or town, of Okfuskee during the eighteenth century, historian Joshua Piker argues for the importance of a local focus to understand the complexities of both indigenous life and "broader connective systems" such as clan, regional, and national affiliations.[22] Likewise, in his study of late-twentieth-century Seminole Baptist churches in Oklahoma, anthropologist Jack M. Schultz demonstrates how analysis of the interactions of members of a community reveals not only social organization but also the values informing such structures and functions.[23]

In lieu of direct participant observation, I located the families in my sample in the documentary record. The Dawes Commission, the federal committee that allotted the tribal republics of Indian Territory, existed for just over twenty years (1893–1914), but the story of Cherokee experiences of allotment cannot be contained by its records. For this reason, I have included evidence about Cherokee family life from before the tribe's removal from its southeastern homeland until after the repeal of allotment policy as part of the Indian New Deal. The majority of information referred to in this study originated between 1880 and 1930, the decades making up the allotment era that are its focus. Because each source of data has weaknesses and inaccuracies, no one record provided a baseline for my interpretation. Rather, I evaluated each finding across time and against multiple sources. In particular, I did this by creating charts for extended families, noting demographic information about members and evidence suggesting how these individuals functioned as a group. Unable to conduct my own interviews with those who experienced this process, I mined government records and oral history collections for the testimony of Cherokee allottees.

A wide variety of sources inform this narrative. Materials published by the advocates of allotment illuminate the importance of family as a social unit and a symbol of civilization and provide useful context for understanding the congressional debates leading up to the passage of allotment legislation. Responses from vocal Cherokee opponents of the policy include their explanation of the actual roles filled by Indian families. These documents also reflect both the Cherokees' need to defend themselves and their society from assimilationist critics and their effort to define the best possibilities for humanity in terms of Cherokee civilization.

The majority of my research, however, focused on this sample of Cherokee families. I traced them through both Cherokee and U.S. censuses beginning with those compiled before the removal era and ending with the 1920 U.S. census. I also drew information from the records of the Cherokee government, although it kept minimal records on its citizens before allotment and operated in a skeletal state after the policy was enacted. For this reason, the archives of the U.S. government provided a wider pool of data. I looked to the Dawes Commission's records, including enrollment packets, allotment jackets, miscellaneous records and correspondence, and maps. I also examined information collected on Eastern Cherokee applications by the Guion Miller Commission. Adair County's probate records were useful, as were those regarding the removal of restrictions against the sale of allotted land and Indian case files that documented a range of concerns related to land use. I further describe these sources in the appendix.

I found yet more information in the *Cherokee Advocate*, the newspaper published by the Cherokee government until 1906, and other contemporary local periodicals, including the *Vinita Indian Chieftain*, the *Oklahoma City Oklahoman*, and the *Stilwell Standard Sentinel*. Oral history collections, particularly the Doris Duke Collection, the Indian Pioneer Papers, and the Oklahoma Historical Society's Oral History Collection, were an invaluable source of information. It was thrilling to read transcripts of conversations with the handful of people included in this study who had been interviewed as part of one of these projects, but the accounts of other Cherokees from this area who experienced allotment also proved to be insightful.

All sources of evidence pose challenges to historians, and I should bring four, in particular, to the attention of readers. First, throughout the records upon which this study is based, given names and surnames vary widely. Many Cherokees used both Cherokee and English names, and individuals often used different names during their lifetimes. Steve Dog, or S-di-wi in Cherokee, was also known as Stephen Glory. His wife, called Day-yeh-ni in Cherokee, appears in the records as both Nannie and Nancy. She also went by several different surnames, including Acorn, her father's name; Mitchell, her first husband's surname; and Whale, a surname used by her mother, Sarah, also known by the surname Foreman. By the late nineteenth century, Cherokee women commonly assumed their husband's surname upon marriage. Consequently, after marrying Steve, Nannie was identified by both of his surnames, too. Families frequently shifted surnames over generations. Most commonly, children adopted the given name of their father as their surname. For example, Oce and Jim Hogshooter also were known by the surname of Harlan. Their father's name was Harlan Hogshooter. Therefore, shared surnames do not necessarily signify relatedness. For example, none of the Harlans in this study were related to the large family of Harlans descended from Pennsylvania-born merchant Ellis Harlan and his Cherokee wife, Catherine Kingfisher, a daughter of Beloved Woman Nancy Ward. Variations of spelling also were normal. Betsy Suake and several of her children are listed throughout the documentary record by the surnames Snake, Suwake, Suake, Suakee, Wickey, and Waker.

I appreciate that this rich variety of names points not to a society-wide identity crisis but to the elegant melding of traditional Cherokee practices with the customs adopted from Anglo-Americans and the English language. There is a wonderful study to be done here by a Cherokee linguist, but that I am not. Expecting readers to keep track of multiple names for the approximately two hundred individuals included in this study would be asking too much. Therefore, evaluating the evidence available to me, I tried to identify one name that each person used for himself or herself within the community during the allotment era, and I used that name throughout the book. Careful to not erase Cherokee names from this story, I used them in their English translation when evidence suggested that their bearer preferred that version of his or her name.

Others identified themselves by English names, and so I used those when appropriate. In reality, many people probably used both interchangeably. I hope readers will forgive my simplification and remember the diversity to which it refers.

Second, the abundance of names contrasts with the lack of clan identification. The function of clans evolved tremendously throughout the nineteenth century, and they ceased to fill the broad sociopolitical and spiritual functions that they did prior to the organization of the Cherokees' constitutional government in 1827. Nonetheless, some culturally conservative Cherokees continue to identify themselves by and value their clan affiliation today. This persistence would suggest that their ancestors, particularly those participating in the Keetoowah Society and the Nighthawk movement (discussed throughout this book), also cared about clans, and understanding their role among late-nineteenth-century Cherokees would help illuminate the worldview and organization of those groups. However, no allotment-era record created by the Cherokee or U.S. government notes clan affiliation. The Cherokee government presumably appreciated the personal and private nature of such information; the U.S. government likely considered such data to be irrelevant and unimportant. In addition, because some traditional Cherokees today consider this topic to be sensitive, it would not have been appropriate to print if it were available.

Third, the misleading and loaded terms "full blood" and "mixed blood" permeate the documentary record. This language of blood quantum was spoken fluidly and freely about Cherokees and sometimes by Cherokees. Although specific meanings are rarely defined, context indicates that the signification of these terms varies throughout the sources in which I conducted my research. I do my best to explain their use when necessary. Readers should note, however, that during this time period, Anglo-Americans tended to use blood as a subjective representation of both ancestry and ability, while Cherokees more often used the same terms to indicate cultural orientation and upbringing. For this reason, many so-called full bloods actually had non-Indian ancestry, and many Cherokees of mixed parentage raised in traditional and conservative communities behaved accordingly. Likewise, when used by non-Indians, the terms tell us more about their own understanding of inherent racial differences and the workings of white supremacy than about Cherokee beliefs about race or belonging. In fact, this binary itself is an imposition upon Cherokee people's history and reflects their colonizers' perspective about what forces were shaping Cherokee society and the inevitable direction of this change, anticipating assimilation into Anglo-American society. Cherokee conceptions of identity were never as simple as this "either-or" model would suggest. They still are not.[24]

When used without explanation, the terms "full blood" and "mixed blood" are racist distractions from the complicated, intricate ways that Cherokees formed and expressed their identities during this era. Mary Evelyn Rogers, a Cherokee genealogist who wrote and privately published an outstanding history of the Cherokee Nation for her family, commented, "I take issue with some of the writers who assumed that the large number of mixed-bloods in the western Cherokee Nation meant a lessening of their Cherokee heritage. White genes did not carry white culture, and outward adaptation to white civilization did not carry with it the abandonment of the Cherokee outlook."[25] I agree.

Influenced by the scholarship about southeastern Indians and cognizant of the common usage of these terms by some modern-day Cherokees, I expected blood quantum to matter more than it did. Instead, I was surprised by its irrelevance as an explanation of behavior, particularly prior to allotment.[26] The terms gained tangible meaning, however, when allotment policy created a range of restrictions on Indian landownership based on these designations. After that point, full blood and mixed blood signified different freedoms, protections, and opportunities. During the allotment era, these words proved to be self-fulfilling prophecies by fostering separate categories of experiences and, perhaps, outlooks among Cherokees, but we should not forget that the meanings then associated with them were defined by non-Indians who believed in the rightness and inevitability of assimilation.[27]

Scholars have struggled to organize this blood discourse we inherited into something useful, but it is hard to write poetry with poison. As a result, we still lack good words with which to discuss the political, religious, and economic divisions that did exist within Cherokee society. Some authors have used "conservative" and "progressive," and although not loaded with the racist baggage of blood, these terms reinforce this same binary view of Cherokee society and tend to obscure the range of beliefs and behaviors common among them. I use these terms sparingly and cautiously. Of all of them, I prefer "traditional" to describe those most concerned with the perpetuation of distinctly Cherokee ways of thinking and being. In this, I borrow from Jack M. Schultz in defining traditional people as those whose adaptation is "structured in culturally meaningful ways, allowing a social group to sustain its identity while being engaged in changing circumstances."[28] When relevant, I noted when Cherokees intermarried with noncitizens, who thus made up part of their families, but I do not assume that sexual relations negated cultural orientation or that biology correlated to ways of life. More often, I did not specify who was of mixed parentage and who was not because I think this information usually conceals more than it reveals, particularly concerning the reasons why individual Cherokees made particular decisions.

This obsession with blood quantum also obscures the ways that self-directed change is normal and enabled cultural survival for all Cherokee people. As Cherokee scholar Julia Coates has observed, Cherokees have been "damned if they do, damned if they don't." She continues, "Rather than equating change with loss, change can be regarded as the very natural and human cultural process that enables individuals and cultures to deal with altered conditions, and thus continue to survive and flourish."[29] If they had not adapted, Cherokee people would not have survived, but because they have changed, their motives, identity, and behavior became suspect and suspiciously un-Cherokee to government bureaucrats charged with policing tribal rolls or when contextualized within the broader Anglo-American discourse on blood, identity, and authenticity.[30] Therefore, I avoid situating the families in this study on the binary of blood quantum because I want to emphasize the shared ways in which Cherokee family life evolved throughout the nineteenth century and how divisions among Cherokees increased in importance and took on rigid meanings as a result of allotment.

Last, while writing this book, I struggled with the legacy of the Dawes Commission as a record-producing body. As a historian, I depend on documents to do my job. As a human being who believes that all of us are equally entitled to basic freedoms and dignity, I often felt outraged and sickened by what I was reading in the archives. I appreciate that the Dawes Commission records, a valuable windfall for historians, were created at an enormous cost to the Cherokee people, even beyond the ultimate loss of their resources and national independence. Their right to privacy was violated. Their articulations of their own identities were ignored. Their lives were interrupted by government employees knocking at their doors and demanding personal information. They were the ones who repeatedly left their families and fields to appear before government agents and fill out paperwork. They endured personal, sometimes offensive, often frustrating questioning from strangers in public hearings. A pointed comment by Steve Dog, responding to the peppering of questions about his family by federal officials, has lingered in my mind since I first read it years ago: "I don't know anything myself and I don't know who does and you can let go, I reckon." But he did know a lot more than he told them; he was unwilling to tell these outsiders within the context of a process that was hurtful to him and those he loved. Working in these records requires filtering responses to separate a lack of knowledge of specific information from the lack of willingness to share it.[31] Recognizing that many of the records I utilized for this book were the products of experiences that were time-consuming, irritating, and degrading to Cherokees, I approached these sources with gratitude while never forgetting the injustice of their very making.

THIS PROJECT IS PART of the second generation of scholarship on allotment. The first studies of the policy expertly documented how it devastated communal land bases, suppressed tribal governments, and undermined indigenous cultures.[32] More recent scholarship on the era has not refuted these earlier assertions but rather has added depth and nuance by explaining how, within such an abusive, limiting system, American Indian communities survived. Scholars have demonstrated that Indian people responded to the policy not only to mitigate land loss but also to further individual or collective goals. In her study of Southern Ute women during the allotment era, Katherine M. B. Osburn explains how Indian women creatively retained a role in communal decisions and control over their personal lives, particularly their marital and sexual choices. By reading non-Indian documents for evidence of Ute agency, Osburn demonstrates how Indian Service staff misunderstood the Utes' selective compliance with policies and strategic manipulation of their enforcers as the internalization of assimilationist beliefs.[33] The ability of Indian people to adapt to new economic circumstances also makes up an important theme of this second group of studies. Analyses of allotment are just one example of the scholarly attention now being paid to American Indian approaches to resource use and development. That historians increasingly recognize the range of ways in which changing strategies for physical survival have enabled cultural survival in the past creates a more fertile, respectful environment for tribes to continue this ongoing process.[34]

The classic "first generation" study of allotment specifically among the Five Tribes, including the Cherokee Nation, is Angie Debo's *And Still the Waters Run: The Betrayal of the Five Civilized Tribes.* Although first published in 1940, Debo's study has stood the test of time. She "named names" by openly writing about those who exploited Indian allottees and expertly documented how they got away with it. She did not talk much about how Indian people actually experienced the abusive system she described, however.[35] Carolyn Ross Johnston devoted a chapter of her more recent book on Cherokee women during the late nineteenth and early twentieth centuries to allotment, and she describes the policy as particularly devastating to women, who lost any remaining legacy of their customary authority.[36] I respectfully disagree with this conclusion in an otherwise valuable study. My interpretation does not wholly deny negative outcomes, but it explains the persistence of the Cherokee communities thriving in northeastern Oklahoma today in spite of them.

Scholars have written about this assault on Indian cultures and resources from other angles. Allotment was one phase of the colonization of indigenous America, and during the late nineteenth and early twentieth centuries, this policy worked in conjunction with others intended to assimilate tribal people, particularly that of raising Indian children in boarding schools staffed by non-Indians who neither understood nor appreciated their students' cultures. The land reform plan was intended to shatter extended Indian families into nuclear units, and the residential school system was designed to isolate Indian children from the relations who could teach them indigenous ways of being that challenged lessons about the superiority of Anglo-American society. Historian K. Tsianina Lomawaima calls Chilocco, opened near the Cherokee Nation but in Oklahoma Territory in 1884, part of "an educational crusade—vast in scope, military in organization, fervent in zeal, and violent in method." As the allotment era neared its end in 1925, 26 percent of the students at Chilocco were Cherokee. In other words, although Cherokees did not experience the brutality of reservation life as did those tribes settled in what became western Oklahoma, their exceptionalism eroded during the allotment era as they—and their children—suffered from the same assimilationist policies as other indigenous Americans.[37]

Such bureaucracy was brutalizing. Scholars of assimilationist initiatives such as boarding schools and home matron programs have demonstrated that the U.S. government's policies toward Indian people that followed the end of warfare with Indians on the Plains were no more benign and no less brutal than bullets. White supremacist laws created complicated programs that empowered outsiders whose work in Indian communities was to change the ways that Native people loved one another by destroying customs of kinship and networks of relatedness.[38] In this sense, allotment was an attack on not just the land bases but also the intimate lives of American Indian people. In her study of a comparable policy enacted upon Native Hawaiians during the early twentieth century, J. Kehaulani Kauanui points out that the denial of indigenous sovereignty includes both the appropriation of land and resources, a process that is visible, and the undermining of traditional means of constructing identity and relatedness, an invisible theft that is felt in the families and communities of Native people for whom kinship has become contested.[39]

These assimilationist policies also were profoundly gendered in their application and outcomes. American Indian women and men experienced these assaults in particular ways. At least since the Red Power movement of the late 1960s and 1970s, female indigenous activists have called for an understanding of how European Americans' dismissal of Indian women as rapeable has enabled systemic violations not only of women's bodies but also, and in particular relevance to this study, of their mothering and familial relationships, their homes and communities, and their land. Indigenous community leaders and healers, artists and authors, and mothers have argued for an expansive definition of sexual violence that delegitimizes laws and institutions that construct indigenous women and the resources that enable their survival as intimately and infinitely exploitable.[40]

At the same time, indigenous women have called for healing to recognize gender difference and to restore balance not only between women and men but also among human societies, non-human beings, and the land. The late Wilma Mankiller, the beloved former principal chief of the Cherokee Nation, suggested that traditional Cherokee gender relations provide a model for this healing, and Mankiller called for historical scholarship to play a part in restoring women's authority by acknowledging its presence in the past.[41] For this reason, I write about Cherokee women's power as normative, and although I discuss evidence pointing to the loss of status in particular circumstances, I also identify cases in which women maintained and even gained it. In particular, I do not assume that the presence of white men in Cherokee households correlates to the declension of Cherokee women's authority in them, because evidence concerning the balance of power in intermarried women's relationships in this study usually suggests otherwise.

I consider allotment in the context of historical scholarship on gender, sexuality, and family structure and function in the United States. Family history has evolved from its early focus on the experiences of white, middle-class families as normative to reveal the processes through which such ideals were created and enforced and deviants from them punished. Recent literature exploring government initiatives to regulate and reform sexuality and family formation in general during the late nineteenth and early twentieth centuries provides valuable context for understanding assimilationist policies targeted at American Indians. As historian Peggy Pascoe explains, private lives were public business during this era: "The many functions of marriage—the gendered molding of husbands and wives, the containment of sexuality, the raising of children, the linking of the private family to the political and economic figure of the male householder, the orderly handing down of property from generation to generation—made it an institution of singular importance to the state."[42] Thus inspired, I expanded the scope of this study of allotment to examine not just which Cherokees held onto their land but also, and more important, who sat at their kitchen tables, who worked in their fields, who slept in their beds, who parented their children, and who cared for their sick. I want readers to understand that allotment was not solely about property but about families and their role as basic units of social and economic production, reproduction, and political authentication.

BUILDING UPON THIS SCHOLARSHIP, this book explains how Cherokees adapted to allotment policy and used allotted land to meet the needs of their families. If reformers intended the policy to assimilate them to Anglo-American ideals, grafters plotted to rob them, and federal, state, and local officials often failed to protect them, how then did Cherokees survive as individuals and as a tribal people? How did they come to be currently the second largest Indian nation in the United States? The continuity of family life enabled functional responses to private landownership and the exploitation that this transition from communal ownership entailed.

I tell this story in eight chapters. In the first two, I trace the arrival of the families in my sample to Goingsnake District and explain how they lived there prior to allotment. In chapter 3, I explain why the nature of Indian family life was central to the application of and opposition to the policy. Chapters 4 and 5 explore how Cherokee families enrolled with the Dawes Commission and the creation of the Dawes roll, which signified inclusion or exclusion from the distribution of tribal resources. In chapter 6, I discuss the division and distribution of land among Cherokee families, and in chapter 7, I explain how Cherokee families adapted to the evolving management of their estates. I conclude the study with an eighth chapter revisiting the basic components of Cherokee family life in the decades after allotment.

CHAPTER ONE

⚘

Arriving

The story of the Cherokee people begins with a family undergoing tremendous change. In the version of "Origin of Corn" that ethnologist James Mooney learned while researching among the Eastern Band of Cherokees during the late nineteenth century, the central characters are a couple, Selu and Kana'ti, and their unnamed biological son. Selu means "Corn Mother," but her significance is transcendent and multifaceted.[1] The first woman and man at once represented the ideal division of labor in Cherokee society, explained the origination of dietary staples, and modeled standards for proper behavior. Selu and Kana'ti knew only harmony and, therefore, abundance until they adopted another son, an outsider, a boy born of pollution, of blood mixed with water, who brought chaos and suffering into the world.[2] This Wild Boy did not respect boundaries, and the Cherokee world hinged upon the careful balance of many opposing categories. Lacking his adoptive parents' sagacity, his understanding of how to survive was simplistic and irreverent. He had no interest in the long process through which wisdom was acquired, nor did he care to know the deeper significance of the work humans did to live rightly in the world.[3]

As a result, Selu and Kana'ti's household suffered through tragedy of their own making, but they responded as a family, including Wild Boy. He had inadvertently caused the dispersion of the resources, technology, and knowledge essential for Cherokee survival and shaped the natural environment into the one Cherokees recognized and in which they prospered. Instructed by his parents, he at last learned behaviors essential for community well-being, especially making recompense through the assumption of individual responsibility and generously sharing food and labor with the earliest Cherokees. That Wild Boy's mistakes, the release of game and the spread of agriculture, ultimately produced positive results should not be surprising, considering the emphasis on restoration in the traditional Cherokee worldview. Selu and Kana'ti are not Adam and Eve. The change that took place in their idyllic home was not an irrevocable loss of harmony because, although there was no restoration of what had been, Selu's children made amends together and in doing so restored prosperity to a world forever transformed but still fundamentally good.[4]

This chapter tells the story of how Selu's descendants adapted to enormous changes taking place in their southeastern homeland even prior to allotment. Emphasizing the major transitions defining Cherokee history during the late eighteenth and early nineteenth centuries, I historicize the experiences of the families in this study as they adjusted to non-Indian encroachment, relocated to the Goingsnake District, and rebuilt their households in Indian Territory. The Henderson roll, compiled in 1835, and the Eastern Cherokee applications collected by the Guion Miller Commission between 1906 and 1909 provide the core of this chapter.[5] Many scholars have ably conceptualized this period, and the causes, outcomes, and nature of the profound political, religious, and economic developments that characterize this era remain a subject of debate. As historian Theda Perdue has argued, however, the overall persistence of traditional gender roles made possible adaptation to and even mastery of new resources and technologies prior to removal.[6] This consistency suggests the overall stability of Cherokee family life. As the chaos of colonization buffeted them, Cherokee households remained egalitarian, flexible, inclusive, and decentralized.

The Old Nation

This story begins in the southeastern homeland of the Cherokee clans. Prior to the early nineteenth century, these seven interconnected, extended families that traced their ancestry back to a common maternal ancestor formed the basis of Cherokee sociopolitical organization.[7] Cherokees recognized matrilineal descent, meaning that anyone born of a Cherokee mother belonged to her clan and was a person with rights and obligations to other "Real Human Beings," or Ani-yun-wiya, as they called themselves. Because clan affiliation was fixed and did not change, people knew who they were and relied upon maternal relatives to provide care, companionship, and protection throughout their lifetimes. Within clans, individuals related to each other in precise ways informed by gender, age, and type of connection, but this specific and complicated system for positioning oneself in relationship to others should not be confused with hierarchy. Clans provided order rather than rank. Forbidden from marrying members of their own clan, Cherokees were exogamous, and through intermarriage with members of other clans, they further connected themselves to one another. The clans thus permeated the Cherokee world, infusing it with structure and meaning.[8]

As important as kinship was to Cherokees, however, it often was incomprehensible to Europeans and their American descendants. In part, this lack of understanding resulted from outsiders' belief in female subservience and disdain for the powerful and important place women held in matrilineal societies. Unable to comprehend clan law, early outsiders who observed and wrote about Cherokees anglicized their way of life by focusing on identifiable geographic and political units and their male leaders. Prior to the French and Indian War, approximately sixty Cherokee communities were scattered among four distinct regions: the Lower Towns in South Carolina; the Middle Towns in western North Carolina; the Valley Towns in southwestern North Carolina and northeastern Georgia; and the Upper or Overhill Towns in eastern Tennessee and northwestern North Carolina. Linguistic and, to a lesser extent, cultural and economic differences distinguished them.[9]

Cherokee towns were autonomous settlements in which households related to each other through ties of kinship and patterns of reciprocal interaction for subsistence, spiritual, and political purposes. These ties and patterns—the presence of family throughout their communities and their obligations to one another—united the Cherokees, not allegiance to a particular headman or ideology. Like other Indian towns throughout the Southeast, these communities ranged in size from dozens to many hundreds of residents. They typically were composed of residential structures and fields clustered around a council house complex or, if the landscape dictated it, a trail of sleeping and working quarters that stretched outward from the common buildings. These communities always were located near water, the constant mooring connecting the physical and spiritual landscape. Rivers, lakes, streams, and springs influenced the shape of towns and shaped life within them.[10] Anthropologist Charles Hudson describes these settlements as "small, bounded, and composed of intricate, many stranded relationships." The hospitality and reciprocity necessitated by Cherokees' ways of reckoning kinship were such regular occurrences that practitioners understood them as normal and universal. They must have thought the relatively disconnected and unattached Europeans who identified themselves by their different churches and distant kings to be as profoundly strange as those outsiders thought Cherokees.[11]

Larger Cherokee towns, called mother towns, were surrounded by satellite communities. Within these settlements, households organized themselves into similar patterns. In addition to being a matrilineal people, Cherokees were matrilocal, meaning that women remained with their birth families throughout their lives and, after marriage, a husband relocated to the home of his wife. Extended family households were organized around matrilineages comprising elder women and their descendants through their daughters and granddaughters. Maternal uncles filled a paternal role toward their nieces and nephews, but because they often stayed in the homes of their own wives, male leadership was not essential to the day-to-day operation of Cherokee households. Instead, these homes were the centers of women's authority, and their households were the primary unit of reproduction, production, and distribution in Cherokee society. Hudson describes these residences as clusters of buildings including rectangular summer shelters; solidly constructed winter houses; cribs and storage buildings for other foodstuffs; covered work spaces; and menstrual houses. These improvements belonged to women, and the relationships connecting their inhabitants existed through women.[12]

Cherokees practiced a gendered division of labor that empowered women and men as autonomous producers of the diverse range of foods needed for survival. Women worked as the gatherers, growers, and processors of foodstuffs. They collected a prodigious amount of wild edibles from forests and fallowed fields grown over with semi-domesticated plants. Historian Tom Hatley suggests that these sources provided as much as half of Cherokees' non-meat calories during the eighteenth century.[13] Acorns, hickory nuts, black walnuts, berries, seeds, grasses, greens, tubers, roots, bark, and leaves nourished Cherokees because women were skilled in their collection, storage, and preparation.[14]

Women also grew corn, the Cherokees' staple, and their gender identity was inseparable from that of their primary crop. Women raised food in multiple locations throughout their communities. Planting the majority of their corn in large, communal fields outside their towns, they also grew "intensive gardens," as Hatley calls them, next to their households. The "three sisters"—the name given to the ecologically sound co-cultivation of corn, beans, and squash—occupied the majority of tilled space, and Cherokee women hedged their bets against crop failure and diversified their menu by growing at least three types of corn: a small, quick-growing variety; a large, yellow one used for hominy; and a large, white, fluffy type used for bread.[15] Men provided meat, using bows and arrows, traps, snares, deadfalls, clubs, and blowguns to hunt white-tailed deer, bear, elk, and smaller fur-bearing animals and fowl as well.[16] Both men and women fished.[17] Although forests provided valuable hunting grounds and opportunities for significant male contributions to familial subsistence, as archaeologist Max White notes, Cherokees relied most on the resources obtainable on river bottomlands, places where women did the majority of their productive work.[18]

Cherokees had developed a proficient system for exploiting the resources in their environment, but their towns proved vulnerable to attack by English colonists seeking to control the economic development of the Southeast. Throughout the eighteenth century, these communities were lightning rods for assault, and Cherokees soon concluded that concentrations of population were a liability in the age of empire. When they established permanent diplomatic and trade relationships with European colonists during the 1690s, Cherokees were integrated fully into the intricate networks connecting communities throughout the Indian South. The arrival of Europeans, who brought new people, worldviews, and material culture, accelerated the pace of change in an already sophisticated, complicated world.

Europeans also introduced new microbes, and although Cherokees may have succumbed to earlier epidemics, certainly smallpox decimated their towns during 1738 and 1739. Casualties may have totaled half the population, leaving 8,000 to 12,000 grieving kin. The survivors likely abandoned some towns and consolidated in others. These settlements became targets in wars involving Europeans and their colonial descendants. In 1760 and 1761, within the larger conflict known as the French and Indian War, the British, although nominally allied with some Cherokee leaders, attacked the Lower, Middle, and Upper Towns. According to British trader and historian James Adair, 40 percent of Cherokee towns were burned to the ground during this conflict. In addition, smallpox, and perhaps other diseases, again struck in 1759 and 1760. The Cherokees sided with the British during the American Revolution, and the Patriots responded by engaging in scorched-earth warfare that destroyed approximately 80 percent of their homes and fields, sparing only the Valley Towns. Smallpox also struck the survivors of war in 1783, and a third of the population died that year.[19]

The Treaty of Hopewell, signed in 1785, marked the formal end of warfare between the Cherokees and the United States but not the cessation of violence between the Cherokees and the new nation. Sporadic attacks and raids on Cherokee towns continued throughout the end of the century. The Revolutionary War had been the second time in a normal lifespan that Cherokees had experienced such brutality in communities simultaneously ravaged by disease. Their population hovered around 9,000, the lowest on record. After having already ceded much of their land base in colonial-era treaties, Cherokee leaders acknowledged the sovereignty of the United States and gave up what was left of their hunting grounds. This era in Cherokee history is one of loss, shock, grief, and dispersal. Despite its optimistic name, then, the gathering at Hopewell was an ominous moment for Cherokees. Their survival depended on their ability to adapt, and they were poised for dramatic change.[20]

In the decades between the American Revolution and removal, Cherokees reestablished their households, but they did not do so in towns. The survivors who rebuilt their homes were a different kind of Cherokee from what their ancestors had been. Smaller, less concentrated groupings made sense to those who had lived through epidemics and total warfare, and although not all Cherokees abandoned towns, the majority did.[21] For this reason, traditional residence patterns changed as most Cherokees dispersed into communities characterized by smatterings of farms strung along waterways and separated by woodlands.[22] These were the homes made by the ancestors of allotment-era residents of Chewey, and we first meet these specific families here amid their recovery.

Rivers continued to define and connect settlements. Huckleberry, Nelson Crittenden's father, lived with four other family members along the Ellijay River, which flows into the Coosawattee. Lewis Bird's ancestors lived to the southeast along the Etowah River, which, like the waters of the Ellijay, eventually joins the Coosa River. His father, Jeh-si, and nine more of his ancestors lived among three houses.[23] Tellingly, pre-removal census takers commonly noted households like Jeh-si's whose members resided in multiple, connected farms. In other words, these extended families lived in close proximity to one another, even though they were scattered among several houses interspersed by fields.[24] For example,

Steve Dog's ancestors made up a family of eight who lived among three houses located on six acres of cultivated land.[25] Will and Dicey Proctor, the maternal grandparents of Fannie Turtle, Betsy Suake, and Nannie Dog, belonged to a family of ten. Among them, they had built two farms that included four houses on twenty-five acres of land.[26] Census takers did not note who lived in these houses, and Perdue has suggested that the more dispersed settlement pattern prompted a shift toward nuclear family organization.[27] Without knowing the age and gender of family members, it is difficult to know conclusively. The clustering of farms, however, makes clear that Cherokees continued to live and work among their kin. Those who once shared a household within a town remained near one another. Likewise, it is logical to presume that they worked together and shared resources.

Those who intermarried with whites during this era had larger families and tended to live on one farm, but they nonetheless remained close to kin. Although they did not define their methodology, American census takers noted the presumed racial makeup of each Cherokee household prior to removal.[28] Eliza Brown grew up in a family of nine descended from an intermarried white father, Jesse Raper, and Cherokee mother, Mary McDaniel, on one farm along the Nottley River, near Murphy in North Carolina. The two neighboring households were those of her father's kin, Thomas and James Raper, who also had married Cherokee women, at least one of whom was a relative of her mother.[29] Mary Ghormley, who became Eliza's daughter-in-law, was the descendant of Cherokees from Tennessee. Her maternal grandparents were Andrew and Jennie Taylor. Andrew was a white man, and Jennie belonged to the Bigby family, which had intermarried in at least one previous generation. They lived with their four children on a farm near Mouse Creek. Her siblings and maternal relatives, the Foremans, also lived along Mouse and Candy Creeks, both of which fed into the Hiwassee River. The Hiwassee ran through Cherokee settlements in Georgia, North Carolina, and Tennessee. Jennie's sister Mary Ann, who had married Andrew's brother David Taylor, lived with her children along the Valley River across the North Carolina border. The Valley River also is a tributary of the Hiwassee. This extended family, although not neighbors, lived near each other, connected by the water. In other words, the state boundaries imply a distance between families that is misleading.[30]

At the same time, intermarried Cherokees did not segregate themselves from those who had married other Cherokees. Elizabeth Cannon was born in her family's home along the Etowah River in what became Lumpkin County, Georgia. Her parents, Silas and Sarah Palmour, ran their farm in an area that was predominantly settled by those identified by census takers as full bloods. One of those households was that of the Chewey family.[31]

Settled onto homesteads, Cherokees also reinvented their domestic economy, but what that meant varied. Necessity forced innovation and concessions. Cherokees already had adopted some elements of Anglo-American food production that they then readily adapted to their newly dispersed settlement pattern. Scattered farms provided room for plowed fields and orchards and range for livestock. Women and men gravitated toward that which improved their lives without undermining their identities, particularly their gendered sensibilities about appropriate work, but women likely found this transition to be less disruptive than men. Hatley suggests that Cherokee women had "held their ground" throughout the colonial era and, therefore, were better positioned to make this leap. They had obtained new plants and domesticated animals from Europeans and adapted them to the Cherokee system of agriculture such that they maintained a diverse diet despite the loss of access to some natural resources as settlers encroached on their homeland. He concludes, "Cherokee agriculture, the clearest domain of women, was a conspicuous success in adapting new crops and techniques of cultivation." Sweet potatoes, peas, peaches, watermelons, hogs, and poultry were common by the mid-eighteenth century, and these resources and technologies were easily transferred from towns to dispersed settlements.[32]

Women also seized the technology of cloth production.[33] First distributed by the federal government in the 1790s, cotton combs, spinning wheels, and looms became valued possessions because Cherokees began growing cotton to clothe themselves and to sell during the early nineteenth century.[34] The extent of this transition is evident in the 1835 census: the families of Huckleberry Crittenden, Jeh-si, Silas and Sarah Palmour, Will and Dicey Proctor, Jesse and Mary Raper, Polly Rattlinggourd, and George and Margaret Welch all included one weaver and two spinners. The division is suggestive of the skill required to do these tasks, which young women seem to have mastered. Those families with more daughters had a distinct advantage. Andrew and Jennie Taylor's family, which included three daughters, had three weavers and three spinners. Michael and Nannie Hilderbrand's household included five unmarried daughters old enough to weave and spin, and in 1835, they all did this work. Domestic cloth production was so widespread that only one family, that of Steve Dog's ancestors, did not identify women in their family as engaging in it.[35]

Men may have struggled more to make the transition to dispersed settlements. After some Cherokee leaders ceded their hunting grounds and signed away their right to be warriors, Cherokee men were no longer able to contribute to their families' survival or earn status in traditional ways. Moreover, they needed to adapt to working in what had been feminine spaces, fields and homes. Through its "civilization" policy, the U.S. government and Christian missionaries hoped to show men the way by turning them into yeoman farmers, but men needed ways to be productive that felt appropriate. After initial opposition, they embraced livestock production because it enabled them to provide meat. As Perdue explains it, "Cherokee men had found a new use for their 'hunting grounds,' that is, land they did not cultivate. They simply restocked hunting grounds with cattle and hogs." Likewise, some created appropriate agricultural tasks by adopting the plow, equipment not associated with female work, but hoes nonetheless remained the more popular agricultural tool and women the predominant farmers in the early nineteenth century.[36]

Although many Cherokees were growing cotton and spinning cloth, only a minority adopted the system of agriculture that would be associated with this crop in the Old South. These Cherokees incorporated the ownership of enslaved Africans and their descendants into their way of life. Several ancestors of members of this study were slave owners. All belonged to families that had intermarried. Silas and Sarah Palmour owned one slave. So did George and Margaret Welch. Jesse and Mary Raper owned two slaves, and Polly Rattlinggourd possessed three. Michael and Nannie Hilderbrand owned five slaves.[37] Some of these families also developed other means of generating income, and several ran businesses that made Anglo-American technology available to Cherokees. Silas and Sarah Palmour owned a gristmill and a sawmill and were part-owners of a threshing machine.[38] George and Margaret Welch owned a mill and a blacksmith shop.[39] The Rapers owned a store.[40] The Hilderbrands claimed two mills and a ferryboat. One member of the family also was a mechanic.[41] In other words, the Cherokees who owned slaves were those who were most directly and aggressively participating in the developing commercial market of the American South.

By far, however, the technology that Cherokees embraced with the most vigor was literacy, which was widespread among them. The families of Polly Rattlinggourd and Huckleberry Crittenden included a member literate in Cherokee.[42] George and Margaret Welch's family included two readers of English.[43] Of the nine members of the Hilderbrand family, six read English and two read Cherokee.[44] Five members of the Taylor household read English, which raises an interesting question. The four children likely were literate, but which parent was? Should we assume that Andrew, an intermarried white, read his own language? I do not. I think he was the illiterate member of the family. His wife, Jane Bigby, came from an extended Cherokee family that included many readers of English and Cherokee, and I speculate that she was the literate adult in their household.[45]

In the decades after Hopewell, Cherokees rebuilt and recovered. Their range of adaptation is notable, and the diversity among them was obvious by the 1830s. Nonetheless, it is important to remember that the majority of Cherokees, including the ancestors of those in this study, remained simple subsistence farmers profoundly connected to their kin and their common land. After all, even the Palmours, slave owners who claimed improvements valued at over $3,000, lived in a log house. Tellingly, they left a second house on their property half-built when they were forced out by Georgians to march to a new homeland.[46]

Removal

The removal of the majority of the Cherokee population from the Southeast between 1817 and 1839 inflicted a dreadful wound that left gaping holes in Cherokee families and traumatized the survivors. The separation of families began generations before the Trail of Tears, however, as the wars of colonization tore through Cherokee lands. Some looked to the mountains of North Carolina for security and opportunity. Mary McDaniel was a Cherokee woman from a prosperous extended family whose members lived in what became Cass County, Georgia. She married Jesse Raper, a white man from South Carolina. After the birth of their first child, Martin, in 1808, the couple moved north to Cherokee County, North Carolina. Some of her kin joined them, but the rest of the McDaniels seem to have removed to Indian Territory during the 1830s. The Rapers would rejoin them there forty years later.[47]

Others moved west before the main body of Cherokees. Historical demographer Russell Thornton suggests that groups of Cherokees had been migrating to territory beyond the Mississippi River since as early as 1721.[48] In the 1830s, the pace of this self-directed emigration increased. Lydia Quinton, whose grandchildren Rosanna Mounce, John Kelley, and Laura Kirk are included in this study, survived a pre–Trail of Tears migration to Indian Territory. Her family remembers her story. Lydia lived along the Etowah River, which Cherokees called the Hightower River, in the Old Nation. She was married to a white man, Samuel Quinton Jr. In 1834, their household included six members, one of whom was Nellie, whose descendants lived near Chewey during the allotment era. The Quintons lived in a prosperous part of the Old Nation, and Lydia was a woman of means. Georgians coveted the area's established plantations and productive fields, and during the winter of 1833–34, they seized the homes of the wealthiest Cherokees, including "Rich Joe" Vann and John Ross, the principal chief. The most powerful Cherokees had lost their material possessions and nearly their lives and seemed helpless to do anything in response. This assault fueled the fears of other Cherokees who owned nearby farms. At least six signers of the Treaty of New Echota, the controversial, fraudulent removal treaty negotiated by an unauthorized faction of the tribe, were neighbors to the Quintons. This included Stand Watie and Elias Boudinot. In 1834, Lydia Quinton's family decided to move.[49] Perhaps she sought to escape the factionalism and violence that troubled her people; she also could have feared the brutality of the Georgians who stole from and harmed Cherokees with impunity; or she may have thought that the best chance to maintain or improve her family's comfortable lifestyle lay in the West. Whatever motivated her, Lydia bought a flatboat to transport her family's material possessions. Her family, including ten-year-old Nellie, left their home and moved with approximately sixty other emigrants. The party joined a larger group led by U.S. Army lieutenant Joseph W. Harris, who described what happened to material pieces of Lydia's old home that she was trying to bring with her: their boat was "lashed abreast of the keel [of a steamboat]—filled in the night and went down. The people on board had barely time to save themselves. They lost most of their property." Lydia lost all of her material things, but her family survived.[50]

And, unlike many others, they remained together. Families routinely became separated during the removal process. Of his party, Harris wrote:

> The parting scene was more moving than I was prepared for; when this hour of leave-taking arrived I saw many a manly cheek suffused with tears. Parents were turning with sick hearts from children

who were about to seek other homes in a far off and stranger land; and brothers and sisters with heaving bosoms and brimful eyes were wringing each others [sic] hands for the last time. And often I observed some young man whom the spirit of roving or adventure had tempted to forsake all that was dear to him, to seek alone an uncertain future in other climes; or some young wife who was tearing herself from father and mother, "kith and kin," to follow the fortunes of her husband whithersoever they should lead, turn again and again to the embrace of those they loved and were leaving.[51]

Although perceptive of the sadness to which he bore witness, Harris did not question his interpretation of Cherokee behavior. He saw the exodus of the young, particularly newly married women, as normal. Among Cherokees, however, such separation had no precedent, especially for women, who were accustomed to living their lives among their natal families.

Mary Brown's family provides another telling example of how this decades-long process separated families, some of whom never reunited. In the February 1819 Treaty of Washington, Cherokee leaders ceded the part of eastern Tennessee north of the Hiwassee River known as the Hiwassee District. That is where Mary's ancestors lived, and in 1820, her great-grandparents James and Catherine Bigby were forced from their home. Several of their eight children already were grown and married with children of their own, and this generation made different decisions about how to respond to the crisis. Most of the siblings eventually moved west with the majority of the Cherokee Nation. At least one, Thomas Wilson Bigby, settled in Goingsnake District. Mary Ann, who had married David Taylor, a white man from Virginia, eventually moved to a Cherokee community in North Carolina. Jennie and her husband, Andrew Taylor, took a reserve within the Hiwassee District, but this proved to be a temporary solution to their displacement. By 1849, the family again had lost their land in a ruling by the state court of Tennessee, and so Jennie, Andrew, and their children removed to Indian Territory. They, too, settled in Goingsnake District. Some of Mary Ann's children then also relocated there, but others remained in North Carolina.[52]

Cherokee families also lost enormous numbers to death. Historians do not have tools to measure heartbreak. I was not able to determine exactly how many ancestors of those in this study did not survive removal, but every family endured tragedy. The unspeakable suffering caused by the forced migration of Cherokees from their Old Nation to Indian Territory is nearly incomprehensible. The number of Cherokees who died along the "Trail Where They Cried," or Trail of Tears, is debated, but as many as 4,000 people, a quarter of the Cherokee population, lost their lives.[53] That number does not include those killed prior to the Trail of Tears or those who never recovered from removal and who subsequently died in Indian Territory.

Although a small number of Cherokees escaped removal in North Carolina and an even smaller number renounced their tribal citizenship and remained in Georgia or Tennessee, most Cherokees were removed between 1838 and 1839. Those who survived the trip made a place for their families in Indian Territory. Beginning in 1841, the Cherokee Nation extended citizenship to those who had not removed if they joined their kin in their reestablished homeland. The brutal guerrilla fighting of the Civil War between 1861 and 1865 heightened the importance of this mechanism for reunifying Cherokees. The tribal government promoted the restoration of families as a means of healing for its own citizens, but statesmen also had practical motivations. Beginning in the Reconstruction era, this generous immigration policy served as a means to deflect criticism from advocates of opening Indian Territory to non-Indian development about the supposed mistreatment of intruders, some of whom falsely claimed to be Cherokee citizens. The policy also stemmed from opposition to sharing settlements and tribal wealth with those Cherokees who lived outside of Indian Territory, specifically the Eastern Band of Cherokee Indians in North Carolina. Offering to include those who relocated justified the exclusion of those who remained apart from the Cherokee Nation.[54]

Family and community were important to the relocation process. Through years or even decades of separation, families maintained ties, and those petitioning for citizenship as Cherokees had to demonstrate a connection to living members of the Cherokee Nation as well as prove their Cherokee ancestry. Both were necessary for readmittance to Cherokee citizenship. For example, on September 14, 1883, the *Cherokee Advocate* reported on the reunification of the Nicholson family, some of whom had left Indian Territory for Texas during the Civil War. Richard, who had traveled to the Cherokee Nation in advance of relocating the remainder of his family, was the subject of the story, which emphasized his joy: "He left here yesterday for home well pleased with the hearty reception given him by his people after his thirty odd years separation from them. Give them time—and they will all come home."[55] Although the tribal government experimented with different means of evaluating citizenship applications beginning in 1869, these criteria demanding both biological and social ties did not change.

Most migrants came from North Carolina, where a growing Cherokee population remained after removal, but they also came from Georgia, Arkansas, and Texas, places where smaller populations of Cherokees lived due to the tragic realities of Cherokee history. For example, Jesse and Mary Raper's eleven children ended up divided in a pattern not unusual for Cherokee families of the era. Shortly after giving birth to the last of her ten children in 1871, their daughter Eliza Brown moved her family from Cherokee County, North Carolina, to the Cherokee Nation. Eliza's sisters Caty Johnson and Nancy Holland and their families also made the journey at the same time. Her brother Martin and sister Martha followed between 1880 and 1890. By the allotment era, over half of the Raper siblings either were living in Indian Territory or had died there, while the rest remained in Cherokee County.[56] Eliza may have made the journey to complete a process that their father had started. Jesse Raper seems to have visited Indian Territory in 1860, returned to North Carolina, and then relocated to Goingsnake District with Mary, where the couple are buried.[57]

Likewise, when Elizabeth Cannon's family left Georgia for the Cherokee Nation in 1870, they were greeted by relatives at the end of their journey. Elizabeth was the daughter of Silas and Sarah Palmour. Sarah was a daughter of Cherokees James Dougherty Jr. and Mary Dean. The Dougherty family, in particular, was a large, prosperous one. Rather than remove with the majority of her kin, Sarah chose to stay with Silas on 160 acres of their improved land in Lumpkin County, Georgia. In 1838, the state of Georgia admitted Sarah and her children, including Elizabeth, to citizenship. In 1851, Elizabeth married Irby Cannon, a white man, who worked as a miner and farmer. After surviving the Civil War, Elizabeth and Irby, who had ten children, decided to move west rather than face Reconstruction. Elizabeth joined her extended family in the Cherokee Nation and was readmitted to citizenship.[58]

As much as family pulled them, poverty pushed Cherokees toward Indian Territory. George and Margaret Welch were wealthy by the standards of removal-era Cherokees, but their descendants who remained in Georgia became landless within a generation. Their son George, who married a white woman, Nancy, continued living in Cherokee County, Georgia, after removal. In 1860, this younger George owned $800 in real estate and an additional $1,300 in personal property, but a decade later, he owned no land and only $150 in property. George's occupation likewise had changed. He farmed his own land in 1860. By 1870, he and his oldest son, Tom, were farm laborers. Within another year or two, the family moved to Indian Territory. The last thing Tom remembered of his old home was an aunt running after them with food for their journey west.[59] Once again, the Welch family was separated.

This same decline in status was reflected in the story of their cousins, other descendants of George and Margaret Welch through their son Lemuel, or Less. He also married a white woman, Mary, and they started a family in Georgia. By 1860, he was a laborer who owned no land and only $50 in personal property. The couple had seven children. The family's prospects improved some after they moved to Alabama. In 1870, Lemuel was a farmer with $775 in real estate, and his oldest son, George, owned an additional $50 in property. Nonetheless, the family moved to Indian Territory the following year around the same time that their cousins set out from Georgia. Both families settled in Goingsnake District near each other, and this particular group of Welches was reunited. Either these kin remained in contact over the years and across the distance, or their simultaneous arrival in the Cherokee Nation was a tremendous coincidence.[60]

Removal created a highway along which Cherokee people moved back and forth between the Old Nation and Indian Territory. Although displacement from their southeastern homeland was not reversible, many Cherokees, particularly those who had intermarried with whites, remained in contact with the few kin who had stayed behind. Two stories exemplify this. Malachi Parris, the father of Martha Phillips, came from a wealthy intermarried Cherokee family that left the Noonday Creek area of the Old Nation in 1832. They ultimately settled in Cane Hill, Arkansas. Malachi went back to Georgia as a young man, and there he met and married a white woman, Mahalia. They returned to Indian Territory and settled in Goingsnake District in 1851, prior to the birth of the last of their nine children.[61]

This mobility was not unusual. One of Eliza Brown's oldest granddaughters, Hattie, was born in Georgia *after* the whole family had moved to Indian Territory. Eliza's mother came from the area of the Old Nation that became Cobb County, Georgia, but she had moved her family to North Carolina shortly after 1808. In 1871, Eliza and her children moved from North Carolina to Indian Territory, but Eliza's daughter Love then traveled back to Georgia for the birth of her daughter Hattie in 1876. It is unclear who else made the trip with her. Love returned to Indian Territory with Hattie and gave birth to and raised the rest of her children there. Such incredible stories of migration suggest the persistence of familial bonds and the expectation of hospitality among family. That these aspects of Cherokees' ancient kinship system survived generations of intermarriage, removal, and thousands of miles of separation testifies to their durability.[62]

Indian Territory

Violence and factionalism characterized post-removal Cherokee history and erupted again during the Civil War. Some Cherokees remained apart from the nation during this period, some twenty years, as a result. Lydia Quinton and her family, for example, had left the Old Nation in 1834 and briefly settled in Goingsnake District but then moved across the state line into Arkansas, where other members of her extended family joined them. In other words, when the main body of the Cherokee people arrived in Indian Territory in the late 1830s, the Quintons moved away from them.[63]

Although there is no analysis of the political leanings of those who lived in the Goingsnake District of the Cherokee Nation during that tumultuous time, we can learn something about them by understanding whom local residents chose to honor when they named their new home. Goingsnake District, one of the original eight geographic and civic subdivisions within the Cherokee Nation, was established in 1840. The approximately 350-square-mile region was named after Going Snake, a venerated elder statesman aligned with the Ross Party, which opposed removal. Born in approximately 1758, Going Snake earned status, and probably his name, as a warrior, one who struck swiftly and quickly like a snake. During 1813 and 1814, he served in the Red Stick War and fought alongside Andrew Jackson and against the traditionalist faction of the Muskogees, or Creeks, longtime enemies of the Cherokees. Around the same time, he also began to serve as a representative to the National Council from Amohee District, and in 1827, he was elected to serve as speaker of the National Council. In other words, the same year that John Ross was elected to be principal chief, Going Snake also was tapped to serve the Cherokee people because of his oratorical skills and ability to negotiate and bring divergent groups to consensus. During a time when a minority of Cherokees asked the majority to support a radical experiment with republican government, Going Snake gave voice to the traditionalists.

His people continued to look to him for leadership during the removal. In 1838, he left the Old Nation for Indian Territory on the Trail of Tears.

According to one account, the old man, then in his eighties, led John Benge's contingent: "There was not a cloud in the sky that morning when the wagons lined up. Near the head of the line, sat Going Snake. . . . The old man, with hair whitened by eighty winters, bowed his head in prayer. When the order came to move out, the old man straightened his wiry body and led the way west. It is said that at that moment a dark cloud appeared in the distant west and thunder pealed forth, but no rain fell. It was as though a divine voice of indignation was protesting the brutal exodus." Going Snake built a new home in the hills of eastern Indian Territory. On July 12, 1839, he, along with Principal Chief John Ross and president of the National Council George Lowrey, signed the Act of Union with the Old Settlers. The old Cherokee nationalist had lived to see his people reunited, at least in ink on paper, and he likely died during the fall of 1839.[64]

The district was named after him the following year. It was probably during this time that those who were sympathetic to the Treaty Party, which had agreed to removal and opposed John Ross's authority, were uncomfortable living among these neighbors. This might have been the reason why Lydia Quinton's family moved across the state line into Arkansas, where they prospered. In 1860, the family owned $1,500 in real estate and $5,425 in total property. After the Civil War, Lydia moved back into Goingsnake District, where many of her descendants lived at the time of allotment."[65]

Little specific information exists about how the residents of this particular region of Goingsnake District experienced the American Civil War and the factional warfare that rent Cherokee society during the mid-nineteenth century. Much of the Cherokee Nation was destroyed, however, and civilians abandoned their homes to escape raiding and guerrilla warfare. Staying in the nation in the 1860s meant choosing a very difficult life. Cherokee genealogist James Carselowey recorded in his journal a story of a Cherokee mother who followed government wagons full of army supplies that passed by her home. She gathered the corn that fell from them. When she had an apron full of corn, she returned home. Her children would eat that day. Others relied on a traditional Cherokee food that passing armies had little interest in—acorns, which they hulled and pounded with a mortar as their grandmothers had once done east of the Mississippi River. Depending on their loyalties, others clustered in refugee camps across the border to the north in Kansas or fled south to Texas.[66]

Several ancestors of people in this study fought on the side of the Union and John Ross. Joe Chewey, the father of Bill Chewey, served as a lieutenant in the Second Indian Home Guard.[67] Yellowhammer Suake, who was married to Betsy and fathered Tom, Nannie, and Lawyer, also served in this unit.[68] Men from this area may have served under Stand Watie in the Cherokee Mounted Rifles of the Confederate States of America, but I was not able to find any with certainty.[69] This is probably because Goingsnake District was an area populated largely by "Pin Indians," or those affiliated with the Keetoowah Society and loyal to John Ross. Moreover, those loyal to Confederate general Stand Watie tended to settle to the west in the Canadian District after the Civil War.[70]

Tension continued to exist locally between those who had supported, or at least conceded to, removal and were more likely to sympathize with the Confederacy and those who had opposed removal and endorsed John Ross and the Union. Malachi Parris was the son of slave owners who had left the Cherokee Nation in 1829 to settle in Arkansas. He had returned to Georgia, where he worked as the weighmaster of a gold mine located in what had been Cherokee territory, but he eventually came back to the Cherokee Nation in the 1850s. Although the exact reasons are unclear, Malachi became a target of the sectional violence. A detachment of Union scouts that included some fellow Cherokees assassinated him near Cane Hill, Arkansas. Fearing for the lives of their sons, his wife and seven daughters went to claim his body for burial.[71]

It is relatively easy to trace the movement of large Cherokee populations and to describe the factional violence that plagued them in the aftermath of removal. Understanding the evolution of the Cherokee kinship system in these years is much more difficult. In part, this difficulty results from the secrecy that in the past shrouded and even today continues to shroud clan affiliation. At least since the tumultuous removal era, when violence divided Cherokees against themselves, people have kept clan affiliation close to their chests, because they believed that witchcraft was effective only when the clan affiliation of the intended victim was known. Even without access to such information, scholars still debate how the role of clans in Cherokee society evolved in response to the European invasion and American efforts to assimilate Indian people. Scholars argue that the centralization of the Cherokee government into a republic, the conversion of some Cherokees to Christianity, the participation of an increasingly wealthy minority of Cherokees in the market economy, and the intermarriage of some Cherokee women and men with non-Indians undermined the place and power of the clans. Others have pointed out that as it reorganized itself during the early republic, Cherokee society incorporated the values of kinship into its new government and laws.[72]

Undoubtedly, the clans changed throughout the nineteenth century, but as Cherokee anthropologist Robert K. Thomas suggests, a reorientation of clan affiliates does not necessarily correlate with the loss of the behavior and values of kinship associated with the clan system.[73] An increasingly inclusive understanding of relatedness may have enabled those who survived disease, war, and dislocation to rebuild and recover. Likewise, although the clans did not fill the formal, public, and political roles that they did earlier in the century, kinship continued to inform everyday life among Cherokees at the end of the nineteenth century in places like Chewey.

CHEWEY, A COMMUNITY along the Illinois River in the Goingsnake District, was named after Joe Chewey. He was a teenager when he crossed from the Old Nation to Indian Territory, and he was a grown man when he served in the Second Indian Home Guard during the Civil War. As a veteran, he was elected to the Cherokee legislature.[74] Joe Chewey died in the early months of 1894.[75] When elders like him passed away, their families lost more than grandparents. Cherokees of Joe Chewey's generation connected them to the Old Nation and the way of life Cherokees had known there. They were born just right. They were old enough to have known elders who had made their homes in the towns that existed prior to the American Revolution, and they were old enough to remember life in the east before removal. At the same time, they were young enough to have grown up as Cherokee society moved into what historian William McLoughlin has called the "Cherokee Renascence." They were the ones who had to reestablish the Cherokee Nation west of the Mississippi River and guide it through the Civil War.[76] Joe Chewey died as the Cherokee Nation faced allotment. He left few material possessions. As his legacy, he left children and grandchildren who knew something of change, survival, and persistence.

CHAPTER TWO

~~◅ ▻~~

Belonging

In the early 1880s, two boys approached a farmhouse on the Niescoop Prairie in Goingsnake District. They were brothers whose family had been traveling for days and was camped at nearby Tyner Creek. Exhausted and low on supplies, the parents sent their sons to a neighboring farm to buy food. Upon nearing the house, one of the boys, Gus, was struck dumb by the yard full of girls and hound dogs. He noticed one of them in particular, and she returned his attention. Ten or so years later, that girl, Ollie Brown, married Gus Hart. He later said, "Some might say that was just happenstance, but I believe it was Providence." Gus and Ollie stayed near her family. In fact, when they first married, they lived with her parents, John and Emily Brown, and her six siblings. Eventually, they established their own home. They had two daughters and a son. Gus and Ollie farmed. Along with her brothers, he ran a mill. They prospered and lived a good life.[1]

Ollie was a granddaughter of Eliza Brown, the matriarch of a large Cherokee family that emigrated from North Carolina to the Cherokee Nation in 1871. Gus Hart was an American from Texas, and when his family immigrated into the Goingsnake District in the 1880s, they were intruders, non-Indian squatters on tribal land whose presence helped to precipitate allotment.[2] But Ollie was doing what her elders before her had done. Her father, grandmother, and great-grandmother had married outsiders yet stayed among their own people. Ollie's great-grandmother Mary was a member of the McDaniel family that lived along Salequoyah Creek in the Old Nation. She had married Jesse Raper, a white man from South Carolina, who was one of three relatives, likely brothers, who

40

Eliza and James Brown. Photo courtesy of Jack D. Baker.

married Cherokee women. While members of their extended family moved back and forth between the Old Nation in Georgia and Cherokee County, North Carolina, Jesse and Mary had settled in North Carolina by the time of Eliza's birth in 1827. They first lived along the Nottley River but then moved northeast across the Hiwassee River to the Valley River region. Eliza married James Brown, a white man from nearby Tennessee. The family did well until the 1860s, but Cherokee communities in the mountains suffered during the Civil War and Reconstruction. Still, there was some happiness. In 1870, Eliza's son John married Emily McTaggert, a white woman from a neighboring family. The following year, the whole family moved to the Cherokee Nation. There they settled on the Niescoop Prairie. John and Emily had eight children, and seven lived to adulthood. Ollie, who married Gus Hart, was the oldest. One of Gus's sisters, Ida, married Cap, another of Eliza's sons. The rest of Gus's family moved on and settled to the west in Oklahoma Territory.[3]

How different was the household of Ollie Hart from that of her grandmother Eliza or her great-grandmother Mary? Would Selu, the first Cherokee woman, have felt comfortable in any of their homes? These family stories are riddles of persistence, and to understand them, we must focus on Cherokee households as sites of historical importance. Many sources of evidence provide insight: the 1880, 1890, and 1893 Cherokee censuses; the 1900 U.S. census for Indian Territory; records created by the Cherokee government; and the Eastern Cherokee applications. (See the appendix.) I use these sources to describe the composition of a typical late-nineteenth-century Cherokee family immediately prior to allotment, and I then explain the ways in which these people interacted with one other and how these exchanges exemplify the perpetuation of longstanding Cherokee kinship practices and values. Throughout this chapter, I emphasize the continuity of purpose amid changes in the forms that families took. Families remained egalitarian, flexible, inclusive, and decentralized, and extended families continued to provide needed order and stability through difficult times.

Cherokee Family Organization Prior to Allotment

The Cherokees who lived in Goingsnake District during the late nineteenth century were the survivors of the colonization of their southeastern homeland. Their elders bore witness to undeniable change throughout their lifetimes, and yet a remarkable stability nonetheless characterized the daily lives of common Cherokees. They fostered such normalcy by adapting the form of their households to broaden the bonds of relatedness. Betsy Oakball's life provides an outstanding example of this process and indicates how such adaptation reflected the persistence of the values and behaviors associated with kinship. Betsy, or Gar-de-tlo-a, was born in the Old Nation.[4] As a toddler, she survived the Trail of Tears, but her mother, Tsi-gu-mi, did not. Years later, Betsy remembered that her mother never left Georgia and died in 1839. Tsi-gu-mi may have died in one of the thirteen stockades in northern Georgia where Cherokees were briefly held during May and June 1838, or disease and despair could have caused her death in one of the eleven internment camps in Tennessee and Alabama, where imprisoned Cherokees waited to begin the march to Indian Territory in November 1838. Tsi-gu-mi also could have died on the long walk west. The last of the thirteen contingents did not arrive in Indian Territory until March 1839. It may have been comforting for this little girl who lost both her home and her mother (and probably other close relatives) to remember them as they once were—together. Betsy had four siblings, at least two of whom also survived. She knew little else about her extended biological family, including her father, A-ma-ga-na-hi. She did not know her grandparents. I do not know who raised her.[5]

Betsy grew up while the Cherokee Nation rebuilt itself west of the Mississippi River. She married a man named Oakball, or Omnagu, who also had been born in Georgia. He had at least four siblings, two brothers and two sisters. Betsy became a mother to sons White and John. Her husband died in 1873, the year after John, the youngest, was born, and Betsy did not remarry. Her boys knew both their paternal and maternal uncles and aunts, and so she maintained some type of relationship with her late husband's family. By 1880, she had settled in Goingsnake District. She remained close to her sister An-ne-wa-ke, whose death may have left her with no living direct maternal relatives by the time allotment began. Or, if she had them, she was not living with them at the turn of the twentieth century. By then, when she was in her seventies, her sons were grown and married with children of their own. Her younger son, John, lived nearby with his wife's family. Betsy likely shared her home with her older son, White, his wife, Susie, and their children, including Alisa, born in 1904. Among Cherokees of this era, the name "Alisa" was used interchangeably with "Betsy," and the girl was named to honor her grandmother. The elder Betsy died on September 26, 1910.[6]

The loss of loved ones characterized Betsy's life and shaped the options available to her, but so did flexibility. Betsy was bound by traditional conceptions of kinship to her maternal relatives but in life to other survivors. Some, like her sister, were maternal kin. Others, like her daughter-in-law Susie and granddaughter Betsy, were not, but throughout a lifetime so emblematic of the decimation of her people, Betsy Oakball made her home among those who were left—her sons *and* their families. Her life story hints at the causes for the shift toward the bilateral reckoning of kinship that had taken place among Cherokees by the late nineteenth century. Prior to allotment, most Cherokees saw themselves as related to both maternal and paternal relatives, an adaptation that facilitated physical survival while perpetuating the behaviors and commitments associated with traditional familial relationships.

Such inclusiveness did not mean the total demise of matrilineality, and Cherokees continued to favor their maternal relatives, particularly when crises necessitated care for survivors. Dan Downing's life provides a good example. Born on January 1, 1888, he was an infant when his father, James, died. His mother, Lucy, died in 1894, but Dan was not alone. Several maternal relatives cared for him temporarily until his mother's maternal first cousin, Noah Sand, took him in to raise along with his own sons.[7] According to Cherokees' traditional kinship system, Noah would have been like a brother to Dan's mother, and his relationship with the boy would have been a close one. For all the purposes that clans no longer served in Cherokee society, the obligation to care for children persisted.

Dan Downing grew up among Cherokees considered to be full bloods and traditionalists during the allotment era, but the tendency for maternal relatives to care for orphaned children defied the categories of blood quantum. Although the Cherokee Nation established an orphanage after the Civil War, no family in this study sent a child to it. Instead, relatives became the guardians of the children of their deceased kin. Take Nancy Allen, for example, who took in her sister's children. Nancy was the daughter of Rachel, who had married Reese Mitchell, a white Virginian. Nancy also married a white man, C. H. Allen. The couple had eight children of their own whose ages ranged from twenty to four when Nancy's sister Louisa died in 1882. Nancy took in Louisa's four children by three different men. She raised Birch and Cleo Anderson, Ida May Lane, and Alice Round along with her own children until Alice finished school, when she moved into the home of her maternal cousin, Fannie Welch.[8]

Such support transcended age. Maternal kin cared for each other throughout their lives whenever necessary. In 1898, Martha Phillips's household changed dramatically when her husband, James, to whom she had been married since before the Civil War and with whom she had six children, became paralyzed and died. His death left her and fifteen-year-old Jennie, their youngest child, in the family homestead. The rest of her grown children remained close, however. James Jr., in fact, lived next door. Soon after James's death, their daughter Maggie and four small grandchildren moved back in. Maggie's intermarried white husband, Tilman Chance, was serving a sentence in the federal prison in Jefferson City, Missouri, for perjury. Jennie soon married Ed Hines, a twenty-year-old white hired man from Arkansas then working for her eldest brother, John. When Tilman returned from prison, Maggie and her children reestablished a separate household with him nearby, but Jennie and Ed stayed with her mother on the family farm. Martha died in 1933. Jennie and Ed left the home in 1954 when their well dried up. Did Martha provide a home for her daughters, or did her daughters take care of her? Both. Cherokee households often contained extended maternal relatives because the kin of one's mother—and especially one's mother—remained a safety net.[9]

Residence patterns likewise show evidence of flexibility. No longer strictly conforming to matrilocal customs of household occupation, some Cherokees lived near paternal relatives. Susie Sante Fe, who grew up to marry White Oakball, was raised by her parents near her paternal grandmother, uncle, and aunt. When she married White, she moved into what was probably her mother-in-law Betsy's house.[10] On the other hand, Jennie Fields, who grew up to marry John Oakball, was raised by her mother, Celia. When Jennie and John married, John moved into the Fields family household. When Jennie's older brother Charlie married, however, he did not leave his family as John had. Instead, his wife, Carrie, also moved to live near the extended Fields family.[11] In short, matrilocal residence patterns were no longer the rule but one possibility. By the late nineteenth century, Cherokees were ambilocal, meaning that adult children tended to join or establish households near *either* the wife's or husband's parents.

Cherokees who married other Cherokees lived near either maternal or paternal relatives, but the families who continued to practice matrilocal residence patterns most consistently in the late nineteenth century were those families in which Cherokee women had intermarried with white men over successive generations. The family of Nellie Kelley, the daughter of a white South Carolinian and a Cherokee woman, and her husband, Joel, a white Georgian, exemplifies this trend. Of their nine children, eight survived into adulthood, and six of those eight children lived in close proximity to their parents when grown. Daughters Melvina, who married a Choctaw, and Laura, who married a Cherokee, did not but remained in Goingsnake District. Of the six adult children who lived near their parents, at least two daughters and one son intermarried with whites. Grandchildren also remained close, and even those raised farther away returned when starting their own household. For example, Melvina's daughter, Elizabeth, settled near her grandmother Nellie when she married a white man, John Washington.[12] In other words, families in which Cherokee women intermarried commonly remained matrifocal, and offspring who intermarried favored their relationship with their Cherokee parent and siblings over that with non-Indian relations.

Martha Phillips also lived surrounded by her adult children. Both she and her husband, James, were from Cherokee families that had intermarried with whites for several generations. When their children married and began families of their own, they overwhelmingly chose white partners and then remained in or near their parents' household. In 1890, the extended household included forty-year-old Martha and James;

twenty-one-year-old John and his intermarried white wife; twenty-year-old William and his intermarried white wife and their baby, Martha; seventeen-year-old Maggie and her intermarried white husband and their newborn, James; and unmarried children James Rufus, Sallie, and Jennie. Ten years later, James and his intermarried white wife were living next door to his then widowed mother. Maggie had left and returned to her mother's household. Jennie, Martha's youngest daughter, and her intermarried white husband still lived with Martha on the family farm and remained there with her.[13] While such arrangements could point to the persistence of matrilocal residence patterns, they also could be the logical outcome of intermarriage. Although some whites intruded into Indian Territory in family groups, many others lacked local relatives and, more important, the access to material resources that being a member of a Cherokee family entailed. Unlike individuals with Cherokee relatives on both sides, then, those with only one set of Cherokee kin, typically through the maternal side, tended to cluster by them.[14]

The mobility that Martha Phillips's children enjoyed was common among Cherokees, regardless of their preference in marital partners. Residence patterns were fluid throughout familial life cycles. Communal property ownership made it easy to move and build a new homestead or repair and improve an unoccupied one, and the customs of hospitality and reciprocity ensured familial support during these transitions. For example, Tom and Fannie Welch started their family near her kin, the descendants of Reese and Rachel Mitchell. In 1890, the young couple and their first two children lived near three of her maternal uncles and their families.[15] By 1900, however, their closest relatives were Tom's kin, including his brother James Mack and his sisters Eliza and Donas and their families along with his widowed mother, Nancy.[16] Young couples typically remained in or near parents' or other older relatives' households before building a farm of their own nearby after they had begun having children, but they sometimes stayed or, as often, left and later returned. Notably, building a separate house near relatives did not entail any attenuation of interaction, and family members continued to share resources and labor. Extended families, or two or more nuclear families made up of three or more generations sharing living and working environments, were the rule when considering clusters of homes and fields, their occupants, and their connection to one another.

Although households usually were no longer exclusively matrilineages, elderly women remained the core of Cherokee families. A historically matrilineal people, Cherokees were a people of mothers and, perhaps even more so, of grandmothers, because a person's physical connection to his or her nation derived from the oldest living female ancestor. But grandmothers served more than a symbolic role. They were vitally important to the day-to-day well-being of their descendants because they did much of the work associated with mothering by attending to the care, education, and loving of the young, thus freeing young, able-bodied women for more arduous work. A less tangible role was perhaps their most important— they passed on their knowledge and interpretation of the Cherokee world-view.[17] Known for her hospitality and her cooking, especially her hominy and bean bread, Martha Phillips, for example, also was a renowned story-teller who preserved the family's oral *and* written history, including a daybook written by her Cherokee father.[18] Throughout the last decade, while scholars have debated whether or not Cherokee women's status worsened as a result of the Euro-American conquest of their homelands, they have given little attention to the status of elders. Perhaps this neglect is because their continued authority is obvious in Cherokee communities even today. Especially among nonelite families, women maintained sig-nificant power over their households, and the most powerful among them were the gray-haired. They remained matriarchs of their families.[19]

With grandmothers at the core of their kin networks, Cherokees con-tinued to live in extended family groupings clustered among multiple homesteads. The occupation of individual homes was fluid, and members commonly included elderly parents, adult children, grandchildren, and other relatives. For example, in 1900, seventy-five-year-old Kate Sixkiller lived with her thirty-two-year-old grandson Sam. Her immediate neigh-bors were son Abe Sixkiller and his wife, Margaret, their five children, and Stan Watie Gibson, Abe's nephew and Kate's grandson. In the next house over lived William, a white man who had been married to Kate's late daughter Ellen, and five more of her grandchildren. Kate likely was involved in raising those children.[20] Women past their own childbear-ing years usually remained primary caregivers to multiple generations of children and relatives. In that same year, Betsy Suake, whose husband, Yellowhammer, passed away in 1898, led a household that included sons Jim and Lawyer, daughters Nannie, Linnie, and Mary, grandson William, and an elderly male cousin. Betsy was in a transitional moment in 1900. Her children were starting their own families, and she was beginning the next phase of her life, during which she would raise her grandchildren by two of her daughters and one of her sons.[21]

Adult children who established their own households away from parents tended to do so next to siblings. In other words, Cherokees who did not form extended families often belonged to joint ones. Such proximity between grown brothers and sisters was normal among both those whose families had intermarried with whites and those who had not. Although such lifetime bonds among sisters would be expected, this pattern is particularly noticeable among brothers. This visibility may reflect the increased difficulty of tracing Cherokee women in the documentary record, however, because they usually assumed the surname of their husbands by the late nineteenth century. When researching, I tried to find all family members in every source, but sometimes I could not. In other words, sisters may have formed these joint households as often as or even more often than brothers, but it was more likely that I could identify the latter in the documentary record, and so I make this conclusion with a caveat. For example, John and William, Martha and James Phillips's two oldest children, moved away from their widowed mother's household by 1900, but the brothers continued to live nearby as neighbors.[22] That same pattern describes the Cannon brothers, whose mother was Cherokee and whose father was an intermarried white man. Edwin, Oscar, and John were neighbors, and Wilson and sometimes Sterling lived a short distance away.[23] Oce and Jim Hogshooter, traditionalists who opposed allotment, lived next to each other throughout most of their lives. They also raised their families together. Such a close bond among siblings pervaded Cherokee society and spanned lifetimes. These relationships often were more durable than those between spouses.[24]

Because they were not exclusively nuclear, Cherokee households often included unmarried adult family members, especially men. Women almost always married, but some men did not. These bachelors typically remained in their natal home. Martin Raper, the eldest son of Jesse and Mary and the older brother of Eliza Brown, never established his own household. He shared a home with his parents until their death and after that with his sisters Martha and Eliza along with her husband, James.[25] Likewise, the sons of Noah Sand provide a telling example of the range of acceptable roles for young men in late-nineteenth-century Cherokee society. Noah Sand was in his late fifties by the end of the nineteenth century, and he was the father of three adult sons. Steve, who was in his late thirties, was married with children of his own and lived separately from his father. Will and John, both young men in their twenties, continued to live with their father and younger cousin Dan Downing. Anglo-Americans expected men to establish a separate household before fathering children, but Cherokees usually did not do so. Although he had a child with Sissa Mitchell, Will Sand continued to live with his family and she with hers. Both later married other people and had additional children. When Will eventually married, his wife moved into the home he shared with his father, Noah. There, they raised their children. John Sand, having never established a separate household, passed away in his thirties.[26]

The reasons why some men did not marry are difficult to discern. Only one healthy woman in this study remained unmarried throughout her adulthood, and yet I believe at least six men in this group who never married were able-bodied.[27] Why did they choose to remain single? Perhaps these men never met a suitable Cherokee or non-Indian partner. A lack of interest in marriage for reasons of sexual preference is a possibility but can remain only that; no documentary evidence points to the existence of open homosexuality among late-nineteenth-century Cherokees. Likewise, sexual activity was not confined to marriage, and bachelors were not inherently celibate. I suspect that these men's labor was essential to their natal household. Sam Sixkiller, who lived with his grandmother, seems never to have married. Did he assist Kate Sixkiller with the heaviest farmwork? Likewise, Ned Turtle stayed on with his mother, Fannie. After his father Arch's death, was his contribution essential to provide for the rest of his siblings and his niece? Men's ability to remain unmarried reveals the persistence of traditional conceptions of Cherokee masculinity. Men were valued for meeting the needs of their natal family members instead of being expected to form their own households. Because Cherokees owned their land in common, manhood did not require amassing a patrimony to bequeath to biological heirs, and so bachelorhood was a possibility for Cherokee men that did not deny them status, opportunities, or even sexual pleasure.[28]

By the late nineteenth century, Cherokee households commonly included members who were not biologically Cherokee. In 1835, just over three-quarters of Cherokees had no non-Indian ancestry.[29] By 1890, when the Census Bureau first tallied the residents of Indian Territory and noted the supposed blood quantum of Indian people, the Cherokee population was of markedly greater mixed heritage. The census takers reported that just over half of Cherokees were "pure bloods."[30] The presumed Cherokee proclivity toward intermarriage with Europeans and their descendants has transcended the scholarship on historical demography and entrenched itself in popular mythology as the "Cherokee grandmother syndrome." Russell Thornton offers several historically plausible explanations as to why so many Cherokee women may have married white men: a demographic imbalance resulting in a shortage of Indian men; immigration patterns resulting in a surplus of non-Indian men; and matrilineality preventing stigma against interracial children.[31] Scholars generally have focused on Cherokee women's intermarriage, but within this community, more Cherokee men married white women than the other way around.[32] In particular, men in the Cannon and Welch families chose white spouses over multiple generations. After the family relocated from Georgia to the Cherokee Nation, however, Welch men tended to choose Cherokee spouses, particularly women from other Cherokee families with their own history of intermarriage. The increased availability of Cherokee marriage partners in Indian Territory may have made intermarriage less likely.[33]

Nonetheless, children of an intermarried parent were more likely to intermarry than those whose parents had married other Cherokees. In other words, intermarriage "ran" in families. Eliza Brown and Elizabeth Cannon both chose non-Indian spouses as their mothers had done, and both had children who also intermarried. Of course, both also had children who married other Cherokees.[34] Indeed, children of intermarried parents routinely married other Cherokees. Mary Ghormley married Eliza's son Marsh, although her mother had intermarried, and so had her grandmother and great-great-grandmothers.[35] Cherokees whose parents were not intermarried with whites also had their choice of marriage partners and could choose non-Indians.[36] In short, intermarriage was a common choice that many Cherokees made, but it was not the only choice, because siblings within the same family often married other Cherokees.

Lacking clear, discernible patterns delineating these individual decisions, we are left, essentially, with love stories. The existence of love is a challenge to prove historically, for although marriage may attest to love, it could result from practicality, convenience, and dependency as well. Anthropologists Michael H. Logan and Stephen D. Ousley characterize relationships between Cherokee women and white men as love matches that provided economic benefits for Cherokee women.[37] Other scholars, such as Theda Perdue, have pointed out that these marriages entailed significant economic benefits for European men.[38] Marriage to a Cherokee woman had provided the social start-up capital for many a successful intermarried merchant or trader. In this area during the late nineteenth century, it primarily provided access to land. Some European or American men who married into Cherokee society did quite well for themselves and established their descendants as elites. The family of John Ross, principal chief during the removal and Civil War eras, is a good example. None of the Cherokees in this study attained wealth, though. On the contrary, intermarried families in the area surrounding Chewey in Goingsnake District had more in common with their kin and neighbors who did not intermarry than not. They shared a pattern of behavior characteristic of ordinary, subsistence-farming Cherokee families.

Cherokee Family Behavior Prior to Allotment

Throughout the nineteenth century, Cherokee family structure had evolved in response to war, disease, and dislocation, but family members continued to treat each other in ways consistent with their ancient kinship system. Cherokee families were still egalitarian, flexible, inclusive, and decentralized. Although the role of clans had diminished greatly, the values and customs associated with them continued to inform the everyday lives of Cherokees in discernible, predictable ways.

Relations between men and women remained egalitarian. Women and men alike owned improvements, including houses, farm buildings, and livestock, and this pattern transcended divisions within the community. Rosanna Mounce, whose grandmother Lydia Quinton was the woman of means who lost her possessions while migrating west to Indian Territory, was herself a woman who attained some level of material comfort. Her farm included two houses and a field of about fifteen fenced acres in cultivation. Rosanna's sister Melvina, the widow of Choctaw Levi Folsom, owned and ran her own business, a livery stable.[39] Women also continued to inherit improvements. Rosanna Mounce probably fell heir to and continued to improve upon her mother's farm. Although they lived with their mother, Nannie, and stepfather, Steve Dog, on another farm, Rachel, Sissa, and Dora Mitchell owned a farm of their own. Lacking more detailed probate records, it is impossible to know precisely who built it, but there are two possibilities. The farm could have belonged to their grandmother Sarah Proctor. It was located close to the homes of her brother Zeke and her other daughter, Betsy Suake. In 1890, she would have shared it with Nannie and her granddaughters. Sarah died in 1899. On the other hand, the farm could have belonged to the girls' father, Reese Mitchell. It was located near three of his siblings. Considering that Reese passed away in 1889 when he was only in his mid-twenties, the first possibility—that the elder Sarah had built this farm throughout her lifetime and left it to her granddaughters—seems a more likely choice.[40]

Historians Devon A. Mihesuah and Carolyn Ross Johnston have argued that at least some Cherokee women internalized Anglo-American ideals of "true womanhood," including sexual chastity, throughout the nineteenth century, but in comparison to their white counterparts, late-nineteenth-century Cherokee women retained enormous autonomy to engage in a range of sexual relationships. In other words, the ideological innovations adopted from Anglo-America that may have appealed to some elite Cherokees did not limit the romantic and reproductive choices of the rest. In fact, they seem not to have applied much at all in Goingsnake District. Serial monogamy remained the norm, and most Cherokees, including women, had multiple sexual partners throughout their adult lives.[41] Because I usually was able to identify definitively only those relationships that resulted in children, I likely grossly underestimated the number of sexual relationships that many Cherokees had. For example, take Sarah Proctor and just her female descendants through 1900. Sarah, who was born before removal and crossed over to Indian Territory as a young girl, had five children with Ned Foreman before they separated: Stephen, Joe, Thomas, Betsy, and Fannie. She then had Nannie with Rider Acorn. Acorn died shortly before or after Nannie's birth, and Sarah may have married again. In the 1880 census, she is listed under the surname Whale. Her daughter Fannie was married once, to Arch Turtle, whom she outlived by decades. Betsy had at least two relationships. She was married to Yellowhammer Suake, and after her husband's death, she lived with John Blackfox. Nannie was married to Reese Mitchell and then Steve Dog. Sarah's granddaughters had just begun their reproductive lives by the time their grandmother passed away in 1899. That same year, two of Betsy's daughters each had their first of two sons by two separate relationships. Fannie's eldest two daughters were married, and the oldest was pregnant with her third child. Nannie's eldest daughter, Sissa, who was not married, was pregnant with her first baby.[42] In other words, women consistently demonstrated that they had considerable sexual autonomy, but the pattern is incomplete because it is evident primarily through successful pregnancies. It is difficult to track this behavior once women's reproductive years ended, although many women, like Sarah and Betsy, may have continued to enjoy their sexuality after they were no longer able to bear children.

This pattern of behavior remained consistent among those whose families had repeatedly intermarried with Anglo-Americans as well as those who had not, and if intermarried Anglo-American fathers had sought to impose the value of sexual purity on their Cherokee daughters, they failed. Throughout Cherokee society, sexual and marital relationships were characterized by fluidity rather than permanence or exclusivity. Louisa Mitchell was the product of four generations of intermarriage that began with her great-great-grandmother Nancy marrying Bryan Ward. Louisa also intermarried a man named Daniel Anderson and gave birth to two children, Birch and Cleo, thirteen months apart. Daniel died the following year. Louisa remarried and, five years later, had another daughter, May, or Mabel, Lane. It is unclear whether she again was widowed or if she left this husband. Five years later, in 1880, however, Louisa, then thirty-two years old, was married to a fifty-one-year-old Cherokee man named James Round. She gave birth to another daughter, Alice, later that year. Louisa died in 1882.[43]

Although some Cherokees took vows and registered their relationships with the tribal government, marriage remained a product of communal validation. Some Cherokees did marry before a minister. Reverend Adam Lacie, a Cherokee Baptist minister, administered vows to three couples in this study, and they provide a perfect snapshot of both the diverse ancestry and common culture shared by the families of this area. He married Oscar Cannon, the son of a Cherokee woman and an intermarried white man, and his wife, Annie, a white woman.[44] He administered vows to Cherokees Mose Crittenden and Minnie Proctor.[45] Lacie also officiated the ceremony of Tom Suake and his first wife, Charlotte, who were from families considered to be full bloods.[46] However, most couples did not marry formally. Community recognition remained an important and common means of validating marriages. Years later, when asked if her son Tom had been legitimately married to Charlotte, Betsy asserted that he had been, but not because the couple had taken formal vows; rather, it was because "I gave them a supper."[47] For couples whose families did not honor them with a public feast, living together and raising children signaled to community members that they were committed, and although Cherokee law provided for marriage either by a judge or a clerk, most Cherokees in this study were married by community recognition instead. Cap Brown, a son of Eliza Brown, remembered most folks in the area practicing common-law marriage.[48]

Divorce, therefore, remained accessible and common. Rosanna Mounce's life reflects the range of consensual sexual relationships that could be considered to be marriage and likewise the various ways of separating that could be considered to be divorce. Her first son, Wyly Beavers, was born during her teens as a result of her relationship with George Beavers. Because she never lived with George, she did not consider herself to have been married to him. Her second son, Jesse, was the product of her marriage to Bill Smith, a noncitizen, to whom she was not legally married according to Cherokee law but from whom she was divorced by the state of Texas (the divorce was not legal as Texas had no jurisdiction over marriages in the Cherokee Nation). Her third relationship was with James Garner, a non-Indian carpenter a dozen years her senior. They separated within a year. Finally, she married Joe Mounce, another non-Indian, according to Cherokee law. They had two sons, Thomas and Ellis, and remained married until her death in 1911. The boundary between "common-law" and "by law" was open to interpretation, too. Rosanna testified before the Dawes Commission that she considered herself to have been married three times "lawfully" and excluded the relationship with Beavers, of which the commissioners seem to have been unaware, although they enrolled Wyly. In 1910, the census taker identified her marriage to Joe as her second, but he did not specify which of her three previous relationships counted as her first marriage. After her death, an Adair County probate court determined that Mounce had been married three times because they counted only those relationships that had resulted in children. In other words, they included her relationship with Beavers and excluded that with Garner.[49]

Ending romantic relationships remained easy, in part, because the customs of matrilineality continued to govern child custody arrangements. There is no evidence that separating parents fought over their children. In fact, every woman in this study retained custody of her children when a relationship ended. Nannie Wolfe, for example, had children by William Batt, Jesse Sunday, and Bill Chewey. She raised them, and by the mid-1890s, the youngest two lived in a household that included Tom Wolfe and his sons. Nannie and Tom had one son who died as an infant.[50] Nannie's oldest daughter, Jennie, also retained custody of her son Martin after she left his father, Will Foreman, and married Nelson Crittenden, with whom she had nine more children.[51] Widows likewise retained custody of their children. When Nellie Kelley's oldest son, Wiley, died in 1872, neither she nor his adult sisters raised his children. Instead, his widow Sarah remarried and moved the children to the Canadian District, where she and her second husband made a home. Wiley was not forgotten, however. His sister Rosanna named her first son after him.[52]

As Tom Wolfe's story suggests, however, customs concerning the custody of children whose mothers had died but whose fathers remained alive had changed. Maternal kin no longer automatically assumed responsibility for children when their family members died. Instead, some fathers, especially those who remarried, continued to raise them. When Tom Wolfe's first wife, Jane, died, he moved away from her family and closer to his, where he continued to raise sons John and Jesse. He remarried twice, first to Annie and then to Nannie.[53] Maternal kin nonetheless remained a presence in the children's lives. After the death of Sam Crittenden's wife, Annie, in 1900, he continued to raise their three children. Their maternal grandparents, Isaac and Nancy Youngbird, remained close to them.[54] When his first wife, Carrie Cannon, died, John Welch's in-laws continued to be a presence in the lives of the couple's children. Dovie, their eldest maternal aunt, became especially invested in them when she became John's second wife. The couple had at least five more children of their own.[55]

The conception of parenthood expanded as biological fathers and stepfathers assumed some roles traditionally filled by maternal uncles. In other words, men were parenting the children in their households, regardless of whether or not they were the biological fathers. It is difficult to find evidence of caregiving in the historical record because so much of the work of parenting went (and still goes) undocumented. For example, I do not know who taught any of the boys in this study to hunt, a responsibility that had been performed by maternal uncles traditionally but likely was filled by biological fathers by the late nineteenth century. Such intricate details about relationships were not recorded. Surnames, however, were written down. By the late nineteenth century, Cherokee men identified their biological children as their own, but some even claimed the other children who lived in their household as theirs, too. Louella Sunday and Sam Chewey were listed under the surname of "Wolfe" in the 1896 Cherokee census. Was it the census taker's mistake, or had their stepfather, Tom, truly bonded with them such that they were his family?[56] Likewise, Nelson Crittenden claimed his stepson, Martin Foreman, as his own son in his Eastern Cherokee application from July 1907. After listing his minor children with wife Jennie, he added her son from a previous relationship, then seventeen years old, as "Martain Crittendon."[57]

Raised by his maternal uncle Noah Sand after the death of his parents, Dan Downing also was known socially as Dan Sand.[58] Of course, the use of surnames passed through fathers was not part of precontact Cherokee culture, but Cherokees incorporated the custom by the early nineteenth century after they began to intermarry with British officers and traders. Still, such fluidity in naming had deep roots in Cherokee culture, and the assumption of these names may have reflected the bond between these men and the children with whom they shared a household. In this sense, blood remained only one indicator of relationship and not the most important.

As the personal histories recounted above demonstrate, marriage was not the only context in which Cherokees had sexual relationships. Premarital intercourse was common. Rosanna Mounce is just one example. Annie Bearpaw is another. She remained in her parents' household after giving birth to an infant son, William Chewey, named after his father. The baby soon died. She was fifteen. She eventually married Bill Chewey, and the couple had a daughter in 1898 and another in 1901 before separating. Annie remarried Tom Suake and had another son, Frankie, before she passed away.[59] Young mothers, however, did not necessarily marry the fathers of their infants. After the birth of her son Dachichi Bear, Betsy Wilson continued to live with her mother, Diana Wilson, and her brother Jim until her marriage to Lewis Bird.[60] Cherokees did not stigmatize unwed mothers, who enjoyed the support of their natal families and the same range of opportunities for future relationships, including marriage, as any young Cherokee woman who did not have a child. Sissa Mitchell, the daughter of Nannie Dog and Reese Mitchell, had a baby with Will Sand. She continued to live with her parents until she married Jesse Bird, Lewis and Betsy's son.[61] This lack of stigma and punishment for premarital sexual activity and unwed motherhood sharply distinguished Cherokee norms from those of the surrounding Anglo-American society, which had become increasingly punitive toward those who engaged in this behavior and their offspring over the course of the nineteenth century.

Although Cherokees enjoyed considerable sexual freedom as young adults, most eventually settled into a committed relationship, and that pattern characterized the people in this study. Lewis Bird, for example, had at least two relationships. In 1880, he was twenty-five years old and married to a twenty-three-year-old woman named Susan. Betsy Wilson was then fifteen and the mother of an infant by a man she never married.

By 1890, Lewis and Betsy were married, and their household included Betsy's first son and their first two children together, Jesse and Lucy.[62] For many, the creation and maintenance of a long-term relationship likely was a mark of maturation, though whether motivated by resignation or affection is difficult to prove. History may have provided us just a glimpse into Lewis Bird's heart, however. In 1907, he submitted his Eastern Cherokee application and responded to the question about his marital status by saying that he was married to Betsy. She had been dead for four years. He had been happily married to her for about twenty years. He did not remarry.[63]

Like Bird, most Cherokees seemed to prefer marriage, and most children, therefore, were the product of long-term, if not always permanent, relationships. Nelson Crittenden's life best reflects this trend. Nelson married Mary Sweatbee in his early twenties, and beginning in 1868 the couple had four children before separating. He remarried to Katie Hart, with whom he had one daughter. He then married a third time to Jennie Bat, Nannie Wolfe's daughter. They had nine children together. Their youngest son was born in 1913. In other words, Nelson fathered fourteen children over forty-five years, and all of them were within his three marriages.[64]

Cherokees remained flexible and inclusive in their selection of sexual partners and mates. In particular, they did not let the factional divisions emphasized by modern historians limit their pool of potential spouses. This pattern transcended generations. Lydia Quinton, Rosanna Mounce's grandmother, married a white South Carolinian. The man had fought on the Patriot side during the American Revolution, and the South Carolina militia had waged scorched-earth warfare against the Cherokee Nation because of its alliance with Great Britain.[65] Margaret Sixkiller's father, Aaron Crittenden, was from an Old Settler family, or those who had migrated west to Arkansas beginning in 1817 and who relocated again into Indian Territory in 1828, and her mother, Catherine Foreman, was the daughter of survivors of the Trail of Tears. Relations between these two factions were acrimonious in the aftermath of removal, but the birth of Margaret in 1857 suggests that at least some Cherokees put their grievances aside.[66] Likewise, Tom Welch's paternal grandfather, George Welch, was a member of the Treaty Party, yet he married a descendant of survivors of the Trail of Tears as well.[67] Although Cherokee society was wracked by the same factionalism that plagued most Indian communities in the course of war, removal, and revival, subsequent generations promptly and intimately defied those divides. Sexual relationships were one way to unify a community and restore or even extend the bonds of reciprocity.

Likewise, the lines based on blood quantum that the Dawes Commission would draw seemed to have little relevance to those picking mates during the late nineteenth century. Cherokees commonly married across the boundaries of full blood and mixed blood that would feature so prominently on the Dawes roll. The descendants of Reese and Rachel Mitchell provide one example. Reese Mitchell Sr., a white man from Virginia, married Rachel Hilderbrand, a Cherokee woman from Tennessee whose family had intermarried with whites for three generations before she was born. The eleven children of Reese and Rachel Mitchell had one full-blood Cherokee great-grandparent. In the math of blood quantum, they had one-sixteenth Cherokee ancestry.[68] Five are included in this study. Nancy married a white man. Jane never married but had a daughter, Fannie, with a white man. Rebecca married Zeke Proctor, identified as a full blood. Louisa married three times, and at least one of her husbands was a white man and another was a Cherokee of mixed ancestry. Reese Jr. married Nannie Acorn, considered to be a full blood by the Dawes Commission but who had mixed ancestry. In other words, the children of Reese and Rachel Mitchell formed relationships that reflected the range of Cherokee society.[69]

Closer analysis of a few of their children's relationships further demonstrates the irrelevance of blood quantum as a factor in family formation and, as will be discussed in greater detail in chapter 5, how grossly inaccurate the Dawes Commission's evaluations were of the actual ancestry of Cherokee allottees. Fannie, Jane's daughter, married Tom Welch, the son of George and Nancy Welch, another family that had intermarried with whites for several generations.[70] Rebecca had four children with Zeke Proctor, including triplets: Minnie and Linnie both married Cherokee men with some non-Indian ancestry; William, the other triplet, had a child with Nannie Palone, the daughter of Betsy Suake.[71] The Suakes were considered to be full bloods, and William and Nannie's boy, William Jr., was designated as a full blood by the Dawes Commission.[72] Louisa's son Birch and daughter Cleo also married into families with their own history of intermarriage. Birch married Eliza Brown's granddaughter Lizzie, and Cleo married Mack Welch.[73] Reese Jr. married Nannie Acorn during the early 1880s. Barely in their twenties, the couple had three daughters in quick succession: Rachel (named after Reese's mother), Sissa, and Dora.

Reese died before 1890, leaving his wife, then twenty-six, with seven-, five-, and three-year-old daughters. Nannie then lived with her mother, Sarah Proctor, who helped care for the girls. Sarah was the daughter of Will Proctor and Dicey Downing, two extended Cherokee families with a history of intermarriage. By the time of allotment, Nannie had remarried Steve Dog, and the Dawes Commission listed the entire family, including Rachel, Sissa, and Dora Mitchell, as full bloods.[74] In short, one does not have to trace out too many of these families' relationships to realize that sexual attraction bore no correlation to blood quantum in the late nineteenth century.

There was one sexual boundary that Cherokees did not cross. No formal law enacted by the tribal government forbade marriage to maternal relatives, but Cherokees nonetheless observed such a prohibition. This custom, originating in clan law that labeled such relationships as incestuous, persisted. Although Cherokees in this study married a wide range of their neighbors and outsiders, I found evidence of only one relationship between maternal kin prior to allotment. Hattie Thompson, a granddaughter of Eliza Brown, married James Holland, the son of her maternal great-aunt Nancy, who was her grandmother Eliza's sister.[75] On the other hand, Cherokees in the allotment era did not give preference to paternal kin or even the kin of their maternal grandfathers, as had been custom when clan affiliation strongly influenced the selection of marital partners. Some extended families did intermarry among successive generations, but these unions do not seem to follow customary patterns.[76]

Residence patterns also were flexible. Cherokees commonly moved across geographic boundaries within and beyond the Cherokee Nation. People frequently relocated among the districts of the Cherokee Nation, and kin seem to have been widely dispersed. For example, Nannie Wolfe was born in Goingsnake District, lived briefly in Tahlequah District during her twenties when married to Jesse Sunday, but then moved back to Goingsnake District, where she lived the rest of her adult life.[77] The man who would be her fourth and final husband, Tom Wolfe, and his first wife were not living in Goingsnake District during the 1880 census, but Tom's father enrolled the couple there anyway. They may have been living on a farm to the north of Goingsnake District on the Buffalo Prairie. By 1890, Tom had returned to his home community and remained in the area for the rest of his life. His reasons are unclear, but perhaps the death of his first wife, Jane, prompted his return to his kin. By then, Tom, then thirty-five, was married to Annie, who was nineteen, and in addition to

Tom's sons John, age twelve, and Jesse, age ten, the couple had an infant son named Davis.[78]

Young men commonly left the Cherokee Nation for several years as a normal part of their maturation process. Some traveled east to pursue a higher education. For example, William Potter Ross attended Princeton. Ross ultimately returned to his family, married, made a home, and served his nation as principal chief. Others learned through their travels by taking odd jobs and by seeking their fortunes, especially in the West. In 1841, a young Dennis Wolf Bushyhead left Goingsnake District to study at Princeton but returned home after the death of his father, Reverend Jesse Bushyhead, a minister and the chief justice of the Cherokee Nation. The young man worked in Lewis Ross's store for three years and also served as the clerk of the Senate. Two years later, in 1849, he left for California among a group of over a hundred young Cherokee men participating in the gold rush. He returned nearly twenty years later, in 1868, married in 1870, and was elected to serve as the treasurer in that same year. In 1879, he was elected to be the principal chief.[79]

This regular outmigration of young men likely had its origins deep in Cherokee history. Although Cherokees had been an agricultural people who lived in towns, these communities were populated predominantly by women. Men were absent for long periods of time when fulfilling their duties as hunters or serving as warriors, traders, or diplomats. In other words, the periodic absence of a father or husband was normal in Cherokee society, especially prior to the late eighteenth century, and although Cherokee men became more settled following the Revolutionary War as the occupations of warrior and hide hunter became politically and economically irrelevant, young men retained the right to leave, at least for a while. Writing in the 1960s, anthropologist Albert L. Wahrhaftig explained that this persistent custom was a means through which Cherokee communities safely incorporated outside knowledge. Upon their return, community leaders and elders reintegrated the men by listening to stories of their experiences and, more important, by helping them to use their acquired skills and wisdom for the benefit of their community.[80] This custom contrasted sharply with expectations for self-sufficiency and individual success embraced by young men in Anglo-American society, who were encouraged to establish themselves as independent from their families.

During the late nineteenth century, Cherokees continued to rely on a range of resources and practiced a decentralized division of labor. Although some in the Cherokee Nation were quite wealthy, the families in this study were not. Cherokees who lived in and around Chewey were just beyond the subsistence level. They traveled to commercial districts to trade the little surplus they produced, but the majority of their productive work took place within their homesteads and the surrounding woods and nearby streams. Some, like the Browns, settled in prairie land, while others, like the Dogs, nestled their farms higher into the hills, but all built along stream banks and near springs. Late-nineteenth-century Cherokees were sedentary people who did not confine their productive labor to a few crops or activities but practiced a wide range of subsistence activities. Their farms, in other words, should be seen as hubs for a range of group and individual tasks that collectively contributed to familial survival. As their ancestors had done, late-nineteenth-century Cherokees implemented a mixed subsistence strategy that combined agriculture and the management of livestock with hunting, fishing, and the harvesting of natural resources such as nuts, wild fruits, and plants.[81]

The typical pre–allotment era farm in the region consisted of between ten and thirty acres, although a few families farmed more.[82] Wyly Beavers, a son of Rosanna Mounce, remembered growing up on his maternal grandparents' farm, which included about thirty acres in cultivation.[83] He recalled this spread as relatively large for the area. Cap Brown, a son of Eliza and James Brown, remembered his parents' farm as about the same acreage at the time. He considered his family to be well off.[84] Families grew a range of crops. The most common included corn, peas, squash, sweet potatoes, and pumpkins. Cherokees continued to practice polycropping, meaning the cultivation of multiple crops immediately adjacent to each other. As result, their fields, while small, were less vulnerable to pests and disease and probably more productive per acre.[85] It is not clear who completed which particular tasks, but women and men both performed agricultural labor. Nellie Wolf recalled that her husband, Jack, had always helped her put in their large garden, and while both participated in the work of farming, she identified it as her primary responsibility, whereas he also hunted.[86]

Most families also owned livestock, especially pigs but small herds of cattle, too. Communalism informed the management of these resources. The animals, though owned by individuals, roamed and grazed freely about the countryside with only their owners' marks in their ears. Families registered their marks and brands with the Cherokee government, but that served to identify animals that wandered too far rather than to protect them from use by others. The honesty of neighbors was the only barrier to the animals' becoming someone else's supper.[87] Most men continued to provide meat through hunting, and venison remained a seasonal staple of their diet. Nellie Wolf remembered her husband's skill as a hunter, noting that Jack used a muzzle-loading rifle, a bow and arrows, and even rocks to kill wolves, bobcats, minks, opossums, raccoons, skunks, badgers, and, above all, deer.[88]

Animal products provided most families' only way of getting money and, therefore, trade goods prior to allotment. Until the end of the century, Cherokees continued to sell pelts, especially otter, beaver, and mink, to fur buyers from St. Louis who came to the area to trade with local merchants.[89] Families also carried on a small-scale trade in livestock and dressed meat with local merchants. Although hunting and trapping were men's work, women also engaged in this form of meat production. In particular, cured hams provided an easily transportable, reliable source of revenue with which to purchase supplies that families could not produce themselves, such as coffee and sugar. Jess Wright, who lived in the area, remembered that his family grew, raised, and preserved nearly everything that they needed, but his mother-in-law traded a ham for what they could not make themselves or barter for among neighbors.[90] During the late nineteenth century, families from the area surrounding Chewey typically traveled across the border into Arkansas to shop at Cincinnati and Siloam Springs. They traveled on foot or horseback but rarely by wagon. Roads were dirt paths, and travel by team and wagon was difficult.[91]

Cherokees' diverse farming strategy proved sound. The region's thin soil was easily sapped, and it was not prudent to gamble survival on tilled fields alone in such an environment. Maintaining broad networks of reciprocity also remained a priority. Cherokees tended to work their fields with household members, whereas gathering and fishing were tasks often done alongside neighbors and other kin. Although there is no evidence of communal labor organizations, called *ga-du-gi*, like those that existed in Cherokee communities in North Carolina, Cherokees in Indian Territory tended to do some work, like berry picking and gathering nuts, in groups. Jensie Dick, who grew up in the region, recalled that extended families came together for extended periods of work intermixed with relaxation, and reestablishing fellowship with one other was as important as the food resources obtained.[92]

Such communalism also is evident regarding the sharing of new information and technology. Wash Lee, a Cherokee Civil War veteran who lived near Baptist Mission, purchased the region's first thresher, an

Innerless Chain Thresher brought from Cincinnati, Arkansas. Although corn remained the predominant grain planted in the Cherokee Nation, Cherokees grew small amounts of wheat. Without a thresher, however, it was difficult to process; people typically cleaned it by hand on a flat rock. Lee coordinated with a group of neighbors, including Soldier Sixkiller and Tom Suake, to take the thresher, pulled and powered by a team of horses, from farm to farm at harvest time. Lee's efforts gave the community greater access to a viable food source while reinforcing existing relationships among the Cherokee families of the region. Tellingly, the thresher, a machine run by horsepower, empowered men with the means to increase production of a crop not associated with women like corn was. Was the thresher the new plow? Equally suggestive is the fact that all of the men involved were veterans, Cherokee Baptists, or traditionalists, hinting that the bond among them was more specific then neighborliness. They likely were Keetoowahs.[93]

Not surprisingly, literacy was a tool Cherokees also shared widely. Cherokee parents in this study generally were educated people who, in turn, educated their children. By the late nineteenth century, families commonly had been literate for several generations. Catherine Tarepin could read and write, and so could her daughter Margaret Sixkiller, who was sending her children to the school at Baptist Mission during the late nineteenth century. In 1900, Abe and Margaret Sixkiller were educating three of their five children, and they were typical of the parents in this study. Only their oldest son, Dennis, a teenager who had already completed his education, and the youngest, Retta, a small toddler, were not attending school. Two of their children later specified the outcome of their education. Dennis and their daughter Kate had learned to speak, read, and write English. They, like their father, spoke but did not read or write Cherokee. It is likely, then, that Cherokee was spoken in their home, and literacy in English did not correlate to the abandonment of the Cherokee language. Bilingualism, rather, was one more shared resource.[94]

Even within this small study, there was a wide range of educational experiences and outcomes. Moreover, degrees and types of literacy are difficult to discern from the documentary record. Few people in this study were like Sam Chewey, Nannie Wolfe's son. He was a year younger than Dennis and four years older than Kate. He was fully bilingual in that he read, wrote, and spoke both English and Cherokee.[95] He did not note which local school he attended, but it might have been the Joe Chewey School, which existed briefly during the 1890s. This Cherokee Nation school was taught by Bluford Sixkiller and Oce Hogshooter. Hogshooter seems to have been one of the most educated members of this study; he attended the Cherokee Male Seminary for two years after completing six years at a local school. In addition to serving his community as a schoolteacher, he also later served as the secretary for the Nighthawk Keetoowahs. Oce was fully bilingual. Jim, Oce's brother, attended school through third grade, and he read, wrote, and spoke English. He spoke Cherokee, but whether he read and wrote it is unclear.[96] Even within families, then, Cherokees attained varying levels of education that differed among siblings in no discernible pattern. For example, Sissa Bird is identified as unable to read and write, but her younger sister Dora attended school through the fourth grade and was fully literate in English and could speak Cherokee. Their half-brothers Johnson and Arch were literate enough to sign their names, but their younger half-sister Tinna was so proficient in English that she wrote scathing letters to the Indian Office, a story told in chapter 7.[97]

Few Cherokee were fully bilingual, but even fewer were totally illiterate. Literacy was the norm in this study, especially among those considered to be full bloods, and in fact, the two extended families that had the most illiterate members were those who had intermarried with whites for generations and had relocated to the Cherokee Nation late: the Phillipses and the Kelleys. Martha Phillips could read but not write. Her daughters Maggie and Jennie attained the same small level of literacy, but her sons William and James could not read or write. Only her oldest son, John, was listed as able to both read and write English. None appear to have been able to read, write, or speak Cherokee.[98] Lydia Quinton was illiterate, and so were her daughter Nellie and Nellie's intermarried husband, Joel. In turn, their daughter Rosanna and son John were illiterate, but their younger daughter Laura may have been able to read and write. This improvement might have occurred because the family was able to educate the younger children in the Cherokee Nation schools after they moved from Arkansas to Goingsnake District in 1867. Rosanna was thirteen and John was eleven by then, and Laura was only three. Most, but not all, of the next generation received some education, but some degree of illiteracy persisted.[99]

For those who did reunite with family and rejoin the Cherokee Nation after removal or the Civil War, Cherokee Nation schools provided a venue in which to educate children and foster a common identity among them. The Cannon brothers exemplify this. When the family relocated from Georgia to the Cherokee Nation in 1870, Edwin was fifteen, Wilson was ten, Sterling was seven, Oscar was four, and John was one. Edwin was able to read and write English, but there is no evidence that he attended the Cherokee Nation schools. Wilson, however, did, and therefore those younger than him probably did, too. They are listed as literate in English in subsequent documentation. Wilson began school in the spring of 1871. His teacher was Cary Bushyhead, the sister of Dennis Wolf Bushyhead, who would serve as the principal chief of the Cherokee Nation between 1879 and 1887. Wilson learned to read and write English, which he already spoke, but he also learned to speak Cherokee, starting with how to count and the names of the local animals he trapped to earn extra money for the family. His teachers were the boys his age who were his playmates and hunting companions. Likewise, his Cherokee mother reinforced his reading skills. Wilson did not mention whether his father was literate or not, but his mother had some few years of education such that she could help him continue his studies when he had to skip school to work on their farm. Between these two Cherokee women, his mother and Cary Bushyhead, Wilson received enough of an education so that when he had children of his own, he knew the value of learning. In 1902, he led the parents in his community in establishing the Beaver School. His six children graduated from the eighth grade, and he served on the school board for twenty-seven years.[100]

Power also was decentralized. No institutions competed with extended families for importance, and those that existed were nonhierarchical and localized. Christianity was important to some families in this study, and it had been since before removal. Evan Jones began preaching among Cherokees in 1821 in the Valley Towns, and because his inclusive interpretation of Baptist Christianity encouraged acceptance of Christian teachings through Cherokee culture, especially the language, Cherokees embraced the Baptist practice. In 1832, the ordination of Cherokee minister Jesse Bushyhead further invigorated the acceptance of Baptist Christianity even among those considered to be traditionalists. The earliest churches in the Goingsnake District were established by those whose faith had survived the Trail of Tears. In 1839, Jones and Bushyhead established Baptist Mission. Abe and Margaret Sixkiller were active members, and Abe served as one of its directors in the 1890s. Throughout the region, small churches were established as its satellites, and although many had meetinghouses, open-air services remained common.[101]

Cherokee churches in the immediate vicinity of Chewey were loosely organized and nascent during the late nineteenth century. James and

Eliza Brown and their daughter Polly were three of the first converts received into the fellowship of New Hope Church, where they were baptized on October 13, 1887, five days after the church was organized. The church was Baptist in its orientation.[102] Likewise, several members of the extended families in this study were buried at the Baptist Mission Cemetery and New Hope Cemetery.[103] Although the desire to be buried in consecrated ground at death likely signifies the importance of Christianity to these individuals in life, oral histories make little mention of churches as a powerful influence in the community until after the allotment era. They are best understood as small congregations of affiliated families served by a Cherokee preacher who was a member of their community rather than as hierarchical institutions administered by ministers who were missionaries sent from the East, as was common in other Indian communities at the time.

Political participation in the nation was widespread and intensely localized, and the application of authority was diffuse. In a republic as small as the Cherokee Nation, Cherokees were neighbors and kin to their elected officials. Zeke Proctor, the father and grandfather of several individuals included in this study, served as a sheriff. So did Tom Welch. Both men were elected directly by the voters for two-year terms.[104] Men who served in the National Council included those considered to be full bloods, such as Abe Sixkiller, and those whose families had intermarried extensively, such as Tom Welch.[105] Cherokees experienced politics through these family members and sometimes in their homes. For example, for many years, voting took place at the homes of district superintendents.[106] District courthouses were the hubs of Cherokee politics. Originally, the Goingsnake District courthouse was located in Court House Hollow south of Chewey. In addition to the courthouse, the community boasted a mill and a general store and stocks made of 2 x 10 timbers. In the early 1870s, following a shootout involving Zeke Proctor that became the stuff of legend, the courthouse was moved to Peacheater Creek in the northern part of the district.[107] Wyly Beavers remembered that court days were social events, and families attended even when they had no member involved in the proceedings.[108]

In addition, many Cherokees participated in the Keetoowah Society, a group whose purpose had evolved dramatically throughout the nineteenth century.[109] Originally a loose network of practitioners of traditional Cherokee religion, being Keetoowah signified a commitment to living in harmony according to Cherokee values rather than membership in a fraternal organization or political party. Nonetheless, some Keetoowahs espoused a political agenda at troubled times in their history. During the Civil War, the Keetoowahs, known as "Pin Indians" for the way that affiliated men identified themselves with two crossed pins in their lapels, defended Principal Chief John Ross, opposed slavery and secession, and waged guerrilla warfare against Confederate Cherokees, those aligned with Stand Watie. Although Baptist minister Evan Jones claimed to have founded the Keetoowah Society in the 1850s as an abolitionist organization, modern traditionalists claim the group's origins lay much earlier in Cherokee history. By the 1850s, many had incorporated a distinctive Cherokee variation on Baptist Christianity into their worldview, but they retained a commitment to harmony and sovereignty.

Following the Civil War, the Keetoowah Society held on to this dual role as a religious and a political network—at times quite awkwardly, as the most spiritually devout among them shunned activism while the leaders of the Keetoowah Society wielded enormous influence over elections and council votes. The group extended to all the nation's districts, each organizing its members under the leadership of elected captains. The majority of Keetoowahs in this study were from families who had lived in Chewey for generations prior to the allotment era. The adults had grown up together, and their families had intermarried. They also had participated together in the governance of the Cherokee Nation for generations. They were not isolated people removed from centers of understanding about allotment policy. On the contrary, they were living in the heart of everything they would need to resist it.[110]

IN THE HUNDRED YEARS following the devastation marked by the Treaty of Hopewell, Cherokees rebuilt their homes and nation on the solid foundation of kinship. Cherokee society was profoundly changed, but the values and behaviors associated with the seven clans remained recognizable. Cherokee families were egalitarian, inclusive, flexible, and decentralized. Their perception of relatedness had broadened to include paternal kin, but the expectations for hospitable and reciprocal interaction with family continued to shape daily life. Against the odds, Cherokees had survived and even thrived in Indian Territory. Dora Wolfe, Nannie Dog's daughter, never understood why this way of life had to change. She and her husband, John, the son of Tom Wolfe, suffered following allotment. They were poor and struggled to provide for their large family. Perhaps because her adulthood was so difficult, she remembered her childhood with fondness. She never forgave the U.S. government for allotment. She felt robbed and cheated. "That's what I always wonder sometimes," she said. "Why did we have to live like that?"[111]

Non-Indian reformers did not understand Wolfe's attachment to her extended family, homeland, and way of life. At the end of the nineteenth century, they insisted that American Indian people participate in American society on assimilationists' terms, and they would not consent to the maintenance of their cultures or the communally owned land that perpetuated them. These reformers called themselves the Friends of the Indian, and they launched a campaign against Indian family life that resulted in sweeping policy reform unprecedented in the history of U.S.-Indian relations.

CHAPTER THREE

~❦~

Debating

In 1896, Samuel Houston Mayes wrote an impassioned letter in which he described his countrymen as the quintessence of virtuous, modern manhood. He used evocative words with strong connotations to convey his pride: these men were "sober," "industrious," and "independent." He explained that the common people he lived among "earned [their] daily bread by honest labor upon the soil," and each was "an equal participant in God's great gift of liberty." Mayes urged his readers to open their minds and accept the superiority of his way of life because, he insisted, their assimilation promised the "one solution to the many vexed problems already upon [them]." Writing in the heyday of the movement to assimilate American Indians, Mayes was not a reformer peddling the benefits of Anglo-American culture to indigenous people. He was the principal chief of the Cherokee Nation, and he wrote this letter to the U.S. Congress, then debating whether to allot the Cherokee Nation. Turning the popular discourse about assimilation on its head, Mayes offered to uplift Americans by nurturing them in the superior Cherokee culture. From the perspective of this Cherokee statesman, the accomplishments of American civilization paled in comparison to those of his own society.[1]

Mayes's letter contributed to a fierce debate about the value of Indian societies and their persistence in the late nineteenth century, a debate finally resolved through the allotment of Indian lands between 1887 and 1934. Both the partisans of this policy and Cherokee statesmen understood that allotment was designed to force fundamental changes in Indian family life through the redistribution of resources. Each worked to mobilize support for their cause through public relations and propaganda, but the assimilationists proved more powerful. I do not recount the history of that movement here because other historians have written eloquently about it.[2] Rather, I focus on the debate between reformers and Cherokee statesmen specifically over the nature of Indian families and their place in late-nineteenth-century America.

In this chapter, I first briefly describe who the pro-allotment forces and their Cherokee opponents were and what resources they drew upon in making their arguments. I then recount the ideological campaign for assimilation, which culminated in allotment policy, by explaining how reformers correlated landownership and use, family structure and function, and civilization. The privatization of Indian land was the means to the end of remaking Indian families into the idealized, nuclear type embraced by Anglo-Americans at the time. Finally, I summarize the response of Cherokee leaders and discuss their understanding of the role of families in social organization as expressed in their several-decades-long opposition to the policy. In other words, what follows is a debate over the value of Indian family life and what allotment would make of it.

The Nature of the Debate

During the last quarter of the nineteenth century, public interest in American Indians surged, and a movement coalesced to reform federal Indian policy. The reformers who theorized and lobbied for the passage of allotment legislation differed markedly from those who subsequently enforced and amended the laws. Whereas personal financial interests corrupted many who implemented allotment, ideology drove the social activists who proposed and advocated for the policy. Their contemporaries were other educated white Protestants of the middle and upper classes who contributed to comparable campaigns, including missions to foreign nations and settlement houses among immigrant communities. Together, these activists participated in a movement for moral reform that they believed would both purify and demonstrate the superiority of the United States. They concerned themselves with the social disorder that they believed threatened American society by uplifting racially and culturally divergent groups. By imposing order, they believed that they reinvigorated American society; they also reinforced their hegemony over those powerless to defend themselves.[3]

Several prominent organizations made up the movement to reform U.S. Indian policy. All were national in reach but were based in the Northeast, where they overlapped with other philanthropic networks and drew from the region's rich history of religious and social movements. The members of the Women's National Indian Association (WNIA), the maternal arm of this crusade, involved Anglo-American housewives by using women's social and familial networks for the household-to-household dissemination of information. Subtly critiquing male authority, they asserted that a shared, universal female morality united them with all women, and biological determinism, rooted in motherhood, justified their work to uplift Indian women.[4]

While the Indian Rights Association (IRA) may have been no more influential with the general public than the WNIA, this men's organization generated interest in policy change by working directly with lawmakers and forcing their agenda onto that of elected officials. Unlike modern defenders of the civil liberties of Indians, the IRA did not interpret "rights" to mean that Indian people enjoyed particular privileges and protections guaranteed them by treaties as members of sovereign tribal nations; instead, the organization focused on the right of Indian people to assimilate into U.S. society, even if most Native people opposed doing so. The very existence of the federal government's Indian Service, the IRA asserted, perpetuated communalism in defiance of the U.S. Constitution and must be eradicated as soon as possible. This sentiment was shared by some on the Board of Indian Commissioners, a committee within the Department of the Interior that directly affiliated the Indian Service with Christian and secular reformers and constituted the third major reform organization.[5]

Although they did not agree on everything, members of the WNIA, the IRA, and the Board of Indian Commissioners shared common goals and worked together with remarkable cohesion. Beginning in 1883, Albert K. Smiley, a member of the Board of Indian Commissioners, hosted an annual gathering of these self-proclaimed "Friends of the Indian" at his resort in Lake Mohonk, New York. Here, advocates of assimilation met to strategize and commend one another on victories in their shared struggle. The Friends of the Indian were no voices in the wilderness; they were powerful people with important allies among the most influential Americans of their time.[6]

Motivated by the need to share information with one another and to document evidence of their success as a means to generate additional support, reformers associated with the Friends of the Indian published voluminously. In this, they were joined by scholars affiliated with the Bureau of Ethnology and the Peabody Museum of Natural History at Yale University, and as the fields of anthropology, archaeology, and ethnology developed, professionals with such training at other institutions also worked with reformers to legitimate their research and advance their careers.[7] Indian Service personnel provided additional demographic and anecdotal information to reformers and scholars alike. All were committed to a social evolutionary framework that prevented accurate analysis and contextualization of information about Indians. Although not oblivious to cultural differences among indigenous societies, they primarily noted how Native people differed from their idealized standard. The Friends of the Indian understood that tribal people did not share one common culture, but their extraordinary cultural diversity mattered less than their common deficiencies. Advocates of assimilation therefore exaggerated dire reports as an asset to their cause. Their repetition of common stories and themes also suggests that they were influenced as much by each other as by direct contact with American Indians, and their bleak conclusions justified intervention, even though it often was unclear whether or not Indian people sought it.[8]

In an era during which few Native people had access to the media, these reformers and scholars served as the most viable sources of information for non-Indians about the status of indigenous people. They interpreted American Indian cultures for the American public and, at the same time, rallied people to the cause of Indian uplift. Their status as educated, traveled, articulate, literate Anglo-American professionals of means lent them an air of credibility with which Indian leaders could not compete in this contest to sway public opinion. Proponents of allotment articulated concise critiques of Indian families in their pamphlets, articles, and speeches, and supportive policy makers in Congress echoed these beliefs in their debates, reports, and bills. These documents are the basis of the first half of this chapter. I use the term "civilized" when referring to the standards they advocated to justify their supremacy.

There was little in Native life that reformers admired or that escaped their critique, and that little did not include the Cherokees, who had once been the darlings of the reform movement. Advocates of Indian uplift throughout the nineteenth century had praised the Cherokees, along with the Choctaws, Chickasaws, Muscogees, and Seminoles, known collectively as the Five Civilized Tribes because they had successfully adopted elements of Anglo-American culture. For many assimilationists, the Cherokees were proof that Indians could learn to live like Anglo-Americans and that the U.S. government could and should assimilate Indians as a matter of policy. By the late nineteenth century, however, it was clear that Cherokees did not want to assimilate fully and that their statesmen opposed allotment. Advocates of the policy explained this contradiction—that the very tribe seemingly most suited to a change in their land tenure most vociferously opposed it—by dismissing Cherokees' dissent as evidence of the limits of gradual, tribally directed adaptation. When Cherokee leaders challenged self-proclaimed non-Indian experts on indigenous affairs, the Friends of the Indian retaliated by attacking the Indians' credibility and comprehension of the situation. Most commonly, reformers blasted Cherokee chiefs as hopelessly corrupt while characterizing themselves as selflessly devoted to philanthropy on behalf of their inferiors.[9] Certainly, Cherokees were not "wild Indians," a reference to those tribes more recently confined to reservations in the West, but as the Department of the Interior reported, "Their condition is not the civilization of the Anglo-Saxon." The difference, assimilationists concluded, stemmed from their communal title.[10]

Throughout the debates about allotment, advocates of the policy continuously returned to the ambiguous situation of the Cherokees and the other tribal republics in Indian Territory. These Native societies both defied the negative generalizations about Indians and also offered the fiercest resistance to any change in the absolute title by which they owned their land. As they came to see land reform as the cure-all for the problems faced by Indian people, the Friends of the Indian failed to defend the rights of any tribe, including the Cherokee, to own land communally. Simply put, these Anglo-Americans believed themselves to be better able to make decisions than even the most "advanced" of their Indian adversaries. Senator Henry L. Dawes, a proponent of the policy whom Cherokees had once considered a close ally, believed that they had evolved as far as they could go under their system of common resource ownership: "It has been up to a certain stage a help in the advancement of these Indians, but in my opinion it has now reached its limits, and hereafter as they continue to hold [land] in common it is difficult for me to see how much progress beyond that will be made."[11] Once the symbol of the limitless ability of Indians to adapt, now Cherokees exemplified the limitations of communalism.

Despite the advantage that the Friends of the Indian had in the media, late-nineteenth-century Cherokee statesmen also wrote prolifically about

Indians. The men who served in their nation's highest elected offices, especially that of principal chief, and represented the Cherokee Nation to the other tribes, Congress, and the American public were educated and fluent in English.[12] Most were products of the Cherokee school system, and some also attended American academies and universities.[13] They were comfortable communicating with both Cherokees and Americans and easily engaged in debate with their peers in the U.S. government. These statesmen published their writings in a variety of ways. Principal chiefs regularly shared their views with the citizenry through the *Cherokee Advocate*, the tribal newspaper published in Tahlequah, seat of the Cherokee government. Sometimes they sent a brief letter in response to a particular concern, but more often they crafted formal statements, including annual state-of-the-nation addresses. Cherokee political leaders also reached out to American politicians and audiences through petitions, editorials, and speeches, which they also reprinted in the *Cherokee Advocate*.

Cherokee statesmen were not unique in their opposition to assimilation and allotment. Many Indian leaders protested ethnocentric policies and explained that while they understood what the Friends of the Indian asked of them, they spoke for their communities when they said that they preferred their own ways. Even those Native leaders open to assimilationist policies nonetheless sought to shape their direction and pace. What makes Cherokee leaders unique, then, was that they debated the critics of tribalism on the intellectual merits of assimilation through the American press, in the halls of Congress, and in the federal courts. In doing so, they subjected themselves to criticism and abuse from the champions of allotment. In retrospect, it was a daring move.

Assimilationists and the Critique of Indian Families

By the early 1880s, most critics of federal Indian policy had reached a consensus on how to solve the "Indian problem," the refusal or inability of indigenous people to assimilate fully into American society, and they promoted allotment as the answer. The most vocal critics of Indian policy were genuine reformers, including academics, clerics, and philanthropists, but others with less altruistic goals joined their cause. Railroads sought to dissolve Indian nations so that they could clear the title to their rights-of-way, and "boomers" agitated for the opening of Indian land to homesteaders. For these groups, land acquisition was a primary motivation.[14] But to the reformers responsible for allotment legislation, land presented a problem primarily because tribes owned and used it collectively: communal land empowered social systems based on kinship. These institutions impeded both Anglo-American acquisition of land and the kinds of changes in tribal cultures that reformers believed were necessary to enable Indian people to blend into the American population. Because Indian people organized their societies according to the rules of kinship, reformers believed that extended families were the dysfunctional core of a flawed social system. They further believed that by subdividing communal land into individual homesteads, they could fracture these networks into nuclear families, modeled after those typical among middle-class Anglo-Americans. This process would foster individualism, promote economic self-interest, defeat tribalism, and instill the core values of American culture in indigenous people.

A scathing critique of American Indian families fueled late-nineteenth-century assimilation efforts. In fact, reformers identified Indian families as the root of the "Indian problem." They did not understand or appreciate the diversity and complexity of the kinship systems through which most Indian people organized their societies. Kinship strictly determined Indians' roles and dictated the standards of appropriate behavior, but these social activists saw organization into clans and other extended groupings as chaotic and anarchical. They did not comprehend the rights and obligations that membership in an Indian family entailed, but they understood that Indian people valued these relationships and that they formed the basis of tribalism. Reformers did not differentiate among the various ways that indigenous people defined family and ordered their domestic lives. They generalized that all Indian people prioritized relationships with their natal kin over the marital relationships that formed the basis of civilized families, and they criticized both the behaviors and the values associated with extended Indian families. They reasoned that the obligations of kinship, including living communally, visiting, redistributing goods and food, feasting, participating in ceremonies for extended periods of time, and sharing labor prevented Indian people from working steadily and accumulating wealth individually, a behavior valued in Anglo-American society. As a result, they believed that these customs fostered a degrading dependency among Indian people by encouraging them to rely upon each other, their tribal leaders, and the federal government for their subsistence. Indian men and women, reformers concluded, put immediate communal interests above their long-term individual interests, and they feared that Indian people and society as a whole suffered for it.[15]

Assimilationists believed communalism kept Native people in a perpetual state of homelessness, and they emphasized Native peoples' need for "homes." In using this particular term, the Friends of the Indian rarely referred to actual physical structures. Rather, they usually meant the groupings of people who lived together and how those people behaved. In particular, they meant that Native people lacked nuclear families.[16] They recognized that Indian people had families and places to live, but not the right kind, and this supposedly pathological lifestyle justified legislation intended to destroy communalism. It is revealing that congressmen often referred to allotment bills up for debate as plans "to provide homes for the Indians."[17]

The gendered division of labor common to most Native societies also marked them as inferior, according to the evolutionary ways of thinking popular with Anglo-Americans, who believed that men should work for wages and wealth, whereas women ideally should confine their labor to their houses and biological children. These critics of Indian cultures characterized Native men as eking out their subsistence on the backs of Indian women. Even those Anglo-Americans who advocated women's rights did not appreciate the status accorded Indian women as owners of their labor and its products.[18] In most Native communities, including among Cherokees, women worked alongside their female kin while farming, gathering, and producing the necessities of life. Because Indian women worked in fields or at other arduous tasks, reformers stereotyped Indian women as drudges whose lazy husbands exploited them.[19] Nineteenth-century ethnologist Alice C. Fletcher attributed Native women's heavy workload to the fact that most Native societies never domesticated animals. Literally, she implied, Indian women worked like animals, like dogs.[20] Reasoning that Native women spent more time doing men's work with their female kin than exclusively tending to the welfare of their husbands and children, female missionaries concluded that Indian women lacked an understanding of homemaking and desperately needed instruction in the domestic and maternal arts.[21] Of course, this supposed failing on the part of Native women justified the presence of Anglo-American domestic missionaries, or home matrons, in their communities.[22]

Such attitudes also ignored the spiritual significance of women's work for their families. Laguna feminist literary theorist Paula Gunn Allen has challenged this now centuries-old trope of the Indian woman as drudge, calling Indian women "vitalizers." She explains, "Through their own bodies they could bring vital beings into the world—a miraculous power whose potency does not diminish with industrial sophistication or time. They were mothers, and that word did not imply slaves, drudges, drones who are required to live only for others rather than themselves."[23] Reformist literature denied the meaning of women's labor and, therefore, its value. Instead, reformers understood themselves to be emancipating yet another group of slaves, a comparison intended to provoke a reaction from those with memory of the moral arguments calling for the liberation of African American women from slavery because the institution debased them as wives and mothers.

According to the Friends of the Indian, while women worked tirelessly, Native men failed to work at all. By the late nineteenth century, the profession of warrior was no longer a viable one because the U.S. government had forcibly demilitarized Indian societies. Likewise, few non-Indians appreciated how the gendered division of labor, seasonal cycle, and spiritual beliefs and obligations dictated the times of year in which men and women performed their respective subsistence activities, and they did not consider some of the tasks men did, particularly hunting and fishing, to be work. Although rural non-Indian Americans hunted and fished to contribute to their subsistence, the middle and upper classes dismissed these activities as hobbies; they were not suitable occupations for men. While some reformers acknowledged that many Native men could no longer contribute to their own subsistence in the ways that they had traditionally, most seemed to believe that Indian men could not or would not support themselves properly, even if they had the opportunity to do so, as long as communal land enabled them to avoid the hard labor involved. By the late nineteenth century, most Cherokee men combined hunting and fishing with farming, but reformers still frowned upon this because they recognized that communal title sustained this behavior as long as men hunted on common land and fished in tribal waters.[24]

Frustrated that Indian men continued to work in customary ways and adopted civilized skills and occupations selectively, reformers retaliated by generalizing that most Native men, regardless of their tribal identification, coasted through life half-starved and half-supported by their female kin or their Indian agent.[25] Commissioner of Indian Affairs Hiram Price put it bluntly when he said that the average Indian man lived a "shiftless, do-nothing, dependent life."[26] That dependency was obnoxious to reformers, who saw it as a stain on their nation and a threat to its supremacy. When Commissioner of Indian Affairs Ezra A. Hayt said that "the Indian, in his savage state, is the only born aristocrat on American soil," he alluded to the corrupting influence of indolence on a society that touted the manly virtues of work.[27] If men anywhere in the United States did not behave rightly, men everywhere in America were vulnerable. So was the nation itself. No longer perceived as a violent threat, Indian masculinity was instead perceived by reformers as a depleting drain on the otherwise young, growing, and vital America. Even those who acknowledged the skill and ferocity of earlier generations of tribal warriors saw little to admire in the Indian men now confined to reservations and living in Indian Territory. For example, President Theodore Roosevelt, an avid outdoorsmen who fashioned himself to be an ideal American man because of his shrewd, self-disciplined outlook and rugged physical prowess, felt that Anglo-Americans had gleaned what benefit they could from their Indian adversaries as they pushed the American frontier westward and now, having defeated them, were poised to tame nature itself and spread American civilization throughout the world. Like the president, many contemporary Americans believed that Indian men were irrelevant and had nothing to contribute to the country.[28]

Within the larger debate about whether or not there was a place for American Indian men in the modern United States, reformers were those who believed that Indian men could change, learn to work like Anglo-American men, and be valuable members of society. Many non-Indians questioned whether indigenous people were mentally capable of doing civilized work, but the Friends of the Indian argued that the nation would never know the answer to that question as long as Indian men enjoyed common title to land. In other words, even those who believed Indians to be the potential intellectual equals of whites advocated allotment as a demonstration of the validity of their theories; responsiveness to assimilation served as an IQ test of sorts.[29]

The Friends of the Indian agreed that the communalism practiced in most Native societies had been particularly problematic for Native men because they believed that it discouraged individual men from advancing themselves above and apart from their extended families. As a result, they thought that Native men lacked the knowledge and the motivation, although not the ability, to be self-supporting and self-sufficient.[30] Ignoring the precedent of many Indian men, including some Cherokees, who had Ivy League educations and accumulated wealth, reformers lamented that Native men scorned opportunities for individual advancement. As Commissioner of Indian Affairs Hayt remarked, "The system of title in common has also been pernicious to them, in that it has prevented advancement and repressed that spirit of rivalry and the desire to accumulate property which is the source of success and advancement in all white communities."[31]

Whether nature or nurture proved to be the cause, reformers considered Indian men to be fundamentally lazy and in need of rehabilitation. Long before the scandalous "welfare queens" were the talk of the 1980s, Indian men were the "welfare kings" of the 1880s. Buzzwords such as "idleness" and "laziness" enabled non-Indians to label Indian men as the undeserving poor, and these judgments obscured greater understanding of Indian people's problems and possible solutions.[32] As historian Anne McClintock notes in her study of race, gender, and sexuality in the British empire during this period, settlers imported this trope of indigenous laziness into colonial settings around the world: "The discourse on idleness is, more properly speaking, a discourse on work—used to distinguish between desirable and undesirable labor. Pressure to work was, more accurately, pressure to alter traditional habits of work."[33] In conjunction with the destruction of ecosystems and the dismantling of economies, this critique of Indian men's work habits was part of the process of assuring that they were unemployable in the traditional professions and pursuits that challenged American hegemony.

This construction of indigenous men as refusing to change also obscured the ways that Native people had been adapting their economies to colonization, had taken an active role in the development of markets throughout what became the United States, and were continuing to evolve. Anthropologist Ty P. Kāwika Tengan summarizes the comparable discourse about indigenous Hawaiian men that American planters promulgated beginning in the mid-1850s in response to the resistance of Hawaiian men to giving up their traditional roles as fishers, farmers, cooks, sailors, canoe builders, and warriors to become laborers on American-owned plantations. The act of creating these labels and categorizing indigenous men by them pathologized traditional masculinity and justified intervention; to the extent that indigenous men believed it, the discourse crippled their ability to respond with effectiveness and dignity to their own exploitation.[34]

This discourse also enabled colonizers to emasculate Native men. When judged by the gender roles that reformers considered natural and normal, most Indian men were deviants: males who did not work to support their wives and biological children or who were not possessive of them simply were not men. Adult males who lacked property—land, slaves, or wives and children—were considered effeminate, dependent, and submissive.[35] Also, because they correlated a proprietary interest in property and women, assimilationists lamented that without concern for the transmission of a privately owned patrimony, Native men had no reason to assure the fidelity of their wives. They were a race of cuckolds. This dismissal enabled Anglo-Americans to deny Native males the rights accorded to men in Western societies and, therefore, treat them as wards and dependents. Now defeated, the brutes once seen as a military threat to the United States were now impotent weaklings. Their supposed lack of civilized, virile manliness constituted both a lament and an accusation used by reformers to justify intervention.[36]

The outcome of this perverted gendered division of labor, assimilationists bemoaned, were societies in which the institution of monogamous, permanent marriage, considered sacrosanct by Anglo-Americans, did not matter. Reformers saw no benefit to egalitarianism and flexibility, particularly relating to marriage and family structure. They disliked the informality of many Native marriages and considered the combined families that resulted to be breeding grounds for social anarchy. In particular, they scorned the ease with which Native men and women married and divorced, and they thought practices like serial monogamy, polygamy, and sororal polygamy degraded Indian women. The result, in their view, was sexual degradation and exploitation, especially of women. In short, advocates of assimilation described Indian wives as disposable: after Indian men wore their wives out through overwork, excessive sexual intercourse, and frequent childbearing, they discarded them and took other child brides. Letters written by WNIA matrons described the bleakest of conditions among Indian communities that placed little value on women and recounted heartbreaking tales of the suffering of women and girls. Many of these accounts were graphic. A few were even erotic.[37] Some appear contrived. All justified intervention.[38]

Because Native people lacked permanent, exclusive unions in which to confine their sexuality, reformers considered them to be debauched. For centuries, missionaries believed that Native cultures encouraged men and women to experiment sexually, promoted ritual and bestial sex, normalized prostitution, and degraded Native women by treating them as sexual objects, even within marriage. Advocates of allotment inherited this discourse on sexual depravity and elaborated upon it to attract attention to their cause precisely because vice issues, including prostitution and sex slavery, were popular causes among the general public. Strategically, "sexing up" the problems with federal Indian policy made sense for these moral crusaders, but it also drew attention to ideological contradictions within the movement.

Although portraying women as the victims of insatiable male lust, late-nineteenth-century Anglo-Americans also characterized Native women as sexually libidinous.[39] Women unclaimed and unrestrained by husbands and fathers were considered suspect in nineteenth-century America, but even more so were women who expressed sexual desire. White middle-class Americans associated sexuality primarily with reproduction, not pleasure, and they conceptualized marriage as an institution that promoted morality.[40] Because of the impermanent nature of many Indian marriages, reformers characterized Indian women as immoral and as available to whites as their presumably unused acres.[41] Without acknowledging the sexual violence that Indian women experienced as a result of warfare and economic dislocation, many reformers characterized Native women as functional prostitutes if not actual ones. For a movement that considered motherhood and morality sacrosanct, such permissiveness in Indian communities was intolerable.[42]

Reformers lamented that Indian societies socialized their children to perpetuate these beliefs and behaviors. Because they did not conform to the standards of manhood and womanhood that assimilationists believed to be natural and normal, Indian men and women also were subject to scrutiny for their parenting. Failing to understand the system of child-rearing dictated by the rules of kinship, reformers believed that Native parents did not bond with or love their children. In part, these outsiders believed so because they did not comprehend how Native people reckoned kinship, particularly in matrilineal communities where maternal uncles assumed a central role akin to that of fathers in Anglo-American society. Although fathers were not exempt from this critique, the majority of criticism fell upon Indian mothers, whom reformers characterized as both too often pregnant and negligent. Among native-born white women during this period, family size was declining. The average Anglo-American woman had only 3.56 children in 1900.[43] Fertility rates among American Indian women likely were higher; historian Nancy Shoemaker estimates that the average Cherokee woman of reproductive age in 1900 had 6.7 children.[44] This, many moral reformers concluded, was too many children for deficient mothers to care for properly. They did not understand that in many Native cultures, female kin shared childcare responsibilities, and elderly members of families often cared for their youngest relations while women of childbearing age worked. Reformers interpreted these traditional caregiving arrangements as abandonment on the part of biological parents and an outcome of supposedly dysfunctional marriages.

Even when Native people parented, however, they did it wrong. The Friends of the Indian complained that deficiencies in tribal child-rearing methods thwarted the efforts of missionaries and matrons to teach morality to rising generations of Indian youth. They disapproved of Native parents' expectation that their children would learn appropriate behavior by modeling that of older siblings and adults. Accustomed to the personalized, intensive parenting aspired to in·their middle-class families, female moral reformers equated this "outsourcing" with neglect and the encouragement of unruly behavior. Vivid accounts of physically and emotionally abused children fueled these judgments and, again, justified intervention.[45]

Assimilationists considered the refusal of many Native parents to send their children to boarding schools to be particularly egregious, arguing that by choosing to raise their children in "the demoralization and degradation of the Indian home," they were endangering the moral and physical well-being of their children.[46] In comparison to the institutions run by missionaries and the Indian Service, Indian homes, as characterized by Commissioner of Indian Affairs Price, were notorious for "heathenism, ignorance, and superstition that will extinguish all the flames of intelligence and virtue that have been kindled by contact with civilization."[47] For this reason, the Friends of the Indian dismissed the rights of Native parents to raise their own children and advocated for the federal government to assume guardianship over all Native youths.[48]

Reflecting their belief about the evolutionary nature of social organization, the Friends of the Indian concluded that because Indians lacked functional nuclear families, their societies were in anarchy. As reformer Merrill E. Gates commented, "The family is God's unit of society. On the integrity of the family depends that of the state."[49] Reformers argued that because indigenous families lacked the kind of order and discipline that they recognized, tribal societies bred chaos and crime rather than men who could govern justly.[50] They characterized tribal leaders, therefore, as abusive, manipulative monopolists who kept their people in oppression and poverty by denying them their fair share of resources and opportunities for individual advancement.[51] These chiefs, they insisted, opposed assimilation because it promised to undermine their tyrannical authority and control over communal property. These critics considered the tribal republics in Indian Territory to be particularly good examples of the failings of Indian leadership; they called it a haven for lawlessness on the verge of a race war, not just between Indians and non-Indians but also between the mixed- and full-blood factions of the tribes.[52]

This social chaos was by no means exclusive to those in Indian Territory, however, because reformers equated all participation in Native political organizations to subjugation and enslavement.[53] As members of tribes, Indians had no more freedom than slaves had, reformers concluded. They had no rights to real marriage, to their biological children, or to individual property. As Gates simply put it, "The tribe dwarfs and blights the family."[54] According to the Friends of the Indian, tribalism could not coexist with civilized family life, representative democracy, and modernity. If Indian people were to survive, they must do so by assimilating into Anglo-American society. And so at its heart, then, reformers believed that the Indian problem was a family problem. Common title to land and resources enabled Indians' dysfunctional behavior, whereas allotment promised to replace chaos with the order of nuclear families. Allotment, therefore, was a means to an end. Although land was an issue for many interested parties, the allotment debates were not about land: they were about the kind of societies created by different systems of property ownership.

Reformers asserted that private property created superior families and better citizens, and by the early 1880s, most believed that other efforts toward assimilation, such as education, proved ineffective unless legislative force destroyed communal title and shattered extended families. In 1878, Commissioner Hayt observed, "In the process of Indian civilization, it is necessary to build from the foundation, and therefore, it is proper to begin with the family relation."[55] In unifying behind allotment, they resolved to start from scratch with Indian policy and to use the might of the federal government to give Indians a solid footing upon which to advance.

The Friends of the Indian thought that allotment would assimilate Indian people within a generation by freeing them from their extended family relationships and enabling them to participate in American society as individuals. For this reason, they frequently called the assimilation process "individualization" and equated "to allot" and "to individualize."[56] Assimilationists predicted that once liberated by private landownership, Indians would embrace "the trinity upon which all civilizations depend—family, home, and property."[57] Reformers saw themselves as igniting a chain reaction that would allow Indian men and women to distance themselves from the family and tribal ties that hindered their personal growth, inspire Indian men to take up civilized labor, free Indian women to care for their children and households, motivate men and women to take a proprietary concern in their possessions and families, and cultivate interest in American culture, which would encourage individualism and materialism and prepare them for citizenship. With their tastes for self-interest thus whetted, allotted Indian men and women would assimilate themselves. Reformers' predictions of the impact of allotment on Indians bordered on the magical, and it is easy to marvel at their childlike faith in the policy's positive results. They peddled allotment as an elixir designed to cure all the social ills that they had diagnosed among American Indians.[58]

Allotment was a profoundly gendered policy. Although the Friends of the Indian did not ignore Native women, they understood allotment as a policy particularly suited to the interests of Native men. After all, private property ownership and political participation were rights generally considered within men's sphere in late-nineteenth-century America. Therefore, the Friends of the Indian emphasized allotment's impact on male behavior, although they expected the status of women to improve as well. Men's assumption of their proper roles as heads-of-households and providers was essential to Indian assimilation. Even those most concerned with Indian women's status, the members of the WNIA, recognized the centrality of Indian men to the success of this policy: in 1884, the organization committed itself to "[raising] the Indian into his true and rightful manhood and citizenship through legislation."[59] C. C. Painter of the IRA remarked upon allotment, "The fact is, we have entered upon the beginnings of a new dispensation, and we shall find it necessary that all things in the methods and machinery of our Indian policy, shall be made new and adapted to the growth and development of men."[60] A specific goal of allotment, then, was to create the gender inequalities that characterized civilized society by creating male-dominant, nuclear families.[61] Although amended to include married women in 1891, the Dawes Act initially severely restricted Indian women's access to property because many reformers staunchly refused to consider granting married women separate allotments; they saw exclusive land grants to married adult men as a means to force them to assume domestic leadership as husbands and fathers.[62]

Some assimilationists were not beyond compelling American Indian men to farm their individual allotments, even at the risk of starvation, but most reformers believed that the policy itself was so enticing that Native men would comply eagerly.[63] By the early 1880s, they agreed that in addition to granting them private property, they must guarantee Indians' title for a generation, which they believed would dispel fear of alienation. As agent John W. Douglas said, "Contrary to the popular impression, I believe that the Indian will work patiently and continuously if the fruits of his labor are secured to him: first, against the encroachments of his own tribe, who prey upon the frugal and industrious ones and eat up their substance, and secondly against the encroachments of white men."[64] In other words, while they conceded that non-Indian intruders threatened Native property rights, reformers believed that kin posed the greater threat by preventing Indians from working consistently, accumulating surplus, and relying only on themselves for their subsistence. Assimilationists believed that private landownership turned Indian males into individual men and encouraged them to treat extended family members with a coldness, skepticism, and defensiveness foreign to their kinship systems but central to civilization.

Allotment would thus enable Native men to accumulate material goods and, perhaps, even take joy in them.[65] As Commissioner Hayt explained, "With the Indian as well as the white man, industry and thrift have their root in ownership of the soil. The patenting of lands in severalty [that is, allotment] creates separate and individual interests, which are necessary in order to teach an Indian the benefits of labor and induce him to follow civilized pursuits."[66] Separating Indians from their tribes was, many reformers concluded, as simple as stoking the fires of pride that civilized men feel in the ownership of nice things.[67] Senator Dawes remarked that one of the most important goals of the movement was to teach Indians "to keep."[68] In short, reformers designed allotment to make Indians, particularly Indian men, greedy.

Although they predicted that allotted Indian men would work willingly and eagerly, the Friends of the Indian admitted that they would have to train them how to labor properly. Once initiated, however, gender-appropriate work perpetuated itself, according to reformers. Civilized labor, they believed, developed valuable character traits that would inspire Indian men to continue assimilating themselves with increasing vigor. Market-oriented farming, in particular, cultivated frugality, self-reliance, perseverance, and industriousness. As Commissioner Price said, "Labor is an essential element in producing civilization. . . . The greatest kindness the government can bestow upon the Indian—is to teach him to labor for his own support, thus developing his true manhood, and, as a consequence, making him self-relying and self-supporting."[69] Reformers thus equated the physical act of working with an acceptance of the value system associated with Anglo-American manhood. In short, as Gates put it, "Labor makes men manly."[70] Of course, the specific economic goal for Native men articulated by the Friends of the Indian, to be self-supporting and to provide for their wives and children, would relieve the U.S. government of its financial obligations to Indian people as specified in treaties, which reformers did not consider to be permanent or binding. Policy makers easily combined allotment's altruistic and nationalist aims.[71] This was, as one congressman euphemistically put it, "[harmonizing] the interest of civilization and the interests of Indian tribes."[72]

Reformers predicted that Native men's self-interest would then extend beyond property and physical possessions to the people in their nuclear families. Once allotted, men's proprietary concern for their patrimony would encompass their wives and children. Assimilationists saw allotment as a revolutionary compact negotiated between Anglo-American and Indian men, who would assume their rightful role as protectors of Native women and children and thus join the ranks of civilized men. The Friends of the Indian anticipated that once allotted, Native men, motivated by self-interest, would eradicate the egalitarian sexual and marital practices that reformers found objectionable. Private landownership, they thought, would ensure that Indian men would form monogamous, legal unions guaranteeing the chastity of their wives and the well-being of their biological offspring, particularly male heirs.[73] Senator George Hoar of Massachusetts called this "[awakening] the dormant manhood" of Indian men by granting them "the privileges, the opportunities, and the comforts of landowners."[74] Like Hoar, reformers thought that private landownership encouraged Indian men to take advantage of the entitlements associated with manhood in their own culture, particularly exclusive relations with women in permanent, monogamous sexual unions, which, as the commissioner of Indian Affairs proposed, was a "safeguard in perpetuating title to lands in severalty."[75] Allotment, then, enabled Indian men to attain what Anglo-American men enjoyed—"the integrity of the family and the home, the unit of Christian civilization."[76]

At the same time, reformers believed that allotment would uplift Indian women precisely by creating male-dominated households. Commissioner of Indian Affairs Thomas Jefferson Morgan hoped to see assimilationist policies lift Indian women "out of that position of servility and degradation which most of them now occupy on to a place where their husbands and the men generally will treat them with the same gallantry and respect which is accorded to their more favored white sisters."[77] In allotted homes, as an agent writing to the IRA explained, "the relation between husband and wife is strengthened. The wife, once a 'hewer of wood and a drawer of water,' becomes a companion."[78] In an unusual twist of the moral reform ideology of the late nineteenth century, then, reformers empowered men, not women, to reform their homes and, from their homes, presumably their societies.[79] The Friends of the Indian proclaimed that allotment would free Native women of their supposedly unnatural burden of labor, such as farming, to focus on the more appropriately feminine tasks of tending to their homes and children. In short, allotment would enable women to be feminine as that ideal was constructed among middle- and upper-class Anglo-Americans.

Reformers committed themselves to teaching Native women what to do with their newly found free time. The WNIA, in particular, affirmed the importance of Native women's domestic work by committing resources to training women through home matron programs, by enabling Indian boarding school graduates to establish their own homes through home loan programs, and by sending Indian women boxes of domestic goods through the mission box program. Home matrons enabled Indian women to use donated domestic goods by teaching them skills like sewing and decorative needlework. Reformers intended these boxes of fabric and other household materials to inspire Native women to beautify their bodies with appropriate, modest dress and their homes with decorative flair. Appropriate women's handiwork symbolized the success of assimilationist policies.[80]

The Friends of the Indian believed that allotted Native parents would raise their children properly. As Gates remarked about the homes of allotted Indians: "Family affections and care for the education and virtue of the young are promoted."[81] In other words, reformers believed that allotment would free Indian parents to love their children and, more important, raise them with respect for the law of the land rather than the rules of kinship.[82] Senator George Vest of Missouri called the home the "germ of civilization," and reformers believed that allotment created stable, permanent parental homes that stirred in Native people the desire to assimilate.[83] Children accustomed to modeling the behavior of adults would have appropriate role models in allotted homes, but many Friends of the Indian still did not wholly trust allotted parents and continued to advocate for the education of Native children in mission and boarding schools, where Indian children were taught their new gender roles directly. At Hampton Institute, a secondary-level boarding school for African Americans and Native Americans in Hampton, Virginia, teachers used a particularly creative method: they taught their students new songs to replace tribal songs. The lyrics of one equated cleaning house with waging a just war: "Yes, our house is the fort we are keeping, / And our foe is the dust on the floor." Laundresses, too, contributed to the process because "A civilizing power is the laundress with her tub; / We are cleaning more than clothes as we rub, rub, rub." By making civilized homes for their families, Native girls undermined their tribal identities. They washed them away.[84]

Thus, the Friends of the Indian predicted that allotment would end Native people's supposed homelessness by enabling them to create the physical and emotional settings necessary for civilized family life. Reformers pointed to the civilized homes popping up throughout Indian communities. Individual houses, particularly log cabins, were physical symbols of assimilationists' success because they assumed that nuclear families lived in them and used them in the same ways that Anglo-Americans did.[85] The WNIA even assisted young Native couples in making these homes on their allotments through home loan programs, which made available the resources to build them, and through home matron programs, which provided the instructions to run them appropriately.[86] Above all, these homes signified changing gender roles and the successes of allotment policy.[87]

Once Indian people established stable families, reformers posited that allotment would create a hunger for law among them, particularly for the protection of their material possessions. Having cultivated a taste for self-interest, allotment presumably undermined individuals' commitment to kin and reliance on communal property. J. F. Kinney, a member of the IRA, asserted, "The general effect of the Severalty Law is beneficial to the Indians. By taking land in severalty, the Indian becomes individualized. Disintegration follows. Fealty to chiefs is destroyed. Submission to their authority is no longer rendered. The Indian on land of his own, separated from the general mass which belong to all in common, for the first time becomes conscious of his own manhood."[88] Since they believed that tribal leaders oppressed their people, advocates of policy change thought that the security provided by private landownership enabled Indian men to free themselves from that yoke by giving them the economic means to resist their chiefs. At the same time, their new needs as owners of personal wealth interested them in the government that protected their property rights, the United States of America.[89] In short, allotted Indian men would taste political freedom in the same way the Founding Fathers had by rebelling against the British crown, and like the men of the Revolutionary generation, they would throw off their oppressors and cast their lot with other free men in governing their communities democratically.[90]

For this reason, after asserting their individuality, settling down with their wives and children, and distancing themselves from their tribes, Native men, many reformers believed, should be "clothed with citizenship."[91] Throughout the allotment debates, reformers and policy makers argued whether Indians should be granted citizenship with allotment or whether private landownership would prepare Indian men for citizenship, which the United States would extend at a later time.[92] Many, such as Representative Thomas Skinner of the House Committee on Indian Affairs, advocated allotment as "the most direct route to citizenship for the Indians."[93] Although not all agreed, most of the Friends of the Indian clearly understood that by taking private ownership of land, Indians also would be assuming the legal, political, and social rights associated with property ownership and heretofore unknown to them. Consequently, they saw citizenship as Indians' best and only defense against further exploitation.[94] Calling citizenship a fundamental right, the members of the IRA believed that allotment with citizenship fulfilled the government's obligations to Native people as specified in their treaties.[95]

Reformers, including Dawes in the Senate, strongly backed the plan, and unlike earlier versions of allotment legislation, the General Allotment Act extended citizenship with allotments.[96] As the members of the Board of Indian Commissioners explained, "After securing to the Indian a home and placing him under law, we shall hope to see him soon invested with the full rights of citizenship and treated as an individual man."[97] Once Indian men participated as equal citizens in the United States, the "Indian problem," and the financial commitment of the federal government as agreed to in treaties, would be no more.

On February 8, 1887, President Grover Cleveland signed the General Allotment Act, or Dawes Act, into law. Senator Dawes captured the joyous emotions he shared with all reformers when he called the General Allotment Act the "Indian Emancipation Act."[98] The word "emancipation" is significant. Advocates of assimilation believed that they had abolished the institution that oppressed Indian people no less than the system of chattel slavery had done to African Americans: they had freed Indians from their extended familial and tribal relations and offered them the possibility of participation in Anglo-American society. In the years immediately following the passage of the Dawes Act and at centers of social reform such as Hampton Institute, advocates of allotment celebrated Indian Emancipation Day on February 8.[99] This holiday, according to promotional literature, marked the "nation's first recognition of the Indian as an individual. It secures to him Land, Law, Citizenship, and Manhood."[100]

The Dawes Act excluded the Cherokees and other tribal republics of Indian Territory, but it signaled an imminent change in their situation. The Cherokee Nation held its land by absolute title granted and guaranteed by the federal government in compensation for their removal from their southeastern homeland. Dawes considered this agreement a travesty, and while he wished to include the Cherokees in this legislation, he appreciated that their situation demanded a separate law. He and the other members of the House and Senate Committees on Indian Affairs promised it would soon follow the Dawes Act.[101]

Cherokee statesmen did not interpret their exclusion from the Dawes Act as a reprieve from allotment, either. Instead, they recognized it as a clear threat to their sovereignty. Although they had protested allotment since the earliest debates of the 1880s and had ensured their exclusion from the Dawes Act, Cherokee statesmen lost no time in lobbying to prevent Dawes from ever proposing the promised bill to allot them. In this, they faced an enormous challenge because reformers' negative characterization of Native societies dominated debate and obliterated alternative views of Indian people. Often speaking to hostile or indifferent audiences, Cherokee statesmen responded to this critique of their culture and themselves. Cherokee leaders challenged the Friends of the Indian, questioned the existence of an "Indian problem," and demanded recognition of their treaty rights—all in defense of what they believed was their superior civilization rooted in Cherokee families.

Cherokee Statesmen and the Defense of Indian Families

Although advocates of assimilation framed the allotment debate in gendered language, Cherokee statesmen largely deflected the discussion from an evaluation of their manhood. In only one exchange did Cherokee delegates to Congress pointedly offer themselves as virile examples of Cherokee civilization in a defense of their republic: "Is it to be doubted that a people fostering and encouraging such institutions have all the finer sensibilities of education and Christian manhood that will be found among similar communities in the United States? Could a nation of irresponsible, corrupt, criminal people produce such conditions?"[102] Such flaunting was rare, however, because Cherokee statesmen realized this line of argument was problematic. Many were of mixed heritage, and they knew that the reformers therefore considered them as inherently manipulative and unrepresentative of their full-blood contemporaries. Likewise, Cherokee gender roles *were* different from those of Anglo-Americans, a reality that statesmen logically concluded was best left out of this debate. Lastly, a defense of Cherokee masculinity to match the reformers' critique would have required elaboration on the intimate details of individuals' lives, and that openness would have been unlikely among late-nineteenth-century Cherokees. As an alternative, Cherokee statesmen emphasized the outcomes of their gender roles and the public manifestation of their private lives in their government and civic institutions. If reformers argued that dysfunctional families resulted in anarchic tribes, Cherokee statesmen offered their civilization as evidence of the superior homes that thrived on communal property.

During the allotment era, both those who sought to terminate their common title and those who sought to defend it politicized Cherokee families. In their annual messages, memorials, and other public papers, successive Cherokee principal chiefs articulated common themes. Like their contemporaries in the United States, Cherokee statesmen were politicians motivated by their civic duty, their personal ambitions, and their party alliances.[103] A small minority of Cherokees, including W. P. Boudinot, a frequent editor of the *Cherokee Advocate*, proposed that the Cherokee Nation allot itself as a means to protect citizens' land from encroachment and ensure the survival of the tribal government.[104] The majority of Cherokee leaders, however, including those who led the prominent Downing and National political parties, were in agreement on their opposition to federally imposed land privatization. Read for unity instead of factionalism, the papers of these leaders reveal not only their political strategies for responding to the allotment crisis but also the common values that motivated them.

Late-nineteenth-century Americans who decried the possibility of Indian extinction assumed the desirability of their assimilation, but contemporary Cherokee statesmen had no intention of merging their nation's course with that of the United States. Collective independence was the core of Cherokee culture. Cherokee leaders defended their system of use ownership because this practice permitted familial sufficiency and sustained civic bonds. Statesmen explained that because Cherokees shared land, they valued their relationships with each other in a particular and unique way that Americans did not. They believed that their common interests motivated them to work toward shared prosperity, which they argued was a superior alternative to the excessive individuality and greed that they associated with Anglo-American society.

The familial use of common land made possible everything that was of value to Cherokee people: their homes, communities, and nation. Principal Chief C. J. Harris articulated the significance of the public domain in his 1893 address to the Cherokee people: "This [our communal land] means our country. It means everything to us—life, self control and prosperity. Without a country, we are simply a people without lands, we have no governments. Without homes, we are paupers and vagabonds. How jealous should we then be of our common property and how well we should guard it!"[105] In other words, while the Cherokees did not equate themselves with their land, they believed that they, as a people, were inseparable from it because it provided the foundation for their families, their way of life, and their existence as a distinct people.

Common resource ownership enabled distinctly Cherokee values and behaviors. Cherokees praised hospitality, and they believed that communal landownership made generous giving and reciprocity among citizens possible. Late-nineteenth-century Cherokees shared the sentiment voiced by Joel B. Mayes: "Charity is the greatest of virtues."[106] Mayes was not referring to almsgiving as was practiced among Anglo-Americans but to the comprehensive, pervasive transfer of food and material goods among neighbors who understood hospitality as a process of giving and receiving that benefited all who participated in the transaction. Robert K. Thomas suggests that this effort toward maintaining "harmonious interpersonal relationships" through the sharing of resources and even labor was central to Cherokees' value system.[107] This custom likely had a long history among Cherokees and proved remarkably enduring throughout their adaptation to colonization. Anthropologist John Gulick led a team of researchers working among the Eastern Band of Cherokees in North Carolina during the 1950s. At that time, many Cherokees continued to participate in *ga-du-gi* organizations, or work teams that shared labor and other support, including food and cash, among members. Gulick theorizes that these organizations had their roots in aboriginal town organization and adds, "The persistence of this form of social organization shows no little resilience and adaptability to changing conditions, together with the continued forcefulness of values which encourage such non-individualistic activity."[108]

Cherokees in Indian Territory did not create formal organizations like their kin in the Carolinas did, but the values and behaviors fostering hospitality and discouraging "stinginess," as Thomas puts it, remained central to Cherokee culture there.[109] Cherokee Richard Manus remembered the importance of communal working and eating during his youth near Chewey at the beginning of the twentieth century. He described how Cherokees in his community routinely helped each other take in crops and freely performed other household labor, like chopping firewood, for neighbors who were sick. He remembered, "Cherokees loved one another . . . they done for one another." He also recalled how they ate together during these times of shared work and grief: "Everybody brought their dinner. And the funniest part of it, when it come dinner time, they'd all put it together. . . . They're afraid some fellow didn't have as much as another. It didn't make no difference then. They just all spread it out there and everybody ate."[110] Notably, receiving hospitality did not detract from one's character or manhood, as reformers, who equated such behavior with dependency, believed. Accepting was as Cherokee a behavior as giving, and reciprocity was an ongoing process that fostered civic unity among Cherokee families and distinguished them from those who did not participate, particularly American intruders who squatted on Cherokee land and used tribal resources without permission or payment.[111]

Communal resource ownership balanced individual gain with public good by enabling the success of the industrious while providing for the subsistence of those unable to accumulate property and resources. Thomas calls Cherokee customs of hospitality "one of the most highly developed 'social security' systems in the world."[112] Communal resource ownership functioned as a social welfare system of sorts by preventing profound poverty and the social ills created by extreme disparities in class. Rebuking their American contemporaries, a convention of delegates from the Five Tribes pointed out, "We have no rich men among the Indians, in the sense the word is now used in the United States. . . . Potter's fields and poor houses are unknown to our civilization."[113]

Perhaps statesmen were being too modest. There were wealthy men and women who belonged to each of the tribal republics, but their societies did not suffer from the extremes that characterized the United States, which by the late nineteenth century struggled with the obviously negative outcomes of the concentration of wealth. Certainly, there was no conspicuous consumption or leisured class in Chewey, just farmers living at or just above their subsistence. As historian Andrew Denson has pointed out in his study of Cherokee rhetoric, although late-nineteenth-century tribal leaders were not aligning themselves with the radical thinkers and organizations critical of private property ownership in the United States, they were aware of these voices and willing to engage with their language if it served the Cherokee cause.[114] In arguing that their society produced a superior citizenry because communal landownership balanced individual independence with common interest, Cherokee statesmen performed a brief solo among the chorus of voices calling for economic reform in the United States.

Cherokee leaders argued that this virtuous citizenry proved better at self-government than its American counterpart. Common resource ownership enabled social stability because it guaranteed economic security. According to Dennis Wolf Bushyhead, Cherokees held to communal landownership because "in this way every one of our citizens is sure of a home."[115] Late-nineteenth-century Cherokee men and women worked mostly as farmers and stock-raisers, and communal landownership guaranteed each citizen's access to the one thing needed to support his or her family—land. And this, statesmen argued, guaranteed political independence, an essential component of representative government. As Samuel Mayes and other Cherokee delegates put it to the U.S. Congress in the gendered language that they understood, "The common tenure of land makes every man independent—no paupers, no beggars . . . Every man is a peer of his fellow-man, an equal participant of God's great gift of liberty."[116] And independent people had something those bound to another by economic interest did not have: the ability to choose freely.[117]

Statesmen believed that this security encouraged a sense of responsibility for fellow community members among Cherokees. Because competition for resources and status was mitigated by shared resource ownership, Cherokees saw beyond the needs of their immediate families to the betterment of the larger Cherokee family, the citizenry of the Cherokee Nation. Beholden to no one and secure in their rights, Cherokees sought the protection of their common interests rather than the unnatural increase of their individual estates at the expense of others in their community.[118] Harris explained, "Land in common is common interest, and common interest implies equal benefits whenever the people as a community demand their share of equal rights and benefits in the common property."[119] In other words, Cherokee statesmen considered excessive greed to be an abomination, a sign of social sickness that required legislative attention. In this, they disagreed with the American reformers who considered self-interest to be a hallmark of civilization and the acquisition and transmission of wealth to be a primary function of the family. Bound to one another as shared property owners, Cherokee citizens looked beyond the greed that they believed corrupted non-Indian men and crippled American society to the common good. Their shared homeland perpetuated a community of self-reliant individuals by giving Cherokees the economic freedom to stand together by choice.[120]

Common landownership provided the foundation for Cherokee culture, and homes served as the Cherokees' most important sociopolitical institutions. Late-nineteenth-century Cherokees had a nuanced, layered understanding of the word "home," and they defined it in a collective sense. The term conveyed two meanings, neither of which referred to the actual physical structure that reformers so closely equated with the attainment of civilization. Home referred to a permanent place of settlement, and it referred to collectively owned land.[121] Cherokee statesmen rarely used the word to refer to individual households; we might use the word "homeland" to convey their commonly used meaning. Simply put, home was not the place where one Cherokee family lived but where all Cherokee families lived in relationship with one another.[122]

Because they shared a common home, Cherokee statesmen referred to their government as a family. Joel Mayes called the Cherokee Nation "this great family government and estate." He also referred to the National Council as a "family" and a "household located on their [the Cherokees'] home." Membership in and ownership of this home gave Cherokee statesmen authority to govern, and political power began with common interest in the Cherokees' home.[123] Cherokees maintained that they bought their home at an enormous cost to their ancestors and referred to their treaties as evidence. They pointed to their fee simple title and proudly insisted that they owned their homeland. In other words, they were not a race of dependents or renters but a nation of homeowners.[124] Because Cherokees referred to their nation and land in familial terms, or "this great family of ours," they spoke of allotment as abandonment, not just of their communal title but also of each other.[125]

Cherokee statesmen explained that the legitimacy of the tribal government extended from that of their homes, and, therefore, they believed that their government was accountable to the citizenry, not the other way around. Cherokees traditionally understood power to be representative rather than coercive. Final authority on important matters regarding title, such as land sales, rested with the people, the members of the Cherokee national family.[126] Although statesmen were obligated to regulate the use and occupancy of the land, all decisions relating to its title belonged to the people, and any such decision was not the National Council's to make, even though the federal government pressured it to do so.[127] For this reason, statesmen commonly endorsed the idea of putting issues directly before their citizens, particularly in matters of local concern, such as education, and of local expertise, such as the census.[128] For example, in 1895, Samuel Mayes urged that the National Council revise the census by putting it before the Cherokee people for scrutiny. He believed that the general population, rather than a special government officer or committee, could best correct the roll.[129] In their handling of their people's affairs and their relationship with their citizenry, Cherokee statesmen believed that their civic life demonstrated their civilization precisely because it was nonhierarchical and egalitarian.[130]

Part of the Cherokee government's trust was to manage the communal resources of the people, including minerals, timber, and grass as well as land and to raise revenue to support services for its citizens.[131] Another primary purpose of the Cherokee government was to further the well-being of its citizens by enabling Cherokee families to maintain their subsistence. The chiefs and the National Council experimented with legislation protecting and balancing communal and individual rights.[132] Cherokee statesmen took this job seriously. When Joel Mayes was considering running for the office of principal chief, he wrote to Stephen Teehee, "What ever may be the future destiny of the Cherokees, my greatest purpose shall be to protect their property rights and make it realize its full value."[133] It was a struggle made worse by limitations the federal government placed on Cherokee efforts to raise the revenue needed to pay for administrative and social services.

Another primary function of the Cherokee government was to extend hospitality to its citizens. Communal landholding engendered a political ethic and concern for social welfare that distinguished the Cherokee Nation from other governments of its time. According to Joel Mayes, "The greatest purpose for which all government can thus extend over its citizens is a protecting hand, thereby creating in the citizen a feeling of security and contentment."[134] Decades before the U.S. government committed itself to social welfare through the New Deal, Cherokee statesmen, sharing the values of their citizens, embraced economic egalitarianism as a primary goal of government. For example, the Cherokee government repeatedly distributed per capita payments among its citizens. The need to distribute cash for "bread money" resulted in the census of 1880, and additional lists were made to distribute "grass money," earned from the leasing of the Cherokee Outlet, which was tribally owned grazing land rented to non-Indian ranchers.[135] The Cherokee government concerned itself with the fiscal well-being of its citizens in a way that distinguished it from that of the United States.[136]

The localized nature of Cherokee society fostered Cherokees' familiarity, and their political system reinforced local authority. Their constitution guaranteed that the nation's highest officer remained in contact with the citizenry, for the principal chief was required to visit each of the eight (eventually nine) districts every two years. Most Cherokees interacted with their government through district judges and sheriffs and representatives, individuals who were first and foremost their kin and neighbors. Although Cherokees commonly settled grievances among themselves, they occasionally had business with the court, and yet local officials handled even these matters according to local preference. Since people equated the administration of justice with the restoration of social harmony in their small, interconnected communities, local officials treated suspected or convicted Cherokees with familiarity and dignity.

Moses Welch remembered that his father, George, although not the sheriff, often housed prisoners awaiting trial at the Goingsnake District court. In this way, many repeat offenders under Cherokee law developed a relationship with George Welch and visited him when traveling near his farm. He recalled that Belle Starr, an infamous outlaw, occasionally visited his parents. When in the Welch household, she treated George and his wife, Lizzie, like kin: "She always pushed her Winchester under the bed, and pulled her forty-five off and laid it on the bed. Then she sat around and visited and joked just like she was carefree." Moses saw no contradiction in this. His father, he noted, "was a peace loving citizen, who helped to enforce the law when called upon, but refused to meddle in matters in which he had no interest."[137] Because Cherokees valued nonaggression, hospitality among them was normal, even under such circumstances.

This familiarity among local officials and neighborhood lawbreakers created a distinctively personal criminal justice system. For example, when Mose Crittenden of Chewey was accused of a crime, the district judge sent a court official, White Whitmire, to bring him in. Unable to find him at home and suspecting that Crittenden was at the house of the woman whom Whitmire knew him to be courting, the official traveled to her home, where he found and arrested Crittenden. But it was late in the evening, and Whitmire decided to bed down and take Crittenden in the next morning. During the night, Whitmire awoke to the sound of an ax slicing into a tree just above his head—someone had thrown it at him in an attempt to free Crittenden. Rather than taking advantage of the commotion to escape, Crittenden calmed the startled Whitmire by promising that he would not run away, and the two men traveled to court together the next day. Crittenden was not bound and came peacefully.[138] Advocates of allotment considered the Cherokee criminal justice system to be lax and devoid of impartiality because of such familiarity, but relationships between officials and the accused fostered social harmony in Cherokee communities.

The counterpoint to this kindness was self-sufficiency. Cherokees had never been a dependent people and sought independence from the United States through their tribal government. Statesmen repeatedly reminded congressmen and other non-Indian audiences that the Cherokees maintained their own common school system, asylums, and government without assistance from the United States.[139] Throughout the late nineteenth century, Cherokee leaders struggled to collect the revenue needed to provide services to their citizenry. Even when it was barely or imperfectly attained, this self-sufficiency was celebrated.[140] Bushyhead praised his fellow citizens for working through a drought and pooling resources rather than selling land to provide relief money: "Present industry and economy are our true and only certain refuge against the recurrence of bad seasons."[141] In their families, communities, and nation, Cherokees looked, above all, to care for themselves and their own.

Cherokees took immense pride in their civic institutions, especially their educational system. Unlike other Indian nations that relied on the federal government or Christian missionaries to educate their children, the Cherokees established a public school system following their removal. Through the primary level, education was free to all citizens, and most took advantage of it.[142] Students attended local district schools taught by Cherokee teachers. At the turn of the twentieth century, over 150 schools served Cherokee communities.[143] From these schools, some students advanced to the male and female seminaries, equivalent to modern high schools and equal if not superior to any other west of the Mississippi River.

A few graduates of the Cherokee school system attended the best universities in the East. The seminaries were not reserved for the children of the wealthiest Cherokees. At least one resident of Chewey attended the male seminary—Oce Hogshooter, the brother of Jim Hogshooter and the secretary of the Nighthawk Keetoowahs.[144] Notably, Cherokees supported male and female education alike. Cherokee women had equal access to all levels of education, including seminary. This commitment to public education and women's education was unequaled in Anglo-American society well into the twentieth century.[145]

Cherokees were wary of interference with their educational system because, unlike reformers, they did not equate education with assimilation and believed that education instead served the interests of Cherokee nationalism.[146] Statesmen considered their common school system to be the logical complement to their practice of communal resource ownership. Cherokees understood the practical and ideological basis for common education in a republic. By reaching the vast majority of Cherokees and promoting literacy in their own language and English, the school system facilitated participation in the nation's civic and economic life. Above all, in a society that had grown out of town councils and into a republic, literacy enabled the continuation of popular involvement in government affairs. The *Cherokee Advocate* reflected the nation's commitment to literacy and reported on public affairs in both Cherokee, using the Sequoyah syllabary, and English. Disseminated throughout the nation, the *Cherokee Advocate* served the interests of Cherokee communities by reporting on local matters and promoted national identity by informing citizens of their government's affairs.[147]

The Cherokee common school system served another important purpose in fostering common values, particularly devotion to the Cherokee Nation. While they realized that most Cherokees worked on farms throughout their lives, statesmen saw their schools as more than vocational programs. Although Cherokee politicians sometimes debated about pedagogy, they generally agreed that the main purpose of education was to inspire and inform their citizenry. They wanted their schools to train youth in skills that would benefit their communities, develop their minds with knowledge of their history, and reinforce values that fostered social harmony.[148] Cherokee leaders intended for their education system to produce good citizens who were productive farmers, shrewd businesspersons, eloquent orators, learned scholars, deft poets, and, of course, able statesmen. In particular, they believed that their schools should encourage young Cherokees to be "useful" to their people in defense of their common rights and interests against intruders, corporations, and the federal government. In other words, Cherokee schools were the front line in the nation's defense against encroachment.[149] Looking to the future from 1890, Joel Mayes commented on the Cherokee school system: "The Cherokee Nation must anticipate a community inferior to none, who will be competent to know and defend every right that belongs to them."[150] Cherokee statesmen rightly understood that the future of their nation depended on the education of Cherokee children, and they believed that a primary purpose of the national government was to nurture all young members of the Cherokee family.

Because they believed that the combination of familial development of common resources and republican institutions struck a balance that fostered social harmony, Cherokee statesmen boldly asserted that they considered their society to be superior to any, including that of the United States.[151] While they saw themselves as fellow participants in the republican experiment initiated by the U.S. government, their adaptation of republican institutions to common landownership created a society that they claimed the world's best minds admired and to which the suffering people of the world looked for hope. Cherokee statesmen believed that they must continue their way of life, not only for their own benefit but for the good of humanity: "Our system of government must be perpetuated. . . . The system is well worth preservation to mankind. The burden of other governments is the unequal distribution of their territory. Out of such injustice—a relic of times when might was right, a few men were absolute and many slaves—all sorts of evils have sprung and increased. The principle of common property in land is the principle of universal brotherhood and is the leading feature of our government. It recognizes the right of every citizen to his just share of the bountiful gifts of Providence to all—land being one."[152] William Potter Ross even prophesied that the Cherokee Nation was poised for greater things than its American counterpart because Cherokees were of a "higher civilization."[153]

In this, Cherokee statesmen refuted the suggestion that their society had evolved to its greatest capacity, as anthropologists and advocates of uplift theorized. Rather, they insisted that the development of Cherokee civilization was a process of continual adaptation, one characterized by an infusion of innovative ideas and practices into their time-tested way of life. Such adaptations, such as the adoption of a republican-style government modeled after that of the United States, did not replace traditional

Cherokee culture but perfected it.[154] As C. J. Harris explained it, the Cherokee Nation always had been a "free, happy, and civilized people."[155] They were not waiting for uplift from anyone. Likewise, rather than preventing progress, common landownership was the engine of Cherokee adaptation.[156] Its commitment to the traditional method of communal resource ownership and development ensured that the Cherokee government would remain forward-thinking.

The proponents of allotment, Cherokee statesmen thus implied, were the ones truly unable to grasp the situation. Statesmen sometimes grouped Americans together as the target of their criticism, but they more often attempted to drive a wedge between reformers and those more aptly labeled exploiters, those whose priority was the opening of Indian Territory to American economic development. This group included corporations, especially railroads, and intruders squatting on Indian land. Statesmen chided their critics in reform circles for naively enabling the violation of Cherokees' rights by those who cared little for Indian welfare. Samuel Mayes charged that lust for "gain, so evidently the ruling passion of your civilization," drove Americans to commit illegal and uncivilized acts against Cherokees, and the Friends of the Indian supported this behavior.[157] An anonymous author identified as a citizen of Goingsnake District who wrote to the *Cherokee Advocate* put it more bluntly when he described the civilization of the intruders: "If Christ was to come among them he couldn't possibly live half an hour, if that long."[158] Advocates of uplift justified allotment by publicizing behaviors that they found objectionable in Indian communities; Cherokee statesmen responded in kind. In the context of a debate in which Anglo-Americans routinely denied the full humanity of Indian people by labeling them as heathens, Cherokee leaders responded that Americans were soulless. In a letter to his peer, the chief executive of the United States, President Benjamin Harrison, Joel Mayes explained that Cherokees "have souls and are responsible for their conduct to the law of God and man." He went on to imply that the behavior of Americans suggested that they did not.[159]

Accusing their American contemporaries of failing to appreciate whose interests they truly represented, Cherokee statesmen criticized them as puppets of their society's robber barons and rabble. Civilized nations kept their word, as Joel Mayes explained, because their leaders "[had] the manhood" to do so even when difficult decisions were unpopular. Mayes and other Cherokee statesmen chided American politicians for their ignorance of the diplomatic history their nations shared and for failing to honor their treaties, which were federal law, because they frustrated the economic agendas of those who advocated for the development of the West.[160] Cherokee leaders also cautioned congressmen to consider the long-term outcomes of their actions. Dennis Wolf Bushyhead warned that by privileging corporate interests, American leaders ensured that "gigantic corporations and federations of corporations" ultimately would grow more powerful than state governments and even the federal government. Suggesting that congressmen were showing a remarkable lack of foresight, he predicted that they would prove a greater menace to American progress than Indian nations ever could.[161] Cherokee statesmen thus refused to concede to the assertions of those who believed themselves to be the superiors of the Cherokees.

Throughout the late nineteenth century, then, Cherokee statesmen staunchly opposed allotment, both their own and that of other Indian nations, as a regressive policy advocated by the uninformed and ill-intentioned.[162] According to William Potter Ross, allotment was "a nut without a kernel."[163] Statesmen resented the intervention of "self-constituted guardians and interested intermeddlers" in the affairs of the Cherokee Nation, and they balked at the prospect of its being administered by a bureaucracy of non-Indians.[164] Bushyhead and a Cherokee delegation explained to Henry Teller, then the secretary of the interior, that there was "no excuse for this attempt to reduce the Cherokee Nation to the status of Wild Indian tribe, and make them the dependents of the Indian Office."[165] Statesmen feared that allotment, by subdividing their communal land, would impoverish their families, destroy the fabric of their culture, and prevent their society from evolving further. Above all, they loathed the possibility of being subject to an administration not accountable to them in a system not of their own making.

Statesmen equated allotment with homelessness. The loss of access to land would produce social instability and poverty, and Cherokees did not consider this a step forward in their evolution as a people. The Five Tribes delegation to Congress explained, "Lands in common means perpetual homes to [us] and [our] posterity, [we] know that under that system, [we] can never become homeless." Allotment threatened them with "certain loss of home if not to [us] certainly to [our] children and ultimate pauperism to [our] race, no thought troubles [our] hearts so much."[166] Unlike their American contemporaries who considered poverty a social inevitability and an indication of personal moral failure, Cherokees considered homelessness and poverty to be unnatural, an indication of social disorder that needed righting. Turn-of-the-century Cherokee statesmen, some of whom had traveled widely in the United States, including its northeastern cities and its western mining camps, recognized that communal land enabled families to live and work independently, an impossibility for an increasing number of turn-of-the-century Americans, for whom economic stability and independence were unattainable.

Communal landownership enabled self-government: under allotment, statesmen knew that their tribal government faced extinction. Joel Mayes insisted that communal land, or, as he phrased it, their "perpetual home," provided the basis for Cherokee liberty and enabled the Cherokees to make decisions of conscience for themselves and their posterity. Mayes believed that Cherokees could live by their shared values only on their common land.[167] Harris echoed that sentiment when he insisted that "the fact cannot be denied that the lands of our nation are the very foundation of our political existence and the source of our livelihood." Outsiders considered allotment to be a shrewd business deal, particularly for those Cherokees, including most statesmen, who could have prospered as private landowners. Harris proclaimed that no patriotic Cherokee, however, could put a price on "home and country." They were inseparable and inviolable.[168] By critiquing American governmental affairs and noting the experiences of previously allotted tribes, Cherokee leaders understood that allotment meant the loss of self-government, not liberation from tribalism.

BEGINNING IN 1881 with the debates over the Coke bill, the movement in favor of allotment gained momentum. For two decades, however, Cherokee statesmen thwarted efforts to dismantle their nation. Following the passage of the Dawes Act in 1887, Congress progressively undermined the sovereignty of the tribal republics. Established in 1889 to negotiate the purchase of land in Indian Territory that included the Cherokee Outlet, the Jerome Commission forced the Cherokee government to sell these acres for a pittance by denying its right to lease it for revenue generation.[169] In 1893, Congress created the Dawes Commission to negotiate allotment agreements with the Five Tribes.[170] Because Cherokee statesmen refused to deal with the commissioners and in response to charges of corruption and social unrest, Senator Henry Teller chaired a special investigation on the conditions in Indian Territory, which was released in May 1894. Using much the same logic as the reformers who favored allotment, Teller's report offered a scathing critique of the tribal governments and urged the dissolution of the Indian republics. In another report released in the fall of 1896, the IRA affirmed Teller's interpretation and solidified the support of reformers behind the immediate allotment of Indian Territory by the Dawes Commission.[171]

Cherokee statesmen continued to stall the commissioners until, in the Curtis Act of 1898, Congress empowered the Dawes Commission to allot Indian Territory without the consent of the tribal governments. Supporters of the Curtis Act believed that they had succeeded in opening up the area for development and settlement by non-Indians, a process they predicted would take two years.[172] Cherokees then initiated negotiations that lasted for four more years and, ultimately, conceded to allotment under the Cherokee Agreement of 1902, a version of the policy more favorable to them than the Curtis Act.

The Cherokees had been first in resisting allotment, and they were the last of the Five Tribes to submit to the policy.[173] The resulting tragedy makes their resistance for over two decades no less remarkable. As Julia Coates remarks, "Much as in the removal era, this most acculturated of the Five Tribes, with the highest proportion of mixed-race citizens, unexpectedly exhibited the most conservative behavior while also engaging in the most sophisticated legal/political battle of any of the Indian nations."[174] To any student of Cherokee political history, the innovative, determined resistance of Cherokee leaders was neither unprecedented nor unexpected. For the Cherokee people to acquiesce to infringement upon their homes and families without a fight would have been unthinkable. The same persistence that described Cherokee statesmen throughout their opposition to allotment also characterized Cherokee families.

CHAPTER FOUR

Enrolling

In 1902, as summer aged into autumn, Simon Walkingstick scoured the rugged terrain of Goingsnake District for Cherokees who had not enrolled with the Dawes Commission. This was no easy task. Residents of this area clustered their farms in valleys shielded by ridges. For millennia, water had eroded the limestone and dolomite bedrock, but the Ozark Plateau had not disappeared. If anything, it seemed like it had dug in deeper and pushed down farther into the earth's crust. The dissolution of the Ozark Plateau's subterranean layers had created springs where the groundwater met the topsoil, resulting in hundreds of verdant rooms within this larger mansion of stone. These made secure, healthy, viable sites for small farms, and smatterings of wooden buildings and fields dotted the lush pockets nestled into the shallow soil of the mountainous Ozarks.

Since primordial times, Cherokees were a people of water, a force shaping their settlement patterns and infusing their spirituality. They built their ancient villages in the Appalachian Mountains along waterways that they believed were portals to the underworld, and they revered the power of water to purify and rejuvenate in this world. Those who settled in Goingsnake District following removal rebuilt homes along streams and near springs, an auspicious setting for a people thirsty for regeneration. The name given to these springs was "resurgences," as though to remind the ever-present winds and rains that although they could erode rock, these deep layers of the earth were tough and capable of changing in order to survive, too. So were the people who lived there. A source of destruction could instead spark adaptation. The Ozarks certainly proved that.[1]

This was the ecoregion through which Walkingstick followed the well-worn footpaths that traced the relationships connecting the Cherokees who called this place home. He depended on locals for information, directions, and hospitality, things that, under normal circumstances, they would have been inclined to give to a fellow Cherokee. But these were abnormal times, difficult and dangerous, and Walkingstick was seeking answers to questions that many of the people of these hills did not want asked. He worked for the Dawes Commission, the agency responsible for allotting the Cherokees. Although the policy remained unpopular, the passage of the Curtis Act in 1898 had prompted most Cherokees to conclude that allotment was inevitable, and some, like Walkingstick, found good jobs with the commission. After all, most of the Cherokee Nation's citizens were educated and literate, and some were bilingual in Cherokee and English. Federal jobs paid well and provided opportunities to earn cash money, which was not plentiful in an area then transitioning from a subsistence and barter-based economy to a market-driven one. Other Cherokees cooperated with allotment to retain some control over decisions about local matters. John Brown, to give one example, assisted in drawing section lines and plotting roads through his township.[2]

Walkingstick worked for the Dawes Commission in the official capacity of an interpreter, but he functioned as an investigator by necessity. Some Cherokees would not go before the Dawes Commission, and some who would spoke only Cherokee. Charged to gather specific information that would help the commission complete its census of the Cherokee Nation as the first step toward determining who would receive a share of tribal resources, Walkingstick sought answers to questions about the most personal details of peoples' lives, such as the paternity of their children and the stability of their marriages. Such intrusiveness made many Cherokees uncomfortable, and it made Walkingstick a target of animosity from those who opposed the policy.

The majority's acquiescence to allotment did not equate to a popular endorsement, and many Cherokees continued to challenge federal authority throughout each stage of the process. Many criticized the federal government's usurpation of the right to determine individuals' eligibility to share in communal wealth without accountability to the Cherokee Nation. They explained that citizenship was a decision informed by kinship and pointed out that the Cherokees had their own rosters created at the local level by district officials, and through this means they had conducted several censuses among themselves. In short, they knew who belonged, and they wanted to produce their own list of those eligible to receive an allotment. But in response to accusations of corruption by intruders, many of whose claims were dubious but who nonetheless charged that leaders of the Cherokee Nation had wrongfully denied their tribal citizenship, Congress instructed commissioners to create a new list, which would come to be called the Dawes roll.[3]

In 1896, the Dawes Commission began this massive, complicated process; it would not end until 1914. Most Cherokees registered with the Dawes Commission in 1900 by reporting to enrollment centers opened throughout the Cherokee Nation. At the same time, a significant minority believed this whole process to be so profoundly evil that, in accordance with Cherokee custom, they withdrew from it altogether. Such people identified themselves as Keetoowahs and, after 1901, as Nighthawks; among them were many residents of Goingsnake District. Directed by Congress to complete the Cherokee roll in 1902, the Dawes Commission sent staff to find them and obtain needed information by force, including the possibility of arrest, if necessary. Nighthawks had avoided going to enrollment centers, but men like Walkingstick brought the allotment crisis to their doorsteps.

This was the context in which Walkingstick approached the home of Jennie Oakball, a thirty-three-year-old farmer, wife, and mother. She had given birth to her first child, Ski-yos-ty, or Dave, in 1895, and her daughter, Ah-no-he, or Annie, was born two years later. In 1900, she gave birth to another son, named Cull, or Coo-wees-coo-wee in Cherokee. This was the Cherokee name of the beloved principal chief John Ross, and giving it to a newborn was a gesture akin to a citizen of the United States naming her son "George Washington." The Dawes commissioners had sent Walkingstick to investigate reports that Oakball recently had given birth to a daughter. According to the Cherokee Agreement of 1902, which elaborated upon the provisions of the Curtis Act of 1898 and in which the National Council of the Cherokee Nation conceded to allotment, all children born prior to September 1, 1902, to Cherokee parents were entitled to a portion of tribal wealth. Was Oakball the mother of a Cherokee newborn? Walkingstick was ordered to find out.

The Oakballs were Nighthawks, and when Walkingstick approached Jennie's home, she showed him no hospitality. To those who refused to enroll, Walkingstick was a menace and a reminder of the precariousness of their nation's existence. In this context, the names of Cherokee babies were political statements. Their inclusion or exclusion from the Dawes roll signified the parents' willingness—or lack of—to participate in allotment, a covenant with the U.S. government that resistant Cherokees believed violated their earlier treaties and broke the more important agreement that they had had with their Creator since ancient times. And so Jennie Oakball faced down Simon Walkingstick. He repeatedly asked her for information about her newborn as her other children played nearby. The young mother responded with stone-faced silence. Oakball would not tell him anything that he wanted to know about a child who may never have been born, who may have been born and died, or who may have been sleeping quietly in the house that he could not see into because she blocked the doorway with her tense body.

Her silence no doubt confirmed the view of the members of the Dawes Commission that the Nighthawks were backwards, unintelligent, and easily duped rather than proactive, rational, informed, conscientious, and committed. Whereas the commissioners' comments about the male leaders of the movement were both condescending and romantic, female Nighthawks remained invisible to them. That was their oversight. Jennie Oakball was not dumb. Jennie Oakball was angry, and her passion fed the cause of her people. Whether or not the commissioners acknowledged it, patriotism had deep roots in tribal communities and came in a female variety.

Accepting the futility of his efforts, Walkingstick turned to leave the Oakball homestead, but not before he asked one last question: Who fathered the child? "Chu-nu-lur-hunks," Oakball said. Walkingstick must have been stunned that his persistent questioning had yielded a result, at least to confirm the birth of a baby. But it would be a mistake to read her answer as a concession. Jennie Oakball knew her husband's English name—John. Instead of answering Walkingstick's question in the language the commissioners expected and preferred, however, Jennie said her husband's name in the mother tongue of their nation. "Chu-nu-lur-hunks," Oakball said, "Chu-nu-lur-hunks." In the context of this meeting during a great crisis among their people, one word shared between Simon Walkingstick and Jennie Oakball spoke volumes. It represented a worldview. In the end, Jennie's defiance did not prevent the Oakballs' enrollment, because Walkingstick obtained needed information from neighbors and the local midwife. He took that information back to the Dawes Commission, which recorded it, compared it to existing tribal rolls, and allotted land to the Oakball family, but among all the forms and transcripts documenting the transition of this family from tribal members to private landowners, there would be a record of Jennie making it very clear that the Oakballs did not consent.[4]

The story of this brief encounter between Walkingstick and Oakball draws us away from the perspectives of the Dawes commissioners and toward those of Cherokee people participating in or resisting this process. It consequently restores some complexity to the historical narrative of allotment, which rationalizes the commissioners' points of view as normative while obscuring the many and complicated ways that Cherokees thought about and experienced the enrollment process. The Dawes roll was a product of a contest between the agents of a movement to assimilate Cherokees into Anglo-American society through land reform and Cherokees who rejected the legitimacy of both the mission and the process.[5]

This vignette also focuses us on the central institution through which Cherokees mediated allotment, their families. For advocates of assimilation, allotment was about remaking Cherokee families in the Anglo-American model, and enrollment was the first step in this process. It was the means through which the federal government co-opted a duty that traditionally had been performed by those families: the determination of who was kin and who was not. Told from the vantage point of Cherokee people, then, the story of the making of the Dawes roll, this most intimate form of colonialism, is about resistance to the loss of autonomy and privacy in family matters—the nation's sovereignty abrogated on the threshold of its homes. It is also a tale of creative adaptation, selective collaboration, and informed resistance in defense of the families that were the foundation of Cherokee society. In this chapter, I show what Cherokee families made of the Dawes roll and what the Dawes roll made of Cherokee families.

By contextualizing the testimony and evidence compiled by the Dawes Commission in the making of the Dawes roll, I explore some of the many ways that Cherokees experienced this process and influenced the final product. Some Cherokees enrolled themselves and shared information about family and neighbors who were unwilling to participate. Cherokees complicated enrollment through their active participation in defense of those who they believed rightly belonged to them, but they also undermined the Dawes Commission's authority through casual and willful noncompliance. The places where the commissioners' expectations confused Cherokees and where Cherokee norms frustrated the commissioners provide a fertile ground for a discussion of the values and behaviors common among Cherokee families at the beginning of the twentieth century.

The Enrollment Process and the Mission of the Dawes Commission

In 1896, after decades of wrangling over the accuracy of Cherokee rolls and the unwillingness of the U.S. government to remove its citizens from Cherokee land, Congress stripped the Cherokee Nation of its sovereign right to regulate tribal membership. Instead, it charged the Dawes Commission with creating a roster of the Cherokee Nation intended to serve several functions. First, the Dawes roll was supposed to provide a complete list of those eligible to receive an allotment, or a share in the distributed material wealth of the Cherokee Nation. Second, the Dawes roll was intended to organize the population of the tribal republic into categories that facilitated the management of Cherokee property owners and, more important, their property. Toward this end, blood quantum emerged as both an organizing system and a symbolic language referring to competency. Third, the Dawes roll was designed to facilitate the transmission of newly privatized property through sale and inheritance in the future, and for this reason, the documentation of paternity and maternity was essential.[6]

Congress gave the commissioners this assignment nine years after the passage of the Dawes Act and two years before the passage of the Curtis Act, and the process represents a transitional moment in the evolution of allotment from a visionary, if misguided, plan for the inclusion of Indian people into Anglo-American society to the creation of a bureaucracy designed to regulate them at its margins. By 1896, the U.S. government had been in the wholesale land privatization business for nearly a decade, and officials appreciated that the administration of Cherokee property owners would be an enormous task. Seemingly everything about the policy's application to smaller, less wealthy tribes mushroomed in complexity and controversy when applied to the large, prosperous Cherokee Nation. In addition, those who assumed the work of allotting Indian Territory generally lacked the belief in uplift that had characterized the early proponents of the policy. The Friends of the Indian had never been in the business of pleasing Indian people, but the initial disappointing results of allotment, leading to drastic revisions to the Dawes Act as early as 1891, prompted many of the policy's advocates to retire from Indian uplift and take up other, less bleak causes. As a result, the Friends of the Indian did not allot the Cherokee Nation. Rather, they abandoned the project to political appointees who were poor stewards of both the integrity of the reformers' vision and the well-being of those who would be allotted.[7]

Serving on the Dawes Commission was an opportune appointment for men of ambition if not necessarily charity and character, and many looked to benefit from the opening of the region to non-Indians. The corruption that accompanied the allotment of Indian Territory is documented by historian Angie Debo, who describes in detail how graft was built into the administration of Indian allotments. In the polarized political climate, those tribal leaders who could have called attention to fraud were silenced. Other prominent tribal members who benefited from this system legitimized it.[8] This factionalism was compounded by the lack of external oversight from the Department of the Interior and Congress, which supported the goals of assimilation and the interests of boosters. Nonetheless, the Dawes commissioners and their staff were not rabid Indian haters. They were ambassadors who held the widely shared Anglo-American view that Indians were backward relics of broken cultures whose rights, particularly to resources and self-determination, no longer mattered as the United States look forward to the twentieth century.[9]

The commissioners and their staff sought to create an accurate, detailed roll that would facilitate the economic development and administration of the region. As such, it needed to be intelligible to the non-Indians who would be using it regularly, and there was no incentive to reflect Cherokee understandings of relatedness. Like their Progressive contemporaries elsewhere, the Dawes commissioners also saw the regulation of sexuality and reproduction as an appropriate focus of state power, particularly when the goals were the eradication of poverty and the generation of individual wealth. If Cherokees were to assimilate into American society as individual property owners, their extended family structures would not do. Therefore, the commissioners' task of producing a roll entailed the use of Anglo-American categories for reckoning kinship and belonging.[10] In this, the Dawes Commission diverged from precedent. Allotment agent and ethnologist Alice C. Fletcher studied and documented the kinship systems of the tribes among whom she worked, particularly the Winnebago. Intrigued by their way of reckoning relatedness, she created a registry correlating Winnebago kinship to that of Anglo-America.[11] Likewise, the Census Office, established in 1840, usually defined a family as those who shared a household whether or not they were biologically related or conformed to the nuclear ideal.[12] The Dawes

Commission did not organize its roll to provide a comparably accurate reflection of Cherokee society, however, but instead enrolled Cherokees in the units preferred in Anglo-American society, whether or not they accurately represented actual living situations.

Enrollment consisted of three stages. First, the Dawes commissioners arranged for public hearings to be held in fourteen towns throughout the Cherokee Nation between July and December 1900.[13] Rather than canvassing the Cherokee Nation, following the model of the U.S. census, the Dawes Commission instructed Cherokees that all heads-of-households were to appear before it to enroll their families. Throughout the spring of 1900, the commissioners advertised these dates and locations in English and in Cherokee, both on flyers and in local newspapers.[14] Most families in this study who participated enrolled in Westville in July 1900 or in Tahlequah that December. Cherokees who appeared before the commission were asked a set of questions designed to obtain the information necessary to fill in preprinted enrollment cards. When needed, Cherokee-speaking translators facilitated the interviews on behalf of the English-speaking commissioners. Stenographers recorded the interviews in English.[15]

Second, commissioners verified the information given to them. This investigative component was the most arduous part of the Dawes Commission's task. Most often, clerks cross-checked individuals with the 1880 and 1896 tribal rolls. The latter was the final census taken by the Cherokee government, although the National Council never validated the results. Criticized by those who sought to open Indian Territory to non-Indian development as plagued by irregularities, the 1896 roll was nevertheless endorsed by Congress, which instructed the Dawes Commission to use it to certify the legitimacy of prospective enrollees. Other documents were less frequently noted. Clerks also requested documentation of marriages, births, and deaths. Because few Cherokees kept such records and because commissioners did not assume the accuracy of answers given to them, the Dawes Commission also questioned neighbors about the veracity of each other's testimony. In particular, they asked about sexual fidelity, or the paternity and maternity of minors, to determine whether or not the children living in a household were the biological offspring of the adults caring for them. Commissioners also obtained information about those who refused to enroll themselves from their family members and neighbors.

Third, clerks entered the information on preprinted 14 x 17 inch cards. They wrote the name of the person whom they considered to be the head-of-household at the top left of the card, then listed others beneath that person and specified their relationships. The commission further identified enrollees by age, sex, perceived blood quantum, history of tribal enrollment, and history of their parents' tribal enrollment. Other miscellaneous, relevant information was noted on the bottom and back of the cards. Clerks then categorized the applicants as "regular," "doubtful," or "rejected." Each card was numbered.[16] Finally, clerks assigned each approved individual a Dawes roll number, which was listed before his or her name.[17]

The Dawes commissioners believed that they had used their experiences enrolling citizens of the other tribal republics to create a straightforward protocol that would result in an accurate roster of the Cherokee Nation. It quickly became clear, however, that this process was neither simple nor pleasant for those involved. As the *Cherokee Advocate* reported, "The proceedings have a tendency to irritate the Commissioners and their applicants alike."[18] Even for those Cherokees who spoke English, words as well as worldview separated them from commissioners, and cultural differences became starkly apparent. During the early weeks of enrollment, the *Cherokee Advocate* published an "account" of the taking of oaths that preceded commissioners' questioning of Cherokees that humorously hinted at the divide separating them. They simply did not understand one another:

"Witness, have you been sworn?" asked the Commissioners the other day of a witness after he had testified. His answer was—"I don't know." Commissioners, "Well do you feel like you have been sworn?" Witness, "Sorter that erway—not much."[19]

Cherokee conceptions of the expected and customary did not correspond with those of the commissioners. What resulted was a series of struggles among individual Cherokees, their families, and the commissioners over what would end up on those preprinted cards.

Cherokee Experiences of Enrollment

Although the population of the Cherokee Nation had attained widespread literacy during the 1820s and several generations of Cherokees had had the means to document their lives in writing by the allotment era, the transitions of human existence largely remained collected in the oral library of the Cherokee Nation: its people, especially its elders. Births, marriages, divorces, and deaths remained recorded in the memories of the living and the stories passed down to those who came later.[20] Considering the widespread attainment of literacy within Cherokee society, the lack of written documentation provided to the Dawes Commission is notable. Important information was remembered and organized locally, and this system was fluid and accountable to those it served and validated grassroots knowledge and authority. Such a method of record keeping, however, was not readily accessible to outsiders, including commissioners and their staff, who interpreted the lack of vital statistics as confirmation of the ineptitude of the Cherokee government and the inferiority of Cherokee society.[21]

The demographic information, such as names and ages, written down on late-nineteenth-century Cherokee censuses often was inconsistent across sources, and clerks noted these discrepancies and other miscellaneous data on the bottom of the enrollment cards. The accuracy of such information simply was not important to the functioning of the tribal government or Cherokee families because presence in one's community was evidence of existence, behavior indicated one's stage of life, and relationships with kin and neighbors validated one's rights.[22] Testifying before the Dawes Commission in 1907, Betsy Suake was not unique in responding to a question asking her age by stating, "I *guess* I am fifty-six" (emphasis mine). Existing Cherokee records suggested that she could have been as young as fifty-two or as old as sixty-two.[23] Commissioners perceived this paucity of accurate written records as a void rather than as evidence of a vibrant, predominantly oral archival system with which they would have to work in tandem.

When they started gathering data on Cherokees to compile the Dawes roll, commissioners nonetheless sought documentation, and they began with the beginning of life. They requested affidavits confirming the birth of children too young to have appeared in the 1896 Cherokee census. In other words, the Dawes Commission expected parents to provide birth certificates. The concept of documenting a birth by giving a voluntary written statement affirmed by an oath administered by an authorized government representative was foreign to Cherokees. Instead, midwives served as the repositories for such information in late-nineteenth-century Cherokee society. Traditionally, four female relatives tended to a birthing mother and welcomed her baby into their world. The group was led by a midwife, an expert who possessed experiential, medicinal, and spiritual knowledge and guided the new mother through rituals that strengthened and purified her, protected her child, and enabled both to rejoin the community. For that, the midwife was accorded respect.[24]

It is not clear if late-nineteenth-century residents of the Cherokee Nation provided care for mothers and infants in traditional ways, but midwives continued to serve an important role, and Cherokees still deferred to them. One particular incident involving a midwife must have caused commissioners to scratch their heads. In July 1900, John Cannon appeared before them to enroll his wife, Lee, and their son and daughter. Although his task seemed relatively simple and his interview uneventful, Cannon later discovered that he had made a grievous mistake. In a subsequent letter to the Dawes Commission, Cannon explained that he had enrolled his daughter under the wrong name. Rather than "Beulah," the name he gave to the Dawes Commission, her name was "Bular." He requested that they change their records. Who better than a father knew the name of his own child? Cannon answered that his wife and the midwife named her, and they called her Bular. In John's understanding of the situation, they spoke with authority on the identity of the child.[25] As they struggled to complete their roll, the Dawes commissioners came to value the knowledge of midwives, too. When enrollment began in 1900, they did not subpoena midwives to verify the information they were collecting, but this oversight proved to be a mistake. By 1902, they sought out their testimony, particularly to confirm the births of infants and children whose parents had not provided affidavits.[26]

Most Cherokees ignored the Dawes Commission's request for birth affidavits. While Nighthawks, like Jim and Mary Hogshooter, returned commissioners' letters requesting such documentation to signal their rejection of the enrollment process, most Cherokees did not provide affidavits simply because they did not have them.[27] When parents did supply them, clerks noted the date of submission but did not record copies, and so the date when the documents were created is impossible to know. Because Cherokees rarely brought such papers to their enrollment interviews but returned with them months or even years later, these certificates likely were created in response to the Dawes Commission's request rather than at the time of birth. After all, if John Cannon had had his children's birth certificates, he would have known what his wife and midwife had named their daughter. He left his interview promising to supply them. He did—three months later for son Walter and four months later for daughter Bular.[28] As late as the spring of 1900, shortly before the Dawes Commission opened enrollment centers throughout the Cherokee Nation, Cherokees were not routinely creating birth affidavits for their infants. John's nephew Ira Cannon also enrolled his family in July 1900, and Ira, newly married with a newborn daughter, also told the commissioners that he had no certificate but would obtain one, which he provided the following month.[29]

Throughout the enrollment period, however, Cherokees learned from each other's experiences and came to understand the importance of affidavits to the Dawes Commission. For this reason, Cherokees who enrolled later sometimes brought certificates for their young children. Oscar, the last of the Cannon brothers to enroll, had an affidavit confirming the birth of his toddler, Wirt, at his enrollment interview.[30] By the time the enrollment period closed in 1902, Cherokees routinely supplied affidavits to the Dawes Commission in order to enroll their newborn children. Oscar Cannon returned to enroll daughter Maggie with an affidavit in December 1901, and a few days later, his brother John enrolled his newborn daughter, Cora, in the same way. Their niece Dovie's first son, Harry Welch, was enrolled via affidavit in January 1902, which completed the enrollment of the extended Cannon family.[31]

Although some Cherokees learned to comply with the Dawes Commission's expectations for documentation, the commissioners ultimately deferred to Cherokee custom and enrolled children of Cherokee parents whether or not the parents provided birth affidavits. They had to, because by the time enrollment closed in 1902, the Dawes Commission had sought but not received written confirmation of the births of all Cherokee children under six years old. In other words, although some Cherokees had accommodated the Dawes Commission's preferences for written documentation, commissioners ultimately changed their policy to accommodate Cherokee custom because the majority of Cherokee parents did not provide affidavits, and their children were enrolled anyway.[32]

Like birth, death also complicated enrollment. The majority of Cherokees left life as they entered it, witnessed by family and neighbors who loved and knew them. Although some left wills, most Cherokees died intestate. Cherokees did customarily report deaths to their government in order to settle any outstanding debts their late loved ones may have had or been owed. The settlement of debts entailed administrators appearing in district court and informing the judges if they had collected or parted with any property on behalf of the deceased. These statements, typically only a few sentences long, were written down.[33] During the enrollment period, the Dawes Commission expected Cherokees also to report to it deaths that occurred.[34] Deaths mattered because in the Cherokee Agreement of 1902, the National Council and Dawes Commission set the cutoff date for inclusion on the Dawes roll as September 1, 1902. In other words, any Cherokee alive on that date was entitled to an allotment, but Cherokees who enrolled during the previous two years but then died were not. Martha Raper, who had been enrolled by her maternal nephew John Brown in December 1900, passed away in September 1901, and commissioners struck her from the roll.[35] Clerks did not explain how they learned of Martha's death. There is no record of the Dawes Commission having sent requests for death affidavits like they did for those confirming births, and so Cherokees seemed to be self-reporting, albeit slowly.[36] Hattie Holland was widowed in May 1901 when her husband, James, passed away, but she did not send notification of his death to the Dawes Commission until January 1903.[37]

The ability to select an allotment, which mostly took place in 1904, probably motivated Cherokees to report deaths because, again, commissioners expected documentation and denied surviving family members who did not have it, even when they were the rightful heirs. Mose Crittenden did not know this, and he did not come prepared. His son William died on February 24, 1903, when the boy would have been about two years old. On December 29, 1904, Mose selected allotments for himself and the rest of his family, but the Dawes Commission would not allow him to claim land for William until he filed a death affidavit, which he did on January 5, 1905. Crittenden had to go to federal court to be named the executor of William's estate before he could select his late son's allotment in March 1905.[38]

On the other hand, Marsh Brown did come prepared. His experience affirmed the Dawes Commission's expectation that Cherokees would go to the federal court to have themselves declared the executors of their deceased kin's estate, which typically consisted of an allotment, before claiming land in their own name. On September 4, 1904, Brown's teenage daughter Eliza died, and on September 24, he went to the federal court in order to be declared the administrator of her estate, which was her allotment. When he appeared before the Dawes Commission in late October to select his family's allotments, he brought the paperwork empowering him to claim Eliza's, too. Brown may have been prepared to handle his daughter's affairs, but the U.S. federal courts were not. Their preprinted forms referred to those property owners who died intestate as male. The clerk had to type "her" over the preexisting "his" throughout the document.[39]

For the purposes of enrollment, commissioners sought definitive answers, but Cherokees responded to death, particularly concerning how surviving children received care, with flexibility. Take the children of George and Lizzie Welch, for example. George died in February 1900, and his wife died that July. The couple had six children ranging in age from seventeen to four years old. Two weeks after Lizzie's death, Mack Welch, the children's half-brother and George's son from a previous marriage, enrolled them. Commissioners wanted to know the whereabouts of the children and who claimed custody of them, and Mack explained that he and his wife, Emma, were caring for the youngest child, a girl named Lee, and that other relatives, including his sister and brother, were caring for her older siblings. But, he emphasized, the family was reeling from the death of Lizzie, and they had made no permanent decisions. Lee died that next month, and sixteen-year-old George passed away the following year. By 1905, John Welch, Mack's older brother and another half-brother of the children, served as their legal guardian and claimed allotments for three of the surviving children (twenty-year-old Moses selected his own), but, in reality, Mack and John both continued to share in the care of their father's second family. In 1906, the Dawes Commission notified the family that it had officially stricken Lee and George from the roll, but no such erasure of the bonds of kinship occurred within the Welch family. The two youngest children, Mollie and Nay, continued to live with their older half-siblings in 1910.[40]

The mobility of Cherokee people also challenged commissioners to understand the role of displacement and reunification in Cherokee history when determining who belonged on the Dawes roll. To a more compassionate audience, the history of Cherokee dispossession would have been shocking, but in the context of the creation of the Dawes roll, it proved to be just another complication to be factored in by already overwhelmed clerks. Although Cherokees were not a migratory people according to an anthropological understanding of the term, in the course of their contact with Europeans and their American descendants, their homes had been repeatedly destroyed, they had been expelled from their land, and their communities had been fragmented. Although the federal government created lists in 1835, 1848, 1851, and 1852 that counted eastern and western

Cherokees before and after removal, the Cherokee diaspora largely went undocumented. The pain of the separation it caused did not go unfelt.

Beginning in 1841, the Cherokee Nation extended citizenship to members of the Eastern Band of Cherokees, who remained in the mountains of North Carolina, inviting them to rejoin their kin in Indian Territory, and eventually this invitation included Cherokees who had relocated elsewhere during the Civil War. The documentation that the Cherokee Nation issued to Cherokee immigrants, however, was unsatisfactory to commissioners. In 1900, Eliza Brown's son John tried to enroll his elderly parents, including his father, James, an intermarried white man. The two were in fragile health and could not travel to the enrollment center themselves. Their absence raised commissioners' suspicions. In particular, they questioned why John did not provide a marriage license for his parents. The couple, he explained, did not register their intermarriage with the Cherokee Nation because they had married in North Carolina approximately *thirty years* before moving to Indian Territory. After relocating, Eliza applied for admission, and in November 1876, Principal Chief Charles Thompson signed an act conferring the rights of citizenship upon Eliza and her family. Did that include her husband of over thirty years? The Dawes Commission wavered. They heard testimony that James and Eliza had always lived as husband and wife and that James had voted in Cherokee elections since relocating to Indian Territory and was listed as an adopted white in Cherokee censuses. Ultimately, in February 1907, the Dawes Commission decided that James was eligible for an allotment. Although she had not been physically well enough to make the trip to appear before that time, commissioners nonetheless subpoenaed Eliza to testify and finally resolve this matter. She never did. Perhaps she was not able, or perhaps she was too grieved. James, her husband of over half a century, had died on Christmas Day 1903.[41]

In addition to the dispersal caused by Cherokee dispossession, traditional gender roles made young men mobile, and economic necessity may have encouraged their temporary outmigration from the nation. To facilitate their task, the Dawes Commission specified that they would not enroll anyone who had left the nation following the 1880 census without proof of readmission from the National Council, and they asked questions to confirm residency during enrollment interviews. The Cherokee constitution did state that only the National Council could readmit persons to citizenship, but neither the Cherokee constitution nor the National

Council specified what period of time necessitated a subsequent appearance before them. Likewise, because Cherokees considered it normal for young men to leave seeking education and life experiences and because these men stayed in touch with their families with the expectation of returning home, Cherokee men often did not apply for readmission. Even when they did, their certificates did not always satisfy the requirements of the Dawes Commission. The cases of two of the Cannon brothers exemplify this.

Edwin Cannon was a middle-aged father of seven by the time he stood before the commissioners seeking to enroll. Born in Georgia, he had migrated to the Cherokee Nation during the early 1870s with his Cherokee mother, intermarried white father, and siblings. The family was admitted to citizenship. In 1873, when he was eighteen, Edwin married Lucinda, a white woman, in Arkansas, and after living in the Cherokee Nation for two years, the couple left and traveled elsewhere together, including as far away as Idaho, where their son Ira and perhaps their daughter Dovie were born, before returning to Goingsnake District in 1885. There they built a home among the extended Cannon family and raised their children for the next fifteen years. Then Edwin found himself standing before the Dawes Commission explaining the decisions he had made as a youth. Commissioners questioned Cannon about his reasons for leaving and returning after a decade. When they challenged him regarding his eligibility for the rights of citizenship, he showed them a certificate of readmission dated August 13, 1887, but they scrutinized him further and questioned the breadth of this document's application. His certificate of readmission did not include Lucinda's name. Why, they asked, did he not remarry her in 1887? From Edwin's perspective, the question was nonsensical. Cherokee law did not require him to do so, and neither did his family or his neighbors, who understood Lucinda to be his wife in 1887 no different than she had been for the previous fourteen years of their marriage. The 1890 Cherokee census lists Lucinda as an adopted white. The Dawes Commission's rigid interpretation of Cherokee law highlights the strength of the flexible, localized system through which Cherokees interpreted such policies. What was obvious was not problematic.[42]

Cases like Sterling Cannon's also troubled the Dawes Commission because although the Cherokee Nation issued documents verifying readmission to citizenship, Cherokees did not universally or uniformly seek them, especially when those who left did so for work, did not give up their home in the Cherokee Nation, communicated with their families, and returned regularly. Sterling was younger than Edwin but older than Oscar and John. He never married but had a cabin among the farms of his siblings, closest to his oldest brother, Wilson. Throughout his adulthood, Sterling traveled throughout the Cherokee Nation and beyond for work. Although in 1880 he lived in the Goingsnake District with his family, by 1890, he had moved to the Canadian District. In 1900, Sterling was working in Washington when he became sick and did not have the money to return home to appear before the Dawes Commission. Wilson tried to enroll him, and when two years later commissioners demanded additional information about the duration and reason for Sterling's absence, Wilson had to go back for an additional interview. Wilson attempted to confuse, rather than clarify, his brother's status. He explained that Sterling had been back home and had left again for health reasons, but he would not identify the particular illness his brother suffered from more specifically than it was "something peculiar to men" and "I can't tell you." Wilson also would not specify the length of his brother's absences other than to say that in the past he had left home for months or even years.[43] Commissioners interpreted men's absences from their homes as abandonment when they were, in fact, often normal and temporary separations. Leaving did not negate belonging as long as one remained in contact with family and, above all, returned home to their welcome, the only validation of their citizenship most Cherokees received. In this case, the family's certainty finally proved good enough for the Dawes Commission. Because of the persistence of his brother Wilson, commissioners ultimately enrolled Sterling, who appeared before them himself to select an allotment in 1904.[44]

Marriage, too, usually lacked certification among Cherokees. Beginning in 1819, the Cherokee government required white men to obtain a license before marrying a Cherokee woman if they also sought the privileges associated with Cherokee citizenship. Both of the white men in this study who married Cherokee women after relocating to Indian Territory did so.[45] No such regulation pertained to marriages between Cherokee citizens, and for this reason, Cherokees rarely obtained affidavits documenting their marriages to each other.[46] Rather, couples celebrated unions before family, and, above all, the acknowledgment of their community validated their bond.

Even within families, some couples documented their marriages and others did not. Take Edwin Cannon's siblings. In 1887, Wilson Cannon married a white American woman, Sarah Bell, and he registered their marriage with the tribal government.[47] In 1890, Ophelia Jane Cannon registered her marriage to white American Scott Harless, who was granted a license.[48] That same year, Oscar Cannon married a white American woman, Annie, but did not register the marriage with the tribal government; when the Dawes Commission later asked him for documentation, he responded that "Parson Lacey" (*sic*) had administered their vows and could corroborate Oscar's testimony.[49] Reverend Adam Lacie, a minister associated with the Baptist Mission located four miles north of Westville, witnessed many such ceremonies. He was reputed to be tireless in his work as both a man of the cloth and a representative to the tribal government. John Cannon told the commissioners that he had no marriage certificate verifying his relationship to Lee, a fellow Cherokee, but his older brother Wilson confirmed John's testimony and added that the couple were married in his home in 1896.[50] Even for those married just before enrollment, such certification seemed unnecessary. Edwin Cannon's son Ira married Lizzie, an American, in 1899, and the following year, Ira explained to the Dawes Commission that he, too, had "no certificate handy."[51] Marriage affidavits may have followed the same pattern as birth certificates; Cherokees routinely obtained them only when the Dawes Commission began requesting them. Dovie Cannon, Edwin's daughter, supplied one in January 1902 verifying her marriage to fellow Cherokee John Welch in November 1900.[52]

Cherokees' attitudes toward divorce also contrasted with the expectations of the Dawes Commission. Divorce, as historian John Phillip Reid points out, was an awkward term to use in reference to Cherokee marriages because in the American legal system, it refers to the breaking of a legal contract regarding material concerns rather than affection, whereas among Cherokees, marriage involved no such lifetime commitment to support.[53] Cohabitation and separation are more accurate terms for describing the nature and dissolution of Cherokee marriages. Members of the Dawes Commission equated marriage with a permanent bond, however, and that it was not always so among Cherokees confused them. As Rosanna Mounce explained when they sought documentation of her previous marriage's end, "There was no such thing as divorce when him and me was married, [but we] just lived together and parted the same way." Mounce was referring to the early 1890s.[54]

Shameful and secretive in Anglo-American society, divorce bore no such stigma among Cherokees, who spoke readily about the end of each other's relationships because such transitions were not abnormal. Informant

Rider Hammer matter-of-factly informed the Dawes Commission that his neighbor Nannie Palone's husband had left her. Did commissioners interpret his comments as casting aspersion upon her? Perhaps, but it was not likely that Hammer considered Nannie's circumstances to be scandalous because serial monogamy was common. He likely expected the young woman to pair up with another man soon.[55]

Although they preferred written documentation, Dawes commissioners accepted and, ultimately, solicited verbal corroboration of the information they were receiving from witnesses and informants. In traveling to enrollment centers and, eventually, to Tahlequah to speak on behalf of one another, Cherokees shaped the decisions made by the Dawes Commission. Most witnesses were kin and neighbors to those about whom they testified, but not all were comfortable speaking openly before the commissioners. For example, lacking a marriage certificate, Mose Crittenden asked neighbor John B. Morris to confirm that he and Minnie truly were married. Although he admitted knowing them and their children and having been in their house, Morris would not directly state that the couple were married. Instead, he said, "It was the rumor that he was married," and, in doing so, Morris situated authority over such a decision in the neighborhood court of public opinion as a way of negotiating his role in this awkward, unfamiliar situation.[56]

Informants usually also testified about family and neighbors. The difference was that they provided information about those who had not enrolled themselves. Did those who enabled the inclusion of the Nighthawks on the Dawes roll violate their right to dissent and undermine their cause, or did these fellow Cherokees act selflessly to assure that those they knew to be eligible did not lose their homes and farms? It is difficult to determine intent from the transcripts compiled by the Dawes Commission's clerks, but informants did not openly criticize those who opposed the process with which they were cooperating.[57] For example, Reverend Lacie provided information about several Nighthawks. In doing so, he usually explained the context in which he knew them. In other words, his relationships motivated his testimony. For example, Lacie had married Tom Suake to his first wife, Charlotte, who passed away prior to enrollment. He provided information on Tom, his mother, Betsy, and her other children.[58] In his testimony about Abe and Margaret Sixkiller, Lacie began by explaining that they were "neighbors," although they lived five miles apart. Their children attended school together at Baptist Mission, and Margaret was kin to his wife, Jennie. Lacie did not mention the strongest bond between them. The Sixkiller family had long been active at Baptist Mission, where Abe served as a director. The men knew each other well. If Lacie struggled over whether or not to enroll his friends, he did not share his concerns with the Dawes Commission; the extent of his justifications suggests his decision to serve as an informant may have been a difficult one for the community leader.[59]

Lacie's testimony may have been the most evocative in suggesting how deeply connected by blood and life these factions of Cherokees were, but most informants knew an enormous amount of specific information, suggesting that these people were close to one another, neighbors and even family. Isaac Youngbird, for example, provided such specific details about John and Jennie Oakball that although he did not explain how he knew them, it was clear that he had been witness to their lives for a long time. He knew their names in English and Cherokee, their ages, and the names and ages of their children. He also knew the couple's parents, who were close to his own age. His tie to another family in this study is more obvious, however. He enrolled his grandchildren against their father's wishes. Youngbird's daughter Annie, who had died in 1900, was married to Sam Crittenden. The couple had three children together. On May 28, 1902, their grandfather enrolled them and his son-in-law.[60] Consistent with Cherokees' traditional means of organizing such demographic material, informants tended to be elders like Youngbird. Only one of the five men in this study who testified about the unenrolled was younger than fifty.[61]

That exception was forty-three-year-old Rider Hammer. He provided specific information about nearly all the Nighthawks in this study. Unlike other informants sought out by the Dawes Commission who served in roles that entailed their having obvious specific knowledge, such as midwives recalling births, ministers testifying to vows taken, and sheriffs speaking about papers served, Hammer seemed not to have had any official capacity.[62] He gave no specific information about his relationships with people except to explain that he had known most of them for decades.[63] And whereas Lacie did not openly discuss his neighbors' political views with the Dawes Commission, Hammer did. He knew that those he was helping to enroll, including the Birds, Hogshooters, Sands, and Turtles, opposed allotment, but he shared information about them anyway.[64]

Hammer is intriguing because his motives are unclear. Lacking evidence that he bore ill will toward Nighthawks personally or opposed their movement, I can only speculate that perhaps his testimony reflected his usual role in his community. Hammer had a finely tuned memory, and he was a repository of demographic information. Another way to say this is that he could have been the neighborhood gossip.[65] No note in the record clarifies whether he took it upon himself to go before the Dawes Commission or, on the other hand, if the Dawes Commission subpoenaed him or even paid him. By May 1902, however, the commissioners were actively seeking those who would share the information they needed to complete their roll. They returned to Goingsnake District, and both Lacie and Hammer appeared before the commission over multiple days in May and June. In the following few months, staff of the commission, men like Simon Walkingstick, canvassed communities throughout the Cherokee Nation to find more people who would talk. Commissioners could not have finished their job without informants, and they could not have completed the Dawes roll without access to the oral archives of the Cherokee Nation.

Although such informants were valuable resources for the Dawes Commission because they knew a remarkable amount of data that was not available through any documentary records, Hammer told the commissioners some things that were not correct. The presence of these inaccuracies in the Dawes roll reflects the weakness of commissioners' methodology, which in turn reflects their lack of respect for the Cherokees' oral history and kinship networks. Relying on only a few local informants rather than opening the process to grassroots scrutiny and feedback meant that knowledgeable Cherokees did not catch and correct mistakes. The Cherokee government had done precisely that in compiling and authenticating the 1880 census. By not immersing themselves in Cherokee communities, there is a lot the Dawes Commission did not learn.[66]

ONE CANNOT BE LONG in the research room of the Oklahoma Historical Society, where I conducted much of the archival research for this project, before hearing a patron refer to the Dawes roll with near biblical respect: "So-and-so was on *the roll*," implying that this person, without question, was a *real Indian*. The Dawes roll is equated with the truth. But *whose* truth? Although the contested process through which it was created has been forgotten, the Dawes roll is alive and well today. A century after its creation, it continues to influence Cherokee affairs. The Cherokee Nation recognizes it as the primary documentary source validating claims to tribal citizenship, and many Cherokees and non-Indians alike point to the Dawes roll as an authentic expression of who the Cherokees were at the moment of their republic's dissolution and, therefore, who they are today. Accepting the Dawes roll as inherently accurate ignores that this important and useful record is essentially a catalog of decisions made by non-Indians about what it meant to be Cherokee. Contemporary Cherokees understood this and frequently challenged these outsiders' conclusions.

The transcripts of Cherokees' interviews with the Dawes commissioners may seem uneventful on first reading, but upon further scrutiny, they reveal how contested the enrollment process and the commission's decisions were. Placing these brief exchanges in the context of both the stories of these individual families and the larger history of allotment is revealing. Cherokee cultural norms permeate the documents. They shaped the responses of those who enrolled and those who refused to do so and highlight the disjuncture between Cherokee and Anglo-American ideas about family, gender roles, and sexuality. The Dawes Commission was charged to create an index that would facilitate the application of a policy that Cherokees generally did not support, and their compliance was unenthusiastic. Enrollment was inconvenient and its outcomes unknowable. Most Cherokees complied, however, because they sought to secure a future that ensured their families' welfare. From their perspective, then, enrollment was an act of love and faith. Cherokees did not know what information the final roll would include, and they did not know how this document would shape their lives and those of their descendants. That uncertainty hung thick in the air of the enrollment office. It was a witness to all that was said and written down, and its presence was recorded between the lines.

CHAPTER FIVE

~❧ ❦~

Dividing

Rosanna Mounce was flustered. The Dawes commissioners were asking questions about her former lovers and ex-husbands, and they expected her to answer them in this public place, the enrollment office. It was the fall of 1902. Having sent her current husband, Joe, to speak on her behalf as was customary and appropriate from her perspective, she had been waiting outside in the family's wagon. Joe had represented her once before. In 1900, he had enrolled Rosanna, her son from a previous relationship, and their sons. But his testimony was no longer acceptable to commissioners because they no longer believed with certainty that he was her rightful husband and, therefore, entitled to represent her. A man she had lived with over a decade earlier was claiming an allotment through her, and so commissioners wanted Rosanna to answer directly to them and clarify with whom she had ever had sexual intercourse, lived, and conceived surviving children. And so commissioners called her down from her wagon and put her under oath. During her interrogation, Mounce was surrounded by strangers and outsiders, probably all of whom were men. A stenographer clicked away as she spoke, and her responses became part of the public record. This likely was the first time this common Cherokee farmer and mother in her mid-forties had testified to anything, let alone spoke openly about topics so private. Her answers were short and staccato. Perhaps she was uncomfortable. She might have been angry. She and Joe had married according to Cherokee law and had shared a home for a dozen years. They had three sons together. Who had more right than she to decide to whom she was married? In 1902, the five white men who made up the Dawes Commission thought that they did.[1]

As strange and disconcerting as this experience was for Mounce, it was a normal one for the Dawes Commission. Allotment policy was a tool of American hegemony over indigenous people, but such abstract and complicated processes were experienced very personally by those being allotted. Mounce's final enrollment card looks like any other in the Dawes roll. It provides no hint that there was any conflict over which man would be listed next to Rosanna as her husband. The transcript of this interview also is part of the records compiled by the Dawes Commission, however, and it and many other similar exchanges demonstrate just how thoroughly land privatization was interconnected with the regulation of Indian sexuality and reproduction, especially that of women.

The purpose of the Dawes roll influenced its final format. It was the means through which federal officials began keeping extensive data on Cherokee domestic life for the purpose of methodically enforcing assimilationist policies. Told from the vantage point of Cherokee people, then, the story of the making of the Dawes roll, this most intimate form of colonialism, is about resistance against the loss of autonomy and privacy over family matters. It also is a story about the bureaucratic reinvention of Cherokee family life and about making Cherokee people appear to be something on paper that they were not, in their daily reality, and then working to make the reality match the records on file.

Although Cherokees advocated for their families' interests, the Dawes Commission never shared the power to draw final conclusions, and, ultimately, the Dawes roll misrepresented Cherokee families in fundamental ways. When categorizing Cherokees on the Dawes roll, commissioners denied the flexibility and autonomy that characterized bonds between Cherokee spouses, and they diminished the importance of kin. To a people who conceptualized prosperity as a reflection of their interconnectedness with one another, such a reduction was pauperizing. In other words, a precursor to privatizing tribal land was robbing Indians of their extended families.

Documenting Sexuality

Commissioners did not understand all of the information that they gathered. In particular, Cherokees' conceptions of normal and appropriate sexual relations contrasted with the expectations and values of Dawes commissioners, who had to investigate and document the intimate histories of enrollees in the creation of the roll. Although at times their interest appeared to be prurient, the commissioners' concern also reflected the logistical necessities of allotment policy. The goal of allotment was to assimilate Indians and, more so over time, their property into the mainstream of American society, including its civil legal system through which material resources were transferred. In other words, because thorough documentation of maternity and paternity is essential for the inheritance and sale of land under American property law in a way that it had not been under late-nineteenth-century Cherokee law, which mandated common title, the Dawes Commission sought to learn and permanently, publicly disclose the biological relationships connecting Cherokees. In order to facilitate this process, commissioners imposed their notion of relatedness upon Cherokee families rather than discern how Cherokees perceived themselves to be tied to one another.

This component of the Dawes commissioners' job description was an innovation in allotment policy that reflected another of assimilationists' goals, the regulation of Indian sexuality. Since at least the late 1870s, moral reformers had advocated federal intervention in the reproductive and marital choices of Indian people. At the urging of groups like the WNIA, in particular, successive commissioners of Indian Affairs recommended that Congress criminalize cohabitation (serial monogamy), polygamy, and other practices common among Indian people that many non-Indians considered to be morally objectionable and socially degenerative. They also wanted Indian Service employees to register and license couples in the hopes that such documentation would inspire, or perhaps require, Indian couples to treat their marriages as permanent. The Dawes Act lacked such a provision, but reformers continued to agitate for its modification, which began in 1891 and culminated in the passage of the Burke Act in 1906. Although the Dawes Act did not apply to Indian Territory, as the predominant allotment legislation, it did set a precedent, and the concurrent debate over how to fix allotment policy through the addition of this regulatory component pertaining to marriage influenced the Dawes Commission's conception of its task. In 1901, five years after the Dawes Commission began constructing its rolls in Indian Territory, the Department of the Interior instructed reservation officials to begin creating such marriage registers. Thus, the regulation of Indian families must be understood in conjunction with the privatization of communal property and the Dawes roll seen as a step in the progressive intervention into Indian people's private lives.[2]

Those who advocated intrusion into the personal lives of Indian people in the name of public welfare found themselves in good company by the late nineteenth century. As the Gilded Age evolved into the Progressive Era, a chorus of voices from across the United States warned that private debauchery had public consequences, and they advocated action. These campaigns for public morality and social purity entailed the expansion of state authority into the most intimate matters of citizens' lives; the criminalization of private behavior seen as threatening by those in power; and the elevation of supposed experts, including academics, to positions of authority over marginalized and disempowered populations who had little recourse to prevent such intrusion. Some of these programs, such as those created to curb the spread of venereal diseases, responded to critical threats to public health, but those that criminalized interracial marriage and stigmatized multiracial people, sometimes resulting in their sterilization, stem from the same impulses to restrict bodies perceived as dangerous. Reflecting the political leanings of those in power, the majority of men who served on and worked for the Dawes Commission during enrollment were Republicans, the party of Progressivism. Much of the actual allotting of the Cherokees took place under Republican president Theodore Roosevelt, a champion of interventionist government, social reform, and vigorous physical wellness.

The Progressive spirit infused the dismantling of the Indian republics and the formation of the state of Oklahoma, but this celebrated fervor came at a cost for Indian people, whose privacy over matters of sexuality was threatened.[3] Emboldened by Progressive Era justifications for intrusiveness, commissioners ran roughshod over Cherokees' expectations that government would respect the autonomy and privacy of individuals. Indeed, during their enrollment interviews with the Dawes Commission, Cherokees answered questions not about property but about their personal histories. Reflecting their interest in clarifying biological relatedness for the purpose of facilitating the transmission of land, commissioners sought to determine the marital and reproductive histories of Cherokee citizens. For this reason, they needed to know when and how couples were married and whether those individuals had been married previously. They inquired whether married couples then lived together and whether they had done so continuously since their marriage. They intended to confirm marital fidelity by asking for the names and ages of children in the household and confirmation of their parentage. Commissioners not only compared these answers against tribal rolls but also often corroborated testimony by asking relatives and neighbors to confirm information about others during their own interviews. Although gossip played an important role in Cherokee society as a means to curb and correct inappropriate behavior, there were contexts in which it was and was not acceptable. Cherokee gossips faced consequences for offending others, and many avoided speaking ill of one another in public because they feared retaliation, especially in the form of witchcraft.[4] Commissioners, however, were unconcerned with fostering goodwill among neighbors and individual well-being.

Because the Dawes Commission's protocol for enrollment created discomfort and the probability for discord, Principal Chief T. M. Buffington issued a precautionary statement in May 1900 explaining the process and preparing Cherokee citizens for the commissioners' questions about their ancestry, families, and improved property.[5] Officials of the Cherokee government, in particular, were expected to share information with commissioners, but such collaboration conflicted with the expectations of the communities that they served. For example, take Tom Welch, whom the citizens of Goingsnake District elected to serve as their sheriff in 1891. In 1902, commissioners called on him to clarify the marital history of his neighbor, Rosanna Mounce. Two non-Indian men claimed an allotment through intermarriage with her, and the Dawes commissioners looked to Welch to provide unbiased testimony on the circumstances that led to his delivery of a citation of divorce to her nearly a decade earlier. Although, or perhaps because, he knew Rosanna well, Welch did not want to answer questions more specifically than, "No, sir, I don't know anything about it." When the commissioners asked him directly to discuss "on what grounds that suit for divorce was brought," he replied, "I would rather not state." The commissioners asked him to file a copy of that citation with them, and he complied, but he avoided publicly discussing the private life of a neighbor. Welch's discomfort was palpable. His reticence contradicted commissioners' assumptions that the state had a right to investigate the behavior of individuals deemed to be requiring moral correction, including someone the Dawes commissioners suspected of adultery.[6]

Was the Dawes Commission the sole cause of Welch's nervousness, or did Mounce's behavior leave him unsettled, too? By the standards of non-Indian society, she was an adulteress, but among Cherokees, serial monogamy and divorce by mutual consent were normal. Mounce had at least four sexual relationships throughout her adult life, and the last three were of concern to the commissioners. Before she was twenty years old, she had her first son, Wyly, with noncitizen George Beavers. They seem not to have married according to Cherokee law. Next, she had son Jesse with a white man named Bill Smith between 1884 and 1887, but the couple separated shortly after the baby's birth. They also seem not to have married according to Cherokee law, and Smith left the Cherokee Nation. Mounce then had a relationship with James Garner, a non-Indian carpenter a dozen years her senior. Their relationship also ended within a year without legal marriage. Finally, in October 1890, she married Joe Mounce, another American. Joe obtained a license and married her according to Cherokee law. They had three sons: Joel, Thomas, and Ellis. Although it confused the commissioners, Rosanna's behavior was not deviant within her community.[7]

It is probable, then, that Welch was disconcerted with the public airing of matters that he considered personal. He also may have realized that the commissioners' interests were legally irrelevant. In December 1893, Smith's divorce was issued by the state of Texas, which had no jurisdiction over marriages in the Cherokee Nation, but Smith and Rosanna had parted ways years before anyway. Likewise, Smith was not claiming an allotment through intermarriage to Rosanna. Garner was, but he had no permit from the Cherokee government, and Joe Mounce, who also was claiming an allotment, had a marriage license issued by the Cherokee Nation, which the Dawes Commission had no authority to invalidate. In other words, the commissioners investigated a nonissue because Cherokee law was clear—Joe Mounce was Rosanna's husband. He was her preference, too, and she was confused by their interest in her past. When commissioners asked her to present the divorce certificate, she retorted, "I have not got the divorce now. I don't know what I done with it. I reckon I lost it. I haven't got it now; couldn't keep anything that long." The Dawes Commission's investigation into Mounce is revealing because it suggests that despite their exposure to Anglo-American gender norms for over a century, common Cherokee women continued to enjoy sexual freedom and remained relatively unrestricted by the expectations of so-called true womanhood and uninhibited by the stigma of divorce.[8]

Women's sexual autonomy was difficult for members of the Dawes Commission to understand. Their treatment of one particular unwed mother reveals how their biases shaped decisions about Cherokees who engaged in sexual behavior that was frowned upon among Anglo-Americans. In 1902, the Dawes Commission enrolled twenty-year-old Nannie Palone, the daughter of Betsy and the late Yellowhammer Suake, apart from her mother and siblings. They separated her even though she lived with them in Betsy's household at the time of allotment and during the taking of previous Cherokee rolls and the 1900 census. Why? Nannie had two children by two different men. She was not in a relationship with either of them at the time of enrollment. She named both boys after their fathers, Andrew Palone and William Proctor.[9] Nannie had been married to Palone, but she never married Proctor. Commissioners obtained information about the Suake family from informants, one of whom explained that Andrew had left Nannie. Considering she gave birth to a son by another man within the year, the Dawes Commissioners probably assumed that he had abandoned her for infidelity. They likely figured that the father of the second child refused to marry her because of her supposed lack of morals as well. From the perspective of the Dawes Commission, Nannie bore the double stigma of an abandoned woman and one who subsequently bore a child out of wedlock. Such assumptions were inconsistent with Cherokee sexuality, however, and young Cherokee women commonly had a child, remained in their parents' household, and subsequently married.[10]

Apart from situations like Nannie's, the Dawes Commission did not separate young, unmarried women from their families because they considered them to be dependents until they married, but they treated Nannie as she would have been treated in their own society, isolated from family and community. Why? Rider Hammer shared an intriguing bit of evidence about Nannie's life, and it is likely that commissioners misinterpreted it. When asked if he knew why Nannie, who came from a family of Nighthawks, had not enrolled herself, Hammer responded, "Has no home." But Nannie had a home and was part of a family. She and her children lived in her mother's household. In fact, Rider saw them there "two weeks ago last Sunday."[11] Rider likely meant that Nannie had no separate farm. Her relationship with Andrew Palone did not last long enough for the couple to establish their own household, which would have resulted in improvements for her to claim. But the Dawes Commission understood Hammer's comment to mean that Nannie was homeless and that her family had abandoned her because of sexual indiscretions.

The commissioners' decision to separate the Suake family on paper had dire implications. Nannie and her boys were assigned land at a distance from her mother and siblings in what became Craig County, two counties north and east of Adair County. Likewise, because she was considered an unfit mother, her boys were assigned a court-appointed guardian in Craig

Andrew Palone and William Proctor, two sons of Nannie Suake and grandsons of Betsy Suake. Andrew also was known as William, and William also was called John or Johnny. Photo courtesy of Gail Crittenden.

County the following year. As Angie Debo explains, such officials typically robbed their charges, and they were enabled by the sentiment common among non-Indians that full-blood families were dysfunctional and that children like Andrew and William were not looked after or cared for properly, one of the arguments used by assimilationists to justify allotment. And yet, the boys likely had a stable childhood because they continued to live in the same home they had always known until the 1920s; their grandmother Betsy raised them.[12]

In part, commissioners' confusion about sexuality resulted from their erroneous belief that relationships between spouses, as opposed to those with other family members, were of primary importance to Cherokees. Grouping heterosexual couples together on the Dawes roll wrongly suggested that the bonds between them were permanent when, in reality, Cherokee adults commonly separated and remarried before, during, and after their enrollment. Nannie's brother Tom provides a useful example. Tom Suake's first wife, Charlotte, died prior to enrollment. At the time of allotment, he was married to Nancy, who had previously been married several times. In 1902, Rider Hammer struggled to recall her sexual and marital history so that commissioners could find her on previous Cherokee rolls, but he concluded, "She has lived with several different men. I couldn't say exactly." Nancy's marriage to Tom did not last much longer than her earlier ones. By December 1906, he was married to Annie Bearpaw, who had been married to Bill Chewey during enrollment. Annie passed away within a few years. Within the next half-dozen years, Tom married Annie Hilderbrand. Nancy continued to pursue other relationships, too. By 1913, her surname was Gritts. On the subsequent forms referring to these women, they are identified by a string of names such as "Nancy Suake now Gritts," "Annie Chewey now Suake," and "Annie Hilderbrand now Suwake." This lyrical testament to the persistence of serial monogamy among Cherokees confounded commissioners and defied their preprinted forms. The universality of permanent, monogamous marriage as the norm among Cherokees was a fiction that existed only on the Dawes roll and quickly was proven false by subsequent papers managing allotments.[13]

Sexuality was a hot-button issue in turn-of-the-century America, and Indian Territory sat squarely in the middle of the debate, ideologically and physically. Commissioners recorded their interpretations of Cherokee culture, including sexuality, into the Dawes roll and created a facade that obscured normalcy such that it could be labeled deviant. As the U.S. government tried to regulate and eradicate certain sexual behaviors seen as threatening to society, including premarital and extramarital sexual intercourse, its representatives sought to identify who engaged in them for the purpose of limiting that behavior in the future. During the twentieth century, Cherokee women, like other American Indians, endured the loss of control over their fertility through government-sponsored sterilization programs; the loss of control over their mothering through a predatory, anti-Indian child welfare system; and the loss of control over their sexual bodies through escalating rates of sexual violence. The Dawes roll began this dehumanizing process through its disregard for the privacy and autonomy that had protected the most intimate parts of Cherokee family life.

Fragmenting Cherokee Families

Although Cherokees forced commissioners to make significant and important concessions throughout the compilation of the roll, the final product nonetheless grossly misrepresented Cherokee society in significant ways. Rather than organizing the roll around their extended families, the Dawes Commission subdivided and reorganized Cherokee households into nuclear units. Commissioners designated adult males as heads-of-households and listed wives and biological children, and occasionally grandchildren and stepchildren, beneath them. Other family members, including elderly parents and adult siblings, were relegated to separate cards, even if they shared a home. In other words, the Dawes Commission did not create one card for each Cherokee family. Instead, it administratively divided Cherokees into the nuclear units recognized as legitimate and through which property was transmitted in Anglo-American society. That division necessitated the creation of multiple cards per family. In doing so, the Dawes Commission created an illusion of an assimilated people rather than an accurate representation of Cherokee society. Unfortunately, that illusion exercised great power because it shaped the perspectives of outsiders otherwise unfamiliar with Cherokees who enforced allotment and subsequent policies.

To begin, the Dawes Commission marginalized elders. Throughout the nineteenth century, the status of the aged had declined among Anglo-Americans as their society increasingly championed the nuclear unit as providing the ideal relationship through which each gender fulfilled its appropriate reproductive and productive role, thus promoting social order and furthering civilization.[14] By the Gilded Age, Anglo-Americans had begun to see those in their latter years of life as a drain upon able-bodied family members. They likewise believed that the physical infirmities and mental lapses associated with age were the result of cerebral degeneration, an idea popularized by physicians who called for the treatment of aging as an illness necessitating medical intervention. This attitude led to the establishment of both private and public institutionalized rest homes.[15] Although Cherokees established several social welfare institutions, there was no complementary movement to hospitalize the elderly among them, and the Anglo-American stigmatization of the old sharply contrasted with the treatment of the elderly among Cherokees, who understood the aged to have gained wisdom and status with the years rather than to have lost their wits.

Although no longer exclusively matrilineal or matrilocal, Cherokees continued to treat their gray-haired women with profound respect and deference. The living arrangements of one great-grandmother, Eliza Brown, exemplify elderly women's importance to their families. Eliza Brown was in her late seventies during the allotment era, and she had a large family of ten children. She shared an extended household of at least two houses with her husband, James; their two grown daughters; her elderly brother Martin Raper; and her elderly sister Martha Raper. Although she had buried at least three of her children by the allotment era, she lived in close proximity to several other of her grown children and their families, and she had multiple namesakes among them. Looking at their homes on a map, one sees a cluster of children and grandchildren with Eliza at its core. Nonetheless, the Dawes Commission listed her and James separately along with their two unmarried adult daughters. Her elderly brother and sister, Martin and Martha, were listed on an additional card. Eliza's other sons and daughters and their children also were segregated onto separate cards. Those who were the core of this family thus became its margin on paper.[16]

The long-term consequences of this decision were particularly negative for Cherokee grandparents, especially women, who often were primary caregivers for their grandchildren. In separating grandmothers from their grandchildren, commissioners denied the legitimacy of such relationships and the reality of their being common among Cherokees. Betsy Suake, for example, cared for at least two of her children's children during the enrollment era. She had always helped to raise her daughter Nannie's two sons, and when Nannie died, those boys stayed in Betsy's home. Likewise, two of her son Tom's wives died, leaving small sons. Betsy welcomed both into her home as well. Tom retained a relationship with the boys, but his mother raised them. None of the three boys who were born before enrollment were listed with her on her enrollment card.[17] As will be discussed in chapter 7, this schism created obstacles for grandmothers who sought to administer or protect their grandchildren's estates. It also affirmed for officials affiliated with the Oklahoma courts and social services that such arrangements were deviant and abnormal rather than customary.

The enrollment process was especially difficult for many of the elderly. Dawes commissioners expected Cherokees to enroll at centers established throughout the Cherokee Nation, but the infirm could not travel to them. Nonetheless, commissioners treated with skepticism those who represented kin unable to appear themselves. Eliza Brown's husband, James, was in his early eighties, and a stroke had left his face and hands paralyzed. She had no particular illness but was a small, frail woman. For this reason, her son John tried to enroll them, his elderly aunt and uncle, and his two older sisters, one of whom "was sick with the rising in her head and grip." The other sister, who was the primary caregiver for the rest, "can't leave the old folks." Although existing Cherokee rolls corroborated John's testimony, commissioners did not accept his word and required him to return for two additional interviews and provide witnesses. John learned how to force commissioners to accept him as his elders' representative, however. When he returned to select their allotments in 1904, he brought signed affidavits granting him power of attorney.[18]

The commissioners' preference for documentation also created problems for elders. Written records were unlikely to have been created, let alone have survived lifetimes that included the Trail of Tears and the Civil War. Likewise, the old could not as readily provide witnesses to corroborate their testimony, especially about marriages that began decades earlier. For example, take James Mack Welch, who pled for his mother's inclusion on the Dawes roll. Nancy, an intermarried white woman, was sixty-six when her son testified on her behalf before the Dawes Commission. She was sickly, he explained: a "woman that has done a whole lot of hard work in her day" caring for her husband and children, all recognized to be Cherokees. She had been married to his father, George, for over forty years, but George died ten years before allotment, and since then Nancy had lived with her son and his wife. Although her family had no doubt that she belonged to them, the Dawes Commission was skeptical. Nancy was too weak to appear before them, she lacked documentation of her marriage, and she no longer had a living husband. Her best evidence was her inclusion on previous Cherokee rolls and her grown children, all of whom were included on the Dawes roll. It was not enough. She was denied inclusion. Had her late-husband George been alive, the Dawes Commission's decision likely would have been in her favor.[19]

Commissioners also segregated unmarried young men onto separate enrollment cards from their parents and siblings. Imposing Anglo-American gender norms onto them, the Dawes commissioners assumed that these men would leave their parents and establish their own households, but many Cherokee men continued to live with their parents well into adulthood, and some never left the households of their birth. Take, for example, Noah Sand's sons. At the time of enrollment, Sand was a widower in his late fifties. Will and John, both young men in their twenties, lived with their father and teenaged cousin Dan Downing. In other words, the men formed a household. The Dawes Commission created three separate cards for this family, however: one for John, one for Will, and one for Noah and Dan. Noah, Will, and John continued to share a home until John's and then Noah's deaths.[20]

Deferring to the legal guidelines accepted among Anglo-Americans, the Dawes Commission imposed the twenty-first birthday as a signifier of maturity upon Cherokee men (not women, who were grouped with their parents or, if married, their spouse). For this reason, the commissioners sought to determine the accurate age of young men, an obsession that often confused Cherokees. Setting a particular age for the onset of maturity was nonsensical to Cherokees, among whom adulthood was determined by behavior rather than by date of birth. In 1902, for example, commissioners were gathering testimony about Arch and Fannie Turtle's family. They were Nighthawks who refused to enroll. When informant Rider Hammer began listing the couple's children with their eldest, Ned, commissioners corrected him. They "just want[ed] those under 21—what is the oldest under 21?"[21] Likewise, regarding another young man, commissioners never asked whether or not Sam Kirk was mature. They only wanted to know his age. In July 1900, William Kirk, his father, enrolled his wife and six children. He said that his oldest son was then eighteen years old. In September 1903, the Dawes Commission called William back to provide more information about Sam's birth. William explained that Sam would turn twenty-one the following month and was born in October 1882. Unsatisfied, commissioners pressed a frustrated Kirk:

> Dawes Commission: How did you happen to give his age as eighteen in July 1900 [when] that would make him more than twenty-one?
> William Kirk: I don't know. That is his age.
> Dawes Commission: Do you think you know his age better now?
> William Kirk: I don't know as I do.

The commissioners' attention to Sam's age is notable because they were not questioning whether he was alive, Cherokee, or entitled to an allotment. Rather, they solely sought to determine whether or not he was legally mature in order to clarify whether they would enroll him with or apart from his family. In fact, Sam turned twenty-one between enrollment and the selection of allotments, but this birthday was not a significant event in his daily life. He continued living with his parents as before. For the Dawes Commission, however, this transition was important. Although they did not separate him from his parents on their enrollment card, they segregated him onto a separate form when designating allotments.[22]

Throughout the making of the roll, the Dawes Commission routinely made decisions about Cherokees that corresponded to the standards of gendered behavior among Anglo-Americans, and through the Dawes roll, the commissioners imposed their vision of male supremacy on Cherokee families. Anglo-Americans believed female dependency to be more than simply normal. It was civilized, or superior, to female social and economic self-sufficiency. Female-headed households were considered inappropriate for the purposes of assimilation. Lacking an understanding of norms ascribed to men and women in Cherokee society, commissioners sometimes saw male dominance where it did not exist; more often, they created it on paper in the hopes that it would quickly become reality. The format of enrollment cards sought to permanently document biological relationships, meaning maternity and paternity, for the purposes of the transmission of property, but Dawes commissioners also sought to create hierarchy. In documenting the fidelity of wives and the legitimacy of children, commissioners asserted the dominance of husbands and fathers.

Commissioners arrived in the Cherokee Nation with a protocol and preprinted cards based on the assumption that Cherokee women should be the dependents of their men. The Dawes Commission then mandated that heads-of-households report for enrollment, and commissioners anticipated that men would perform this duty. In this particular circumstance, the expectations of the commissioners coincided with the cultural norms of Cherokees—to an extent. Among Cherokee families, adult males served as representatives to outsiders, a practice with deep roots in Cherokee history. Referring to the "civilization" program of the early nineteenth century, Theda Perdue has noted that "men served as the intermediaries between women and the federal government and as conduits for most of the tools and implements that the agent made available to the Nation."[23] Yet neither in the beginning nor at the end of the century, however, did this role entitle men to make decisions for the rest of the household. Cherokee men appearing before the Dawes Commission were spokesmen who represented their female family members, and had cultural sensitivity been a goal of the Dawes Commission, the term "representative-of-household" would have been more accurate than "head-of-household." John Brown, for example, as mentioned earlier, attended to the affairs of several adult women in his family throughout the enrollment and allotment process: his wife, mother, aunt, and two sisters. John made numerous trips to appear before the Dawes Commission, and, ultimately, his sisters Polly and Florence and his wife, Emily, did, too. It is clear through their testimony that Polly, in particular, and Florence were making their own decisions in dialogue with their family and that they were speaking through John. Polly was John's elder sister, and she owned substantial improvements of her own. John did not speak *for* her. Rather, Polly sometimes handled her affairs *through* him.[24]

Likewise, by organizing enrollment cards around adult men as husbands, the Dawes Commission obscured the fluidity of Cherokee households and ignored the likelihood that the most permanent members of any grouping were mothers and siblings. In short, the presence of any particular adult man who married into a household could be temporary. Notably, commissioners did not ask enrollees who the head of their household was; they assumed that husbands filled this role based on their own notions of appropriate hierarchy and authority. In each family in this study, however, women retained custody of their children after divorce, a practice with its origins in the Cherokees' matrilineal kinship system. This custom sharply contrasted with contemporary practice in the United States. In other words, among Cherokees, subsequent husbands joined family units that already existed, and because Cherokees continued to practice serial monogamy, husbands not infrequently left those family units.[25] During the enrollment period, at least two of the marriages in this study ended, but the commissioners did not correct their roll. By 1902, Annie Bearpaw was no longer married to Bill Chewey but to Tom Suake, who had ended his brief relationship with Nancy Bear. The Dawes Commission nonetheless enrolled and allotted land to the families made up of Bill and Annie Chewey and their two daughters and, separately, to Tom and Nancy Suake and Tom's son from his first marriage, Ezekiel, who had lived with his paternal grandmother, Betsy, since his mother, Charlotte, died years earlier. Simply put, the Dawes roll records a version of the Chewey family on paper that no longer existed and a version of the Suake family that never had existed at all.[26]

Erasing Identity

The Dawes Commission excluded other evidence of the persistence of Cherokee culture from the roll. Although the U.S. census provided a model for documenting this information, commissioners did not record the language(s) spoken, read, or written by Cherokees on their enrollment cards. In addition, the Dawes Commission anglicized names. For example, Rider Hammer testified that Lewis and Betsy Bird's daughters were called Ah-yah-ne and Oo-loo-che. When questioned further about the older girl, he replied, "I don't know of any English name for her." Commissioners nonetheless anglicized the girls' names to Annie and Lucy.[27] In this particular aspect of the allotment process, commissioners treated both genders equally; they also anglicized males' names. When they asked him if he knew the son of Nannie Wolfe and Bill Chewey, Hammer replied through the translator that he did. His name was Oh-kon-stor-ter, but commissioners found the boy listed as Samuel on the unverified 1896 Cherokee roll. Could that be him? Rider said, "I guess so [but] I never heard him go by that name."[28] Commissioners enrolled him as Samuel anyway.

Last, the Dawes Commission incorporated the language of blood into their roll. Their doing so reflected American society's concern with social regulation and purity. Although the terminology of blood quantum was not coined during the allotment era, these socially constructed categories of classification became increasingly potent because of the policy. Blood quantum refers to the presumed degree of Indian ancestry, and percentages correlate with perceived lifestyle and presumed ability. Indianness was stigmatized, and whiteness was preferenced. Inseparable from scientific racism at the turn of the twentieth century, this system of classification was based on the assumption of the supremacy of white people, their civilization, and their physical bodies.[29] Initial allotment legislation, including the Dawes Act, did not refer to blood quantum, but the application of allotment policy throughout the 1890s entailed the development of this system designed to facilitate the administration of allottees. In short, blood quantum is a race-based filing system for human beings. The process had been evolving in the field among allotment agents and staff with the Indian Service for nearly two decades, including by the Dawes Commission, before it was fully articulated in the Burke Act and the Five Tribes Bill of 1906 as a means to expedite competency decisions. The language of blood, then, is a symbolic discourse in which terms represent the freedoms and limitations placed upon those managed by bureaucrats within this system.[30]

Cherokees spoke their own language of blood, but it usually differed in meaning from that used by the Dawes Commission. For example, they used the term "full blood" to refer to those who spoke Cherokee as their primary language and who were perceived by other Cherokees as behaving in ways that were considered traditional. Those individuals may or may not have had exclusively Cherokee ancestry. Among Cherokees prior to the allotment era, then, "full blood" referred to linguistic and cultural orientation rather than race.[31] Indeed, the ways that Cherokees character-ized their full-blood neighbors confirms that this term referred not to heritage but to one's lifestyle and the perception of it by others. When asked to identify the blood quantum of his Nighthawk neighbors, Rider Hammer described them as full bloods who not only were recognized as such by their fellow citizens of the Cherokee Nation but also had always made their homes there. In other words, Hammer synthesized political and spiritual orientation, community recognition, attachment to place, and perhaps linguistic preference into this term, but he never referred to parentage. Another informant affirmed that Bill and Annie Chewey were full bloods, then added how he knew this to be true (through Cherokee translator Simon Walkingstick): "They are so considered."[32] There were exceptions, however, and some Cherokees used the language of blood as a marker of race but not inferiority. Reverend Lacie described Abe Sixkiller as a full blood and his wife, Margaret, as a mixed blood because he knew of her family's history of intermarriage since she was related to his wife. There is no evidence to suggest that Lacie, who identified as a full blood himself, however, used these terms to signify limited intellectual ability. He seemed to have cared deeply for the Sixkillers and thought highly of them.[33]

Although scientific racism shaped the language of blood, the assigna-tion of blood quantum was a not a science. In his discussion of enrollment, Russell Thornton explained that Cherokees identified their blood quan-tum, although commissioners often noted a lower amount on the roll.[34] I did not find evidence that Cherokees routinely self-designated. Instead, commissioners asked only two people in this study to specify their own blood quantum, and their answers were unsure and inaccurate, suggest-ing their lack of facility with this system of identification. In one situa-tion, commissioners directly asked, "What proportion of Cherokee blood do you claim to have?" William Kirk responded, "About 1/8th, I sup-pose."[35] The only man who identified his spouse's quantum was grossly inaccurate. James Holland suggested that Hattie was a full blood; the Dawes Commission listed her as one-eighth. A member of a family with a history of intermarriage, including her white father, Hattie was probably one-thirty-second.[36]

Cherokee rolls were of little use to commissioners in this matter because the tribe did not track blood quantum. Tribal census takers had noted when a citizen was intermarried and designated him or her as an "adopted white," but they otherwise made no effort to determine ancestry or divide citizens by blood quantum. Because detailed information about individuals' racial makeup was not readily available to them, commissioners may have categorized Cherokees based on their appearance, but there are no documented discussions of physicality in the enrollment packets of Cherokees in this study. Instead, interviews focused on the behavior of Cherokees, and commissioners expressed a particular concern with sexuality, especially cohabitation, marriage, and procreation. People who behaved in ways that the commissioners approved of generally earned lower blood quantum numbers; those whom commissioners believed to conduct themselves according to Cherokee values received higher ones.

The Dawes Commission's estimations of Cherokee ancestry are wildly inconsistent and often inaccurate. Most obviously, full siblings commonly have different designations.[37] For example, although they share both parents, the Cannon siblings are listed on the Dawes roll with differing blood quantums. Sterling, Edwin, John, and Ophelia are listed as one-thirty-second, but brother Oscar is listed as one-sixteenth.[38] The adult children of Joel and Nellie Kelley also fit that pattern. John is listed as one-fourth, Laura as one-eighth, and Rosanna as one-sixteenth. Rosanna was married to a white man, and commissioners tended to list a lower quantum for those intermarried to whites.[39]

The quantums listed on the Dawes roll also differ dramatically from those listed on the 1900 U.S. census. The United States took censuses in Indian Territory in 1890 and again in 1900, or at least attempted to, but enumerators faced widespread resistance from the Indian population, and both failed to provide accurate counts. In the 1890 census, the Census Office made no effort to distinguish among Indians according to blood quantum but divided the residents of the territory by race: Indian, African American, and white. Ten years later, the Census Office noted race and blood quantum. In this study, most families of mixed ancestry are not identified by the same quantum that appeared on that document, and the Dawes rolls usually listed a significantly smaller quantum when compared to the census. For example, John Welch is listed as one-eighth Cherokee on the 1900 census, but the Dawes Commission listed him as one-sixty-fourth. Likewise, his cousin Tom Welch is listed as one-fourth in the 1900 census and one-sixteenth by the Dawes Commission.[40] Apparently, the degree of Cherokee blood truly was in the eye of the beholder.

The Divisive Impact of Enrollment

In November 1901, in the midst of the enrollment crisis, traditional Cherokees did what their people always had done when seeking clarity and wisdom. They went to a quiet place near water. The Keetoowahs gathered at Big Tucker's Spring. There they prayed. They talked. And split. The majority, who were Cherokee Baptists, remained affiliated with the Keetoowah Society under the leadership of Rabbit Bunch, who thought landlessness did not serve as the best protest against Anglo-American hegemony. If allotment was inevitable, they concluded that they should compel the Dawes Commission to ensure a just distribution of resources in compliance with Cherokee law and advocate for themselves in the changing political environment. The minority, who practiced traditional Cherokee spirituality, became known as Nighthawk Keetoowahs, or simply Nighthawks, and led by Redbird Smith, they continued to believe that any acknowledgment of or involvement in the allotment process legitimized it. This separation, while significant, was not definitive in that many members, tied by bonds of kinship and friendship, continued to associate with each other. Redbird Smith's sons, interviewed as elders, remembered their father as being unmoved by this development. He considered himself the leader of the majority of the traditional Cherokees who opposed allotment. Likewise, this division suggests the persistence of traditional Cherokee understandings of governance. In a system that values consensus, those who dissent are entitled to leave, and when factionalism provides multiple viable alternatives for the expression of dissent, it serves a constructive purpose.[41]

The Keetoowahs organized to defend their interests in a process they could not stop. In particular, they sought to limit the inclusion of people on the roll that the Cherokee government had not made full citizens. The word used to designate intermarried whites on the 1880 and 1890 Cherokee censuses was "adopted," a word rooted in the language of family and meaning to make as one's own. The Cherokees' localized system was flexible enough to include such family members for over a century, but allotment stretched those bonds to their breaking point and forced Cherokees to confront their divergent views on the rights of intermarried spouses. Those relationships and their entitlements became a focus of Keetoowah activism. In February 1903, on behalf of the Keetoowah Society, Daniel Redbird filed suit against the United States to force the Dawes Commission to comply with Cherokee law by not distributing resources to intermarried spouses. In November 1906, the Supreme Court ruled for the Keetoowahs in *Daniel Red Bird v. United States*. The court ruled that the Dawes Commission must uphold Cherokee law regarding 3,600 intermarried spouses who married after November 1, 1875, and therefore, according to Cherokee law, should not have access to tribal property.[42]

John and Emily Brown were one of the Cherokee families directly impacted by the decision. Like John's parents, the couple had married in North Carolina prior to relocating to Indian Territory. They married in January 1870, then moved to the Cherokee Nation in 1871. In 1874, John voted in the tribal election. He received a certificate of enrollment dated November 16, 1876. The Dawes Commission decided that paper came one year and fifteen days too late for Emily to be enrolled and receive an allotment. The Dawes Commission sought to notify them by letter, but the family refused to accept it.[43] The Keetoowahs continued their lobby. In 1905, under the leadership of Richard M. Wolf, the group filed papers with the federal court in Indian Territory and was incorporated as the Keetoowah Society, Incorporated.[44]

Meanwhile, the Nighthawks still refused to participate, and their resistance took several forms: they ignored the Dawes Commission's order to enroll their families; when the commissioners sent enrollment parties out looking for them, parents sent children away and refused to answer questions; and whole communities left their homes and gathered with other resisters in locations inaccessible to outsiders. Although unwilling to negotiate about their participation, they were willing to explain the reasons for their avoidance, and their leaders gave eloquent speeches and wrote heartfelt petitions. They also created alliances with other traditionalists in the Choctaw, Chickasaw, and Creek nations and, together, established the Four Mothers Society, an intertribal organization devoted to the sovereignty and spiritual revitalization of the Five Tribes. Members of the group sent delegates to Washington, D.C., to seek the restoration of their treaties. Most important, they reinvigorated ceremonies and gathered at fires. The Nighthawks reestablished ceremonial grounds throughout the hills of the western Ozarks, and as the Dawes Commission allotted their land, they came together in relationship with each other and their Creator.[45]

The Dawes commissioners understood none of this activism and characterized the Nighthawks as misinformed dupes being manipulated by mixed bloods who wanted to deny stereotypically ignorant full bloods their just share of tribal land. Toward this end, commissioners even speculated that the *Cherokee Advocate* printed anti-enrollment propaganda in its Cherokee-language columns.[46] Determined to break their resistance, the Dawes Commission turned to the federal courts. In the spring of 1902, the U.S. district court in Muskogee issued an order requiring uncounted Cherokee heads-of-households to enroll their families with the Dawes Commission immediately. The Nighthawks did not waver. Commissioners then appealed to Judge Charles W. Raymond, who issued an order specifically instructing a handful of men known to be leaders of the resistance to appear before the Dawes Commission. At ten in the morning on March 15, some showed up in order to refuse to answer commissioners' questions. They were jailed. Determined to make a public statement of their own, U.S. marshals lined up the prisoners and cut off their hair, worn long as was customary among practitioners of traditional Cherokee religion. The sympathetic *Cherokee Advocate* reported: "The Indians wore expressions of hatred and sullenness that will not soon be forgotten. . . . Although they were humiliated and compelled to obey, it was evident that they were neither defeated nor subdued." To avoid returning to jail, some of the men enrolled, but they frustrated commissioners by failing to fully answer questions about their ancestry, children, and way of life. The commissioners forced resisters to comply with the letter of the law, but these Nighthawks defied the anti-tribal spirit behind it. Their family life remained an enigma to the Dawes Commission.[47]

THE ENROLLMENT OF the Cherokee Nation lasted for nearly two decades, from 1896 until 1914, during which time the Dawes Commission, Cherokee statesmen, common Cherokees, and the federal courts struggled to agree upon a definition of belonging. As a result of legal challenges by the Cherokee government, clarification and directives from the secretary of the interior, decisions by the federal courts, and legislation from Congress, the standards used by the Dawes Commission continuously evolved throughout enrollment. The situation forced the Dawes Commission's clerks, characteristically underqualified and overworked, to reevaluate applications repeatedly. Congress never appreciated the enormity or complexity of the task that they had given to them.

During the creation of the Dawes roll, commissioners divided up Cherokee families, and Cherokees further divided themselves. The tragedy of allotment, then, does not refer simply to the loss of communal resources but to the U.S. government's invalidation of the localized ways through which Cherokees reckoned their relationships to each other. The immediate outcome of the creation of the Dawes roll was the repudiation of Cherokees' traditional means of constructing identity, but the long-term consequences of "blood politics," as anthropologist Circe Sturm has called it, have been far more divisive. Belonging was never a simple matter of ancestry or even presence but entailed the nurturing of relationships. It was about reciprocity over lifetimes.[48]

What the Dawes Commission did still matters today because it created a document that has immeasurably shaped modern-day Americans' understanding of who Cherokees are, and because it is an inaccurate representation, it has fostered enormous misunderstanding about Cherokee culture, including Cherokees' values and norms of behavior. It is not accidental that commissioners broke apart extended families into administrative units compatible with Anglo-American ideals, and then the sociopolitical institutions of the United States, especially the Oklahoma courts and social welfare system, treated Cherokee families as broken because they did not conform to those ideals. Likewise, outsiders' essentialist definition of who is and is not a Cherokee gained legitimacy in the twentieth century. As a result, some people who have no ties to the formally recognized Cherokee governments claim to be Cherokee based on distant ancestry or even the possibility of having had a "Cherokee grandmother" because of a belief that biology correlates with identity. They do unspeakable damage speaking *for* Cherokee people and often profit from their assertions. Stripped of the commitment to reciprocate and show hospitality to one another, identity becomes a statement rather than a way of life.

The Dawes roll was not a Cherokee creation, and it reflects a non-Indian definition of tribal membership from a moment in American history when Anglo-Americans understood indigenous people to be less than fully human. Outdated notions of Indian ability and authenticity—and inauthenticity—rooted in a discredited terminology that perpetuates biological racism and white supremacy constructed the Dawes roll, which continues to shape modern understandings of tribal cultures. During the creation of the roll, Cherokees challenged these conclusions, and some, like the Nighthawks, denied the legitimacy of the Dawes Commission altogether. These stories are as important as what commissioners ultimately included on this list.

CHAPTER SIX

Transforming

In early November 1902, Birch Anderson claimed allotments for himself, his wife, Lizzie, and their infant daughter, Willie Mae. Birch's selections exemplify how familial relationships shaped the ways that Cherokees picked the land that they would own as individuals. Rather than combining the allotments of his family into a large, contiguous tract of land, Birch dispersed them across his community. He chose an allotment near his maternal kin, the Mitchells, for himself, and he picked land for Lizzie closer to her family, the Browns. He selected a homestead for his daughter that included a house and cultivated field belonging to his maternal uncle, John Mitchell. Anderson, in other words, used allotment to further connect his small, growing nuclear family into his and his wife's network of extended relations. Notably, he did not establish a contiguous base for a large farm that included room for future development and growth, a decision that would have geographically isolated the Andersons from their relatives.[1]

Three years later, in the summer of 1905, the Dawes Commission created such a consolidated farm for Anderson's maternal cousins, Rachel, Sissa, and Dora Mitchell. The mother of the young women, Nannie, had been married to Reese Mitchell. Reese was John's brother and Birch's maternal uncle. After Reese passed away, Nannie married Steve Dog, with whom she had had another daughter, Tinna. All of Nannie's daughters lived with her and Steve. John Mitchell remained their closest neighbor. Unlike Anderson and Mitchell, however, Nannie, Steve, and her daughters did not file for allotments. They were Nighthawks. Unable to force these families to participate in allotment, the Dawes Commission assigned land to them. Clerks divided improvements owned by Steve and Nannie Dog between them and their daughter Tinna. Steve received the property upon which was built their house, and all three received adjoining land that included their fields. Clerks then divided another nearby farm that they identified as "belonging to the Mitchell girls" among them and Sissa's baby. They had inherited this farm, probably from their maternal grandmother but perhaps from their father. Clerks gave Sissa the house, and they divided the fields among her, the baby, and Rachel. Dora received unimproved land on the public domain next to her sisters' allotments. An unrelated neighbor, Hattie Holland Lewis, received a small portion of their field in her allotment. The extended family of Steve and Nannie Dog thus received approximately a thousand acres of land, mostly contiguous, but as late as 1908, they refused to claim their allotment certificates. They just went on living on Steve and Nannie's farm.[2]

Allotment proved incredibly complicated. The process defied bureaucratic efficiency, frustrated those demanding its speedy implementation, and prompted countless federal court cases. It did, however, effectively separate Cherokees from their land in the long term. For all of these reasons, historical scholarship has emphasized chaos and corruption in association with the policy. In *And Still the Waters Run*, Angie Debo characterized federal officials as profiting from the discord and disorder that they created and perpetuated. She demonstrates how this contentious environment enabled the swindling of Indian people as overworked officials enforced cumbersome, complicated policies with an eye toward efficiency, expediency, and their own gain rather than Indian welfare.[3] In contrast, in his detailed study of the Dawes Commission, federal archivist Kent Carter characterizes the commissioners and their staff as generally well-intentioned but completely overwhelmed. With neither adequate personnel nor authority, they struggled to enforce policies repeatedly altered by court rulings and congressional legislation, to compile rolls without the assistance of Indian leaders and while facing the resistance of tribal members, and to thwart those, particularly non-Indian grafters, who sought to exploit allotment for personal gain.[4] Historian H. Craig Miner nicknamed the sprawling bureaucracy that allotted the Five Tribes a "corps of clerks," yet he, too, emphasizes that even this small army of secretaries could not accurately implement the policy or effectively protect Indian resources.[5]

Although justified, this emphasis on the pandemonium associated with non-Indians obscures the orderly ways in which Cherokees responded. Scholars know very little about the rationale that guided Cherokees' selection of allotments. Where they have focused attention on specific responses to the division of communal land among other tribes, historians have demonstrated that Indian families approached the policy thoughtfully and with determination to maintain their autonomy and self-sufficiency. Neighboring tribal nations allotted in the 1890s modeled these behaviors. Legal scholar Rennard Strickland refers to the Quapaws as an example of "Indian self-help" during the allotment era. Rejecting a federal plan to allot them eighty acres per individual and sell the remainder to non-Indians, the Quapaws, living on land in northeastern Indian Territory that the Cherokee Nation had sold to them, organized their own allotment program in which each member received two hundred acres. The Quapaws creatively funded this initiative by adopting several noncitizens who paid for their new homesteads. In their records, the Quapaws referred to them as the "fullblood white Quapaw." The only Indian nation to allot themselves, the Quapaws dramatically increased their landholdings and retained valuable mineral deposits of zinc and lead that were mined in the early 1900s.[6]

Other Indian people used allotments to reinforce their relationships with each other. In her environmental history of the Oklahoma Territory, Bonnie Lynn-Sherow demonstrates that although the Kiowas, living on a reservation in southwestern Oklahoma Territory, could not prevent the division of their land or dictate the terms by which it was done, they selected allotments that enabled them to maintain the residency patterns and division of labor associated with their system of social organization of bands interconnected through kin ties. Although allotment dramatically rearranged the composition of their territory, Kiowa social networks sustained customary ways of relating to the land and to each other.[7]

Likewise, order, not chaos, characterized the selection of allotments by Cherokee families. The images of the Oklahoma land runs captured in photographs and reenacted in film show prospective non-Indian landowners—boomers—in competition with one another. These snapshots teem with conflict and hint at the ever-present threat of violence.[8] Looking through the extensive collection of photographs documenting the allotment of the Five Tribes in the collection of the Oklahoma Historical Society, I found no comparable images of Indian people endangering each other to select their piece of private property.[9] Instead, photos of the citizens of the Five Tribes picking allotments suggest that their responses were calm and even somber. Two photos taken at land offices in Indian Territory struck me as particularly telling. One shows Indian men, women, and children clustered together in large, mixed groups as they wait outside of the land office. They are dressed nicely, socializing with each other as though at a picnic. A second picture shows men and women, having divided themselves by gender, waiting on opposite sides in the land office. The participation of families in the selection of land and the presence of Indian women at land offices is intriguing. No captions give further information, but the suggested persistence of their traditional values and behavior provides one explanation for how Cherokees adapted to allotment. They mitigated its chaotic impact by dividing resources according to their customary ties to each other and influenced by the values that they already practiced.[10]

Order also characterized the response of Cherokee families that refused to take allotments, including many residents of Chewey. While their countrymen and countrywomen gathered at land offices, resisters came together at stomp grounds. As the Dawes Commission dismembered the Cherokee Nation, the Nighthawks innovated to revitalize aspects of traditional Cherokee spirituality and ancient customs of social organization. They believed that allotment threatened the world with turmoil, and they sought to maintain the harmony of creation by recommitting themselves to their ways and to each other. At stomp grounds, such as the one near Chewey, Cherokee families socialized and feasted together, and in doing so, they embodied ideals expected of members of Cherokee society since ancient times and celebrated values that continued to be relevant to Cherokee existence at the beginning of the twentieth century. At times, they, too, separated themselves by gender. Around the fire, while men sang, women kept rhythm with shell shakers (pebble-filled turtle shells tied to their legs, which sounded like rattles). In defiance of the most aggressive campaign to assimilate Indian people in American history, Cherokee women and men retained their unique, distinct place in the order of creation.[11]

Cherokee families who accepted allotments shared many of the same values and behaviors as Cherokee families who would not break their bond to their communal land or to each other. A vital value system can sustain multiple possible responses to a situation. The records compiled by the Dawes Commission in the selection of allotments and oral histories conducted with Cherokees who experienced it show that social relationships influenced and orderliness characterized Cherokee responses to the privatization of their land. Those who selected allotments did so with an eye to sustaining the economic well-being of their extended families. The pattern of landownership of those who refused allotments differs, reflecting the values of the men on the Dawes Commission. The experience of both groups, however, demonstrates that Cherokees adapted to the taking of allotments by finding ways to maintain their extended families and their way of life.

The Curtis Act and the Cherokee Agreement

In the spring of 1898, Senator Charles Curtis proposed a bill to disband the Five Tribes without their consent.[12] Since 1893, Cherokee statesmen had thwarted the Dawes Commission's goal of reaching an agreement to allot Indian Territory while advocates of opening the region to corporate and non-Indian economic development had fervently lobbied in Washington, D.C. Although their interests did not otherwise overlap, commissioners, reformers, and intruders each characterized Cherokee society as broken and its leaders as corrupt. Convinced of the backwardness of the tribal republics and the reasonableness of those advocating for their dismemberment, congressmen ignored the written appeals of Indian statesmen, refused to meet with them, and effectively silenced the only opponents to the extension of allotment policy. Likewise, congressmen generally supported the bill despite some serious questions about its legality and practicality.[13] The House passed it after less than two and a half minutes of debate.[14] Following some discussion and amendment in the Senate, President William McKinley signed the Curtis Act into law on June 28, 1898.

The Curtis Act destroyed tribal sovereignty in Indian Territory. First, it suspended tribal laws and judicial systems. Second, it removed tribal control over assets, entrusting them instead to the secretary of the interior. Third, Congress posted an inspector in Indian Territory to supervise and, essentially, cripple the governments of the Five Tribes. Fourth, the Curtis Act provided a framework for dismantling tribal resource bases. The law authorized the Dawes Commission to compile tribal rolls and criminalized resistance. Indians had to comply with their requests for personal information or face punishment. Finally, the law instructed the Dawes Commission to allot tribal citizens "fair and equal" shares of land, which would be nontransferable and nontaxable until their owners gained full title. Yet, the Curtis Act did not rescind the bargaining power of the Dawes Commission, still charged to meet and treat with Indian statesmen to clarify the application of the powerful but ambiguous mandate.[15] Rather than a practical law, this measure enacted by Congress was crafted to break tribal resistance.

As expected, Cherokee statesmen abhorred the Curtis Act, and they immediately set about obstructing the Dawes Commission's implementation of it by turning to the federal courts. Ultimately, the Supreme Court upheld the Curtis Act in the decision *Stephens v. Cherokee Nation*.[16] Denied authority and resources, tribal officials could do little else in defense of their nation's existence. By December 1898, some Cherokee statesmen conceded to the futility of further resistance. In an effort to supplant the Curtis Act with a more favorable agreement, Principal Chief Samuel H. Mayes initiated negotiations with the Dawes Commission. The majority of Cherokee citizens still opposed allotment, but Cherokee leaders struggled to shape the terms of its application to protect as best they could their disgruntled constituents. This acquiescence generated discord with other Cherokees who opposed any negotiation with the U.S. government because it implied the Cherokee Nation's acceptance of the abrogation of its treaties. In particular, conservative members of the National Council, such as those affiliated with the Keetoowah Society, expressed their disapproval by refusing to participate in negotiations or vote on allotment bills, and they blamed those who did for selling out the Cherokee Nation for a pittance.[17]

Congress had instructed the Dawes Commission to implement the Curtis Act with due haste. Nevertheless, Cherokee statesmen stalled the division of their nation's resources for four years. During this time, Cherokee delegations negotiated three alternative agreements with the Dawes Commission, and the generous terms sought by Cherokee statesmen during these meetings suggest that they considered themselves to be far from powerless. During talks held in the winter of 1898 and 1899, Cherokee leaders reached a compromise with the Dawes Commission, which Congress rejected as too generous.[18] In the spring of 1900, Cherokee delegates and the commissioners resumed talks and negotiated a second agreement. Although federal officials approved it, Cherokee voters rejected it because they wanted both larger allotments and clarification on mineral leases, which the Curtis Act separated from land titles and whose status remained unresolved.[19] Outraged, the secretary of the interior ordered the Dawes Commission to allot the Cherokees under the provisions of the

Curtis Act. Principal Chief T. M. Buffington bargained for a final time, however, and during the summer of 1902, Congress approved this third agreement between Cherokee statesmen and the Dawes Commission.

Many Cherokees abstained from voting, but the agreement was ratified nonetheless. The low turnout reflected both the formal boycott by traditional Cherokees and the widespread unpopularity of allotment. There had been a referendum, however, and accordingly, the U.S. government concluded that the Cherokee people had consented to the policy. Had all eligible Cherokee voters participated, the measure would not have passed.[20] Those included in this study looked upon this referendum with disdain. Nighthawks did not participate, but even those who may have voted remembered the plan with ill feelings. Wyly Beavers, the son of Rosanna Mounce, dismissed it as the work of men who did not represent the will of the people.[21] Oscar Cannon remembered popular opinion being decidedly against allotment.[22]

Known as the Cherokee Agreement of 1902, this plan provided for allotment to begin after January 1, 1903. Each Cherokee citizen would receive a selection of land equal to but not more than 110 acres of average land in value totaling $325.60. In assigning allotments, the Dawes Commission was to take into consideration prior occupation and erection of improvements. The agreement guaranteed the exclusive possession of forty-acre homesteads protected against alienation and taxation for twenty-one years. The same safeguards applied to surplus land, remaining acres not included as part of homesteads, for five years. The secretary of the interior would assume authority over remaining tribal business and disband the Cherokee government on March 4, 1906.[23] In 1887, Senator Henry Dawes had predicted the immediate allotment of Indian Territory, but Cherokee statesmen had resisted for fifteen years, until after the other Indian republics had agreed to their allotment. No other tribal nation had bargained so hard for so long.

While these negotiations were taking place, the Dawes Commission already was making preparations for the division of Cherokee resources by surveying and mapping the nation. Between 1895 and 1897, field parties belonging to the United States Geological Survey (USGS) dispersed throughout Indian Territory. They created plat maps that divided the land into uniform townships. Notably, surveyors failed to note the location and type of improvements made to the land or the owners of these improvements, nor did they appraise the land or the improvements. Subsequently, Congress created a Division of Survey and Appraisement to assist the Dawes Commission. From April until June 1901, another set of field parties fanned through Cherokee country to classify approximately 4.5 million acres of land into one of twenty categories. In the Cherokee Nation, the quality of land varied widely from open bottomland with the most productive soil to flint hills, unsuitable for agriculture. Surveyors generally categorized land in the region of Chewey as poor quality unfit for agriculture. They considered most of the region to be flinty hills but classed a small percentage of the land as bottomland subject to overflow, rough land free from rocks, rocky prairie land, and bottomland covered with timber. They classed the smallest portion of the region as prairie land, smooth and tillable, but the area still proved to be substandard for intensive agriculture.[24] Although data gathered in subsequent surveys revealed errors in the USGS maps, the secretary of the interior forbade the Dawes Commission from correcting the maps and ordered the men to begin allotting land without delay.[25]

Instructed to proceed with inaccurate maps, the Dawes Commission also initiated the distribution of land with incomplete tribal rolls. The terms of the Cherokee Agreement provided for the rejection of any application for enrollment submitted after October 31, 1902, in order that the selection of allotments could begin in January 1903, but many questions about citizenship in the Cherokee Nation remained unsettled. In particular, two cases involving Cherokee families slowly worked their way through the U.S. courts. In 1906, the Supreme Court ruled that noncitizens who married Cherokees after November 1, 1875, had no claim to allotments, and in 1912, the Court ordered the inclusion of 5,605 Cherokee infants born during the enrollment and allotment process. Kent Carter describes the chaotic outcome: "Thus, some people were receiving their land while others were still trying to get on the rolls, and court rulings and legal opinions sometimes complicated the situation by forcing the cancellation of the enrollment of individuals who had already selected an allotment." While the Dawes Commission began assigning allotments to Cherokees whose enrollment was without doubt, lingering questions over the status of others, often members of the same family, caused them to undo and redo the cases of thousands of Cherokee families. For example, John Brown began selecting allotments for himself and his children in October 1904, but the Dawes Commission did not resolve the status of his intermarried wife, Emily, until early 1907.[26]

As it had during the enrollment process, the Dawes Commission set up offices and expected Cherokees to come before the board to select parcels of land. On January 1, 1903, it opened a land office in Vinita but relocated it to Tahlequah on May 1. Although the capital city was not a convenient location for many Cherokees, the Dawes Commission maintained only one land office per Indian nation in order to safeguard the accuracy and security of its records. Barely twenty miles separated this region of Goingsnake District from the Cherokee capital to the west, but poor roads made travel difficult. On January 3, 1905, the commissioners opened an auxiliary office at Muskogee in the Creek Nation to facilitate the selection of allotments by those who had yet to do so for reasons of inconvenience, but this site was beyond the boundary of the Cherokee Nation and farther removed from most Cherokees than was Tahlequah.[27]

The commissioners attempted to closely regulate the selection of allotments. To prevent the confusion and corruption that had arisen when they allotted the Creeks, the commissioners agreed in advance upon a procedure for allotting the Cherokees. As Cherokees waited outside the land office, clerks distributed numbered admission tickets. To prevent the sale of these slips, clerks recorded the names and numbers of allottees. Once called into the land office, each allottee approached another clerk, who referred to the Dawes roll to confirm his or her eligibility and filled out a certificate verifying the person's citizenship. With this piece of paper, the allottee advanced to the next clerk, who, using different colors of ink, noted his or her selection of a homestead and surplus land on a plat map. The next clerk located the proposed claim on the township maps to determine whether or not the land had been claimed already. A commissioner then questioned the applicant about the selection of land: Was it currently in the applicant's possession? What improvements were located on the land? Did he or she own the improvements located on it? Did he or she make this claim in good faith? Did anyone else claim the land? A clerk noted the answers on preprinted forms. After review by commissioners, a final clerk marked off the allotment on the official maps. If the claim was contested, however, the allottee faced additional paperwork, including the notification of the other claimant, an investigation, a hearing by commissioners, and review by the secretary of the interior. This process took months or even years.[28]

Cherokee Families and the Selection of Allotments

This procedure suggests that Cherokees experienced allotment as a series of individuals, but in reality, Cherokees made decisions about allotment as families. Before going to the land office, Cherokees planned their selection of allotments with kin. They strategized to retain their improvements and maintain the integrity of extended family settlements. Eliza Brown's family exemplifies this. Several of her adult children clustered their allotments and those of their children around her farm, the first home the family had made after settling in Indian Territory. In the three decades since, the Browns had made extensive improvements to land along a creek, where they dug wells; built several houses, barns, a smokehouse, chicken coops, a flour mill, and stables; and planted orchards and hundreds of acres in many fields. Three months before going to the land office, the family had begun to "post," or mark their possible claims with fence posts, and they had been discussing the division of their improvements since then. As John, Eliza's son who served as her representative and that of two of his sisters, put it, "I came and talked with the other girls connected and they said it was best to go ahead." Only then did he claim their allotments.[29]

Family members frequently represented each other before the Dawes Commission, and the handling of allotment-related business was treated as a collective effort. As during enrollment, adult males usually represented their wives and children to claim land. Women, however, appeared to claim their own allotments more often than they had to enroll themselves.[30] Nonetheless, most families sent spokesmen, in part because participation in the policy was expensive. Cherokees had to travel to the land office, stay in town during their selection, and put aside their work at home and responsibilities to other family members during this time. In his investigation of the allotment process in 1903, Charles J. Bonaparte, a member of the Board of Indian Commissioners, commented that this aspect of the allotment process placed a great burden on average Cherokees, who should not have been asked to travel more than a day's journey from home to select their allotments.[31] Such business trips were not convenient. Mack Welch explained that he made a mistake claiming his land, in part because he had not had the opportunity to properly measure before filing. He had combined his visit to the land office with other errands he had to attend to in town. If allotments had been selected in the field, such errors would have been avoided.[32]

Kin also tended to each other's affairs because some physically could not make that trip. The illness of his young daughter prompted Ira Cannon to send his father Edwin to Tahlequah to select land on their behalf.[33]

Pregnancy, in particular, kept some women from appearing themselves. Tinsie Kelley, who explained that her "condition" prevented her from traveling, sent a letter, likely written by someone else on her behalf, to the commission expressing her wishes.[34] Hattie Lewis was eight months pregnant when she sent her intermarried husband, Fred, to select allotments. He brought a form granting him power of attorney over the land selection for Hattie and her three sons by her late husband, James Holland, who had passed away in May 1901. Lewis represented her, selected land and improvements in her and her sons' names, and identified his wife and her sons as the owners of it.[35] Also comparable to enrollment, appearing to select an allotment proved too difficult for some elderly Cherokees. Again, John Brown represented his elderly mother, Eliza, and his maternal uncle Martin Raper before the commission because both were too infirm to travel themselves.[36] Reformers had anticipated that the lure of landownership would cause Indian people to begin distancing themselves from their extended families, but in reality, many depended on their kin even to negotiate the cumbersome process of claiming an allotment.

Likewise, Cherokees did not select allotments that segregated their nuclear family from their extended relations. Their choices of allotments maintained multigenerational residence patterns. In families lacking elders, adult siblings formed the bases of contiguous land selections. Adjoining allotments between brothers, like Tom and James Mack Welch, are a particularly obvious pattern.[37] When unable to fully connect their allotted land, families picked acres, either surplus or homestead, near their kin. For example, John Kelley selected a surplus piece of timberland adjoining the allotments of his sister Rosanna Mounce and his maternal nephew Wyly Beavers.[38] Notably, Cherokees did not prioritize conjoined allotments with spouses over those with natal relatives, and married couples commonly selected land close to siblings, parents, and cousins. Spouses divided their allotments and scattered their property among both sets of kin.[39] Most families claimed the majority of their acres in land that they had occupied and improved and surrounding unimproved acreage.[40] Cherokees generally perpetuated their existing residence patterns when selecting private property and did not change their living circumstances.[41]

Lacking surveyors' tools, most Cherokees measured the land that they sought to claim by eye or by foot, called "stepping-off" their farms and fields. These imprecise methods resulted in errors when allottees pointed to their farms on the Dawes Commission's maps. In July 1905, Mack Welch returned to the land office and admitted to claiming the wrong land by mistake when he first visited in March of that year. He did not realize that his initial claim missed his field until he received the allotment certificates several months later. He then asked to relinquish his first claim and file on his improvements, which no one else had selected. The commission questioned how this error came to be. Mack replied, "I don't know how unless it was a mistake of the clerk or made myself when I pointed it out to them." The following March, Mack again went to the land office in hopes of switching his acreage. He explained that he "had never went to the corners and measured the land off" until early 1906 and realized that he still was missing some of his improvements. The annoyed commissioners refused his request, and he lost some of his field. Mack's selection of allotments was complicated by the lack of accurate maps. The clerk noted that none of his family's improvements were marked on the plat map used by the Dawes Commission. The USGS maps were notoriously inaccurate, and their use resulted in countless errors because they prevented Cherokees from making accurate claims and commissioners from making informed decisions.[42]

Some selections precipitated conflicts between neighbors. Although members of the Dawes Commission complained that the enormous number of contests over land claims slowed the allotment of the Cherokees, they wrongly implied that Cherokees greedily grabbed up their neighbors' land. Rather, the frequency of contested claims highlighted a flaw in the system imposed by the General Land Office. As historian Bonnie Lynn-Sherow points out, surveyors, using the township-and-range system, mapped and divided tribal land into uniform amounts in order to facilitate its distribution according to estimated monetary valuations.[43] Confused by this foreign system of dissecting land into interchangeable units of measure that were not readily visible on the landscape itself, Cherokees sometimes accidentally claimed land improved by their neighbors. The decision to use the township-and-range system also resulted in contested claims because surveyors' lines did not conform to the geography of Indian communities. Cherokees customarily settled, managed, and used land based on their familial and communal needs, and Cherokee farms conformed to topography to facilitate access to valuable resources, especially water. The layout of houses and fields followed meandering streams and valleys, wrapped around outcrops, and left valued food and fuel sources, such as stands of nut-bearing trees, undisturbed. Ten-acre plots, the smallest possible unit of land that could be claimed, often included improvements owned by two families, particularly if their farms and fields adjoined a shared natural resource, such as a stream.

Likewise, since Cherokees developed land as extended families, the selection of allotments proved tricky when extended families collectively built, used, and maintained certain improvements, such as orchards, barns, fields, and mills. In other words, boundaries drawn decades after the settlement of Cherokee farms cut though homesteads and defied existing patterns of land use. Kin worked out the division of their improvements. The Dawes Commission recorded the outcomes of familial discussions rather than mediated these decision-making processes. The adult sons and daughters of Eliza Brown, for example, returned their original allotment forms and asked the commissioners to make corrections because they had not divided their land properly the first time according to their own understanding of who should claim which improvements. One barn, a field, and a fence, in particular, proved difficult to allot because it was built and used by a different sibling from the one who claimed the nearest house. The siblings were amicable and had worked the division of resources out by themselves, but they misunderstood a clerk's erroneous suggestion that the family members go ahead and file on their lands and then switch among themselves later. When they realized that they needed to appear before the commissioners again to make these revisions legal, they did so.[44]

Neighbors usually also resolved disputes among themselves, and this resulted in the withdrawal of claims on land improved by or sought by neighbors. Baskum Brown, the son of Marsh and Mary, withdrew his claim once Frank Mitchell claimed the same land. Baskum had filed on an allotment in October 1904. He returned the next month to change his request after realizing his mistake. When the commissioners asked him how he knew he had been wrong, Baskum, pointing to the plat map, responded, "Him [Mitchell] and I looked at it right up to this line up here."[45] The men walked what would become the whole property line between them. In a few situations, however, the Dawes Commission investigated dual claims. Most of these contested claims seemed easily and quickly resolved in the favor of the claimant with the most valuable improvement located on the land. For example, they awarded one who claimed a structure versus one who claimed a field.[46] There is no evidence of violence resulting from disagreements about land claims and boundaries: Cherokees filed many contests but typically resolved them peacefully through their social networks or, occasionally, the procedure established by the Dawes Commission.

Cherokee families divided improved property among members in an egalitarian way that suggests the persistence of customary approaches to their domestic economy, and their decisions sharply contrasted with the initial plan for allotment advocated by reformers who sought the centralization of familial resources under the control of male heads-of-households. Resources remained widely distributed among women and men. Cherokee women and men received allotments of equal value, but, moreover, women retained possession of significant improved property. The identity of those claiming the most valuable estates is telling: the elderly widow Eliza Brown and her unmarried daughter Polly each claimed extensive improvements entailing full farms, more than any other individuals studied in this book.[47] Although property ownership remained uncommon among married women in Anglo-American society, marriage did not preclude claims to improved property in the selection of Cherokee allotments. Married women, including Fannie Welch, Mary Brown, Susan Kelley, Rosanna Mounce, and Hattie Lewis, owned houses and other improvements.[48]

In addition, parents generally divided improvements among their children. Not all Cherokee families claimed multiple farms, but those that had the resources to do so distributed improvements among their members rather than consolidated the most valuable improvements under the control of any one member of the household. Over generations, many families had built multiple small houses and other working buildings and had tilled many fields, although not all of these were in use at the time of allotment. Applications make no reference to the quality or state of repair of improvements. Regardless, families ensured that the ownership of those resources was decentralized. Rosanna Mounce claimed her cultivated field in her name but assigned houses and other improvements to her young sons.[49] Although not excluding sons, parents generally seem to have favored daughters when distributing improvements. For example, John Brown apportioned small houses and outbuildings for his two young daughters, but he assigned fields to his minor sons. The allotment of infant Willie Mae Anderson contained a house and field that belonged to her paternal uncle John Mitchell.[50] The preferential treatment of female children points to the persistence of traditional Cherokee patterns of inheritance through the matrilineal line, a custom some scholars consider defunct among the Cherokees by the late nineteenth century.[51] Unlike

Anglo-American families, in which the adult male head-of-household controlled family resources, Cherokees dispersed valuable property and resources in equitable ways that extended the bonds of reciprocity into the rising generations.

A small group of Cherokees claimed land outside of the boundaries of their community, a move that often resulted in contests lasting several years and, typically, the denial of their requests. In February 1905, Fred Lewis, the intermarried husband of Hattie, claimed land for her and her sons by her previous husband in their own community. After giving birth, Hattie visited the land office the following March to select an allotment for her middle son, Robert, whose land had not been chosen along with that of his siblings. She requested an allotment for him in township 23 North, 14 East. In contrast to the local property claimed for his siblings, Robert's allotment was situated on land known for its oil, gas, and coal deposits, which were leased to corporations through the Office of Indian Affairs and managed by the Indian Service. Hattie, however, knew little about its potential for economic development. When the commissioners asked her to describe it, she said, "I have not seen this land but wish to accept testimony of my husband F. M. Lewis as true and correct."[52] Although it is not certain where Fred learned about this opportunity, a neighbor also filed on land nearby. Prospective opportunities for lease revenue probably were discussed among neighbors and kin. William Kirk also claimed land for some of his children in the same region, but he proved less successful in gaining title to it. Kirk initiated a series of claims in the northern townships, but other Cherokees challenged his claims. After nearly two years of filing applications on land and receiving letters of denial, Kirk's family ended up taking the majority of their allotted land dispersed near their home rather than in distant districts after all.[53]

Notably, families that sought land in distant townships generally did so in addition to claiming a consolidated area of land around their homes. The Cannon brothers, for example, took allotments that encompassed their farms adjoining each other. In addition, two claimed land in several northern townships; perhaps they were trying to gain access to oil and gas income. Again, most of their claims were rejected.[54] Those who successfully obtained land located several townships away from their homes usually had purchased improvements there, and these Cherokees went to the land office armed with notarized agreements scribbled on paper and sometimes even with preprinted forms.[55] These Cherokees may have been trying to gain access to more valuable land or even may have been speculating. Residents who did obtain land in distant townships could have done so at the request of a grafter paying them for their claims. The frequency with which the Dawes Commission decided against their claims, however, suggests that this would not have been a reliable or lucrative way to increase familial income.[56] Although the experiences of Cherokees in this study appear to defy perceptions of rampant abuse in the distribution of allotments, I do not conclude that these families were completely protected. Evidence of graft in the circumstances described above would not likely be obvious in the documentary record unless a Cherokee admitted to being paid to make a claim by a land speculator. Likewise, Cherokees who lived closer to more desirable land probably experienced more pressure to participate in these schemes, and their homes would have been vulnerable.

When the grafter was a member of Cherokee family, however, the corruption was readily apparent. One resident, Tilman Chance, the intermarried husband of Maggie, claimed land to which he was not entitled according to Cherokee law and the policies of the Dawes Commission. Because they married in 1887, over a decade after the National Council passed a law that limited the property rights of intermarried whites and that was upheld by the Dawes Commission and the U.S. Supreme Court, Tilman was not entitled to an allotment. He claimed one anyway. He had been outside the Cherokee Nation serving time in federal prison for perjury when Maggie enrolled herself and their children. After his release, he went before the Dawes Commission several times to make a case for his inclusion, it would seem, as a Cherokee. His entreaties seem to have done little good, however, because he remained listed as an intermarried white on the Dawes roll. He apparently proved more adept at bribery as time went on. Beginning in February 1902, Chance purchased several sets of improvements in township 26 North, 19 East, an area north of their home that was rich with oil, gas, and coal deposits. Although he was ineligible for an allotment, Chance was one of the first residents of his community to pick one. In February 1903, he selected allotments for himself, his wife, and their four children. He claimed land near their home for his allotment and Maggie's, but he selected the improved land in township 26 North, 19 East, for the majority of his children's allotments. Chance dispersed his children's land in areas likely to generate income from mineral wealth. No other residents of this area speculated in improvements with the success of Tilman and Maggie Chance.[57]

Whether selecting the allotments of their family members or awaiting the decision of the Dawes Commission concerning their contested
land, Cherokees spent much of the allotment years waiting. Although the
Cherokee land office opened in January 1903, most families in this study
appeared before the Dawes Commission in 1904. Many waited a year or
two to complete their selection, and others did not even begin to select
their land until 1905 or later. In other words, Cherokee families in this
study did not feel rushed or threatened by the possibility that someone
else would lay claim to their homes. In fact, the allotment of the Cherokee
Nation remained unfinished when the Five Tribes Bill of 1906 abolished
the Dawes Commission. The law provided for one commissioner to complete the work. By this time, the staff of the Cherokee land office was
reduced by two-thirds, to twenty-one employees. Clerks notified families who had yet to select land or accept a cash payment as a substitute.
Their deadline to do so was August 1, 1910.[58] By then, even those who had
opposed allotment had been assigned a fraction of their homeland.

The Assignment of Allotments to Resistant Families

After most of their neighbors and kin had selected allotments, other
Cherokees continued to oppose the policy. Many traditional Cherokees,
including the members of the Keetoowah Society, had conceded to what
they perceived to be inevitable and grudgingly claimed allotments. The
Nighthawks, however, continued to resist U.S. intervention in the affairs of
the Cherokee Nation. They withdrew from Cherokee national and territo-
rial politics and refused to communicate with the commissioners or their
staff. For this reason, as the deadline for selecting an allotment neared,
the Dawes Commission arbitrarily allotted them plots of land based on
information gathered from informants. Several of these Nighthawk families are included in this study: the Birds, Cheweys, Crittendens, Dogs,
Hogshooters, Oakballs, Sands, Sixkillers, Suakes, and Wolfes. As the
Dawes Commission dismantled the Cherokee Nation around them, the
Nighthawks revitalized their religious customs and communities. As time
went on, the movement generated more parallels with ancient Cherokee
social organization, and ultimately, the Nighthawks created a network
that unified communities under councils of elders representing the seven
clans. If the customary ways of Cherokee family life had ordered the taking of allotments, family values certainly underlay the resistance of those
Cherokees who refused them.

This movement had roots far deeper than the allotment era, but it was this crisis that reinvigorated traditionalists. By the late 1890s, Keetoowah headmen had expressed grave concern over the situation in the Cherokee Nation, which was overrun by non-Indian intruders and increasingly governed by the Dawes Commission and other federal officials rather than by Cherokees themselves. They concluded that threats to their sovereignty resulted from the failure of the Cherokees to follow God's laws for them, a primordial people whose righteous existence maintained the harmony of creation. The solution, they concluded, lay not in further political wrangling with the Dawes Commission or politicians in Washington, D.C., as many Cherokee elected officials including the principal chief proposed, but in restoring balance through their own actions and beliefs. The headmen instructed Redbird Smith to lead a committee to "get back what the Keetoowahs had lost," and Smith, along with Wilson Girty, Anderson Gritts, Ned Bullfrog, and later Charlie Scott, set about revitalizing traditional Cherokee spirituality at the request of its practitioners.[59]

Over the next several years, Smith talked with and learned from the wisest elders and holy men in Indian Territory, and he synthesized their knowledge, filtered it through his understanding of Cherokee spirituality, taught it to other traditionalists, and practiced it with them. His education with Creek Sam, a Natchez holy man, focused on deepening his understanding of Natchez teachings. Although a separate tribe, Natchez people had lived among the Cherokees and Creeks since the French destroyed their nation, the last Mississippian chiefdom, in the 1730s. Despite their dislocation, Natchez families retained much of their theology, and other traditionalists looked to them for guidance. This blossoming spiritual revival among the Cherokees developed from a composite of Natchez, Cherokee, and Creek cultures, and it was emblematic of the multiethnic nature of Indian Territory. Such a movement was impossible except in a place where the relationships among traditionalists had developed over several generations through friendship and intermarriage. In other words, the concentration of the Five Tribes into Indian Territory during the removal era planted the seeds for this movement.

Outsiders considered settlements like Chewey to be isolated and their inhabitants to be withdrawn, but the families who lived there were connected to a vital intertribal movement that united communities across Indian Territory. Nighthawk leaders joined the Four Mothers Society, a coalition established at Sulphur Springs in the Illinois District of the Cherokee Nation after the arrival of the Dawes Commission in Indian

Territory. Like the Keetoowah Society, however, the members of the Four Mothers Society came to disagree over the alliance's function. While some sought to focus this network of traditionalists on resistance to allotment, others envisioned the Four Mothers Society as a vehicle for spiritual revitalization. Although the Four Mothers Society maintained a delegation in Washington, D.C., that included Eufala Harjo and John Smith, a son of Redbird Smith, many members participated in the organization primarily through the intertribal stomp dances that it organized.[60]

The Nighthawks focused on spiritual revitalization. In 1896, Cherokee, Creek, and Natchez conservatives held the first stomp dance in over a generation. They gathered at the home of Ella Bonarskie, a Creek widow, and after they worked together splitting rails during the day, they danced into the night. Few present knew how to dance. It had been so long since the people had done so. Elderly George Mushingshell, a Seminole, had to teach the women how to shake the turtle shells attached to their legs. Traditionalists soon erected other stomp grounds, the number of which steadily increased throughout the area. These were sacred places where families gathered to dance, socialize, feast, play ball, and discuss matters important to them. Smith established a stomp ground on Black Gum Mountain, the first in the Cherokee Nation for generations. Smith's son John remembered this as the time that the fires "came back up." He was referring to the coalescence of communities of practitioners of traditional Cherokee spirituality. By 1906, Cherokees in about two dozen communities organized fires under Smith's instruction. The families of Chewey erected a stomp ground in their community. The keepers of these fires initially followed intertribal customs, but as Smith's son George explained, leaders continually adapted their practice to correspond with Cherokee culture: "They changed the rule every year. They kept trying to get back what they had lost." For example, in 1905, the fire-keepers from twenty-two Cherokee communities gathered at Sulphur Springs to learn from one another and to codify their practice.[61]

Smith continued to refocus the emphasis of the Nighthawk practice to customs that resonated with Cherokee culture. The Harmony Ethic, as Robert K. Thomas called this system of customary Cherokee values, provided the foundation of Smith's teachings and of the Nighthawk movement. Smith based much of his philosophy in his understanding of seven wampum belts acquired by the Cherokees from the Iroquois in the mid-eighteenth century. Made of shell beads strung in codes and woven with symbolism, wampum belts were a central component of traditional

Indian diplomacy that conservatives believed symbolized the commitment of the Cherokees as a people to behave righteously. Principal Chief John Ross held the belts until the Civil War, by which time Keetoowah elders had lost the ability to translate them. They charged Smith with learning to read them, a process that took years of questioning holy men about the meanings of the beaded patterns and translating this information through his knowledge of Cherokee theology. From all of these sources, Smith eventually preached a message promising the restoration of social harmony through individual commitment to their God and to following the White Path, which Thomas defined as "being peaceful, friendly, and observing the rest of the moral virtues; but also of keeping up the old Cherokee customs such as the fire, stomp dancing, etc." Keetoowahs also called this "God's Law" and the "Seven Clan Rule."[62] According to Smith's teachings, being Keetoowah was a commitment to their God to follow the path set for the Cherokees at creation, which included behaving appropriately toward other Cherokees, honoring their agreements as represented by the wampums and treaties, and turning to their Creator, manifested by their sacred fires, for sustenance and guidance. Nighthawks refused to take allotments, then, not only because private landownership violated God's law for them but also because doing so disavowed their treaties, sacred compacts made between peoples and before God.[63]

The reinvigoration of Cherokee theology included the reorganization of stomp grounds. The layout of Smith's first ceremonial ground mirrored those used by the Natchez and Creeks, four logs, pointing to the cardinal directions, extended from the fire pit to four arbors. Among Cherokees, however, seven and not four served as their sacred number, so Smith and other Nighthawk leaders began to modify the grounds and their ceremonies by replacing Natchez customs with ones that they believed to be authentically Cherokee. In particular, seven clans had once unified the Cherokee people, and the number seven came to permeate the practices of the Nighthawk Keetoowahs, who built seven arbors, one for each clan, around their fire. They used seven different types of wood to start the fire. They entrusted seven men, one representing each clan, to govern each ceremonial ground. While Smith distanced the practice of the Nighthawks from that of other conservatives among the Five Tribes, he did not reject Natchez theology, which he respected deeply. Instead, this initiative pointed to the maturation of the movement and suggested the ability of practitioners to evaluate the information and theorize the concepts necessary to sustain their spiritual growth.[64]

As their practice increasingly centered on Cherokee culture, the Nighthawks disassociated themselves from intertribal political resistance. In the traditionalist Creek communities located just across the southern border of the Cherokee Nation, Chitto Harjo, whom non-Indians referred to as Crazy Snake, unified dissidents from the Five Tribes into a coalition prepared to take up arms against the U.S. government in order to prevent allotment. Non-Indians feared an Indian uprising and called for troops twice, in 1901 and again in 1909, but the Crazy Snake rebellion failed to undermine the Dawes Commission. As the Crazy Snake rebellion among the Creeks grew, many traditional Cherokees further withdrew from secular efforts. Redbird Smith sympathized with Creek militants, yet he opposed violence as a solution to the crisis of allotment. To Smith, such behavior was not consistent with the White Path, the deep personal commitment to harmony, that he urged Cherokees to walk and that he believed offered a more effective means to the restoration of order. The Nighthawks thus withdrew from the Four Mothers Society.[65]

Reflective of the interconnectedness of Cherokee culture, this spiritual revival entailed the revitalization of Cherokee social structure, particularly aspects associated with fellowship among families. Nighthawks participated in the movement as families, and ties of birth and marriage connected most members. Although most Cherokees did not identify as Nighthawks, upwards of 6,000 Cherokees out of a population of approximately 42,000 did, and by 1906, they had organized about two dozen ceremonial centers, including the one at Chewey. Many Cherokees relocated near stomp grounds, at least for ceremonies, causing a consolidation of the traditional population into temporary settlements composed of many families representing the seven clans, an atypical Cherokee settlement pattern since their dispersal following the American Revolution. As Thomas concludes, "Either the revival of this long-dead structure and ceremonies is a great coincidence or else it tells us something about cultural persistence." There is a difference between knowledge that is lost and that which is dormant and waiting to be embraced again.[66]

While their consolidation fostered their spiritual practice, the Nighthawk movement served a distinct social need as well by providing fellowship to Cherokees who lived and worked together and shared resources during this transitional, turbulent time. The rapid coalescence of the Nighthawks points to the persistence of a kinship-based civic ethic and the perpetuation of the family values inherent in such a system.[67] For Cherokees like the residents of Chewey, stomp grounds served as places for families not only to socialize and practice their faith but also to hear important news affecting them. In other words, these were family reunions and business meetings as well as religious services. Outsiders, including members of the Dawes Commission, considered Nighthawks to be grossly uninformed. Alluding to their supposed primitiveness and savagery, one referred to them as a "cry from the wilderness."[68] On the contrary, Nighthawks maintained ties among them that facilitated the distribution of information, particularly about allotment. The Nighthawks built their consensus-based movement through discussion at their stomp grounds. This trend culminated in the reinstating of clan organization between 1910 and 1915. Nighthawks called this the "time when we found our clans" or the "finding of the clans."[69] By the time Redbird Smith died in November 1918, over twenty years after headmen had appointed him to "get back what the Keetoowahs had lost," he had facilitated the reinvigoration of Cherokee spirituality. George Smith observed, "By the time the old man died the rule was complete."[70] Notably, this era of Cherokee spiritual revitalization culminated in the reinvigoration of ancient familial organization.

The revival of traditional Cherokee social structure frustrated the Dawes Commission, which announced its intention to assign resisters their homesteads and then repeatedly attempted to force them to enroll themselves and take allotments. Because these efforts generally failed, the Dawes Commission gathered information about noncompliant Cherokee families from their kin and neighbors who would cooperate.[71] In 1904 and again in 1905, the Dawes Commission sent field parties in search of those who had yet to select an allotment, estimated to be over 775 heads-of-households, including at least 16 families who lived in Chewey.[72] Because Nighthawks typically left for their stomp grounds when these outsiders approached, field parties usually proved unsuccessful because they failed to find these families at home. For this reason, they commonly questioned less hostile neighbors to secure needed information. In spite of the Nighthawks' resistance, members of the Dawes Commission made a concerted effort to identify their homesteads. Their allotment jackets include notations by field clerks trying to identify the rightful owners of farms and other improvements.

In the summer of 1905, the commissioners issued 1,142 arbitrary allotments, whose recipients included Nighthawk families, some of whom lived in Chewey.[73] The documentary record suggests that the Dawes Commission tried to allot resisters their farms, but it is not clear that they always succeeded. Contemporary testimony and oral history suggests that they failed. Traditionalist leaders throughout the Five Tribes claimed their people were robbed of their homes and "pushed out," in the words of Eufala Harjo, a Creek delegate from the Four Mothers Society. In his testimony before a Senate investigative committee, he explained that some resistant families had lost their farms when others wrongfully claimed them as part of their allotments. He said, "The full-blood Indian people are pushed out to-day and they have left their homes and taken what they have, and everything, and are camped out in the woods to-day."[74] The system established by the Dawes Commission made such dislocation possible. In these situations, the Dawes Commission upheld the rights of allottees, whether or not they were the rightful owners and occupants of the property. They then forced traditionalists off the land that they had improved and put allottees in possession of it. Ironically, the Dawes Commission assumed this responsibility at the insistence of Cherokee statesmen who sought to prevent intruders from retaining possession of illegal improvements once those improvements had been allotted to Cherokee citizens.[75] In short, the system developed by the Dawes Commission did not preclude the possibility of land loss, and traditionalist leaders believed it to be common.

The dire situation that traditionalist leaders described did not exist in Chewey. Of the sixteen families in Chewey in this study that received arbitrary allotments, fourteen retained their familial homestead, at least in part. Perhaps the Dawes Commission was more vigilant to allot families their rightful homestead here, but there is no evidence to suggest that. In such a small, close-knit community, neighbors and relatives who provided information for field clerks and commissioners could have been very helpful in accurately identifying the residents of each household. In addition, the land in this region was not coveted by those who sought to defraud allottees. Poor soil quality and a lack of mineral deposits characterized this area. In other areas of the Cherokee Nation where resistant families had improved valuable land, little in the allotment system prevented their dislocation.[76]

At the same time, one group of Nighthawks did experience a severe loss of improved property: women. Under pressure from politicians to complete the allotment of the Cherokee Nation, the Dawes Commission took no time to investigate the individual economic situations of resistant families, and commissioners completed the distribution of Cherokee land as quickly as possible. This meant that surveyors and field clerks struggled to determine only which families owned which improvements, and they did not distinguish among property claimed by different family members. Although married and widowed women who selected allotments commonly claimed property, the Dawes Commission allotted almost no improvements to resistant women. In fact, only two female Nighthawks, Annie Chewey and Betsy Suake, received the fields that clerks believed they had cleared and planted. None received their houses. Resistant Cherokee women, therefore, lost legal title to improvements that they owned under Cherokee law and the resources that they depended upon to provide for their families. The decision of clerks to assign improved land to other family members would have long-term consequences for these women. Once restrictions against the sale of allotted land were lifted, the legal owners of this property were empowered to sell it, or, if they died, it became taxable. The rightful owners had no recourse.[77]

For modern scholars of American Indian women's history, it would be interesting to know whether traditionalist women owned more, less, or the same amount of property as Cherokee women who did not participate in the resistance movement. Logically, these women who were participating in the revitalization of the ancient clan system should have owned homes and other improvements in great numbers. The commissioners were not concerned with this information, however. The lack of notations regarding female traditionalists' property in allotment jackets suggests that rather than trying to consciously undermine these women's authority, commissioners just assumed these women had no power or resources at their disposal at all.

Nighthawk women truly were invisible to commissioners. In part, this is because these outsiders misunderstood the value and meaning of motherhood in Cherokee society. Among Anglo-Americans, motherhood necessitated female dependence on male providers, but Cherokee society accepted the opposite to be true: motherhood empowered women personally and politically and accorded them authority over domestic matters, especially the use of resources for their children. The encounter between Simon Walkingstick and Jennie Oakball, examined in chapter 4, hints at this. Motherhood was the solid ground upon which Cherokee women spoke with authority about things that affected their families. Jennie Oakball's story reminds us that an "indigenous motherhood that was inherently nationalistic," as historian Tiya Miles puts it, survived within Cherokee households. By the time they arbitrarily allotted the Nighthawks, commissioners had heard several years of testimony from

Cherokees who routinely validated women's ownership of property as normal among them. Nonetheless, the commissioners continued to refer to resisters as exclusively male and their improvements as the products of men's labor and, therefore, owned by men. On allotment jackets, the Dawes Commission identified adult men as "Nighthawks" and the owners of improvements but labeled female Nighthawks and their children as "Cherokees by blood." For example, when elderly Betsy Suake did not enroll, the commissioners questioned Reverend Adam Lacie if he knew why she had not appeared before them. He demurred to answer. They should have known, however. Her adult sons and daughters also refused to enroll. Individual men were not Nighthawks, families were, and women were empowered members of Cherokee families. In ignoring this, commissioners robbed these women of their land and denied their identity.[78]

Sexism was compounded by ageism and resulted in the dispossession of elderly women. Betsy Oakball provides a useful example. When the Dawes Commission arrived in Stilwell in 1900, she was at least in her early sixties, if not older. She had raised her two boys, John and White, into adulthood. The brothers were married with young children of their own. Where did Betsy fit into this larger Oakball family? The Dawes Commission left two conflicting pieces of evidence about her living arrangements. A neighbor suggested that she lived alone, although near her son White. Clerks, however, listed her as a member of White's household. The accompanying map is difficult to read, but at least two buildings are noted. Presumably, at least one is a house; the other may have been another house, the common arrangement on Cherokee farms. Most Cherokees living in this area also had smokehouses, chicken coops, and the like, but clerks tended not to note such smaller structures of insignificant monetary value. Clerks did note that the family had improved their land but did not elaborate about what they had done to it. So Betsy may have shared a house with White, his wife, Susie, and their two children, or perhaps, as the neighbor suggested, she lived in that other building just steps away.[79]

Was the whole farm Betsy's? Betsy Oakball certainly could have built it up over her lifetime, and she could have been the head of this extended household. She seems to have been a woman forced to provide for herself by the unfortunate circumstances of history from removal to allotment. She was born prior to the Trail of Tears, and she arrived in Indian Territory without her parents. She married a man named Oakball and gave birth to two sons. Her husband died in 1873, the year after her younger son,

John, was born. She did not remarry. She was close to at least one other surviving sibling, a sister, whom she lived near and perhaps with in the 1890s. Her late husband's relatives may have provided some support, but Betsy Oakball likely did much of the raising of her two boys, and she most likely provided for them by farming and gathering. Perhaps she did so alongside her sister. Accustomed to seeing elders, especially women, as drains on family resources, however, the Dawes Commission did not consider the possibility that the improvements belonged to Betsy. For this reason, commissioners assigned the improvements to her son White, and they became his legal property. The commissioners gendered property, especially a working farm, as a male possession by attributing it to an able-bodied young father and husband when it likely testified to the hard life's work of his elderly mother.[80] Today, robbery of the old is criminalized and called elder abuse, but the allotment process normalized such theft and rationalized it again in the best interests of Cherokees.

Clerks often proved unable to allot families all of their improvements because of the inadequacies inherent to the grid system imposed on them. For this reason, many families lost portions of their cultivated fields. Among them were Tom and Nannie Wolfe; clerks allotted only a portion of their field to them.[81] Cherokees who selected their own allotments worked through these conflicting claims among themselves or filed with the Dawes Commission for resolution. For those assigned arbitrary allotments, clerks made rapid decisions concerning the distribution of resources, and noncompliant residents did not have the opportunity to challenge them. Overall, resistant families experienced land loss along a spectrum: few families retained all of their improved land, and few families lost everything. Most families in Chewey retained much but not all of their improved land. For example, the family of Abe and Margaret Sixkiller retained the majority of their farm with the exception of a portion of a cultivated field. So did Nelson and Jennie Crittenden and Susie and White Oakball. Of course, this means that Cherokees often received a portion of someone else's property; clerks assigned a portion of a neighboring farm to Samuel Chuwee, although the Dawes Commission knew he lived with his own family. The commissioners reasoned that because they had assigned the neighbors, who had improved multiple homesteads, all of their acres already, they could allot this portion of the farm to Chuwee even though he appears to be unrelated to them.[82]

Unlike Cherokee families who claimed their own allotments, the Dawes Commission tended to allot homesteads to the youngest children and rarely distributed resources among family members. This means that clerks usually excluded most family members from a share in their homes. For example, young Oo-dee-wee-ske Chewey received fields owned by her mother, Annie, while her parents and older sister received land nearby on the public domain.[83] Assigning allotments took on great complexity for large families because the majority of land had already been claimed. Clerks allotted Lewis and Betsy Bird's farm to their youngest daughter and assigned unimproved land to them and their other children. Although their allotments were in the vicinity of Luna Branch, the stream upon which their house was located, their tracts did not completely adjoin. The Birds' experience proved common.[84]

Working around a patchwork of claimed land, clerks often could not allot adjoining plots to members of resistant families, and two or more separate pieces of land typically made up the allotment of those assigned land. The variation in outcomes is dramatic. Members of several resistant families received land near each other, and yet the same clerks assigned other families allotments on opposite sides of the township. This seems random and not motivated by any other factor than what land remained available. For example, improvements belonging to Jim and Mary Hogshooter and his parents were assigned to Jim and Mary's youngest daughter. The rest of the family received land in the public domain, and clerks scattered their allotments across the township. Jim received land near his wife, Mary, but the holdings of their children peppered the map.[85] In the case of Noah Sand and his sons, clerks allotted the farm buildings to son John and a small bit of the family's field to father Noah. Instead of allotting the remainder of their field to son Will, clerks assigned to him land in the public domain on the opposite side of the township from his kin. Clerks gave the majority of the Sands' field to Dan Downing, a maternal nephew who lived with the men, and the remainder of it to other neighboring allottees. Still, while many resisters received disconnected allotments removed from that of their kin, most received land within the township.[86]

The evidence concerning the allotment of Chewey suggests that accusations of immediate, widespread dislocation obscure other stories about allotment that perhaps proved just as devastating to Cherokee communities in the long term, such as gender bias and ageism. Evidence of corruption in the initial distribution of land is not hard to find. For example, Tom Suake identified as a Nighthawk, and the Dawes Commission arbitrarily allotted land in Chewey to his family. His ex-wife Nancy later appeared before the commissioners in December 1905. She sought to return her allotment of land in the public domain, and denying that she was affiliated with the resisters, she applied for land in the Cooweescoowee District, a cattle ranching region that was being developed for its mineral wealth. She handed the commissioners a premade plat map. Commissioners were familiar with these maps, often filled out by grafters and given to Indians paid to claim an allotment that they would never use and that would benefit the grafter. The commissioners denied her request and perhaps prevented her swindling.[87]

On the other hand, clerks assigned Nannie Palone and her two young sons land in the oil districts of the northern townships. Palone, the daughter of Betsy Suake, was then unmarried and likely appeared vulnerable to outsiders. The system established by the Dawes Commission included few protections for people like Palone and her sons, and a corrupt clerk could have allotted them oil land knowing they were unlikely ever to receive income from it or even know that they were entitled to it. There is no evidence that Palone benefited from any such revenue before her death in August 1906. The grafters should not have underestimated Betsy, however, because the boys' grandmother ensured that they did benefit from it, and she went to court on their behalf, a process discussed in the next chapter.[88]

While their resistance to the policy should not be equated with an indifference to their homesteads, many Nighthawks did not claim their allotments, even after the Dawes Commission mailed allotment certificates to them. These slips of paper listed their homestead and surplus land. Particularly when assigned land other than their homestead, a common circumstance for many teens and young adults whose younger siblings received the family farm, Nighthawks made no attempt to relocate to them or improve them. Some refused even to accept the certificate. Eufala Harjo explained that when the postmaster, likely the owner of the local general store, handed him an envelope containing his certificate as he did his shopping, he immediately tried to return it. When the postmaster refused to take it back, Eufala Harjo sent it to the head of the Union Agency, the division of the Indian Service in Indian Territory whose presence confirmed the sovereignty of the Cherokee Nation and notably not the Dawes Commission that was trying to destroy it. He described others doing the same. The Nighthawks eventually collected and returned over 1,600 slips to the Dawes Commission. Kent Carter observes that some bore the notation, "I don't want this. If I want it I will come get it." The Dawes

Commission printed the certificates in English, but resisters often boldly wrote their replies in Cherokee.[89]

Settled into communities distant from predominantly non-Indian boomtowns, Nighthawks minimized their exposure to the hostility increasingly targeted at Indian people, particularly those perceived to be obstructing the movement for joint statehood with Oklahoma Territory popular among non-Indians. Reflecting tensions characteristic of such rapid and dramatic transitions and the perpetuation of stereotypes about violent Indians following the end of the Indian wars on the Plains, these non-Indian newcomers, including the staff of the Dawes Commission, fretfully anticipated an Indian rebellion. Even though Cherokee traditionalists simply withdrew, local whites failed to appreciate the difference between them and rebels among other Native peoples, such as Chitto Harjo and his followers among the neighboring Creeks, and considered their reclusiveness to be suspect.

In retrospect, Redbird Smith's teachings on nonviolence and passive resistance bear striking similarities to those championed by other leaders of twentieth-century movements for social justice, particularly Mahatma Gandhi and Martin Luther King Jr., but Smith preached his particular Cherokee version of this philosophy decades before such ideas became familiar and admirable to Americans. Instead, non-Indians who relocated into the Cherokee Nation disparaged the Nighthawks as threatening the social order, their property, and even their lives. This anti-Indian sentiment nearly resulted in the lynching of Redbird Smith. In 1904, U.S. marshals arrested Smith and jailed him in Vian. While they realized that he had committed no crime, they hoped Smith would reveal information leading to the arrest of several Cherokee men, the sons of another Keetoowah leader whom marshals suspected of murder. As the lawmen questioned Smith, a mob gathered outside and called for his release into their hands. The marshals quickly spirited Smith out the back door. In doing so, they probably saved his life. Had he been lynched that day, his martyrdom would have made it harder for history to forget the scorn directed at resisters to allotment. The values that seem admirable and poetic to modern readers came at an enormous cost and great risk to those who lived by them during the allotment era in the Cherokee Nation.[90]

THOSE WHO HAD accepted allotment had not fully conceded the loss of their sovereignty. In particular, Cherokee statesmen spearheaded a movement for separate statehood. The Curtis Act prepared the way for the incorporation of Indian Territory as a state, and although many lobbied for the admission of Oklahoma Territory combined with Indian Territory as one state, Indian leaders from the Five Tribes dreamed of an alternative, the state of Sequoyah. Angie Debo calls the Sequoyah initiative "a most impressive demonstration of the political vitality that still existed in the Indian citizenship."[91] The convention to draft a constitution for the state met in the late summer and early fall of 1905. Led by the same statesmen among the Five Tribes who had negotiated deals with the Dawes Commission, the movement had the support of many of the traditional Indians who still opposed allotment. They all appreciated that separate statehood offered a chance to retain self-government. On November 7, 1905, the citizens of Indian Territory ratified the constitution drafted at the Sequoyah convention and forwarded their proposal to Congress. Congressmen promptly tabled the plan without considering it.[92]

Concurring with Republican congressmen who lamented the increasing power of Democrats in the regions, President Theodore Roosevelt believed it politically expedient to admit the two territories as one state, and a constitutional convention was held at Guthrie during November 1906.[93] One year later, on November 16, 1907, Oklahoma officially attained statehood. Dignitaries representing Oklahoma Territory and Indian Territory paraded through downtown Guthrie to the steps of the Carnegie Library. The leaders of the Five Tribes rode in carriages, but most Indian people present walked and watched from the crowd. Before Governor-elect Charles N. Haskell read a presidential proclamation uniting the two territories into the state of Oklahoma, those gathered witnessed a symbolic union of another sort, the marriage of Mr. Oklahoma to Miss Indian Territory. C. J. Jones, a prominent businessman from Oklahoma City, portrayed the groom, and Mrs. Leo Bennett, a Cherokee woman from Muskogee, played the bride. The two made a striking couple. He was tall, angular, and fair while the petite brunette wore a fashionable lavender gown and styled her hair in a modern upsweep. Their vows were just as notable: the groom described himself as industrious and capable while she characterized herself as an "orphan" and "the last descendant of the proudest race that ever trod foot on American soil." She lamented that she brought to the marriage only a dowry "in fertile fields, and productive mines." In the absence of her supposedly extinct Indian family, he was destined to care for her.[94]

The gendered implications of this union were not lost on those gathered, and they are an easy target for modern scholars. The characterization of Indian Territory as a passive, vulnerable, and fecund virgin awaiting impregnation by her supposedly superior Anglo-Saxon mate is almost too obvious for feminist and postcolonial deconstruction, but the historical narrative implied by this ceremony should not go unnoted. The elegance of the couple and presumed willingness of the bride served to sanitize the arranged marriage of these two territories of its violence. Elegantly adorned and shown off before so many witnesses, she could not be the victim of political and economic gang rape. Or could she? Fanfare and speeches cloaked the unthinkable in normalcy. The horror of this ceremony makes sense only when the context of the routine acceptance of white supremacy and the supposed inevitability of Indian extinction is remembered.

The inherent brutality of this union was painful for many Cherokees, and they could not bear witness. Notably, this ceremony was not discussed in any of the oral histories I read while researching this book. Cherokees from Goingsnake District did not feel this event worth attending or, if they did go, remembering. Edward Everett Dale, the pioneer historian of Oklahoma, did recount a comparable story about another intermarried couple, a real Cherokee woman and her white husband. She chose not to accompany him to these festivities, but when he returned home and told her what he had seen, the reality of statehood overwhelmed her. Thirty years later, she told Dale, "It broke my heart. I went to bed and cried all night long. It seemed more than I could bear that the Cherokee Nation, my country and my people's country, was no more."[95] Unlike the fictitious Miss Indian Territory, this Indian woman was not an orphan or a dependent. She had been a citizen of a self-sufficient tribal republic based on the extended families that were the sociopolitical and economic foundation of Cherokee society, and she was grieving for what had been lost. Did she also worry for what would come? On paper, the Cherokee Nation was no more, and in homes throughout northeastern Oklahoma, Cherokee families faced adaptation to the new order of things.

CHAPTER SEVEN

Adapting

In 1910, Stan and Tinna Gibson bought forty acres of land from Dennis and Bertha Sixkiller for $4.85. Over the next few years, the Gibsons built a three-room house and a barn, dug a well, tilled fields, and put up a fence. In short, they made a home. In 1915, a field clerk working out of the office for the superintendent for the Five Civilized Tribes, D. H. Shannon, learned of this transaction. Legally, the Gibsons' title was worthless. Dennis Sixkiller was restricted and unable to sell his land without authorization. The field clerk nonetheless worried that the Sixkillers were taking advantage of the Gibsons because, he noted, Sixkiller was "three-quarter-blood" and his wife, the daughter of Oscar and Annie Cannon, was "one-thirty-second blood." The clerk rationalized that because Gibson and his wife, the daughter of Steve and Nannie Dog, were categorized as full bloods, they presumably had "no business ability whatsoever." In short, Shannon distrusted Dennis Sixkiller, about whom he wrote, "Does not appear to be to overly anxious to vest good title in Stan Gibson," whom he pitied as a dupe. Shannon also was frustrated that Stan Gibson sought to avoid conflict with his neighbors and was content to receive either a valid title or his money back. If they lost this farm, he said, they would move to and improve his wife's allotment. Shannon would not have that, and by 1916, he arranged for the removal of restrictions against Sixkiller's selling this forty acres and the conveyance of legal title to Stan Gibson.[1]

Allotment complicated things in Cherokee communities, in part because it empowered manipulative and uninformed outsiders to exercise authority over indigenous peoples' lives. Angie Debo considered the staff

Tinna Dog, daughter of Steve and Nannie Dog. Photo courtesy of Gail Crittenden.

of the superintendency to be political appointees who owed their positions to the spoils system rather than to any experience with or concern
for Indian allottees.[2] Simply put, men like Shannon may have understood
the policies they were enforcing through the bureaucracy to which they
belonged, but they knew nothing of the history and culture of the indigenous people among whom they worked. If he had taken off the blinders of blood quantum, Shannon would have seen that there was nothing
inherently suspicious about the arrangement between the Sixkillers and
Gibsons. They had conducted the sale of Dennis's land as Cherokees had
sold improvements to each other for generations. That they needed to go
through the removal of restrictions process to convey legal title may not

Stan Watie Gibson and Tinna Dog Gibson with their daughter, Nannie. Photo courtesy of Jack D. Baker.

have been apparent to either couple. Or, it may have been, but they may have decided not to involve themselves in an evaluation of their own competency by federal officials.

It is possible that Shannon was correct when he accused Dennis and Bertha Sixkiller of being stereotypical manipulative mixed bloods preying on incompetent full bloods, but I doubt it. Why? Kinship. After his mother died, Stan Gibson was raised by his maternal uncle Abe Sixkiller in his household. Dennis was the son of Abe Sixkiller. In other words, Dennis and Stan were more like brothers than neighbors, and Stan was making his home on his extended family's land. Dennis, Stan, and Tinna also were from families who opposed allotment, which likely contributed to their avoidance of the removal of restrictions process. Lacking an understanding of the kin ties relating these people or the sociopolitical

history of their community, Shannon saw stereotypes acting out their prescribed roles rather than human beings negotiating the normal affairs of their lives in customary ways.[3]

Ignorant of the gender norms among Cherokees, Shannon also ignored the wives in these households. That was a mistake. The field clerk made his assumption that the Gibsons had no business sense because they were full bloods. In addition, Stan, in particular, was characterized as an easy-going man of few words. I do not know whether or not Stan was savvy with money, but he did not have to be: Tinna was the shrewd manager of their family's finances. Shannon never explained how Stan got $4.85, which was a considerable amount of money at the time, but Tinna likely designated it for this purpose. She was known for saving up and investing their money in improvements. In addition to the acres they purchased from the

Sixkillers, Tinna managed their other property, 40 acres of her allotment and 118 acres of his allotment. She rented and improved her land, and she managed money received for an oil or natural gas lease on his.[4]

Other exchanges of letters written during the 1930s and after reveal how skillfully Tinna managed her property. She surprised and frustrated the men empowered to make decisions for her because she used the superintendency to serve her family's needs and to demand accountability from patriarchy. Tinna eventually leased her improved allotment to Sam Welch, perhaps the son of Tom and Fannie Welch. When Sam made changes to the property that she did not approve of and did not maintain it to her standards, she involved the field clerk. She demanded that he examine the property and force Welch to restore the barn and some fencing to her satisfaction. Both men did as she wished.[5] Beginning in 1943, Tinna began another letter-writing campaign. She resented the slow pace at which she received checks for Stan's royalty money, and she questioned the amounts that she was receiving. She could do math, and the figures did not add up. When she was not able to find redress through the superintendent, she involved her congressman. This greatly annoyed Indian Service staff, who suggested that she prepare a budget and stop asking for a handout. Tinna was not intimidated, however. After all, this was *her* money she was asking for. In 1949, District Agent A. A. Exendine wrote, "In handling her affairs, Tina [sic] compares favorably with a lot of the men in this district." She had to. By then a widow and grandmother, she was supporting several relatives, including her younger brother, who had been injured in World War II, and seven grandchildren.[6]

In the last series of letters in her case file, Tinna demanded her money because she wanted to buy five dairy cows from neighbor William Turtle. She planned to start two of her teenage granddaughters in business selling cream to bring additional income into their household. Perhaps aware of her reputation among the staff at the superintendency, she promised that if she could make this purchase, she would "appreciate it and quit bothering you." Her written record ends with that letter from August 1949. No field clerk noted whether or not she got her dairy cows, but I believe that she did. When she died in 1958, Tinna's remaining personal property included a two-year-old electric cream separator, which she left to her grandchildren through her deceased daughter Nannie, whom she had named after her own mother.[7]

Cherokee experiences of allotment did not end with the division of their land. The policy created new bureaucracies that allottees had to negotiate in order to use resources and provide for families. These systems were exploitative. In her account of the administration of Indian estates, Angie Debo describes how the mechanics of these federal, state, and local organizations worked to rob Indians, but that does not explain how Indians reasoned their way through them. Other historians of allotment, particularly Katherine M. B. Osburn in her study of the Southern Utes, have shown how Indian people deciphered these new bureaucracies and used them to accomplish their personal and familial agendas. The documentation compiled in the administration of Indian estates suggests that Cherokees did the same. Federal censuses, removal of restrictions applications, Indian case files, and probate files demonstrate that allottees acted as informed agents who responded to restrictions, oversight, and the intervention of outsiders in positions of authority in ways that preserved their way of life rooted in extended families.

Restrictions, Oversight, and the Evolution of Allotment Policy

The administration of allotment policy became increasingly predatory over time in two significant ways: the removal of restrictions and the transfer of oversight responsibilities. First, the Cherokee Agreement of 1902 included protections against alienation. Cherokee leaders had negotiated with the Dawes Commission to obtain the prohibition against the sale of homesteads and their exclusion from taxation for twenty-one years. Surplus land was inalienable for five years.[8] Before the Dawes Commission had finished allotting the Cherokees, however, boosters began clamoring for the immediate removal of restrictions against the leasing and sale of allotted land in order to encourage economic development. They began in 1904 by winning the lifting of restrictions against intermarried whites and freedpersons selling surplus land. Congress also empowered the secretary of the interior to remove restrictions on adult Indians seeking to sell their surplus on a case-by-case basis.[9] The Five Tribes Bill of 1906 enabled the sale of all inherited land but also forbade full bloods from selling their allotments for twenty-five years. In an effort to protect these Indian landowners, whom they considered to be the most vulnerable to graft, Congress also set guidelines for the administration of wills, inheritances, and leases.[10]

The commitment of Congress to protection was brief. The Restrictions Bill of 1908 was a victory for those who argued against restrictions. They successfully lobbied Congress to permit intermarried whites, freedpersons, and Indian adults and minors registered as having less than one-half Indian blood to sell all their remaining land, including homesteads. They also allowed Indians enrolled as having more than one-half but less than three-quarters Indian blood to sell their surplus land. Protections remained against those in this group selling their homesteads. Likewise, it prevented those categorized as having three-fourths or more Indian blood from selling any of their allotments, but the legislation permitted these Indians or their guardians to lease their surplus land.[11] In 1919, the commissioner of Indian Affairs removed remaining restrictions on all Indians classified as having one-half or less Indian blood. Only those categorized as full bloods remained fully restricted on their land.[12]

Cherokees held varying opinions about the usefulness of these protections. Some detested the heavy hand of federal intervention, and they believed that restrictions encouraged discrimination against Indian people and hindered families in managing their affairs. For these reasons, they wanted all restrictions lifted.[13] Most Cherokees, however, sought the extension of some restrictions on homesteads even while they advocating the limited removal of restrictions on surplus land so that they could rent or sell unused acres.[14] Even Cherokees who sought the continuation of restrictions wanted to minimize federal intervention in their affairs. Non-Indian reformers proposed plans that lifted protections according to the blood quantum or competence of Indian landowners. Cherokee leaders, especially those affiliated with the Keetoowah Society, warned that no such generic policy could meet their needs because their population did not conform to outsiders' stereotypes of Indian ability. Instead, they thought that the removal of restrictions should be at the discretion of the individual landowner. Throughout this debate, Cherokees and non-Indians spoke past each other. Outsiders ought to create an administrative system to determine competency, and they mostly debated what the appropriate percentage of Cherokee ancestry was at which to draw the line demarcating the restricted from the unrestricted. For Cherokees, however, this was not rightly a discussion about heritage but autonomy and the ability to make decisions without interference while remaining protected from exploitation.[15]

Second, throughout this period, Congress incrementally decreased the power of the Dawes Commission and the Office of Indian Affairs and, in response to the vigorous lobby of Oklahoma congressmen, shifted authority over Indian allottees to state and local authorities. This process began in 1905, before the work of allotting the Five Tribes had been completed, when Congress reduced the Dawes Commission to one commissioner to the Five Civilized Tribes.[16] The Union Agency, created by the Curtis Act, oversaw relations with the largely defunct tribal governments and monitored the affairs of individual allottees. In 1907, after the establishment of Oklahoma, the federal government began to transfer management of Indian estates in Oklahoma away from these federal officials, accountable to oversight through the Department of the Interior. Despite concerns raised about the obvious potential conflicts of interest, influential leaders in Indian affairs in Congress and Oklahoma believed that citizens of that state should be trusted to administer the allottees within their borders. They argued that local leaders would tend to their needs with greater concern, efficiency, and economy than the federal government could. Moreover, they believed that they were entitled to some means to make money off of Indian land that was not taxable.

Disillusioned with the long, expensive process of enrolling and allotting the Five Tribes, congressmen were happy to shift the administration of this policy to someone else, particularly Oklahomans eager to develop valuable Indian property. Although the superintendent of the Union Agency in Muskogee retained jurisdiction over Cherokees in some matters, including the removal of restrictions, local authorities, particularly lawyers and judges, assumed control over the day-to-day management of estates, including probates. This trend was exacerbated in 1914 when Oklahoma's congressional delegation successfully championed legislation combining the offices of the commissioner to the Five Civilized Tribes and the Union Agency into the superintendent for the Five Civilized Tribes located in Muskogee. They also reduced the staff. As a result, Stilwell (county seat of Adair County), Muskogee, and Washington, D.C., became as important to Cherokees in Adair County as Tahlequah, the former capital of the now defunct Cherokee Nation, had once been.[17]

Many Cherokees were unsure of how to manage their estates within this ever-changing new system. Familiar with a different system of resource management and self-governance, they were not informed about the policies of the Dawes Commission and the Office of Indian Affairs or the laws of Oklahoma. Ironically, allotment actually had made it more difficult for many Cherokees to learn about them. Keetoowah Society leader Levi Gritts pointed out that in 1906, when the federal government suspended publication of the bilingual *Cherokee Advocate*, which was the official newspaper of the Cherokee government, many Cherokees, particularly those who read only Cherokee, were cut off from their primary source of information about current affairs. Although there were other newspapers in Indian Territory and Oklahoma, none filled the same civic roll that the *Advocate* had, nor did they publish in the Cherokee language. Cherokee communities thus lost the most efficient print means to familiarize themselves with new laws and civic institutions.[18]

In the state of Oklahoma, newspapers facilitated the sale of Cherokee land, and boomers and grafters used newspapers to serve their interests, which often were predatory. These local newspapers were the mouthpieces of the new towns being organized throughout the state, and because the fate of these newspapers and their owners was tied to the growth of the region, they promoted economic development and encouraged the quick transition of restricted Indian land to taxable status. Newspaper owners and editors generally were hostile to protections against the alienation of Indian land. These papers regularly included notices of public auctions of Indian land and ran ads encouraging buyers by offering payment plans and reduced interest rates.[19] As restrictions against more and more Indians selling their land were lifted, local newspapers also published lists of delinquent taxpayers whose lands would be sold to pay their tax debt.[20] They also notified the public of pending probates.[21] In short, the owners and editors of these new periodicals did not necessarily share common interests with most Cherokee readers. For example, David Marrs, a non-Indian who lived in Vinita, owned and edited the *Chieftain*. He also had himself appointed to be the guardian of Nannie Palone's sons, Andrew Palone and William Proctor, until a judge removed him for mismanaging the boys' estates. Such proactive judicial action was exceedingly rare.[22]

Linguistic and cultural barriers further separated Cherokees from the Oklahoma government. Cherokees recognized that the overlap between newly elected officials and grafters made negotiating this system treacherous, particularly for those who did not speak or read English fluently. Unable to trust or understand local and state officials, they lacked confidence in their ability to deal with them fairly.[23] J. Henry Dick, a Cherokee real estate developer who favored the removal of restrictions, commented that many traditional Cherokees opposed the liberalization of protections against alienation because they were certain that they would lose their land and "be a charge on the people." Cherokees feared dependency, particularly upon those whom they considered to be outsiders and with whom they did not have a relationship based on reciprocity.[24]

Locally, Cherokees relied on their own mediators. For example, in Adair County, Dennis Wolf Bushyhead Jr., the son of the former principal chief, served in this role. A well-educated lawyer from a respected family, he represented average Cherokees in local courts, particularly when they had been victims of exploitation.[25] Like generations of other Cherokees before him, Bushyhead served to translate not just the language but also the culture and legal system of non-Indians for his Cherokee neighbors. This role was one that men in his family had filled for at least three generations. His paternal grandfather was the Reverend Jesse Bushyhead, who had worked with Evan Jones to translate the Bible into Cherokee. Both Reverend Jesse and Dennis Wolf Bushyhead Sr. had served as diplomats and ambassadors representing Cherokee interests to outsiders. In his own way in his time, so did Dennis Wolf Bushyhead Jr. The only difference was that by his time, those foreign institutions were located within Cherokee lands.

Federal Paternalism

Allotment introduced a new dynamic into the domestic economy of Cherokee families: federal paternalism. Shielded by their tribal government and living on communally owned land to which their nation held title, late-nineteenth-century Cherokees were not accustomed to the intensive scrutiny associated with wardship that had been commonly experienced by reservation-based Indians. The Cherokees' new relationship with the federal government complicated their ability to maintain their economic self-sufficiency, but, ironically, it also necessitated the perpetuation of the flexibility and decentralization inherent in the division of resources and labor common among Cherokee families. The precarious nature of the natural environment had once been the motivating factor behind this strategy that they easily adapted to the fickle workings of the federal government. The invasive nature of this federal oversight served more often to limit decision making and delay problem solving than to protect Cherokees' property and resources. In other words, it limited their ability to use resources effectively and as they chose.

The abuse rampant in the normal, day-to-day administration of Cherokee estates belied the notion that federal paternalism advanced the best interests of Indian people. It also challenges popular memory of the policy. Throughout the allotment era, sensational stories about graft and kidnappings and murders of allottees whose tracts contained oil and mineral wealth attracted public attention. Stories like that of Jackson Barnett, the Creek millionaire seduced and swindled, are engaging and heartbreaking, but such situations were relatively uncommon.[26] Because their land lacked such enticements, allottees in this study were not prey for fantastic scams. Rather, like most Cherokees, they parted with or were separated from their land through legal, although not necessarily ethical, means. In other words, the abuses most Cherokees experienced were routine parts of the management of their allotments. These patterns of behavior were not seen by Americans as problematic and, in fact, were justified as positive for Cherokee people.

Cherokees experienced the paternalism of the federal government in innumerable ways. Above all, those who were restricted had to navigate the bureaucracy of the superintendency for the Five Civilized Tribes in order to accomplish real estate and financial transactions. Steve Sand knew this cumbersome process all too well. He owned a good team each of horses and mules, but his wagon was falling apart. Sand had an equalization account, $283.75 that was owed him in lieu of having received a full allotment of land. In 1917, Sand decided to spend $40 of his money on repairs to his wagon, but the field clerk in Muskogee questioned Sand's judgment, decided he needed a new wagon, and authorized its purchase. Without Sand's consent, the field clerk paid $97.35 to Lawrence-Wyly Mercantile Company. This store, located in Tahlequah, was not where the Sands normally did their business. Joseph Lawrence, a merchant, banker, druggist, and insurance salesman, had moved to Tahlequah in 1889 from Texas to promote cotton cultivation, but there is no evidence that the Sands had any prior interaction with him. Instead, they usually shopped and traded in Proctor at McClendon's store and at the Proctor Mercantile Company. Apparently, the superintendency preferred spending money with Lawrence, however. Ironically, a policy originally intended to empower Cherokee men in the model of Anglo-American heads-of-households was implemented in such a way that it undermined their authority over even the most minute matters.[27]

This paternalistic oversight also proved to be a cumbersome, time-consuming process, and therefore families could not realistically rely on any one member's resources for survival. This aspect of the implementation of allotment policy thus undermined the consolidation of resources under adult males that allotment was intended to promote. In 1910, Charley Turtle, who farmed 25 acres and owned a team of horses, a cow, and hogs, sought to sell 170 acres of his surplus in order to improve his homestead. The district agent granted his application and specified that his money should be disbursed to him as follows: $300 for a house, $75 for fencing, $50 for assistance clearing his land, and $50 in cash. Over a year later, Turtle contacted the Union Agency, which had yet to release his funds. He had hired help to clear land and had charged groceries, and he had debts to pay. Finally, they approved his expenditures and released his money. Presumably, Charley had assumed these debts based on the kinship-based credit that already existed within the community. In other words, if it were not for the extension of supplies and labor rooted in interrelationship, Charley Turtle could not have improved his land. Only in a community in which nonaggression was valued more than profit could someone withhold payment from his creditors for over a year.[28]

Waiting, in fact, can be seen as an abuse inherent in the oversight system if the outcomes of the denial of timely access to resources are considered. Even though the competency system based on blood quantum was designed to expedite decisions, Cherokees experienced the bureaucracy of the Indian Service as tortuously slow and regularly asserted themselves to insist that clerks move faster to address their concerns and handle their affairs. In October 1949, Jesse Bird wrote demanding to know what would be done about Oscar Wiley, who was squatting on Bird's allotment and not paying rent. Bird was very ill and confined to bed. He may have wanted rent money from Wiley to help pay for his medical expenses, or Bird may have wanted the interloper off his land but was unable to confront the man himself. Finally, in October 1950, clerks moved to resolve the matter for him, or more accurately, for his heirs. Bird had already died.[29] Likewise, in the fall of 1924, Lucy Chewey sought to sell part of her allotment. She wanted money to make improvements to her remaining land, but she also needed cash for medical expenses. In the spring of 1926, she received her money and promptly visited a gynecologist. Had she been waiting all those months for the means to tend to her personal health? In denying Cherokees' timely access to their resources, bureaucrats withheld more than money. They robbed them of resolution, quality of life, and in situations like these where cash was needed for medical treatment, perhaps even their lives.[30]

Moreover, in order to utilize their resources, Cherokees contended with the condescension of Indian Service personnel. These paternalistic attacks could be personal. An undated memo in Tom Suake's removal of restrictions file captures this attitude and behavior. A clerk noted that

Tom originally had been enrolled by the Dawes Commission as "Thomas Snake." That was incorrect. Commissioners indeed had debated what Tom's proper surname was, and although it appeared as "Snake" in some of their records, they asked informants and corrected it to "Suake," the spelling used by his extended family, on the final roll. The field clerk handling the transfer of Tom's surplus to his stepson noted with frustration that Tom "persisted as signing his name as Thomas Swake." The clerk concluded the memo by clarifying that "in the future this office will use his roll name—Thomas Snake." A handwritten memo scrawled across the bottom reads, "Watch name closely."[31] A bureaucratic system that did not acknowledge a person's ability to identify himself properly and as he chose could not possibly treat him with fairness, dignity, and equality.

And it did not. Language hints at the racism that fueled this paternalism. In 1921, Sam Chewey was thirty-four years old and a veteran who had just returned home from a tour of duty in Europe with the American Expeditionary Force. Chewey wanted to learn a trade and enrolled in the Kansas City Auto and Tractor School in Kansas City, Missouri. The cashier from the superintendent's office wrote the superintendent of that school, sending him $60 "to be held in trust by you and paid out for the needs of this *boy* as they arise" (emphasis mine). Sam Chewey was no boy, but this word commonly used by whites to refer to African American men signified his inferiority from the perspective of the cashier. The cashier then added that he would send the superintendent of the school additional money if requested, if Chewey "shows a disposition to work and apply himself." The potential for abuse is obvious, and no further documentation of the expenditures from Chewey's account is included in his file.[32]

Some Cherokees understood how to use paternalism to their advantage, however, and they adapted to negotiate this system. Oce and Jim Hogshooter provide excellent examples. The brothers were educated men. Both had attended local Cherokee day schools, and Oce had spent two years at the Cherokee Male Seminary. With their wives, Jim and Oce built the farm on which the joint family lived. Oce and his wife farmed eighteen acres, and Jim and his wife worked twenty-six acres of fields. The Dawes Commission allotted the farm to Jim's youngest daughter. As Nighthawks, both men had refused to select land and had been allotted unimproved, unusable land on the public domain. In February 1921, the brothers together sought the removal of restrictions in order to sell their unused allotted acres. Between 1916 and 1928, the Indian Office funded a competency board comprising one or two Indian Service employees and a local field clerk who visited homes to give restricted Indians competency tests.[33] The brothers claimed that they sought to sell their allotments in order to purchase a small farm so that they could provide for their families, but in the same application, they admit to already having built their current farm, which was their means of support. Jim, the competency board members noted, "has lived there [on this farm] the past twenty-six years and he says he made the place himself." The board described their house as a "very comfortable farm home." Did these two men, then in their fifties, truly seek to start over economically, or did they appeal to the competency commission's expectations of gender-appropriate behavior in order to get the restrictions removed? The competency board granted their requests, and yet there is no evidence that they purchased other land or moved away from their existing farm.[34] Other Cherokee men's appeals echo the same theme. By claiming to sell some acres in order to buy better ones, they demonstrated a business savvy non-Indian men were sure to recognize and approve. Once their restrictions were removed, however, they used their money in other ways as they saw fit.[35]

Sam Kirk's story exemplifies how Cherokee men learned how to perform to both gendered and racial ideals for competency boards. Kirk was twenty-three when he first requested the removal of restrictions against him selling his allotment and surplus. He was enrolled as one-eighth Cherokee. Sam's father, William Kirk, had selected land for him, and as Sam explained it, "My land is all scattered around, and I want to get it together." Kirk's allotment was near Collinsville, which is northeast of Tulsa and about a hundred miles away from where the Kirks lived. There was a farm, barn, and fields on it, but he did not make those improvements, and he did not want to live there. His surplus was located near Westville, and he had leased part of it to Austin Oil and Gas Company. He did not want to manage this property, either. In fact, he had already lined up a buyer. Kirk wanted to sell this land to purchase a farm near that of his parents. Sam explained that he had some business experience managing money, and he owned some livestock and farm tools. He admitted, however, that he could not read or write because he had suffered from eye problems throughout his childhood. His petition was denied. One year later, Sam returned to try again. This time, he claimed that he was one-sixteenth Cherokee and able to read and write. He diminished the value of the improvements on his land, and he made no mention of an oil and gas lease. Likewise, he claimed that he had no buyers. His application was approved because the competency board, which did not consult its own records, believed that he had a "fair education" and was a "hard-working young man" who owned significant personal property. Sam owned less livestock than he had a year earlier, but he had more skill in presenting himself as the kind of young man whom competency board members would validate.[36]

Paternalism created particular challenges for Cherokee parents. The general acceptance of this system of correlating blood quantum and competence normalized an environment in which non-Indians were considered better able to determine what was in the best interests of Cherokee children than their parents were. The Department of the Interior supported the replacement of parents whom judicial officials deemed unfit to manage their children's wealth with court-appointed guardians. Typically, non-Indian Oklahomans obtained appointments as the guardians of Indian children who owned valuable land or mineral wealth. These guardians made leases, facilitated the development of mineral deposits and timber stands, and collected income, which the Department of the Interior deposited in interest-bearing accounts—in theory. Although guardians were required to report to local courts annually on the status of their wards' estates, this requirement provided little protection against fraud. Tribal leaders complained of rampant mismanagement. Guardians commonly squandered the wealth of Indians minors by stealing from their wards to develop their personal fortunes, and guardians furthered their political careers by treating their wards as part of a spoils system. In spite of widespread opposition among Indians, Congress in 1908 further curtailed federal authority and charged Oklahoma's probate courts with the sole duty of appointing guardians and approving, and monitoring, their decisions. Incompetent and corrupt guardians turned this trust into a thriving industry.[37]

The two young sons of Nannie Suake were swindled by their court-appointed guardian. In 1903, the court appointed David M. Marrs to manage the estates of William Proctor and Andrew Palone. Although no specific reason was given for denying Nannie guardianship, the forms labeled the boys as "illegitimate," and county officials likely were imposing their gendered expectations of appropriate female behavior on her: they considered the divorced and unwed mother to be an unfit parent. Nannie died in 1906, and her mother, Betsy, continued raising the boys, who had always lived in her household. Marrs, on the other hand, paid little attention to their welfare before or after Nannie died. No records suggest that Marrs ever met his charges. A businessman and boomer from Vinita, he selected allotments for the boys in Craig County, where he was their legal guardian. In Adair County, where the boys lived, their grandmother had gone to court to be established as their legal guardian. She had no control over their allotments, however. In his annual reports, Marrs claimed nearly half of the income from rents for his compensation, legal fees, and payments to his associates. He supposedly invested the remainder in the improvement of their allotments, but he did not specify the nature of these improvements, nor did he prove that these upgrades actually had been accomplished. Marrs was robbing the boys with the blessing of the court, and for six years judges approved his reports and did not intervene on the boys' behalf.

In 1913, Betsy did. She returned to court, along with her grandsons, then teenagers, and asked for Marrs's dismissal. The court granted her request, which Marrs did not contest, and appointed Cherokee Dennis Wolf Bushyhead Jr. as their new guardian. Bushyhead initiated a claim against Marrs for the mismanagement of their estates, but the court did not order the boomer to repay any monies. Bushyhead did right by the boys. By the time they reached their maturity, he nearly had doubled their remaining estate by collecting rent, investing the money, and letting it generate interest. Even the judge was impressed by his final disclosure.[38] Unfortunately, Betsy was familiar with abusive guardians and learned her assertiveness the hard way. In 1911, J. E. Smith, the court-appointed guardian of Betsy's grandchildren through daughter Linnie, had reported his expenses since 1908 to the Adair county court. Smith had spent the overwhelming majority on multiple appraisals of the land, paid to his associates, and the rest on legal fees, likely pocketed by himself. He spent not one documentable cent on the children.[39]

In *And Still the Waters Run*, Angie Debo concludes that many guardians, like Marrs and Smith, were despoilers rather than defenders of Indian interests. Guardians avoided providing an accounting of their charges' assets because many county judges benefited financially and politically from the lax guardianship system. Those who sought to protect wards faced intense opposition. In December 1913, Judge John A. Goodall of Adair County threatened to charge any guardian who did not file documentation with the court with contempt, but he softened his declaration by adding that "it is the purpose of the court to assist guardians in rendering their accounts in cases where there has been no intentional violation of the law." With such lenience tolerated, prosecutions for fraud were unthinkable and, therefore, unknown.[40] In 1914, pressure from Commissioner of Indian Affairs Cato Sells pushed the supreme court of Oklahoma to adopt guidelines for such cases, but county judges pushed back and prompted the Oklahoma legislature to abrogate these rules. Instead, state lawmakers instructed local courts to establish their own standards for the administration of Indian estates. In other words, the financial well-being of many Cherokee families was at the mercy of local officials, whose attentiveness and ethics varied widely and competed with their own financial and political interests.[41] Debo notes, however, that Adair County officials proved themselves less predatory than most.[42] This may reflect the high percentage of Cherokees among Adair County's population, including some who participated in local governance. Or, it may reflect the generally lesser value of estates in Adair County than in other counties that included significant oil, gas, and mineral resources.

While enabling an exploitative guardian system, the Indian Service hindered parents' administration of their children's property. In 1903, a federal court ruled that parents could not lease their children's property without a court order, and so the Department of the Interior began requiring Indian parents to obtain the approval of the federal court in order to administer their children's estates. Mack Welch, John Kelley, and William Kirk applied to the court for this privilege. Unlike court-appointed guardians, these Cherokee fathers had to post bond. The Federal Union Insurance Company in Indiana posted Mack Welch's $1,150 security, as it had done when he served as the executor of his late wife's estate. Welch then executed leases on his children's land, and eventually he sold some of it to improve the remaining sections. Welch's case was typical of Cherokee parents in this study who sought to situate their sons and daughters on farms near them, particularly as they approached marriageable age, but who lacked the means to improve their allotments without selling some portion of it.[43]

Ironically, Indian Service personnel often implied that Cherokee parents' decisions were self-serving and challenged them. For example, probate attorney W. E. Foltz, who was stationed out of Muskogee and unfamiliar with the Crittendens, prevented Sam Crittenden from selling his adult son Henry's land because he questioned his intentions. Henry, then forty-two, was deaf and mute and not able to live independently, and his family had cared for him his whole life. In 1930, Sam sought to be appointed Henry's guardian in order to begin the process of selling some of his allotment to pay for his support. The attorney demanded to know why no officer of the court had sought to determine whether or not

Henry was incompetent or if Sam was exploiting his son, but no local official at Stilwell had to because they were familiar with the men and Henry's needs.[44] Cherokee parents generally proved themselves to be better guardians of their children's assets than outsiders. Each parent in this study who had himself or herself appointed by the court as his or her children's legal guardian for the purpose of administering their allotment managed the estate soundly enough that there was something to give them upon their maturity.[45]

The awkward and even humorous situations that resulted from court-mandated parental guardianships are notable. Although minors under the age of twenty-one were not able to manage their own property, children over fourteen years old were required to appear at the appointment of their guardian, even if that person was a parent. Although intended to prevent the exploitation of minors' resources, this process included no safeguards for Cherokee children. Myrtle Welch was asked if she approved her father's request to be her guardian in open court in front of him. There is no evidence of abuse or wrongdoing in their household, but if there had been, it is unlikely that Myrtle or another family member would have been comfortable sharing that information with the court or even seeking protection from it. The case of Wirt Cannon further demonstrates the bizarre outcomes of this policy. Wirt, although not yet twenty-one years old, had already married. His non-Indian mother, Annie, went to court to be appointed as his legal guardian in order to sell land that Wirt and his wife were not living on so that the newlyweds could improve his family's farm, where they were living. Annie had to demonstrate that she, her husband, Oscar (Wirt's father), and Wirt's wife all approved of the sale of her "minor" son's allotment, even though her son had assumed the role of an adult in his community by his decision to marry.[46]

The joint management of married couples' property also proved detrimental to families. This policy denied the commonality of divorce and was a naive attempt to pretend that Cherokee marriages were permanent as a way to encourage them to be so. Clerks routinely failed to determine whether marriages were intact or to ask husbands and wives to consent to transactions that affected each other's allotments. For example, Charlotte Turtle had funds in an equalization account, and her husband, Thomas Swimmer, had money in a royalty account. When either of the pair authorized expenditures, such as the construction of a house and the purchase of a horse and hay, field clerks communicated with the superintendent for the Five Civilized Tribes over which account to take the funds from rather than consulted with Charlotte and Thomas themselves. Clerks eventually realized (although how they did so is not clear) that the relationship had soured and the two were no longer living together as husband and wife. Staff members were in communication with Charlotte, but Thomas was reluctant to respond to their requests for information. Clerks took Charlotte's side, and by 1922, when she was crippled after having part of both of her feet amputated, a field clerk concluded that Thomas had neglected her such that the clerk authorized the speedy disbursement of his money that had been tied up in war savings stamps to pay for her care. While Charlotte's situation may be compelling, this use of her estranged spouse's resources was perhaps inappropriate.[47]

By the end of the 1920s, the Department of the Interior questioned the superintendent of the Five Civilized Tribes regarding whether this practice of joint management was prudent. In particular, the department queried as to whether a spouse who sold his or her allotment to improve the allotment of the other deserved a legal share in that homestead. Apparently, someone—although it is not clear who—realized that the continued management of allotments under current policy was incompatible with the persistence of serial monogamy, and the extent of disenfranchisement was notable enough to spark this inquiry. This became an issue when Jennie Oakball applied for the removal of restrictions. Jennie sought to sell some of her land to improve her family's farm, which was located on her husband John's allotment. The Department of the Interior thought that John should then sell Jennie a portion of his allotment. The superintendent's office said no, and staff members explained that for a decade, they had been using leases to protect spouses who sold their entire allotment. They warned that current policy necessitated the removal of restrictions in order for land to be sold, even to a spouse. Such a sale would render the land taxable. The superintendent's office emphasized that Jennie Oakball was not vulnerable to losing her allotment and being left homeless: "In cases of this kind family relations are such that disturbances or trouble is very improbable." Jennie and John had been married for thirty-one years when she filed the application in 1925. Was the staff of the superintendent's office referring to the durability of their bond or to the fact that the couple lived surrounded by her relatives? Either way, they felt the Oakballs' marriage was secure, removed her restrictions, and arranged for the sale of her land. There is no information regarding a subsequent lease in her file.[48]

Likewise, the Dawes Commission's tendency to allot homesteads to the children of resisters had dire implications for families whose relationships became strained. White and Susie Oakball almost lost their home in 1917 and again in 1920 because of their son Walter. Because the Oakballs had opposed allotment, clerks selected land for them. They did receive their farm, and part of it was allotted to Walter, then seven years old. In 1916, Walter and Joe Downing murdered Bill Hogshooter. Neighbors were horrified by the crime. The young men were drunk, and by the side of a creek, Walter and Joe beat Bill's brains out with a rock. In 1917, Walter sought the removal of restrictions against selling his allotment because he wanted to hire a lawyer. Staff in the office of the superintendent for the Five Civilized Tribes knew that the farm Walter was trying to sell was the one on which his parents had raised him. It was the farm that his grandmother Betsy probably had built. They found a lawyer, E. B. Arnold from Stilwell, who would represent Oakball for what clerks thought they could get for selling the acres that Walter owned but that his family did not live on. By pleading guilty, Arnold got the men a ten-year sentence in the state penitentiary. Observers considered the sentence to be light.[49]

By 1920 Oakball sought to appeal his sentence. He was working as a cook in the Oklahoma State Penitentiary. His neighbors and family members opposed his release, but he wanted to sell the rest of his acres to pay for another attorney to represent him. Walter's second application differed from his first. This time, he claimed that he was literate in English. He also claimed that White Oakball, his father, was his brother and had been renting the land from him for one year rather than farming it since before he was born. The field clerk recognized what Walter was trying to do and denied the application. The land remained in the family.[50]

Consistent with the precedent established by the Dawes Commission during enrollment, field clerks also imposed their definition of legal maturity upon Cherokees. When Charlotte Turtle died in 1923, she left three surviving children between the ages of seventeen and nine. A local law firm, Vance and Bliss, in Tahlequah, closely monitored her children's birthdays because they were leasing the property and sought to purchase it as the children reached twenty-one years of age, the legal age of maturity, at which point they could part with the land. Clerks in Muskogee addressed the issue when Sam, the oldest of Charlotte's children, wrote them. He sought to buy a saw and some hogs with his mother's money, which was distributed to him. His brother and sister should have received their money when they reached their age of legal maturity, but there is no record of the money having been dispersed.[51]

In addition to gender and age, race shaped the way Cherokees experienced allotment policy. The pervasive categorization of Cherokee people by blood quantum facilitated their management by the Indian Service, whose overworked clerks devised this means to ease their workload. The language of blood enabled them to systematically divide Indian people into categories based on their supposed ability. This bureaucratic form of racial profiling undermined the ability of Cherokee families to put their resources to their best use, however, because outsiders with no real knowledge about them as individuals placed limits on them by making decisions based on racist assumptions rather than on thoughtful evaluations of unique circumstances.[52] Both within the Indian Service and in the courtrooms of Adair County, clerks and judges made important decisions that dramatically affected Cherokees based on their impressions of the person standing before them. When making decisions, these officials weighed their standards, based on Anglo-American ideals, against their stereotypes, reducing the range of possibilities for Cherokee behavior to tropes.

Officials made clear distinctions between supposedly mixed-blood and full-blood Cherokees based on perceived behavior. They commonly dismissed full bloods as incompetent but noted when they judged them to be otherwise because exceptions to the rule validated assimilationist policies. Two separate clerks noted that Nighthawk Jim Hogshooter was "a man of good intelligence" and "of excellent character and habits" who "was somewhat above the average full-blood Indian in his community which is a backward one." Having explained their reasoning, they granted Hogshooter's petition to sell a portion of his allotment.[53] Ironically, these outside evaluators sometimes approved individual leaders of the resistance movement against allotment while stereotyping the group as a deficient whole. Impressed by Oce Hogshooter's confidence and command of language, clerks concluded that Oce, who was a secretary for the Nighthawks, had "evidently mingled a great deal with Progressive white people and he has a very good knowledge of ordinary business matters." Oce had traveled to Washington, D.C., in 1914 with Redbird Smith to meet with congressmen and officials in the Department of the Interior, but the men's experiences on the trip had been profoundly negative. Oce may not have considered those white politicians and bureaucrats that he interacted with to be exemplary people, but the two members of the competency board reviewing his application concluded that his intelligence could not reflect the fact that he was Cherokee. They noted that "his home is in a backward and rather unprogressive community." They were referring to Chewey.[54]

Civilization was performed and evident in one's behavior, and officials also held Cherokee women to a standard informed by the gendered expectations of Anglo-American society. They expected capable women to look a certain way. Clerks described Retta Sixkiller, enrolled as "three-fourths" Cherokee, as a "young woman of good appearance, dressed neatly, and is fairly bright and quite well informed . . . she has the ways of a white person, rather than of an Indian." They also granted her application.[55] They also expected women to limit their sexual behavior. In 1918, Lucy Chewey applied to sell ten acres of her restricted land. Chewey was nineteen, had little education, and had already parted with the land she inherited from her parents. She had "sold it to some white man. Don't know his name, nor don't know how much I got for it. Traded it out in a store at Westville, Okla." She admitted to having no experience managing money. There were many reasons for clerks to think Chewey would not use this money to build a house on her allotment, but they denied her request for a reason that had nothing to do with her business sense: "we are advised [she is] living with a man to whom she is not legally married." Although having the funds to build her own house, they denied her request. In 1924, after she married Watt Askwater, she sought to sell the same land to improve the farm they shared, and the field clerk approved her request to sell thirty acres. In 1926, when the couple received payment, they purchased furniture and an array of supplies including house paint, hog wire, barbed wire, a wagon, a harness, a jersey cow and a male calf, canning jars, bed ticking and lace, a sewing machine, a felt mattress, a steel bedstead and bedspring, pillows, a comforter, blankets, a stove and stovepipe, and a dinner pot. Cherokee women who presented themselves as respectable housewives had greater ability to use their resources as they chose, which was typically toward their household expenses.[56]

Suggesting the influence of scientific racism, particularly its correlation of appearance and ability, Indian Service personnel evaluated men's and women's bodies and looked for evidence of competency in Cherokees' physical characteristics. They routinely noted information about body type, such as height and weight, and grooming. In recommending the removal of restrictions on his land, a clerk noted that Lincoln Sixkiller was "five feet, ten inches in height, weighs 185 lbs., and in good health, an intelligent, clean-cut, manly and creditable type." In this, Lincoln apparently took after his father, Abe, who at seventy-one years old was "a good type of healthy, honest Indian . . . he is five feet ten inches in height, weights 150 lbs. . . . active and intelligent, and well preserved." These notations serve to remind us that the acceptance of biological determinism and the influence of physical anthropology had a real impact on Indian people. These theories took on force when believed by those evaluating Indian people who were seeking the removal of their restrictions. In the eyes of one who looked at human bodies for evidence of development, the petitioner became a specimen.[57]

Clerks also had favorable impressions of Cherokees whose behavior or appearance suggested presumed "whiteness" in ancestry or association. Enrolled as a full blood, Lawyer Suake was "stout, husky, dressed quite well, and makes a favorable impression as to capability." He must, the official concluded, "be of part white blood," despite enumeration to the contrary. Moreover, Lawyer had married a white woman, Gertrude, and his profession enabled him to work among both white and Cherokee people. He was a barber in Watts who served a mixed clientele. The field clerk concluded that "he has evidently mingled with white people a great deal." When Suake sought to sell his allotment, it was because he lived in a rented house in town, where he practiced his trade. He wanted to purchase a home and space for his own barbershop. His land was unimproved and brought him no income. Approving of his appearance and his business plan, clerks granted his petition.[58]

In matters of probate, sexuality was a topic of importance. When Jennie Crittenden died in November 1929, her children went to court. They sought to sell her surplus allotment, but the court sought to determine whether all her biological heirs were represented. Crittenden had been married briefly to Bill Foreman, with whom she had son Martin. For most of her adult life, however, she was married to Nelson Crittenden. The court could not determine whether she had been legally married to either man or whether she had been legally divorced from Foreman. Did they have a "ceremony marriage or just a Cherokee marriage?" Although it is not clear why officials needed to ascertain the legitimacy of her children, this issue mattered to them. After asking her children to discuss their mother's sexual history met with little success, they asked neighbor Wyly Beavers to confirm whether or not the couple had lived together throughout her adult life and at the time of Nelson's death. Likewise, the court sought to determine if they were "considered around the neighborhood to be husband and wife." Ultimately, the affirmation of that fact was good enough for the court.[59]

Indian Service personnel used the same racist criteria to decide against other Cherokees, and federal paternalism proved disempowering and frustrating. It severely limited the opportunities available to some Cherokee families. In 1920, Dora Wolfe, a daughter of Reese Mitchell and Nannie Dog, applied for the removal of restrictions against selling part of her allotment. Wolfe, then thirty-six, was married with seven children. She and her husband, John, did not live on their allotments because they considered them to be undesirable places for a home. In particular, they wanted to live close to the school that their children attended, and so they farmed and improved land that they rented. The Wolfes wanted to use the money from the sale of Dora's allotment to purchase and improve land there. Their current farm was estimated to be worth over $1,500, and the couple owned four horses, ten cows, twelve hogs, and a complete set of furniture. Dora also was literate in English. The clerk added that she was "a full-blood citizen of the Cherokee tribe and that she [was] married to a full-blood citizen." Although he gave no reason except for "knowing this allottee as I do," the clerk then decided against her. Her application was denied.[60] As an elder, Dora looked back at the arbitrary application of allotment policy with anger and confusion in equal measure.[61]

The hostility of some Cherokees to their new government was palpable and persistent. Those who had resisted the Dawes Commission's efforts did not set aside their opposition once allotment certificates had been issued. In 1910, three years after Oklahoma became a state, census takers fanned out through the hills of Adair County. Several Nighthawk families refused to share demographic information. In particular, Nighthawk parents would not identify their children to an unknown census taker. These same people had refused to share any information with the Dawes Commission, and less than a decade later, they identified themselves but not their children. Why? Were these parents afraid of the state's intentions toward their children? Did they fear the possibility of a court-imposed guardian intervening in their children's affairs? Did they fear that their children would be removed and placed in a boarding school?[62] All are likely possibilities.

John L. Johnson, an enumerator for Chance Township, where the community of Chewey was located, was an outsider. Several white men named John Johnson lived in Adair County at the time, and I was not able to determine which one he was. He also was unknown to the Cherokees upon whose doorsteps he ended up, and he seemed to know very little about them. When they would not answer his questions, he left spaces blank. In particular, he did not realize that many of them were bilingual but chose not to speak it to him. Rather, he listed them as speaking "Indian."[63] Sometimes when he lacked specific information, he wrote "refused" or "not known," but he seems to have filled in other blanks based on his stereotypes. For example, he listed those who refused to talk to him as uneducated, even though most were literate, because that was how non-Indians perceived resisters. Such misinformation thus became publicly available and used to determine policies.[64]

Generally, Cherokees got whiter over the years, at least according to census takers. Hattie Lewis, a granddaughter of Eliza Brown, was enrolled as one-eighth Cherokee by the Dawes Commission. In the 1910 census, she was identified as one-sixty-fourth Cherokee, and in 1920, she was listed as white. So were her uncles Marsh and Cap Brown and her cousin Lizzie Anderson.[65] This demographic erasure of the Cherokee population was common. It is impossible to know whether intermarried Cherokees were passing for white or, on the other hand, if census takers were identifying them as white. Either way, the whitewashing of the hills of Adair County was pronounced and rapid.[66] This trend held true even for some listed as full bloods by the Dawes Commission. In 1920, Betsy Suake and her grandsons are listed as white. The rest of her family, her children and grandchildren, are listed as Indians.[67]

A comparative look at the documents that did record blood quantum exemplifies how relative these designations remained. Take, for example, the Kelley family. John Kelley was enrolled by the Dawes Commission as one-quarter Cherokee, while his sisters, who shared both parents with him, were enrolled as one-eighth and one-sixteenth Cherokee. On the 1900 census, John is listed as having one-eighth Cherokee blood. By 1910, he is listed as one-sixteenth, while his sisters are one-quarter and one-eighth and his mother is listed as one-quarter. His wife Susan's pedigree varies, too. Enrolled by the Dawes Commission as half Cherokee, she is listed as one-sixteenth Cherokee in 1900 and 1910. Their children were enrolled as three-eighths Cherokee but were identified by the 1900 census taker as either one-sixteenth or one-quarter Cherokee. By 1910, they were also enrolled as one-sixteenth Cherokee. In 1920, the whole family was classified as white. If the outcomes of blood politics were not so horrible, the application of it would be laughable.[68]

There was an exception among the extended Kelley family: Tinsie. John and Susan's eldest daughter married Robert Haze, a white man. The couple briefly moved to Colorado before returning to Oklahoma to live with their three young children in Pottawatomie County. There, the census taker separated intermarried families like Tinsie and Robert's. Robert was listed among their white neighbors. Tinsie and the couple's three children were segregated to a separate Indian schedule and were listed on their own page. The census taker had taken the extra step to separate them from the other intermarried wives in the area, who were Pottawatomies. The census taker also listed her as illiterate, but she was able to read and write. Not only did the categorization of blood quantum differ across time, but it also varied across geographic space and in severity, depending on which federal employee was determining it.[69]

Adapting to Oklahoma and Adair County Jurisdiction

Cherokees' relationships with their new local and state governments varied, with some participating actively and others shunning these non-Cherokee institutions. In Adair County, at least one former Cherokee judge, Bluford West Alberty, continued to sit on the bench for three more years, just as he had in Goingsnake District, and there are several Cherokee names among those who filled elected office in Adair County during the first decades after statehood.[70] John Brown served as a county commissioner between 1911 and 1912. Tom Welch, who had served in the Cherokee council in 1903, was elected to serve as a representative to the Oklahoma legislature from 1915 to 1916. Welch proposed at least one piece of legislation, which was hotly criticized. He introduced a bill to mandate that additional county court sessions be held at Westville rather than only at Stilwell. Westville was in the heart of the area he served, and its residents complained that Stilwell was too far removed for them to access the courts. The bill seems to have died.[71] Mose Crittenden was sheriff between 1917 and 1920 and again in 1923 and 1924. John Welch worked as a deputy sheriff. Notably, none of these men were from the resistant families. Those who opposed allotment remained distant from the new governments established because of the policy, and family names that had been associated with Cherokee National politics, such as the Cheweys, Sixkillers, and Wolfes, were conspicuously absent from new lists of public servants.[72]

Others used these new systems to advocate for their own interests. In 1932, for example, Cherokee Jennette Pathkiller filed an affidavit, signed by a family member and a neighbor, stating that Frank Bird was the father of her son Earl. The document is notable for many reasons. It is the only affidavit of this kind I found in which an unmarried Cherokee woman asserts the paternity of her child. In it, the phrase "out of wedlock" appears. Likewise, Earl is referred to by the surname "Pathkiller" rather than as "Bird," in keeping with Cherokee custom immediately prior to allotment. Lastly, the affidavit clarifies Earl's paternity and his blood quantum. Did Jennette use the affidavit process in order to claim resources for her son that perhaps would someday include a share in his father's allotted land? The ultimate use of the form is unclear, but Pathkiller may have been seeking for the state to intervene in forcing Frank to provide child support for Earl. The Adair County court regularly tried Cherokees for bastardy. Although no one in this study, including Frank, was charged with this crime, the prosecution of Cherokee men for fathering illegitimate children seems to have been a routine means through which county officials diverted the property of some Cherokees for the use of others. It is unclear what role Cherokee mothers and court-appointed guardians played in these situations, and these cases warrant further study.[73]

Cherokees generally became comfortable providing documentation, but they continued to do so at their own pace and to meet their own needs, particularly the protection of their family resources. As early as 1907, Oce Hogshooter, a Nighthawk, obtained a marriage license to legalize his relationship with Betsie Miller. Cherokee genealogist Jack D. Baker has noted increasingly that some (but not all) traditionalist Cherokees legally married. Cherokees quickly learned the value of this certification in the new state, particularly when a spouse passed away.[74] Likewise, providing for the care of family members after one's death was a concern for Cherokees, who filed wills to ensure the distribution of their resources as they saw fit rather than leave them for probate according to the court, which would have meant an equal division among recognized heirs. In 1921, Steve Dog, who was a Nighthawk, wrote a will that specified how his land would be divided in order to maintain the integrity of the farm that provided for his wife and two sons. He left a portion of his land to his daughter Tinna, who was married and owned land elsewhere, but he specified that his wife Nannie inherit the allotment where they had lived and that their two sons, who lived with and farmed for their elderly mother, also take a share in that homestead.[75] Betsy Suake left her entire forty-acre homestead to her grandson William Proctor, who lived there, farmed it, and cared for her. If she had not done so, her farm would have been divided equally among her children, all of whom lived elsewhere. Willing the land to William ensured the survival of the family farm, which would continue to remain a safety net for her descendants. Those who intentionally excluded some family members from inheriting their land kept important resources viable in order to benefit the whole family.[76]

Notably, families often did not necessarily quickly resolve matters related to probate. Rather, they sold property when they needed additional resources, and surplus acres served as a savings account or emergency fund of sorts. The probate process, therefore, was a way for some Cherokees to generate income long after the death of a relative. One or two years between a death and a probate were normal for families in this study, but sometimes family members waited even longer to notify the state. Thomas Mounce died as a child in 1908. His brother Ellis finally probated his land in 1925.[77] In 1934, Tom Crittenden, one of Nelson and Jennie's children, went before the probate court in Adair County. Tom wanted to sell his share of his parents' land. His father had been dead for fourteen years and his mother for eight.[78] Tom attended the hearing alone and without any of his siblings or half-siblings, but descendants usually sold land together, and they often sold it to one buyer. After Lewis Bird's death in February 1929, his five children sold their inheritance as a group to G. V. Murray and S. G. Gregory. Developers seemed most interested in purchasing these larger tracts of land.[79]

For many, particularly those who had opposed allotment, their relationships with local civic institutions changed dramatically following statehood. In particular, Cherokees lost their community-run schools. In 1908, Oklahoma assumed control of tribal schools in the former Cherokee Nation, and schools became government property and educational instruction became subject to bureaucratic control by non-Indian professional educators. In an effort to improve the perceived academic qualifications of the faculty, the first superintendent, John D. Benedict, a non-Indian from Illinois with no experience among Indian people, fired most of the Cherokee teachers who had served in the community schools. He justified his actions by claiming that nepotism had enabled the retention of people whom he did not believe were qualified to teach. Most of the teachers in the Cherokee school system were graduates of, or had at least attended, the male and female seminaries. Benedict did not respect this diploma. He also failed to appreciate that Cherokee communities had managed their schools and that teachers worked with the consent of the parents, whether or not they had degrees. The new cohort of teachers Benedict hired included few Indians, and most were new arrivals to the region. They were unfamiliar with Cherokee history and culture, particularly the tribe's long commitment to public coeducation. Influenced by popular stereotypes of Indian people as inferior, these teachers generally looked down on Cherokee children. State law required that Cherokee children attend these integrated schools, and the federal government paid a modest subsidy to cover the attendance of Indian children who lived on tax-exempt land, ten cents a day per pupil in 1910. New teachers misunderstood this as the students receiving federal aid rather than the government fulfilling its legal obligations.[80] Benedict closed some Cherokee community schools altogether. As a result, education became less attainable for some Cherokee students, especially those in the most rural, isolated communities, such as Chewey.[81]

Within a generation, Cherokee educational attainment declined. Tragically, those who had been among the most educated among rural Americans were rapidly marginalized from public schools. Eufala Harjo explained that many Indian students felt "pushed out" by non-Indian students.[82] Schools became hostile places for Cherokee children, who then behaved according to custom. They withdrew. In other words, they stopped attending. By 1914, the county attorney and superintendent of education were threatening to enforce the state's compulsory attendance law against parents who did not send their children to school.[83] In the 1960s, an older Cherokee man told a story to Albert L. Wahrhaftig that speaks to the rapidity of Cherokee withdrawal from the Oklahoma public school system. The man's eldest brothers, men in their nineties, spoke fluent English. Their father so strongly believed in education that their attendance in school took precedence over other family needs, such as work on the farm. The man remembered that his father once whipped his brothers when they played hooky. The younger brothers in the family, including himself, came of age after allotment, however, and their father refused to send them to school. He grew up speaking fluent Cherokee, not English.[84] Lena Cary, who grew up in northern Adair County during the 1920s, thought that education was not a priority for many Cherokee families of her generation. Parents and grandparents preferred for their children to stay at home and learn from them. She attended school for only a few years.[85] By 1930, although 1,402 Indian students attended school in Adair County, their numbers decreased sharply throughout the grades.

Four hundred Indian children attended the first grade, but only nineteen Indian students completed the twelfth grade. Even their attendance was irregular: the average Indian student in Adair County was present in school in 98.7 days each academic year.[86]

In general, families who had intermarried with non-Indians kept their children in school. All the grandchildren and great-grandchildren of Eliza Brown and Martha Phillips in this study were educated.[87] Even among those who were the least educated prior to allotment, such as the Cannons and the Kelleys, most (but not all) of the children raised in the allotment era had some education.[88] At the same time, not all traditionalists withdrew their children from the Oklahoma public school system. Instead, many, including the Hogshooters, Sands, Sixkillers, and Suakes, educated their children. Some parents did so selectively, and a range of educational attainment within families remained normal. For example, White and Susie Oakball, literate in Cherokee, sent their youngest two children to school. Eldest son Walter seems to have attended only briefly before his parents removed him.[89] Charley and Linnie Turtle, who were able to read and write in English, sent only one of their children to school. In 1920, their thirteen-year-old daughter attended school and could read and write in English, but they were not sending their twelve-year-old and ten-year-old sons Joe and Watie.[90] Within traditionalist communities, families autonomously chose whether or not to educate their children, which ones to send to school, and for how long.

Non-Indians tended to see full-blood Cherokee adults as uneducated and ignorant, which shaped their perceptions of the intellectual abilities of their children. This included those who were literate in Cherokee but who were considered to be illiterate by census takers because they did not read and write in English, and those who did read and write English fluently but who were considered to be uneducated because they did not want to share information about their families with outsiders.[91] Dave and Annie Oakball, the children of Nighthawk parents literate in Cherokee, were attending school in 1910, but the census taker listed only Dave as able to read and neither as able to write.[92] One year later, an Indian Service clerk noted that Dave was illiterate but that Anne could read and write in English. Were the children's teachers equally confused about their academic attainment? Are such evaluations of the intelligence of full-blood Cherokee children accurate, or are they further evidence of non-Indians' misperceptions of them? How can we calculate the cumulative impact of this stereotype of Indian stupidity foisted upon the children of resisters?

Allotment changed not just the physical landscape of Cherokee communities but also the intellectual one.

Adapting to a Changing Environment

By the 1920s, the environmental outcomes of allotment began to undermine the ability of all families, not just Cherokees, to make a living in the hills of Adair County, and this process accelerated throughout the decade. Allotment was intended to bust up Cherokee families, but its more obvious result within a generation was that it broke down the topsoil. By 1920, most of Adair County was slightly to severely eroded.[93] The sale and settlement of landed allotted as "surplus" was a source of the problem. The land was not "extra" but was essential to the well-being of the original community members because it enabled the long-term, slow, sustainable growth of extended families. It was where Cherokees cleared new fields when their existing ones were no longer productive and where their children would have made their homes as they started their own families. Allotment rapidly opened that land for development and attracted newcomers into the area to do that work.[94] Between 1910 and 1920 the number of farms and acreage in cultivation in Adair County increased dramatically.[95]

Escalating demand on Indian land after statehood led to overuse and resulted in a domino effect of negative outcomes. The quick development of the region led to the mismanagement of natural resources. Efforts to regulate use and conserve resources were not enacted until the early 1930s, by which point the damage was done. For over two decades since allotment, timber stands had been cut bare and soil was overfarmed, causing the deterioration of the ecosystem. This led to diminishing wild resources. Groves of surviving nut-bearing trees shrunk because they could not adapt to the denuded land. Game could no longer thrive in the sparse woods, and animal populations declined. Soil runoff reduced the fish population by filling fishing holes and muddying rivers.[96]

Cherokees increasingly depended on their fields for subsistence as other sources of food disappeared. Prior to allotment, Cherokees whose soil was depleted simply would have cleared a new field or moved to a new site. Private property ownership made such mobility considerably more difficult, and for those who were restricted, federal paternalism added another layer of complication. In October 1924, Steve Sand sought to sell eighty acres of surplus land. The rocky, gravelly land covered with scrub timber was located two miles from his farm. It was doing him no good, and he needed money to purchase ten additional tillable acres adjoining the twenty acres the family already had under cultivation. Sand and Maria, his wife, had four children, and the family simply needed more land to feed themselves. Sand's request to sell his land was granted, but it took the office of the superintendent for the Five Civilized Tribes nearly two years to complete the sale. In February 1926, payment was requested of the buyer, C. H. Wingate of Pattin Brothers in Tulsa, a company that supplied engines for gas pumps and oil wells. Interestingly, the deed was issued to Wingate three days before payment was requested of him. In May 1926, the Sands had not yet received the funds with which to purchase extra acreage. Even for those whose fields were quickly being farmed into exhaustion, the Indian Service had only one pace: slow.[97]

Erosion also made it more difficult to rely on other sources of income. As early as 1916, court records show the impact of deforestation on Cherokee land. It was worth less, and buyers were paying less for it.[98] In 1924, a field clerk noted that a strong storm had knocked down what remained of the scrubby timber on Steve Sand's land. The rocky land had little economic value.[99] This same process took place thorough the hills of Adair County, and many Cherokee men thus lost access to the one steady form of day labor they had, which was hacking ties for the railroad. The timber industry quickly abandoned Adair County, and the small railroad lines that had run into it to take its resources out fell into disrepair during the late 1920s and 1930s. Other sources of day labor were few.[100]

The conditions particular to Adair County were made worse by factors beyond the control of its residents. A drought gripped Oklahoma between 1929 and 1941, and although conditions were worse in the western end of the state, especially the Panhandle, farmers throughout the region suffered.[101] Likewise, beginning in the late 1920s, tumbling prices crippled Oklahoma's agricultural sector. In particular, wheat and cotton, two cash crops, were worth fractions of what they had been earlier in the decade, and farmers could not sell them at a price that sustained their families. The Great Depression further negatively affected commodity prices on crops and livestock, especially cattle. Cherokees in this area were not dependent on the market, but they sold small amounts of grain and meat for items they could not grow or make. Therefore, the drop in prices resulted in another lost economic resource.[102]

At the same time, the persistence of customary agricultural practices lessened the blow of these factors, which hurt eastern communities while devastating the western portion of Oklahoma. In particular, because Cherokee farmers in Adair County remained near the subsistence level, they had more and varied resources at their disposal with which to survive the period overall. In 1920, the average farm in the state was about 166 acres and planted mostly in wheat. In Adair County, the majority of farms were between 50 and 99 acres and produced corn, milk, eggs, hay, and strawberries. In the area of Chewey, the normal farm was even smaller, perhaps in the range of 30 acres, and as will be discussed in the next chapter, Cherokees continued to utilize a wide range of food sources.[103] This is not to say that families were not affected. Cherokee families struggled, but they also had larger networks of human resources at their disposal when natural ones were disappearing.

Challenging environmental and economic circumstances nonetheless led to the fragmentation of some Cherokee families in this study.[104] Tinsie Kelley was the first member of this study to leave her home. Before 1910, she and her husband, Robert Haze, moved to Colorado, but by 1920, the couple had returned to Oklahoma.[105] Others followed. By 1920, Edwin and Lucinda Cannon's son Aud was living in Everett, Washington, where he worked in a lumber mill. He had married Nora Stump, a white woman who was working as a servant in his brother Ira's home in 1910. Ira and his family lived nearby. He also worked at the mill. Both Edwin and his brother Sterling had worked in the lumber industry in that area before, so in that sense, the young men were not leaving their family but together returning to a place where their family had been already.[106] These Cherokees usually moved as extended groups, maintained contact with their relatives in Adair County, and frequently returned to northeastern Oklahoma.[107] In her studies of Algonquian kinship networks in the seventeenth-century Great Lakes region, historian Heidi Bohaker demonstrates the durability of these reciprocal agreements among people who saw themselves to be related in that they transcended geographic boundaries and weathered crises.[108] This seems to hold true for Cherokees who left northeastern Oklahoma after allotment. Just as the tragedy of removal had done, allotment once again extended their kinship network even farther west.

Most Cherokees in this study remained in Adair County and the surrounding region. A third of allotted Cherokees in the Oklahoma Ozarks, including Adair County, retained possession of their land into the 1930s.[109] The community of Chewey and the surrounding area proved to be remarkably stable throughout the first decades after allotment. This reflected the circumstances of restricted Cherokees, who were more likely to retain ownership of their allotted land, and even those who had sold some of their land. It also testifies to the conscious decision of Cherokees to stay among their extended families. Although restrictions had been lifted on their allotments, many of the Cannons, Welches, and Browns continued to live on some smaller portion of their allotted land.[110] These patterns of family life are the subject of the last chapter.

THIS "PERFECT STORM" of an environmental crisis compounded by misguided economic and social policy reached its peak during 1930. Cherokee families who remained in the Oklahoma Ozarks suffered. The extreme drought prompted the Red Cross to establish a disaster relief program there, and it reached out to Indian and non-Indian families. In order to identify those in need and distribute resources, the Red Cross tapped into existing local social networks and co-opted established leaders, such as those individuals affiliated with county government and school boards, to assist them. Recognizing that many Cherokees did not have contact with these institutions, the Red Cross included Indian leaders as "key men" in order to assist Indian communities. Many families faced imminent starvation and needed immediate assistance, especially food. In 1930, Red Cross officials in Stilwell, the county seat of Adair County, estimated that drought had negatively affected at least 800 local families (although they did not report what percentage of these were Cherokee), a quarter of whom needed aid to survive until the rains returned. In response, the Red Cross distributed supplies to Cherokees through the "key men" who visited the homes weekly bearing food from the "Great White Mother," as Henry M. Baker, director of drought relief in Oklahoma, called the organization in his report for the Red Cross's newsletter.

Baker's article suggested how thoroughly paternalism and misconceptions of Cherokee culture had warped non-Indians' perceptions of them in the decades after allotment. For example, he stereotyped members of the Five Tribes as having loyal dogs that followed them everywhere and as gratefully thanking Red Cross officials in broken, stunted English with such remarks as, "Heap plenty food little talk."[111] In just over two decades since Oklahoma statehood, the Cherokee homeland in northeastern Oklahoma had been eroded, but so had the Cherokees' ability to represent themselves as a sophisticated people to the rest of the world. Their fields were dust, and they, too, were reduced to Saturday matinee Indians unable to express their perceptions of this crisis or theorize how to end it.

Except that they were positing their own solutions to the problem. In 1932, approximately 120 families living in the area of Chewey withdrew from the Nighthawks and formed the Seven Clans Society. Led by Eli Pumpkin, who lived on land that had been part of Noah Sand's allotment, the organization advocated the communal ownership of land as a means to economic self-sufficiency. They sought to combine their remaining restricted land and manage it collectively because they believed that this would enable them to develop an economic base capable of sustaining their families. The Seven Clans Society saw common title as a solution to poverty and an alternative to outmigration from northeastern Oklahoma. In other words, Cherokees turned to what was time-tested and customary, the familial relationships and common title to land that nurtured them.[112]

CHAPTER EIGHT

Sustaining

Between 1967 and 1972, J. W. Tyner crisscrossed northeastern Oklahoma documenting Cherokee life after allotment as part of the American Indian Oral History Project, commonly known as the Doris Duke
Collection after the foundation that sponsored this massive undertaking.
Tyner, a Cherokee from Adair County, conducted many of his interviews
with elders while driving in his car. Cruising through the back roads
of the western Ozarks, his passengers talked about the journeys of their
lifetimes. They told stories of what had changed, but mostly they talked
about what remained the same and important: family and the land that
sustained them. The countryside itself testified to this. The landscape
still bore the names of Cherokee families that had lived there at the
beginning of the twentieth century when the Cherokee Nation was allotted and, in many cases, continued to live there.

In 1969, Tyner visited with Sam Chewey. Born in 1887, Chewey was
the son of Nannie Wolfe and Bill Chewey. His grandfather Joe had been
beloved for his service to the tribal government as a soldier and council
member, and Sam Chewey's life also was shaped by service. He had been
part of the American Expeditionary Force and served in World War I.
As Tyner puts it, Chewey had "learned many things about the world for
the experience." The right place for him was home, however, and after
he was discharged from the army, he returned to Adair County, married,
farmed, and raised a family. By the time Tyner drove up, Chewey was
an eighty-two-year-old man whose fields were abundant with corn and
whose yard was full of grandchildren and great-grandchildren. A young

teenager during the allotment of the Cherokee Nation, Chewey's adult-hood was shaped by this policy. He witnessed the dispossession and ero-sion that altered his homeland. And yet, as he told Tyner about the things that mattered to him throughout his life, particularly hunting, fishing, farming, socializing with his neighbors, stomp dancing, and caring for his children, he described a life characterized by consistency of belief and behavior in a region that was very much changed.[1]

How did Sam Chewey's family survive allotment? Most studies of the years immediately following the implementation of the policy empha-size the speed and extreme extent of Indian impoverishment.[2] In doing so, these narratives overlook the adaptation of Cherokees to private land-ownership and ignore this example of Indian people ably and adeptly adjusting to changing economic circumstances in order to maintain their way of life. Cherokee families were responsive to allotment, and the goal of maintaining self-sufficiency sparked innovation as they struggled to retain varied, balanced domestic economies against great odds. In other words, the values and patterns of behavior through which they had long attained familial subsistence informed how they incorporated indi-vidually owned land into their system of available resources and took advantage of new economic opportunities resulting from the transition to statehood. Evidence from oral histories, censuses, removal of restric-tions applications, and probate records points to the overall consistency of family life. Cherokees in this region of Adair County continued to live in fluid, extended families and practiced a diversified approach to survival that included farming, hunting, fishing, and gathering. After allotment, they also performed day labor and other wage work. When they needed more cash, they sold surplus land. Cherokees usually (but not always) lived on their own allotments or that of family members, but they did not depend solely on them for survival.

They could not. By the 1920s, allotment had altered the landscape. The removal of restrictions on allotted property enabled the sale of those surplus acres and often led to the loss of access to the natural resources on them, as well as to the overfarming and soil erosion mentioned in chapter 7. Ironically, the survival of Cherokee families in Oklahoma as the Great Depression neared was contingent upon kinship. Traditional customs normalizing reciprocity and hospitality proved invaluable, and those who did not have broad social support and a wide range of resources from which to draw eroded away like the overfarmed topsoil of Adair County. They left. Those, like Sam Chewey, who survived to harvest corn

*From left to right:
Joe Turtle, Sam
Chewey, and Jim
Sand. Photo courtesy
of Jack D. Baker.*

with their great-grandchildren on family land had adapted the best by perhaps changing the least. Their families remained flexible, egalitarian, and inclusive, and their control of resources remained decentralized.

Allotment and the Adaptation of Cherokee Family Structure

Cherokee familial organization remained relatively consistent in the first two decades after allotment. Reformers had predicted that private landownership would spark the reconfiguration of Indian families into nuclear, patriarchal units in which wealth, resources, and power were consolidated under the control of able-bodied adult males. Among Cherokees in this study, however, allotment did not produce this result. Cherokees continued to practice a flexible, bilateral system of reckoning kinship that connected them to maternal and paternal relatives and joined them into extended families. This does not mean that allotment did not change the shape of Cherokee families. It did. The increasingly limited availability of land and other resources perpetuated the formation of some extended households while it divided others. Sam Crittenden's family provides a good example of this pattern. In 1920, Sam, then a widower in his mid-fifties, lived with two of his grown sons, his elderly mother, and his maternal nephew Crust Sulleteskee. Sam's neighbor on one side was his younger brother Charley and his wife and six children. Sam's half-sister Susie and her in-laws, the Mounces, who were a family of intermarried whites, lived on the other side of Charley. Sam's neighbor on his other side was White Youngbird and his wife and two children. White was the brother of Sam's deceased wife, Annie. Both Charley and White were renting land, and Sam owned land. It is likely, therefore, that Charley and White were renting from Sam. Likewise, Sam is listed as a farmer, but his brother, brother-in-law, and son Watt are listed as woodcutters. Sam's father, Nelson Crittenden, and several of his other half-siblings also lived nearby.[3]

Families continued to look to maternal kin to provide support in times of crisis. Maternal relatives, in particular, cared for children when death forced the reconfiguration of households. In 1905, Steve Sand, whose wife Lizzie had died, married Maria Snell. Lizzie's mother, Fannie Turtle, cared for Lizzie's infant daughter, Anna. In 1910, six-year-old Anna continued to live with her maternal grandmother and three unmarried maternal uncles, Ned, Adam, and Joe, who ranged in age from thirty-seven to fourteen years old.[4] Maternal kin also tended to their elders. In February 1909, Martin Raper died. Raper, the elder brother of Eliza Brown, had moved from North Carolina to be with his sisters and their children in 1882. When he passed away, Raper was approximately 100 years old and an invalid. His niece Polly was his primary caregiver, and that entailed an enormous amount of her labor. The length of his life hints at the quality of care she gave him. He lived in her house, which was next to that of her parents. As Polly described it, he "required the same care and attention that would be required by an infant child." Raper's maternal nieces and nephews were his next-of-kin. Eliza's remaining children decided that Polly should inherit what remained of his estate. After his medical expenses were paid for, she received $93.18. It is difficult to prove devotion and selfless love using the documentary record left from the allotment era, but providing care for over twenty-five years for no meaningful financial compensation suggests that the reward of fulfilling duty and honoring the relationship with that elder was compensation enough.[5]

At the same time, it was not uncommon for Cherokees to turn to paternal relatives and even in-laws when necessary. The bonds of relatedness remained broad to include many members of the community in relationships of reciprocity, and these extended throughout lifetimes. After both of their parents died immediately prior to enrollment, Mollie and Nay Welch each moved in with a paternal half-brother; brothers John and Mack Welch were neighbors, and so this arrangement kept the younger siblings in close contact.[6] When Sam Fields died, his widow moved with her children to family land next to her in-laws where Sam's sister Jennie Oakball lived with her husband, John, her children, and her grandchild. Two other in-laws, Jim and Charley Fields, and their families lived nearby. Jennie and John may have been helping the widow care for Jennie's maternal nieces and nephews.[7] In 1920, Lewis Bird, then sixty-three and widowed, lived with fifty-six-year-old Jim Wilson. Jim was the brother of Lewis's deceased wife, Betsy. She had been dead for seventeen years, which was nearly as long as the couple had been married, but the bond between Lewis and Jim apparently endured. Jim owned his land, and it appears that Lewis, then working as a woodchopper, lived there among Jim and his wife, Bettie, their children, and grandchild.[8]

Household membership remained flexible as individuals returned and left as the needs of life required. In particular, adults often remained in or rejoined their parents' household to raise their own children. Charley Kelley's wife died when their two children were small. He raised sons Wyly and John with the help of his parents, John and Susan, in their home.[9] Sam Kirk, Charley's maternal first cousin, made the same decision. When his wife, Bertha, passed away, he returned, along with his son William, to live with his parents, William and Laura Kirk, and his younger siblings.[10] When Ida Oakball's husband went to prison for murder, she returned to her father and stepmother's home and among the extended Hogshooter household with Cornelius, her young son.[11]

The Hogshooter family, in fact, exemplifies the continued normalcy of residential fluidity. In 1910, Jim and Mary Hogshooter's household included their five children between the ages of thirteen and one, Jim's elderly parents, both in their seventies, and his brother Oce's four children between the ages of seventeen and eight. Oce, recently remarried, briefly lived with his new wife, who had two grown children, in Cherokee County. The newlyweds soon returned to Adair County, however, and resumed living with his brother as they had for most of their lives. In

1920, Jim and Mary lived with three of their children and Jim's widowed mother. Next door, Oce shared his home with his wife, children, and grandchildren.[12]

This flexibility characterized those families who were considered to be traditionalists, like the Oakballs and Hogshooters, and those who were not. After her parents died, Polly Brown joined her brother Marsh's household and lived with him, his wife, Mary, four of their five children, and a grandchild. The couple's oldest daughter, Lizzie, lived nearby with her husband, Birch Anderson. The couple shared a home with his fifty-year-old maternal uncle, John Mitchell. Interestingly, although the presence of extended family members in Cherokee households remained normal, this arrangement was considered to be abnormal by census takers, who literally lacked the proper words to describe the relationships connecting residents of the homes they visited. For this reason, these federal officials typically generically identified non-nuclear family members in homes, particularly males, as "boarders." Mitchell may have contributed to the household, but the term "boarder" implies that the relationship primarily was economic and that the Andersons were providing a room and board to Mitchell in return for rent. That is misleading. They were family.[13]

Immediately following allotment, ambilocality remained the norm as couples continued to establish their homes near one set of parents. They often preferred the wife's side, but living near the husband's side was not uncommon. In 1910, Tom and Nannie Wolfe's neighbors were two of their grown children from previous marriages along with their spouses and families. Nannie's daughter Jennie was married to Nelson Crittenden, and Tom's son John was married to Dora Mitchell.[14] Siblings in the same family continued to exemplify both trends, which suggests that decisions about living situations were made on a case-by-case basis. Fannie Turtle's son Charley moved to live near his parents-in-law, Joe and Nancy Vann, when he married their daughter Linnie in 1906, but Fannie's daughter Lizzie had moved to join Steve Sand near his relations.[15] This flexible pattern holds true among both those families who had not intermarried extensively and those who had. In 1920, Reece and Martha Welch were living on land belonging to her parents, Cap and Ida Brown, rather than on land that belonged to his parents, Tom and Fannie Welch.[16]

Reece and Martha Welch were not unique in starting their married life by farming land owned by their parents, but their situation became less common over time among those who were unrestricted. Allotment had made it increasingly difficult for young couples who wanted to establish their own farms to do so if their families lacked acreage to share with them. Both the Welch and Brown families had been unrestricted since 1908 and had sold much of their surplus land, the unimproved acres in between existing farms where the next generation would have settled. By 1920, those able to establish farms near their parents tended to be from families who remained restricted from selling their allotments. These young adults chose to settle near their kin, but they also had the means to do so. For example, when Nelson and Jennie Crittenden's children married, they remained near their parents. In 1920, son William and his wife and daughter Lydia and her husband lived in the neighboring houses. Both William and Lydia were able to do so because the Dawes Commission had assigned this Nighthawk family contiguous allotments on relatively arable land that included their existing farm. Their allotment provided room for the family to grow. Other Cherokee families did not have land on which their children could set up new households.[17]

Likewise, when couples intermarried in the years immediately following allotment, they tended to stay with the Cherokee side of the family, but that trend also changed over time. In 1906, Maud Welch, the eldest daughter of Tom and Fannie, married a white man, Hugh Hess. The couple lived in between her parents and her maternal uncle, James Mack Welch, and his wife. That household also included Maud's grandmother and James Mack's mother, Nancy. None of her younger siblings would be able to do the same, however.[18] By 1910, four of John and Susan Kelley's six children had married non-Indians. Two of those couples were living with John and Susan, and another, whose intermarried wife had passed away, lived there with his two children. Only one of their children who had intermarried, daughter Tinsie, had moved away. By 1920, however, only widower Charley and his sons remained.[19] As restrictions against the sale of allotted land were lifted, families who had intermarried over generations sold land or lost it for nonpayment of taxes. Over time, the material advantage that Cherokee kin had had, particularly access to land and its resources, disappeared. By 1920, this trend of intermarried families remaining near Cherokee kin no longer is apparent. Allotment forced out some members of Cherokee communities by limiting the land base upon which they could live.

Elders remained central to Cherokee families. Again, census takers had no term to note the role the aged played in their families. In 1910, Noah Sand, then seventy-five and still able-bodied, lived with his sons John and Will, who was married with two sons of his own. Misleadingly, a census taker listed all three men as heads of separate households, although the extended family seemed to be sharing two houses next to each other.[20] More often, elderly women headed extended households. For example, after her husband, Abe, died, Margaret Sixkiller shared her home with her unmarried daughter, her elderly mother, her youngest son and his wife, and her teenaged grandson.[21]

After allotment, grandmothers continued to be primary caregivers to their grandchildren. Betsy Suake's second cycle of parenting began before her first had ended. Her youngest children, Mary and Lawyer, were teenagers when her eldest son Tom's first wife, Charlotte, died, leaving a small son named Ezekiel. Betsy took him in. Her grown daughters Nannie and Linnie also continued to live with her, and both were beginning to have children of their own. When Linnie died, Betsy kept her grandson James. In 1906, Nannie died, and Betsy continued to raise William Proctor and Andrew Palone. In October 1906, Annie, Tom Suake's third wife, died. Tom's mother Betsy took in their baby, Johnie. This litany of the loss of Cherokee women in their early childbearing years in one family suggests the impact of maternal death. In such a context, women past their childbearing years provided stable parenting.

Betsy, who had been widowed since 1898, was not past her interest in relationships, however, because by 1910, she was living with John Blackfox. Both were in their sixties. In 1920, Betsy, then seventy-four, shared a household with three of her grandsons, all young men in their early twenties. The Dawes Commission had segregated elders onto separate cards, but Betsy was central to the survival of her family. Ageism and the romantic idealization of motherhood common in Anglo-American society resulted in the lack of recognition of Cherokee grandmothers as legitimate primary caregivers. In 1910, a census taker did not know how else to describe her grandsons, and so he listed the boys whom Betsy was mothering as her "boarders."[22]

Joint families remained common as adult siblings continued to live with and near each other in the decades after allotment. This is most obvious among brothers. Examples include those whose families had intermarried extensively, such as John, Marsh, and Cap Brown, but also those whose families had not, including Jim and Oce Hogshooter.[23] It also occurred among sisters. For example, take the three surviving daughters of Nannie Dog. Dora, Nannie's daughter with Reese Mitchell, married John Wolfe, Tom's son. Sissa, another daughter of Nannie and Reese's, married Jesse Bird, Lewis and Betsy's son. Tinna, Nannie's daughter with

Steve Dog, married Stan Gibson. Dora and John rented land in order to live near her sisters.[24] Gender shaped this decision; examples of siblings of opposite genders living next to each other are less common. Brothers Tom Welch and James Mack Welch formed a joint household throughout their adult lives. In the next generation of this family, Tom's children John and Maud were neighbors once they established their own farms and families, but they were the only such example I found by 1920.[25]

Sometimes, this meant family members rented land to one another, or at least that is how officials recorded it. In other words, family members living on land legally belonging to kin probably were not paying to live there, but outsiders did not recognize hospitality as a form of currency. For example, there are no records showing that Edwin and Lucinda Cannon actually paid their daughter Dovie to live on the land belonging to her, her husband, John Welch, and their children. But in 1920, Edwin and Lucinda, then in their mid-sixties, were living next to their eldest daughter and listed as renters.[26] Edwin's brother John and his wife, Mary, were renting land to their son Walter and his new wife. Their daughter Bular was living on the other side of Walter on land she and her husband Bud Kinnamon owned.[27] Renting, in other words, likely meant "sharing" or "extending hospitality toward" rather than "charging a fixed amount for the use of the land."

These kin-based transactions interconnected extended families that defied the boundary of blood quantum that the Dawes Commission had drawn between supposed full bloods and mixed bloods. For example, Ellis Mounce, the son of Rosanna and Joe, was the center of an extended household connected by multiple layers of land-sharing through matrilineal ties. Rosanna's Cherokee female ancestors had intermarried in several successive generations. Ellis's white father, Joe, was his neighbor, and Ellis's paternal uncle John lived with him. Ellis, who owned his farm, rented land to his maternal cousin Lace Kelley and his wife and children. Lace's household included Ellis's maternal half-brother Wyly Beavers and his wife and child. All three men were grandsons of Nellie Kelley. Wyly's land was being farmed by a relative of his intermarried stepfather, George Mounce, who married Susie Crittenden, the daughter of Nighthawks Nelson and Jennie Crittenden.[28]

After allotment, marriage remained an option but not a necessity, especially for men. Unmarried adult children commonly continued to live with their parents or siblings. Although advocates of the policy believed that it would force Indians to form nuclear families, allotment may have

Some of the sons of Rosanna Mounce. From left to right: Joseph Mounce, Wyly Beavers, and Ellis Mounce. Photo courtesy of Jack D. Baker.

had the opposite effect by making it more difficult for some Cherokees to find suitable partners willing to join their existing extended family households or available, arable land nearby to kin on which to build separate homes. In particular, unmarried adult women began to appear in noticeable numbers. In 1910, five of John and Emily Brown's children shared their home. Ida, Myra, Florence, Robert, and Bertha ranged in age from thirty-three to twenty-one years old.[29] In 1920, most of the Hogshooter children continued to live with their parents, and only the youngest was under twenty years old.[30] Likewise, allotment did not prompt all Cherokee bachelors to take wives. Ned Turtle never married but remained in his parents' household. In 1920, he was forty-five and lived with his sixty-seven-year-old mother, Fannie, by then widowed, and his younger brother Joe, who was twenty-three years old.[31] Although briefly married before he deployed, Sam Chewey continued to live with his mother, Nannie

Wolfe, after her husband, Tom, was murdered and Sam returned from World War I. He eventually married three more times.[32] Although some Cherokees never married, others, particularly men, married for the first time in their thirties. Stan Gibson continued to live with his maternal uncle Abe Sixkiller and his wife, Margaret, well into his thirties before he married Tinna Dog.[33]

Nannie Dog may have explained a reason behind this trend. When she was sixty and her husband, Steve, was seventy, Nannie applied for the removal of restrictions against selling some of her land. In describing her economic circumstances, she explained that their two sons, Arch, who was eighteen, and Johnson, then nineteen, were farming to care for her and their father. Nannie and Steve were no longer able to do the work of the farm on their own. She wanted money to buy tools, equipment, and stock with which to improve their farm. Sons sometimes stayed in their natal home when their labor was essential. With traditional methods of providing income, such as hunting and trapping, less viable and with few sources of paid labor available to them, young men increasingly depended on the family farm as well.[34]

Cherokees continued to marry partners who represented the range of people within their community. Before the allotment era, blood quantum was not a dividing line that extended into Cherokee bedrooms, and it did not become one after allotment. The children of William and Laura Kirk present a good example. Both of their families had intermarried with whites for many generations, but Sam, their eldest son, married Bertha Sixkiller, a woman whose blood quantum was listed as one-half. The Kirks were listed as one-eighth. The Kirks' eldest daughter, Della, on the other hand, married a white man, Wade Hampton. Dennis Sixkiller, the son of Nighthawks who was enrolled as three-quarters Cherokee, married Bertha Cannon, enrolled as one-thirty-second.[35] His younger brother Lincoln married a white woman, Ruth.[36] Notably, those who identified as Nighthawks and opposed to allotment married both other Cherokees outside their movement and non-Indians the least, but even within that group, marriage across boundaries was not unknown. Susie, the oldest daughter of Nighthawks Nelson and Jennie Crittenden, briefly married Lawyer Suake before intermarrying George Mounce, with whom she had five children. George's father and sister, who both also married into the full-blood community, lived next to the couple within this neighborhood of Nighthawks.[37]

Serial monogamy remained normal, and Cherokees continued to enjoy more than one sexual partner throughout their adult lives. The Suakes provide a good example. Shortly after allotment, Betsy Suake and John Blackfox began a relationship when the pair were in their sixties. They did not legally marry, but the couple shared the home in which she raised four of her grandsons. At the time, Betsy's eldest son, Tom, was in his fourth and longest relationship with Annie Hilderbrand, to whom he was not then legally married. She and her five children lived with him. Unsure of how to identify these committed couples who had not legally married according to Oklahoma state law, census takers labeled the women and children in these relationships as "boarders" of the men with whom they shared a home. This label is particularly misleading in Betsy's case because John Blackfox was staying in her house.[38]

Sexual relationships outside of marriage remained common, and, therefore, so did unmarried mothers, particularly among those who identified as full bloods. Emma Hogshooter, Oce's oldest daughter, lived in her parents' home when she had Anna.[39] Likewise, John and Jennie Oakball's oldest daughter, Annie, had a son, Joe Blackfox, but she remained unmarried and lived with her parents. The Blackfoxes were neighbors of the Oakballs.[40] Dan Downing, who was raised by his maternal uncle Noah Sand, had a son with Rosetta Mounce, a non-Indian woman. Their relationship soon ended, and he married Viola Lewis.[41] Abe and Margaret Sixkiller's eldest daughter, Sarah, had a son, Floyd, when she was eighteen and continued to live in her parents' household.[42] Although the state of Oklahoma began prosecuting some individuals for the crime of bastardy, there is no evidence suggesting that women or men within Cherokee communities faced increased stigma for engaging in premarital sexual relations or that their children suffered for it.

Allotment and Cherokee Family Function

Cherokees immediately began integrating allotments into their domestic economies. Those who advocated for the removal of restrictions fretted that Indians would never adapt to private landownership as long as they remained isolated and protected from the market, but in actuality, Cherokees already had begun to adjust. Outsiders simply failed to notice how. Owning land as individuals did not immediately undermine the ways that Cherokees used land as families, as reformers predicted it would, and allotment did not produce the radical changes that its advocates had anticipated. In fact, the goal of Cherokee life remained consistent because rather than accumulating wealth or amassing estates to bequeath to children, Cherokees continued to prioritize the immediate well-being of their extended families. As Richard Manus, a Cherokee who grew up in the region, remembered, "That was the main thing[,] how to make a living. People lived in them days as to make a living. Make a home for his family. And so that's the whole thing." Cherokees continued to measure status through the extension of hospitality, and they put their allotted resources toward that end.[43]

To begin, Cherokee men often sold their land for the benefit of their family. Although they expected men to amass wealth, non-Indian officials approved of the efforts of Cherokee men to part with some of their land to improve their remaining acres because they believed that this signified the adoption of Anglo-American appreciation for investment and long-term financial security. Of course, the sale of surplus land also made property available for non-Indians to purchase. A 1906 editorial in a local non-Indian newspaper, the *New Era*, spoke to this attitude that harked back to an idealization of yeoman agriculture and hinted at the populism that infused the political formation of Oklahoma: "The man who owns a good farm, free from mortgage, and who invests most of his money at home in a better stock or better living—is the center of a financial world of his own. He's the king pin! And many a big city financier envies him his security of possession and freedom from uncertainty."[44] Non-Indians eagerly noted that Indians were selling their surplus, but they failed to understand that they were often using their money for the benefit of extended family members. They did not appreciate that Cherokees measured wealth and security in terms of their relatives and not their land titles.

Because Cherokees typically invested their resources in the property of others, this custom shaped their management of allotments. In particular, Cherokees eligible to do so because of their low blood quantum commonly sought the removal of restrictions against leasing or selling their surplus, which typically was unutilized land that had been part of the public domain. In this, their behavior differed from that of the non-Indian neighbors who were increasingly buying former Cherokee land. They considered real estate an investment and speculated in land for profit rather than immediate use. Most petitioners in this study specified that they sought the lifting of restrictions to lease or sell part of their surplus in order to improve their homestead or, as often, that of another family member. In 1906, for example, John Brown appealed for the removal of restrictions against selling his surplus. Brown and his wife, Emily, farmed their son's allotment. Brown's surplus was located about two miles from their farm, and so it was unusable to him. He sought to sell it to buy new farm equipment. Together, John and Emily and their seven children claimed title to approximately 3,000 acres. Brown already owned some machinery, livestock, and a sawmill. His family was economically comfortable. Still, he chose not to hold onto his extra acres until they appreciated in value because he sought to put his resources to immediate practical use on the family's farm, which was located on his son's homestead. In 1907, the Department of the Interior granted his request, and Brown parted with the land as he saw fit.[45]

Brown was not unusual. Cherokee parents frequently parted with their property during their lifetimes in order to improve that of their children. This was a sharp contrast to the gendered ideals embraced in Anglo-American society in which adult men were supposed to accumulate wealth throughout their lives and bequest it to their children upon their death. Most Cherokees simply did not amass estates. Noah Sand was in his early seventies when, in 1916, his son John passed away. John died intestate, and his property, meaning his allotment, was divided among his heirs, including his brother and his father. When he appeared before a judge to resolve the division of John's estate, Noah requested that his son Will receive his share. The judge was surprised by the elderly man's request and asked him to explain his reasoning. Noah Sand simply replied, "Just because he is my son."[46] Other Cherokee fathers proved equally generous with their children. John Wolfe sold his son Jessie, who was born too late for an allotment, forty acres of land so that Jessie could build a farm near his parents.[47]

Notably, Cherokee parents improved land owned by their daughters as well as by their sons, which suggests the endurance of women's property rights among Cherokees. Retta Sixkiller, who was a toddler at the time, received the family's homestead in her allotment. Between 1911 and 1918, her father, Abe, sold his surplus and then his homestead in increments in order to pay for improvements to the family's home, which legally belonged to her. He used proceeds from the sales for a range of improvements, including the construction of a barn and the purchase of a team of horses. In 1918, the family lived in a comfortable two-story house, and their farm included many cultivated acres, an orchard, a barn, a well, and a large garden. They also owned four cows, three horses, and two hogs. They had accumulated an array of farming implements, including a wagon and many tools. Abe, then seventy-two, was in good health, but

Noah Sand with his grandson Joe Sand. Photo courtesy of Jack D. Baker.

the heaviest labor fell to the children, who remained at home, especially Lincoln, their youngest son, who was four years older than Retta.

Lincoln's situation suggests that siblings, too, used their resources for the benefit of the family, even improving another sibling's allotment. Although he was twenty-one and single, Lincoln did not want to hold onto his allotment in case he should want to marry and move onto it in the future. Instead, he sought the removal of restrictions against selling his surplus land. Although it was rented and generated income, it was located several miles away from the rest of the family's land. Lincoln had no interest in living there, and he wanted to contribute his resources to further upgrades on the family's farm on his sister's allotment. Eventually, when Retta came of age, she sought the removal of restrictions on the whole property. She and her husband, a white man named Jesse Sanders, sought to fence and modernize the property in the mid-1920s.[48]

The story of Tom Suake's family further demonstrates how family members sold land to assist one another as part of their larger culture of reciprocity. In the 1920s, Tom and Annie lived on his homestead, which included a house, fifty cultivated acres, a well, and fencing. Annie had used some of her equalization money to make these improvements to their farm. They also owned two mules and three hogs. When Tom had married Annie Hilderbrand, his fourth wife, she had five children from her previous relationship. One of them, a son named Alex, was a "born-too-late," meaning an infant who was enrolled but whose birth came after the available land had been distributed. The boy therefore received a share of tribal funds equal to the value of an allotment, and his mother and stepfather also used $269.75 of that money to improve their family's farm. By 1922, Alex was nearly twenty years old and sought to establish his own homestead. This prompted Suake to seek the removal of restrictions against selling fifty acres of his surplus land. He wanted to sell twenty acres for cash to make further improvements to the family's farm, but he also wanted to repay Alex by giving him a thirty-acre farm. That land included improvements: a log house, a well, wire fencing, a twenty-acre field, and five additional tillable acres. It took from May 1922 until March 1924 for the Indian Service to complete the transaction, but Alex got his homestead.[49]

Stories like the Suakes' exemplify that Cherokees continued to organize their households collaboratively rather than hierarchically. Property was distributed broadly, and members, including children, contributed to the well-being of the whole. Lawmakers had intended for parents, particularly fathers, to manage the allotments of their children for their future use upon their maturity. Some parents, however, sought to improve their family's immediate circumstances by selling land. In 1910, John Kelley petitioned to sell a portion of his daughter Maud's allotment. It generated no income, and he wanted to invest the proceeds from the sale in stock instead.[50] Many Cherokee parents saw their children's allotments as one more resource available to improve the family's circumstances, and they did not distinguish between their land and their children's but used all available resources to meet immediate family needs. Mack Welch supported his four children as a laborer and farmer. After his wife, Emma, died in 1906, he sold his daughters' share in his wife's estate to pay for the educational expenses of all the children. In 1911, Welch petitioned to sell seven acres of his daughter Esther's land to pay for more expenses. He later sold a portion of daughter Myrtle's land and put the proceeds toward improvements on the family farm. In 1913, Esther, then seventeen, married, and her father formally signed over control of her remaining land. When his other daughters, Myrtle, Georgie, and Ethel, came of age, he did the same for them. Outsiders might have questioned why Welch used bits of his daughters' allotments to raise them, yet using the resources belonging to one family member for the betterment of all was appropriate among Cherokee families.[51]

Although the advocates of allotment expected male dominance to become normal among allotted Indians, relations between the genders remained egalitarian. The proponents of allotment anticipated that private landownership would prompt Indian families to consolidate the management of their resources under male heads-of-households, but unrestricted Cherokee women continued to handle their own affairs. Allotment, therefore, did not rob Cherokee women of their power to make decisions over and administer their family's resources. When she died in 1908, Eliza Brown left ninety improved acres and a gristmill to be divided among her children, daughters and sons alike.[52] This pattern was perpetuated over and over, and parents invested their daughters and other female relatives with land. Their efforts often were unappreciated by outsiders. After her daughter Charlotte died, Fannie Turtle and her son Ned, Charlotte's brother, struggled to convince Indian Service clerks to use money from the sale of Charlotte's land to buy other land for her surviving young daughter, who had not received an allotment of her own.[53]

Fannie and Ned were not the only relatives to do so. Several parents purchased land for their children. John Welch sold his children's allotments to buy better land, some of which he sold and part of which he saved for their later use.[54] John and Susan Kelley sold their daughter Maud's allotment, which was unimproved land, and then bought her another tract of land of better quality.[55] Hattie Lewis, a granddaughter of Eliza Brown, and her intermarried husband, Fred, used her son Robert's oil royalties to purchase a sixty-acre farm in his name, which they then leased. Parents often rented the land of minor children to farmers who would improve it by working it. Hattie's maternal uncle John Brown and her cousin Dick Brown appraised the land and vouched for the investment. In other words, even though her intermarried husband signed the forms, the extended family played a part in deciding and preparing for Robert's future.[56] When family members objected to Fred's handling of affairs, however, they voiced their opinions. Baskum Brown, another of Hattie's maternal cousins, disapproved of her husband loaning his nephew

Arthur's royalty money for a neighbor's mortgage, so Baskum notified the courts and requested to be removed from Lewis's bond. Brown was right. Three years later, the buyer defaulted on the mortgage, and the farm went into foreclosure. The following year, the family sold the rest of Arthur's land, a farm located at a distance from their home that had fallen into disrepair.[57]

Although Cherokees often sold land to outsiders, they sometimes sold it to friends and neighbors. In 1914, Ned Hogshooter died, and in 1920, his widow and three grown children sought to sell 200 acres of his land to their neighbor, Wyly Beavers. Their land butted up against his.[58] Three years after their father Noah died in 1917, Will and Steve Sand sold his allotment to Eli Pumpkin for $500, the smallest real estate transaction in this study. The Sands, who were active Nighthawks, knew Pumpkin through their shared resistance. As discussed in the previous chapter, Pumpkin established the Seven Clans Society there in 1932.[59]

Although advocates of the policy expected Cherokees' homesteads to be the economic engine that drove their assimilation, Cherokee families did not simplify their strategy for survival. Rather, they continued to draw upon a broad range of resources. As they had done before allotment, Cherokee families in the region continued to practice their customary subsistence activities to the extent possible. They combined farming, hunting, fishing, and gathering with lesser amounts of production for sale or trade. Some also worked for cash. In his environmental history of the Illinois River region, historian Robert Krause argues that Adair County was an exception to the rule of rapid commercial agriculture development that characterized the rest of Oklahoma after statehood. Most of the county's farmers remained just above the subsistence level until after the Great Depression.[60] For this reason, Albert L. Wahrhaftig considers the early twentieth century another Cherokee "Golden Age," because he argues that many Cherokee families maintained their self-sufficiency until the 1920s.[61]

In their gardens, Cherokees continued to grow corn, tobacco, peas, turnips, sweet potatoes, and pumpkins.[62] They also maintained their small two- or three-acre orchards.[63] Cherokees were increasingly growing for the market but mostly for trade in nearby towns. In particular, they sold fruits and vegetables, milk and dairy, eggs, and hay.[64] Some Cherokees were growing cash crops, including Oce Hogshooter, who was planting some cotton.[65] Others, like John Brown, were growing wheat.[66] By 1914, farmers throughout the area were producing strawberries, which Adair County still produces in abundance, but it is unclear if Cherokee farmers were growing them.[67]

There was a wide variation in the number of acres cultivated, and the size of Cherokee farms does not fall neatly into any category. Specifically, those of mixed descent were not always farming more than those identified as full bloods. The average acreage farmed among those in this study was thirty-six acres, but some farmed as few as twenty acres while some farmed significantly more. The Browns, the Kirks, and the Sixkillers farmed over sixty acres. Since people sometimes reported acreage as extended families, it is difficult to know which family members claimed ownership of particular fields, if they did at all. For example, Abe Sixkiller's extended family farmed over 114 tilled acres, but this was divided among several fields likely worked by at least five people.[68] Adam and Nellie Turtle, on the other hand, were listed as having no acreage, although they shared a household with her brother Johnson Manning and farmed with him, his wife, and both couples' children. Since Adam and Nellie had married, he had lived in this joint household, and by their own standards, Adam and Nellie were not landless.[69]

In the years immediately following their allotment, Cherokees continued to use local resources communally as long as their environment sustained these food sources and the owner of the land allowed others to do so. Men continued to hunt in the woods, and deer, wild turkey, quail, and other game remained utilized food sources when they were accessible. Newcomers to the community did not always allow hunting on their land, however.[70] Families still raised livestock, especially hogs, which they ran loose on unfenced tracts. Some fenced in their pastureland, however, and new arrivals to the area, in particular, limited the range of their livestock and, thus, of everyone else's.[71] Over time, this seems to have decreased the viability of livestock management for most families. Still, a horse, a mule, a dairy cow, hogs, and poultry remained common.[72] Larger amounts of anything were unusual, but John Brown's family owned a small herd of cattle that ranged from eight to fourteen head.[73]

Cherokee women also continued to gather wild foods, many of which were not located on their own allotments but on that of family or neighbors. For example, families took advantage of berry patches to pick wild strawberries and huckleberries; they pulled wild greens and dug tubers, and they collected nuts, especially hazelnuts and walnuts. Cherokee neighbors perpetuated hospitality toward one another by allowing such gathering and the socializing it encouraged as families came together to share this work.[74]

This diverse range of food sources enabled many families to minimize their need for cash. Walter O. Hale, who grew up during the allotment era, remembered that most Cherokees during his childhood "didn't know what money was. Oh, you would raise your crops and have plenty to live on, but that's about all."[75] Cherokees may not have depended on cash for much, but after statehood, Cherokees wanted some things that required it. The files of restricted Cherokees often include receipts from local stores. Edible household staples were normal: salt, flour, soda, baking powder, lard. Wearable items of clothing and shoes were more common than cloth. Nails, lumber, saws, and other tools were regular purchases. Cleaning supplies and other household needs, such as soap, needles, brooms, and tubs, were less common than food products. Above all, however, Cherokees bought the nonessential things that made life pleasurable then (and still do today): coffee, sugar, and tobacco and snuff.[76]

For this reason, Cherokee families took advantage of new opportunities to generate income. John Welch worked as a deputy sheriff. Lawyer Suake worked as a barber.[77] John Brown and William and Sam Kirk made some money as appraisers.[78] Andrew Palone worked for the oil industry.[79] Women, like Susie Oakball, performed domestic work.[80] Selling agricultural surplus in nearby towns and working for the lumber industry proved to be the most immediate and reliable source of cash for most Cherokees. Throughout the forests of northeastern Oklahoma, divided by the Dawes Commission into small, privately owned timber stands, Cherokee men cut ties for the railroads. This work was called hacking. Lumber companies originally preferred hardwoods, but they became less selective over time.[81] The work was hard, but Indian men willingly did it, in contrast to stereotypes that branded them losers and loafers. Hackers cut trees and hauled them to lumberyards adjoining railroad depots, such as that in Westville, the community with the railroad line in this area. Because of the poor quality of the roads, it could take days for mules to drag the large logs even short distances. The railroads then shipped ties east to Arkansas, to companies like the Hobbs Tie Company that processed and sold them for use on the rail lines expanding throughout Oklahoma and the West. For all this, the pay was low, usually a few cents per tie, but hardworking men earned several dollars per week.[82] Men in this study, including Lewis Bird, Jim Sand, Will Sand, and Steve Sand, worked making ties.[83]

Cherokee men generally used this small income on consumables that they could not grow or make themselves but that were needed by their families. Therefore, the tie industry drew Indian men into the cash economy, both as laborers and consumers. For this reason, the Alberty brothers of Westville catered to this economy by running both the general store and the lumberyard.[84]

Theoretically, of course, Cherokee landowners were earning money for the timber cut on their land, but it often did not work that way, particularly when the land was located at a distance from where the family lived and they did not realize that the timber was removed. Jennie Suake described how her mother, Lucy Bird, was slowly but steadily robbed: "Different ones that cut it, she never did get nothing out of it, go in there and just cut it out."[85] Other Cherokees proved more astute in managing their timber resources. Lewis Bird, who worked in the industry, sold the timber on his two youngest sons' land. He may have cut and transported it himself.[86]

Selling allotted land was another resource that families utilized when they needed cash, and it became an extension of their normal economy. In other words, while some Cherokees were swindled, others made informed decisions to sell land in conjunction with other activities in order to achieve their financial goals, which could be making their subsistence or particular improvements to their farms. Take Susie Oakball as an example. The homestead shared by Susie and her husband, White, included a house and cultivated fields. Susie Oakball also had done work for cash in order to buy items for their farm; thus far, she had purchased a wagon, a harness, a team of horses, and tools. In 1920, she sought to sell ten acres of her surplus in order to make additional improvements. An allotment was just one resource she used to the common end of improving her family's circumstances. In Oakball's case, the land she chose to sell made sense. It was ten acres along the river that was detached from the rest of her land by a public highway cutting through it. Seven of those acres flooded.[87] Susie continued to own the remainder of her land until at least 1930.[88]

Because few members of the community had access to significant amounts of cash, however, reciprocity and hospitality continued to serve as forms of credit. In fact, Cherokee families relied on their customary sources of credit, their family and neighbors, rather than use the banks that were common in the new state. James Brown recalled that "people that needed money" were financed by their neighbors. Cherokees in the region mistrusted banks, including their loans, because they associated

them with speculation, and, more important, they questioned the character and trustworthiness of individuals whose kin would not loan money
to him or her.[89] Moses Welch remembered having "borrowed hundreds
of dollars on my word alone, not a sign of a paper agreeing to pay back
a penny of it."[90] Financial relationships were reflections of the social ties
that bound the community together. It is telling that when Marsh and
Mary Brown signed their will in 1930, they did so in front of their lawyer
and Bill Collyge, the man who had been selling them hardware and supplies for over a decade at his store in Westville.[91]

Family relationships continued to shape the behavior of those Cherokees who did take part in the economic development of the region. For
example, Marsh Brown opened a general store in 1910, but by 1920, his
son-in-law Birch, who was married to his oldest daughter, Lizzie, ran the
store. For a brief period of time, Marsh's son Bill worked as a clerk in the
dry goods store.[92] Meanwhile, Marsh's brothers John and Cap had purchased a gristmill that their sister Love's husband had built. The brothers operated it until John's sons Dick and Bob took over its operation for
several years. Then, they sold it to John's daughter Ollie and her husband,
Gus Hart.[93] Others kept their business in the family in other ways. Edwin
Cannon worked as a carpenter, and he trained his son Caud in this trade,
too. He likely also taught his sons Ira and Aud, who eventually worked in
the lumber industry in the Washington.[94]

Evaluating the overall pattern of their adaptation, Cherokee families
responded to the new opportunities and challenges that resulted from
allotment in ways that reinforced their gendered division of labor. Men
retained their connection with the world beyond their homes and communities. Men performed most hired labor, although women did some
domestic work for wages, such as cleaning and washing.[95] Women continued to prepare food, but men often took foodstuffs to market to sell. Both
men and women farmed. Women's labor was central to the day-to-day
upkeep of Cherokee families, and women described performing a wider
range of tasks. They continued to work in the fields, gather, cook, pre-
serve, sew, wash, and mend to keep their families fed and clothed.[96] Maud
Hess, the oldest daughter of Tom and Fannie Welch, remembered her
adolescence as shaped by the work required on the family farm. She viv-
idly described her domestic chores such as making soap with grease from
meat scraps and lye from wood ashes.[97] Who contributed what suggested
the perpetuation of divisions between genders and among ages regarding

what was considered appropriate work. Such work differed little from earlier generations.

Cherokees incorporated new sources of income in traditionally gendered ways. Richard Manus proudly remembered the time that he "made
[his] manhood," meaning that he began contributing to the subsistence of
his family. Manus described how several men in his family and community helped him to get his start at cutting ties, even though most doubted
that the then fourteen-year-old could make much money at it. It was
physically demanding labor. Manus worked hard, however, and when he
sold his ties, he returned home with a load of groceries that included flour,
tobacco, and lard. Manus earned the respect and gratitude of his family
no less than had he carried home his first deer. In fact, he may already
have been hunting to provide for his family; he did not say. He just said, "I
was a big shot in that home" because "I made a living for all that bunch
and so."[98]

AS THE NEGATIVE OUTCOMES of allotment became obvious to those
within and beyond Indian communities, concerned outsiders, armed with
dire data and fueled with moral indignation, once again sought to save
Indian families. A series of investigative reports undertaken by the federal government and reform organizations drew public attention to conditions in the former Indian Territory. At the request of Secretary of the
Interior Hubert Work, Lewis Meriam of the Institute for Government
Research compiled a study summarizing the state of indigenous people
throughout the nation. Released in 1928, the Meriam Report generated
controversy over the federal mismanagement of Indian affairs and proposed solutions to the many problems identified as directly or indirectly
resulting from the allotment of Indian lands and other efforts to assimilate Indian people. Committed to providing an apolitical and scientific
analysis, Meriam refrained from attacking the Indian Service directly,
but his study emphasized how ineffective administration had undermined
the well-being of Indian people. Critics of the Indian Service called for a
congressional investigation, and in 1930, the Senate Committee on Indian
Affairs visited northeastern Oklahoma. Senators found widespread mal-
nutrition among Indian families subsisting on cornbread and family
members mourning the loss of kin to hunger amid drought gripping the
region. Graphic reports generated sympathy for Oklahoma Indians and
fueled a growing movement to provide for their relief.[99]

As a result of these efforts, reformers again sought long-term solutions to the problems in Indian families in policy reform. Although not everyone associated with Indian affairs abandoned the goal of assimilation, most admitted that allotment had failed to accomplish it and had harmed Indian people. Even the reform organizations that had endorsed the policy now backed the plan proposed by Commissioner of Indian Affairs John Collier in 1933 to protect and nurture tribalism, encourage Indian self-determination, and restore tribal economies. Under pressure from Collier and President Franklin Delano Roosevelt, Congress passed the Wheeler-Howard Act, or Indian Reorganization Act, in 1934. This act repealed the Dawes Act. Echoing the jubilation of Henry L. Dawes nearly fifty years earlier, Collier exclaimed, "One becomes a little breathless when one realizes that Allotment Law—the agony and ruin of Indians—has been repealed."[100]

Reflecting the political clout of Oklahoma's congressional delegation, whose members opposed Collier's reforms, and its leaders' reluctance to share control of Indian affairs in their state with the federal government, the Indian Reorganization Act excluded Oklahoma Indians. Collier, however, quickly proposed a separate and specific bill to include them in the Indian New Deal. Non-Indian Oklahomans resented him for his stinging criticism of their mistreatment of Indians, but even so, Collier found few allies among Oklahoma Indians, particularly those in the eastern half of the state who believed his policies were more suited to reservation Indians rather than those who had once had their own self-governing republics. No different than before allotment, Cherokees resented being the object of outsiders' pity, particularly when it was inspired by stereotypes of them as backwards and degraded.

Nevertheless, everyone agreed that existing legislation failed to provide for the needs of Indian administration in Oklahoma, and Collier worked with his critics to draft legislation designed, if not to fully resolve the problems facing Oklahoma Indians, at least to mitigate the effects of allotment. After extensive debate and revision, Congress approved the Thomas-Rogers Act, which is also known as the Oklahoma Indian Welfare Act, in June 1936. Although it failed to provide for the protection of allotted land remaining in Indian possession or to remove the administration of Indian estates from state to federal court, the law empowered Oklahoma Indians to incorporate for the purposes of land and credit acquisition and self-government.[101] The Cherokee Nation did not immediately reorganize, however. Rather, Cherokee community organizations gradually coalesced into a national government that did not formally reconstitute until the 1970s.

Some Cherokees continued to protest allotment even at the point of its repeal. In 1927, John and Dora Wolfe refused to give information about her allotted land to field clerks.[102] In 1930, Lucy Bird returned a form listing her 330-acre allotment to the office of the superintendent for the Five Civilized Tribes. The tally was an effort by the Indian Service to document who remained in possession of their allotment as plans to end the policy were being debated. Although I have been unable to find documentation explaining why the record was created, it did come in the wake of the Meriam Report, and it might have been an effort to further document the state of Cherokee landownership. Whatever the reasons behind these "Enrollment and Allotment Record: Memorandum for Official Use" forms, Lucy Bird refused to sign hers. So did White and Susie Oakball. The superintendent signed it for them instead.[103]

Conclusion

The community of Chewey and the Cherokee families who lived in the area survived allotment. When anthropologist Albert L. Wahrhaftig conducted his research there during the 1960s, Chewey remained a stable community that still exhibited communitarian ethics.[1] In the decades after allotment, Cherokees there continued to propose their own solutions to the challenges of survival. Allotment was supposed to assimilate them, but Cherokees often have remained at odds with the policies dictated by the federal government and the ideals imposed by the outside world. This is not because Cherokees cannot adapt. As Wahrhaftig put it, "Cherokees innovate when it is necessary to do so in order to keep their way of life intact. Not unchanged, but intact."[2] Cherokees in Chewey organized to develop what Wahrhaftig called a "common and autonomous economic base." The congregation of the Illinois River Cherokee Indian Baptist Church and the members of the Seven Clans stomp ground, for example, sought to establish a cooperative grocery store, a credit union, and a mechanic shop, and they also planned to consolidate and restore their church and ceremonial ground. They proposed purchasing agricultural equipment and employing community members with special skills, such as the graduates of the trade programs popular at Indian boarding schools and veterans who learned how to do specialized jobs while serving in the military. This plan promised to utilize individuals' knowledge for the benefit of community and prevent the outmigration of people with valuable skills who had been seeking work elsewhere. It was a way to bring and keep kin home and make their community prosperous and self-sufficient again.

In the spring of 1967, the two groups combined to raise funds for their development campaign: they built a bandstand and refreshment booth at the stomp ground, and they hosted social dances every weekend through-out the spring and summer. They invited Cherokee and non-Indian musi-cians to play country, rock, and folk music to audiences that included Cherokees and white residents of the community, neighbors from nearby towns, and tourists vacationing in the western Ozarks. Organizers sold sodas and hamburgers to fund their program for economic development.[3] This comprehensive plan for revitalization never materialized in its entirety, but the act of envisioning it and mobilizing community mem-bers to work toward it suggests that what is important about this story is not only the vision of the future that it promised but also the under-lying assumption that the way people there could prosper in the 1960s was with an eye toward harmony and the collective well-being of community members. The persistence of such ways of thinking and acting in the world fails to make sense unless families, the center of Cherokee society, are emphasized.

Also during the 1960s, Cherokee scholars Jack and Anna Kilpatrick recorded another version of the story of the origin of corn (see chapter 1). The storyteller was a fifty-year-old Baptist minister named Siquanid. Origin stories serve a fundamental human need by both explaining the existence of creation and setting the ground rules for interrelationship, and they therefore change along with those who tell and hear them. Siquanid's telling provides a subtle, sophisticated explanation of what was basic and right according to traditional Cherokees living in the mid-twentieth century and in the aftermath of allotment. In other words, it explores the natural law to which Cherokees, and all humans, still are bound to honor if they want to survive.

In this account, Selu shared a home with two grandsons, and although the young men were able providers of meat, she provided what truly nour-ished them, corn from her body that she prepared into delicious dishes. The product of their hunting, meat and fowl, complemented the corn and not the other way around. As in other versions of the story, the grandsons spied on her to learn how she produced this succulent food, but in this account, they then refused to eat. Their rejection of her hospitality sick-ened her, and she died—but not before sharing her knowledge of corn cultivation, instructions that her grandsons followed meticulously to the benefit of humanity.[4]

Selu's household embodied the diffusion of knowledge and power that defined traditional Cherokee society, even after the customary gendered division of labor changed, and emphasized the importance of flexibility.

It also exemplified that being part of the Cherokee family entailed maintaining this balance through generosity and reciprocity. The salvation of Selu's family, moreover, resulted from their commitment to these ideals but also from the adaptability of their young to correct their behavior, adjust to changing circumstances, perfect new technologies, and restore the integrity of their household. In Siquanid's version of the story, this included men learning to farm as they were then doing throughout Cherokee communities in northeastern Oklahoma. As a result, a story about tremendous loss teaches not about downfall and despair but about adaptation and restoration. Those same traits enabled Selu's many descendants to survive repeated tragedies.

Siquanid's version focuses not on the death of Selu but rather on the subsequent actions of the grandsons to right the wrong they committed against their grandmother. As in other versions, these young men already knew how to hunt, but after causing their grandmother's death, they also learned to farm because she told them that perpetuating her knowledge was right. Although they honored her instructions and prospered, that process was not complete until one of Selu's grandsons married. According to Siquanid, one of the young men had no interest in women, but the other did and one day set off toward the home of neighbors who had several daughters. As he neared, he heard them shouting. The girls were roughhousing, and that day, their antics were funny and their laughter was loud. Through all that noise, one of the young women heard a whistle. She turned to see who had called. Like Ollie Brown first taking in Gus Hart (see chapter 2), this young woman liked what she saw. The grandson came closer and explained that he had come looking for a wife. He and his brother had lived alone since their grandmother had died. Selu had been a good provider and a fabulous cook, and the boys had been working in their field like she told them, but the house was not the same without her. Their home needed a woman. The girl must have liked what she heard because she agreed to marry him and move to his home. And so she made it right again; they created a family. He shared the teachings of his grandmother Selu with her. Year after year, the couple hoed a larger field of corn. They grew so much corn that they could share it with the other people, and they extended Selu's hospitality to all Cherokees.[5]

Among all the stories of violence and suffering associated with colonization, there also are tales that bear witness to affection and joy. Adaptation meant survival, and survival can be understood as a series of successful choices made in hopes of living a good life among loved ones. By the time that Siquanid told this story to the Kilpatricks, Selu's family history had been filtered through generations of survivors who endured tremendous loss but who also persisted and rebuilt. Did the decisions that Cherokees made to endure allotment make them less "Cherokee"? Compared to whom? Selu would have understood. She was a woman capable of great love, profound wisdom, enormous change, and remarkable persistence, too. For this, she still is grown and honored by Cherokee families throughout the hills of northeastern Oklahoma.

A century after the passage of allotment legislation, the ongoing political evolution of their nation serves as a reminder of Cherokee durability. In the 1980s, Wilma Mankiller helped to establish the Cherokee Nation Community Development Department. Its first project entailed supporting the residents of Bell, a small Cherokee community in Adair County, and convincing them that they could revitalize their community. Grants paid for the laying of water pipes and improvements to homes, but the work was done by the residents themselves. That one project served as a model and inspiration for Mankiller's administration when she became the first female principal chief of the Cherokee Nation in 1985.[6] At the turn of the twenty-first century, the election of Chadwick Smith as principal chief of the Cherokee Nation is a continuation of this process. Smith's administration has advocated *ga-du-gi*, the ancient Cherokee system of working together as a community to accomplish specific goals, as its formal platform. If the resources made available through the 2010 Cobell settlement to fix the local economies that allotment broke are to accomplish their goal, those who administer them must take into consideration the visions of individual communities, champion their ability to make them reality, and appreciate that the federal government can advocate for *ga-du-gi* as strongly as it once undermined it.

Afterword

After what seemed like a hundred turns down country roads—my queasy stomach feeling every one of them—we arrived at the edge of a field. The scene reminded me of the county fair that I loved as a girl when I would visit my grandma back in the small farm town in Illinois that my dad still calls home. Trucks, campers, minivans, and trailers were wedged into something like rows. I was glad that my friend drove. Having spent most of my life in places where parking spaces were defined by neatly painted lines, I could not have backed a car out of here if my life depended on it. We walked past port-o-johns lining the edge of the field. The smell of food was familiar and good. The soft harmony of music, laughter, and muffled conversations was comforting, too. We filter each new experience through our past, and I fully expected to see the lights of a fair, of carnival rides twinkling in the night sky, but as we wound through the maze of cars and the distance ahead of me brightened, my eyes adjusted to another kind of light altogether.

My friend had brought me to a stomp dance. Dozens of men and women circled the fire. I watched from the edge. As I stood there, late-nineteenth-century ethnologist Alice Fletcher's accounts of learning to understand the language of Indian music—in her case, among the Omaha—came to mind. As she worked past the ethnocentrism and bias of reason, she grew to appreciate what she at first rejected as primitive. Although I never shared Fletcher's confidence in the supremacy of my own culture compared to others, I am guilty of the academic tendency to deconstruct everything. I realized that this was one of those moments in life when I would get the most out of it if I stopped thinking like a scholar. I tried to forget about Fletcher, the proponents of allotment, the ever-vanishing Indian, and all the words written about Native people that

I had ever read. I practiced not-thinking. I listened to what I was told, and I remembered meanings while forgetting the words. I am not a religious person, and so I was surprised by the deep sense of gratitude I felt toward those dancing for themselves and for all of us who seek harmony in our lives, including those whom we love and those whom we do not like and who would do us harm. This is not my belief system, but I know to my bones that the world needs stomp dancers.

Researching this book, I have been humbled many times over by indigenous ways of understanding. Knowing is not a right but a gift given with conditions. This sharply contradicts the freedom of information and expression idealized in Western society, especially in its universities and among its scholars, but these boundaries are what enable cultural survival. I have often heard Indian people speak of things kept hidden from the outside world (including its academics), such as clan affiliations, medicine, and spiritual teachings. These conversations are infused by seriousness, awe, and humor as though it is necessary to acknowledge the importance of such knowledge but also to appreciate this wonderful punch line—that Indian communities have kept some things for themselves. Not everything should be written down, categorized, and published for the world to know. Some things do not belong in an archive. In the age of the Internet, Indian communities retain an *intranet*, where one's ability to know depends on belonging to that network of people bound by family ties and reciprocity.

Armed with a belief in rationality, a prayer for cultural and racial supremacy, and a quest for order, the Dawes Commission entered Cherokee communities demanding information about Cherokee families as a means to gain access to the land and other resources that sustained them. The commissioners and their clerks wrote down a lot of information, but they did not truly listen or learn. Having read through the records created by them during the allotment process with an eye toward answering my specific questions, I am surprised not by how much information was obtained but by what was obscured. Cherokees were remarkably effective in preventing the Dawes Commission from acquiring information that they did not want to share.

I will never find my way back to that stomp ground. I do not know if that was intentional on my friend's part or just his way of taking shortcuts through the back roads of the Cherokee Nation. I suspect the latter, but the former does not trouble me. No GPS could take me back there, and no one who belongs there needs a GPS to find it. When I remember it, I see the handful of small children following the adults around the fire. Some wore the glow necklaces and bracelets that I once loved to wear as a child at Fourth of July celebrations. The smallest ones wore the sneakers that light up with each step. I like this memory because when it was hard to read through the records of the Dawes Commission or write about this egregious mistake in the U.S. government's relationship with indigenous nations, I thought about those Cherokee kids in their light-up shoes taking the fire with them wherever they go in their everyday lives. I envisioned them sparking their way through the hallways of schools in which the Cherokee language is taught once again. Or perhaps they spark down the aisles of the big Wal-Mart in Tahlequah with their grandmas, who remain powerful forces in Cherokee families. In trying to quantify, codify, and reduce what it meant to be Cherokee, the Dawes Commission tried to smother these bonds of family, identity, and community that had brought these children to that ceremonial fire. Allotment wrought unspeakable damage, but, ultimately, it failed. A century after the presumed dissolution of their republic and their proclaimed assimilation into American society, Cherokees survive as families, communities, and sovereign governments. That they have embraced elements of mainstream American life, including even big-box stores, should not be surprising because this is what Cherokee families do—they change in order to persist.

Appendix: Note on Sources

Writing this story was like piecing together a quilt. Connecting the smallest scraps of information into larger pieces, I watched each chapter take shape through many steps of gathering and combining evidence. No one source or set of records tells the story of allotment. That includes the volumes compiled by the Dawes Commission. Likewise, evaluating sources of evidence against one another enables verification of information. I include this brief description of my methodology and key primary sources in order to help those readers who want to do their own research into the allotment era. Whether you are a descendant of allottees, a student of the past, or both, I encourage you to work in these records. There are so many more stories of allotment that should be told.

I began my research in the applications for enrollment compiled by the Dawes Commission. These are called enrollment packets and contain evidence proving rightful inclusion on the Dawes roll. I was most interested in the transcripts of interviews with Cherokees, which provide an enormous amount of demographic and personal information. Not all of this material ended up on the Dawes cards that made up the final roll. I spent my first days researching this book reading through these records, noting information about dozens of individuals. Overwhelmed by the level of detail, I soon created charts for each extended family. Over the decade that I worked on this project, I designed my own system of shorthand to keep track of the names used to refer to individual Cherokees; places of residence and with whom they were shared; age; blood quantum or ancestry; experiences of migration, traveling, or relocation; educational attainment; political orientation and experiences; names of nearest neighbors; proximity to kin and indicators of the type and quality of these relationships; marital, sexual, and reproductive experiences; parenting; sickness and mortality; work and productive labor (both for subsistence and for cash); experiences of the environment, including resources used for food, such as game and wild plants; and land leases and sales.

Having developed a means to bring order to each individual reference to the lives of the Cherokees in this study, I continued researching sources that enabled me to understand how these families evolved over time. I used the Cherokee censuses for 1880, 1883, 1890, and 1893. I also searched in the U.S. census from the mid-nineteenth through the early twentieth centuries. Cherokees who did not remove immediately to Indian Territory on the Trail of Tears often appear in the U.S. census in Georgia and

North Carolina. The United States first took a census in Indian Territory in 1890, but it was lost to fire, and only the cumulative report survived. The U.S. census for 1900 exists but does not include all Cherokee families in Indian Territory. About half of the families I researched were counted. By 1910, census takers included most Cherokee families in this study, but many Cherokees refused to share anything beyond the most basic information. Congress ordered the destruction of the corresponding 1900 and 1910 farm schedules, a tragic loss of information. Most Cherokees in this study appear in the 1920 census and those taken thereafter.

I then compared demographic information obtained from the Dawes roll and censuses to that found on the Eastern Cherokee applications, which resulted in the Guion Miller roll. The U.S. government created this list to determine which survivors of the Trail of Tears and their descendants were eligible to receive compensation according to a May 1906 ruling of the U.S. Court of Claims. The list was completed in 1909. Because claimants had to document their ancestry back to the 1830s, it contains significantly more genealogical information than the Dawes roll or any Cherokee or U.S. census. It is particularly useful when used in conjunction with the Henderson roll, which was compiled before removal in 1835.

Several sources enabled me to learn more about the homesteads and economies of these families. To begin, allotment jackets—files containing applications and maps—often list improvements, including houses and other farm structures, fields, and orchards. Unfortunately, clerks did not always identify the location of these improvements on the accompanying maps, nor do the pre-allotment surveys or plat maps created by the USGS give a detailed or accurate depiction of land use and development prior to allotment. As a result, I made the maps that I wished the Dawes Commission had by laminating their plat maps and, using erasable markers, drawing on and coloring in the improvements and land selections of the families in this study. I appreciate that cartographic software could have done some of this work for me, but mapping by hand proved invaluable, in part, because I colored these maps in a variety of ways several times over the years as I worked on this project and as my understanding of the bonds connecting individuals in this study deepened. In plotting and figuring the relationships among people, homes, and resources, I discerned patterns that I would not have learned any other way. The allotment jackets also include some demographic information about those Cherokees who selected their own allotments, but they contain almost no information on resisters.

Censuses also enabled me to understand the geographic positioning of families. All censuses provide some information about who lived with whom and next to whom. Even the 1880 Cherokee census, which generally lists Cherokees in alphabetical order by surname, sometimes clusters people into extended families. The rest of the censuses group members of households together and enabled me to identify who lived with and near each other, particularly when neighbors were kin. Censuses sometimes provide other data describing characteristics of life such as occupation, marital status, and literacy. The type and quality of this information varies. The educational census taken in 1930 for the commissioner of Indian Affairs to ascertain the economic condition of restricted families and the needs of their minor children provides information on housing, household membership, and subsistence.

Restricted Cherokees who wanted to sell part of their allotments had to file applications for the removal of restrictions. These forms include detailed information about the resources families used to provide for themselves. They also provide information about educational attainment, household composition, marital status, and reproduction. Some include transcripts of interviews with applicants in which they elaborate on their economic circumstances. Indian case files, records kept on restricted Cherokees by the superintendent for the Five Civilized Tribes, also provide information on what resources Cherokees possessed and wanted to obtain. Some of these files are incredibly detailed.

Probate files, most of which were compiled locally by county officials but a few of which were created by federal clerks, also include transcripts of interviews with Cherokees about the status of property. In some cases, the land was legally owned by a deceased loved one, but many probate cases relate to the possession of land belonging to minors attaining legal adulthood or to adults selling land after restrictions were lifted. The interviews vary in specificity, but because decisions regarding the division of property required the participation of or accounting for all legal heirs, these court records include information about relationships, marriage, and reproduction.

Oral histories make up the last group of sources I consulted. I was grateful to find interviews with several Cherokees in this study, especially in the Indian-Pioneer papers and the Doris Duke collection of American Indian oral history. Transcripts of interviews vary in length, relevance to important topics, and depth of questioning. Generally, informants provided information I initially thought to be impersonal, but when I reconsidered these accounts as a group, the story of a generation appeared. That is the story I have tried to tell in this book. I hope it inspires the telling of others.

Notes

ᗒᎻ Ꮍᗕ

ABBREVIATIONS

ARP   Anna Ross Piburn Collection, Western History Collection, University of Oklahoma, Norman, Okla.

CJH   C. J. Harris Collection, Western History Collection, University of Oklahoma, Norman, Okla.

CNR   Cherokee National Records, Oklahoma Historical Society, Oklahoma City, Okla.

DD   Doris Duke Oral History Collection, Western History Collection, University of Oklahoma, Norman, Okla.

DWB   Dennis Wolf Bushyhead Collection, Western History Collection, University of Oklahoma, Norman, Okla.

HAC   *History of Adair County*, by Adair County History Committee (Cane Hill, Ark.: ARC Press of Cane Hill, 1991)

IC   Indian Collection, Hampton University Archives, Hampton University, Hampton, Va.

IPP   Indian-Pioneer History Collection, Oklahoma Historical Society, Oklahoma City, Okla.

JM   Joel B. Mayes Collection, Western History Collection, University of Oklahoma, Norman, Okla.

JMC   James Mansford Carselowey Collection, Oklahoma Historical Society, Oklahoma City, Okla.

LH   Leslie Hewes Collection, Western History Collection, University of Oklahoma, Norman, Okla.

LL   Living Legends Oral History Collection, Oklahoma Historical Society, Oklahoma City, Okla.

SM   Samuel H. Mayes Collection, Western History Collection, University of Oklahoma, Norman, Okla.

WCR   W. C. Rogers Collection, Western History Collection, University of Oklahoma, Norman, Okla.

WPR   William Potter Ross Collection, Western History Collection, University of Oklahoma, Norman, Okla.

1. The Dawes Commission allotted Nannie and her son, Sam Chewey, land that Tom had improved before his marriage to her. It was abandoned and neglected after Tom and Nannie established their home in Chewey. Commission to the Five Civilized Tribes, Applications for Allotment (hereafter known as allotment jacket): Tom and Nannie Wolfe. Indian case file: Sam Chewey. Probate file: Tom Wolfe, Nannie Wolfe.

2. Lewis was the son of Joe Sourjohn, a former deputy sheriff for the Cherokee Nation from Tahlequah. Lewis's mother was Nancy Bearpaw, and her people were from this area to the east of the Cherokee capital. Lewis's maternal aunts and uncles and his sister Jennie still made their homes there. In 1917, Governor Robert L. Williams granted dozens of paroles as part of his birthday celebration, and Sourjohn received one of them. His second chance was short-lived. By 1920, Sourjohn was back in McAlester, and after his subsequent release, Switch Foreman killed him in Tahlequah. Benge, *1880 Cherokee National Census* (hereafter referred to as Cherokee census: 1880). Guion Miller roll (hereafter referred to as Eastern Cherokee application): Jennie Sand. *Adair County Republican*, February 19, 1915: 1; March 12, 1915: 5. *Daily Oklahoman*, December 20, 1917: 1 and 14; November 13, 1920: 7. Probate file: Tom Wolfe.

3. Indian case file: Sam Chewey. Bureau of the Census, 1920 census (hereafter simply given as the year of the census). Probate file: Tom Wolfe. Nannie had helped raise three of Tom's sons from a previous marriage, including John, after she and his father began their relationship following the death of Tom's previous wife, John's mother. They also raised Nannie's two daughters, Jennie and Louella, and her son, Sam, who were the results of three earlier relationships.

4. 1920 census. Probate file: Tom Wolfe. Application for Removal of Restrictions for 1908: Dora Wolfe.

5. I think the stenographer misspelled the buyer's name, which is rightly "Watkins," not "Wadkins." Probate file: Tom Wolfe.

6. There's no evidence of animosity between John and Nannie. Probate file: Tom Wolfe, Nannie Wolfe.

7. Indian case file: Sam Chewey. DD: Sam Chewey.

8. 1920 census. Probate file: Nannie Wolfe.

9. Allotment was not an innovation of the late nineteenth century. For a history of precedents, see Gibson, "Centennial Legacy"; Hagan, *Taking Indian Lands*; and Washburn, *Assault on Indian Tribalism*, 9. In his 1878 annual report, Commissioner of Indian Affairs Ezra A. Hayt, a proponent of the policy, summarized the results of previous allotment laws; his positive narrative is a stark contrast to the interpretations of those who have studied the policy in its aftermath. See pages 7–10.

10. Historian Francis Paul Prucha cites these numbers based on tabulations by John Collier, the commissioner of Indian Affairs from 1933 until 1945 and a critic of allotment. Collier characterized half of remaining land as arid or semi-arid and, therefore, unsuitable for agriculture and grazing. *Great Father*, 895–96. The Indian Land Tenure Foundation suggests there has been little improvement since the repeal of the policy; see <www.indianlandtenure.org/index.html>. The Wheeler-Howard Act, or Indian Reorganization Act, was passed in 1934, and while the act excluded

Oklahoma's diverse Indian population, some of its provisions were extended to the Indian peoples in Oklahoma through the Thomas-Rogers Act, or Oklahoma Indian Welfare Act, of 1936.

11. Warhaftig, "In the Aftermath of Civilization," 33.

12. Smith cited this number while lecturing in the Cherokee Nation history course, which I attended in September 2003 in Oklahoma City.

13. The federal government set up the trust accounts to manage the resources of individual allottees (or their heirs) who received payment for rent or leases on their property or the resources on it or in it. For more information, see <www.cobellsettlement.com/index.php>.

14. Probably because slavery was not practiced there, Chewey lacked a freedmen population. Therefore, I do not comment on the freedmen and freedwomen's experiences of allotment.

15. L. Smith, *Decolonizing Methodologies*, 25–29.

16. The term "thick description" is associated with anthropologist Clifford Geertz and symbolic anthropology. "Thick Description," 3–30.

17. This classic definition is borrowed from James Axtell, an early advocate of the methodology who also has served as its historian. Following Axtell, I define culture as "an idealized pattern of meanings, values, and norms differently shared by members of a society, which can be inferred from the non-instinctive behavior of the group and from the symbolic products of their actions, including materials, artifacts, language, and social institutions." Quote from "Ethnohistory," 2. Axtell, *Natives and Newcomers*, 1–12.

18. Scholars commonly use the terms "upstreaming" and "downstreaming"; Daniel K. Richter coined "sidestreaming" in his *Ordeal of the Longhouse*, 5.

19. Hoxie, "Ethnohistory," 613.

20. Galloway, *Practicing Ethnohistory*, 7.

21. Vine Deloria Jr. is credited with initiating this discussion, described in Biolsi and Zimmerman, *Indians and Anthropologists*. See also Mihesuah and Wilson, *Natives and Academics*.

22. Piker, *Okfuskee*, 5.

23. Schultz, *Seminole Baptist Churches*.

24. These terms have a history in reference to Cherokees. See Perdue, *"Mixed Blood" Indians*. For an elaboration upon this critique of western historical methods, see L. Smith, *Decolonizing Methodologies*, 29–33.

25. Rogers, *Ani-Yun-Wiya*, viii.

26. In this, my interpretation differs from that of other scholars who have written about Cherokee conceptions of race, including Mihesuah, who suggests that some late-nineteenth Cherokees embraced Anglo-American values, particularly notions of true womanhood. See *Cultivating the Rosebuds*. In *Race and the Cherokee Nation*, Yarbrough argues that this gravitation toward whiteness reflected a stigmatization of blackness and those of African ancestry. Saunt has suggested that such schisms were not exclusive to Cherokees. In his biography of the prominent Creek Grayson family, he demonstrates that racial difference mattered enough to divide kin and, thus, a tribal nation. See *Black, White, and Indian*. The class of those analyzed contributes to

the difference in our interpretations. Although one member of this study attended the Cherokee Male Seminary, no one described in this book could be called wealthy or considered to be elite as those examined in the previously mentioned studies tended to be. These were common people who lived in a community with no identifiable families of African ancestry.

27. For an examination of the modern implications of this process, see Sturm, *Blood Politics*.

28. Schultz, *Seminole Baptist Churches*, 4–5. All scholars writing about Cherokees today seemingly are obligated to discuss this terminology at the beginning of their books. My favorite is by Cherokee literary scholar Daniel Heath Justice in *Our Fires Survive the Storm*, xv–xvi.

29. Coates, "'None of Us Are Supposed to Be Here,'" 83.

30. Baird, "Are There Real Indians in Oklahoma?"

31. Eastern Cherokee application: Steve Dog.

32. This group began in the 1930s with Otis, *Dawes Act*. It also includes more recent works including Washburn, *Assault on Indian Tribalism*; Berthrong, *Cheyenne and Arapaho Ordeal*; Hagan, *United States–Comanche Relations*; Gibson, "Centennial Legacy"; and Wishart, *Unspeakable Sadness*.

33. Osburn, *Southern Ute Women*.

34. Good examples incorporating analysis of allotment include Hoxie, *Parading Through History*, and Lynn-Sherow, *Red Earth*. O'Neill's *Working the Navajo Way* provided a model for my understanding of how households adapted new economic opportunities to reaffirm traditional relationships and identities.

35. In her unpublished dissertation, "Divide and Conquer," Odell, like Debo before her, emphasizes economic and political dislocation and assumes a corresponding cultural decline.

36. Johnston, *Cherokee Women in Crisis*.

37. Lomawaima, *They Called It Prairie Light*, quote on p. xi, statistics on p. 15.

38. The best example is Pascoe, *Relations of Rescue*.

39. Kauanui, *Hawaiian Blood*.

40. Jaimes and Halsey, "American Indian Women." Amnesty International, "Maze of injustice."

41. Mankiller, *Mankiller*, 20.

42. Pascoe, *What Comes Naturally*, 23.

CHAPTER ONE

1. Mooney, *History, Myths, and Sacred Formulas*, 242–49.

2. Scholars have elaborated upon the symbolic meaning of blood to Cherokees. See Hudson, *Southeastern Indians*, 319–21, and Perdue, *Cherokee Women*, 28–37.

3. Hudson, *Southeastern Indians*, 120–83. Thomas, "Cherokee Values and Worldview."

4. Mooney, *History, Myths, and Sacred Formulas*, 242–49.

5. I used the published version of this pre-removal roll: Tyner, *Those Who Cried*. For more information about the Henderson roll and Eastern Cherokee applications, see the appendix.

6. Perdue, *Cherokee Women.*

7. Historical names for the clans vary; see Perdue, *Cherokee Women*, 42.

8. Gulick, *Cherokees at the Crossroads*, 64–65. Perdue, *Cherokee Women*, 41–59. B. Smith, "Perspective of the Clans."

9. Most of the allotment-era residents of Chewey whose ancestors I can identify came from what became northeastern Georgia and southwestern North Carolina, but I do not know how long they lived in the Valley Towns region of Cherokee territory, which had shrunk repeatedly and tremendously prior to removal.

10. Hill, *Weaving New Worlds*, 2–7.

11. Goodwin, "Cherokees in Transition," 41. Hudson, *Southeastern Indians*, 193–96, 229–57. Hudson, *Knights of Spain*, 21–22. Reid, *Law of Blood.*

12. Hudson, *Southeastern Indians*, 188–89. Perdue, *Cherokee Women*, 24–26.

13. Hatley, *Dividing Paths*, 64.

14. Goodwin, "Cherokees in Transition," 158–64. White, "Ethnoarchaeological Approach," 119–39.

15. Hatley, "Cherokee Women Farmers," 43. White, "Ethnoarchaeological Approach," 139–47.

16. White, "Ethnoarchaeological Approach," 81–108.

17. Ibid., 108–19.

18. Ibid., 153.

19. In *The Cherokees: A Population History*, Russell Thornton suggests that there may have been earlier population decline due to disease in addition to the tremendous suffering of the eighteenth century. See pages 16–46. Conley, *Cherokee Nation*, 45–71. Hatley, *Dividing Paths*, 119–40.

20. Conley, *Cherokee Nation*, 45–71. Thornton, *Cherokees*, 16–46. Hatley, *Dividing Paths*, 119–40.

21. Goodwin theorized that this process actually began in the late seventeenth century as a result of European encroachment, the extension of trade routes, the depletion of hunting grounds, and warfare; see "Cherokees in Transition," 112–24. Like Thornton, however, I think this trend became more pronounced after the French and Indian War and the Revolutionary War; see *Cherokees*, 24–25. Perdue, *Cherokee Women*, 105–8. In 1824, the Cherokee government passed a law prohibiting settlement within a quarter mile of another's improvements. See Strickland, *Fire and the Spirits*, 215.

22. Goodwin, "Cherokees in Transition," 112–14. The pre-removal census provides vivid evidence of this. Cherokees were grouped by the location in which they lived, and while some lived in towns, most were listed under the water route they lived along. Tyner, *Those Who Cried.*

23. Bird was born in Goingsnake District between 1855 and 1857. I believe Jeh-si's household is that of his paternal relatives. Tyner, *Those Who Cried*, 27, 42.

24. Perdue and Green believe that "house" may refer to other buildings, including barns, smokehouses, and the like; see *Cherokee Removal*, 50. In his study of the valuation records, *Cherokee Planters*, Don L. Shadburn never defines the term but seems to interpret "house" to mean a dwelling structure.

25. Steve Dog was born in Goingsnake District in 1859. I believe this was his paternal grandparents' household. Tyner, *Those Who Cried*, 85.

26. Ibid., 56. Shadburn referred to Will Proctor as a mixed blood. He may have been designated as such by the valuation agents, but he is listed as a full blood in the 1835 census. Such variability of blood quantum designations is common in Cherokee genealogy. Shadburn, *Cherokee Planters*, 16, 108.

27. Perdue, *Cherokee Women*, 107.

28. It is unclear to me whether these census takers asked Cherokees to identify their parentage or made assumptions based on appearance and lifestyle. Likewise, census takers seem not to have made consistent, uniform decisions. In particular, some women who intermarried were identified as having the same blood quantum as their children, although logically they should have twice that amount.

29. Tyner, *Those Who Cried*, 152. I believe Thomas Raper also married a McDaniel woman.

30. See ibid., 132, 173, 179.

31. Ibid., 52. Lorene Phipps Tillery, "Bell, Cannon, Tillery Connection," *HAC*, 688. There were four full-blood Chewey families listed in the 1835 census, and I was not able to determine to which of them Joe Chewey, who settled Chewey, belonged.

32. Hatley, "Cherokee Women Farmers," 41–46, quote on p. 47.

33. Perdue, *Cherokee Women*, 117–34.

34. McLoughlin, *Cherokee Renascence*, 62–64.

35. Tyner, *Those Who Cried*, 42, 27, 52, 56, 152, 88, 188, 178, 54.

36. Perdue, *Cherokee Women*, 120–28, quote on p. 122.

37. Riggs, *Removal Period Cherokee Households*, 255. Tyner, *Those Who Cried*, 52, 54, 88, 188.

38. Tyner, *Those Who Cried*, 52.

39. Shadburn, *Cherokee Planters*, 172–73.

40. Riggs, *Removal Period Cherokee Households*, 275.

41. Tyner, *Those Who Cried*, 188.

42. Ibid., 42, 88.

43. Ibid., 54.

44. Some of these people may have been bilingual. The census does not specify. Ibid., 188.

45. Ibid., 173, 178, 179.

46. Shadburn, *Cherokee Planters*, 227–30.

47. Eastern Cherokee application: Eliza Brown, Martin Raper. U.S. census: 1820, 1860, 1870, 1880. Cherokee census: 1880. Benge, *1890 Cherokee National Census* (hereafter referred to as Cherokee census: 1890). Shadburn, *Cherokee Planters*, 47. Tyner, *Those Who Cried*, 74, 75, 60. According to James Carselowey, some McDaniels moved west in 1834 before the main body of Cherokees. *My Journal*, 18, JMC.

48. Thornton, *Cherokees*, 43–44.

49. Other Cherokees who went west in 1834 were wealthy, including Daniel Ross, William Vann, and their families. Carselowey, *My Journal*, 18.

50. Jack D. Baker, "Joel and Nellie (Quinton) Kelley Family," *HAC*, 401–2. Foreman, *Indian Removal*, 251–63, quote on 254–55. U.S. census: 1860. Other Cherokees from this region may have left before the Trail of Tears as well. The grandparents of James Phillips, who was the father of Maggie Chance, left the Hightower River region for

Indian Territory in 1829. Phyllis Hagan and Soneeta Ballenger, "James and Martha L. Phillips," *HAC*, 514–15.

51. As quoted in Foreman, *Indian Removal*, 254.

52. Arsie Bigby, "James and Catherine Foreman Bigby," *HAC*, 192–93. Arsie Bigby, "David Taylor and Nancy Jane Guilliams Bigby," *HAC*, 193–95. Joseph Tuck, "Ellen Adeline (Dudley) Tuck," *HAC*, 696. Tyner, *Those Who Cried*, 132, 173, 178, 179.

53. Foreman's estimate of 4,000 deaths generally has been accepted as accurate and is popularly quoted. Thornton suggests that Foreman's estimate could be low; see *Cherokees*, 73–77.

54. Finger, *Eastern Band*, 101–7.

55. *Cherokee Advocate*, September 14, 1883.

56. Ibid., November 25, 1876. Eastern Cherokee application: Eliza Brown, Florence M. Brown. Commission to the Five Civilized Tribes, Applications for Enrollment (hereafter referred to as enrollment packet): James and Eliza Brown, James and Hattie Holland. According to Finger, Eliza Brown, who was the daughter of Jesse Raper, came from a family that had been of some means but that had suffered tremendously during and after the Civil War. Finger, *Eastern Band*, 71, 116–17, 128. U.S. census: 1870, 1880. Cherokee census: 1880, 1890.

57. Jesse Raper, a sixty-year-old white farmer from North Carolina, is listed in the 1860 U.S. census for Indian lands west of Arkansas. He lived in the Saline District. Mary (1798–1890) and Jesse Raper (1797–1897) are buried in the Baptist Mission Cemetery near Westville. Carselowey, *My Journal*, 67.

58. U.S. census: 1860, 1870. They lived in Dawson County, Georgia, which was created, in part, out of Lumpkin County in 1857. Cherokee census: 1890. Enrollment packet: Edwin Cannon, Ira Cannon. Eastern Cherokee application: Edwin Cannon. Shadburn, *Cherokee Planters*, 220–30. Lorene Phipps Tillery, "Bell, Cannon, Tillery Connection," *HAC*, 688. "The Wilson Lumpkin Cannon Family," *HAC*, 686–87.

59. George Welch and his family were reinstated to Cherokee citizenship in early December 1877. CNR, vol. 270, p. 118, and vol. 274, p. 32. U.S. census: 1860, 1870. Betty Hess Smith, "Thomas Jefferson Welch," *HAC*, 734.

60. U.S. census: 1860, 1870. Cherokee census: 1880, 1890. Eastern Cherokee application: John Welch, Mack Welch.

61. Phyllis Hagan and Soneeta Ballenger, "Malachi and Mahalia Parris," *HAC*, 504.

62. Eastern Cherokee application: Hattie Lewis. U.S. census: 1920.

63. Baker, "Joel and Nellie (Quinton) Kelley Family," 401–2. The account of the Harris contingent is included in Foreman, *Indian Removal*, 251–63. U.S. census: 1860.

64. Virgil Talbot and A. D. Lester with Betty Barker, "Going Snake," *HAC*, 588–89. "Goingsnake District," *HAC*, 589. The name of the man is spelled as two words, and the district is spelled as one word.

65. Baker, "Joel and Nellie (Quinton) Kelley Family," 401–2.

66. D. M. Starr, "Adair County, Oklahoma," *HAC*, 1–3. Carselowey, *My Journal*, 42–43, 80–81.

67. Jack D. Baker, "Chewey," *HAC*, 54.

68. Gail Crittenden shared with me a copy of Betsy Suake's application to the Bureau of Pensions from 1898. She sought funds for the care of her three children

then under sixteen years old, Linnie, Mary, and Lawyer. Her application was granted. James Carselowey listed the Cherokee men who served with the Union force; see *My Journal*, 29–30, 33. For more information on Civil War–era factionalism, see Confer, *Cherokee Nation*.

69. Several partial lists of Confederate Cherokees are included in James Carselowey's papers at the Oklahoma Historical Society. The longest list is printed in *Cherokee Notes*, 26, JMC.

70. Rogers, *Ani-Yun-Wiya*, 238.

71. Hagan and Ballenger, "Malachi and Mahalia Parris," 504. Carselowey, "An Interview with Sadie Condreay," *Cherokee Notes*, 69–70. The other man killed in that incident was Jonathan Buffington, the brother of Thomas Buffington, who served as principal chief of the Cherokee Nation after the Civil War.

72. This debate is central to the scholarship about American Indian women in which "declension" and "persistence" are major themes. Specifically concerning Cherokee history, Carolyn Ross Johnston argues that women's loss of status was severe and reflected the eroding power of clans, whereas Theda Perdue emphasizes adaptation and persistence. The classic text on the emergence of the Cherokees' republican government is William McLoughlin's *Cherokee Renascence in the New Republic*, a narrative in which the clans' relinquishment of coercive authority prompted their gradual erosion as a force in Cherokee society.

73. Thomas, "Cherokee Values and Worldview."

74. Baker, "Chewey," 54–55.

75. Bill Chewey, his son, probated his estate in June 1894. CNR, vol. 124, p. 28, and vol. 126, p. 37.

76. McLoughlin, *Cherokee Renascence*.

CHAPTER TWO

1. Sue Brown McGinnis, "James Daniel Brown," *HAC*, 229. Justus Hart, "William Hart Family," *HAC*, 367. Enrollment packet: John and Emily Brown.

2. Hart, "William Hart Family," 367.

3. For information on the McDaniels in the Old Nation, see Shadburn, *Cherokee Planters*, 43, 47. Tyner, *Those Who Cried*, 74, 75, 80, 152. Finger, *Eastern Band*, 71, 128. U.S. census: 1860, 1870, 1880. Cherokee census: 1880, 1890. Eastern Cherokee application: Eliza Brown, Martin Raper. McGinnis, "James Daniel Brown," 229. Hart, "William Hart Family," 367.

4. This is the spelling of her name on the 1883 Cherokee census, Oklahoma Historical Society, Oklahoma City, Okla. (hereafter referred to as Cherokee census: 1883). In the Eastern Cherokee application, it is spelled as Gah-dee-klaw-eh.

5. Cherokee census: 1883. Eastern Cherokee application: Betsy Oakball, White Oakball (listed as Charley), John Oakball. White and John's Eastern Cherokee testimony suggests that their grandparents did not remove at all and died in the Old Nation. Foreman, *Indian Removal*, 294–312.

6. Cherokee census: 1883, 1880, 1890. Probate file: Betsy Oakball. Eastern Cherokee application: Betsy Oakball, White Oakball, Susie Oakball, John Oakball.

7. Enrollment packet: Noah Sand. Jack D. Baker, "Daniel Downing Family," *HAC*, 303–4.

8. Eastern Cherokee application: Birch Anderson, Cleo Welch. Cherokee census: 1880, 1890. U.S. census: 1900.

9. In early December 1898, Tilman Chance was sentenced to four years in the federal penitentiary for perjury. *Daily Chieftain*, December 2, 1898. When he appeared before the Dawes Commission, he said that he served two and a half years; he may have been attempting to minimize the time that he was not physically present in the Cherokee Nation because the eligibility of intermarried spouses to receive an allotment was unsettled. Enrollment packet: Tilman and Maggie Chance. U.S. census: 1900. Phyllis Hagan and Soneeta Ballenger, "James and Martha L. Phillips" and "Jennie and Edward Hines," *HAC*, 514–15.

10. Cherokee census: 1890. Eastern Cherokee application: Susie Oakball. Her parents were Sante Fe and Ludi, and her paternal grandmother was Nakey Suwagee, whose other children were Swimmer and Cunyuchee (she may have had additional children not living with her at the time). Enrollment packet: Betsy Oakball, White and Susie Oakball.

11. Cherokee census: 1890. Until he died in 1885, Jennie's father, Richard, also was part of the household. Eastern Cherokee application: Jennie Oakball.

12. Cherokee census: 1890. U.S. census: 1920. Jack D. Baker, "Joel and Nellie (Quinton) Kelley Family," *HAC*, 401–2. Enrollment packet: Joe and Rosanna Mounce, John and Susan Kelley.

13. Cherokee census: 1890. U.S. census: 1900, 1910. Eastern Cherokee application: Maggie Chance. Hagan and Ballenger, "Jennie and Edward Hines," 514–15.

14. This also may hold true concerning the Cherokee fathers who married non-Indian women. The sons of George and Louisa Welch, cousins to Tom, lived next to each other after leaving their parents' household. In 1900, they each lived with their families on either side of their stepmother, Lizzie, a Cherokee woman and recently widowed, and their stepbrothers and stepsisters. Cherokee census: 1890. U.S. census: 1900.

15. Cherokee census: 1890.

16. U.S. census: 1900.

17. Perdue, *Cherokee Women*, 36–37. Sattler, "Women's Status," 224–25.

18. Hagan and Ballenger, "James and Martha L. Phillips," 514–15.

19. The defining texts on the fate of Cherokee women's status post-contact are Johnston, *Cherokee Women in Crisis*; Mihesuah, *Cultivating the Rosebuds*; and Perdue, *Cherokee Women*. Most recently, Miles added to this conversation with an argument specifically for persistence of elderly women's authority in "'Circular Reasoning.'"

20. In 1900, the U.S. census taker listed William as having one-eighth white ancestry and his children as having one-half Indian ancestry. The Cherokee census of 1890 identified him as an intermarried white man, and therefore so have I, because I believe the 1890 Cherokee census to be the more accurate of the two.

21. Eastern Cherokee application: Tom Suake. U.S. census: 1900. In the 1900 census, Betsy Suake is listed as Betsie Wickey. The elderly relative is either Jess or James Crittenden. Linnie is called Lillie.

22. U.S. census: 1900.

23. Ibid.

24. Cherokee census: 1880, 1890. U.S. census: 1920.

25. U.S. census: 1820, 1860, 1870, 1900. Cherokee census: 1890. Enrollment packet: Martin and Martha Raper, James and Eliza Brown.

26. U.S. census: 1900, 1910, 1920. Enrollment packet: Noah Sand, Steve Sand, Will Sand, John Sand, Steve and Nannie Dog. Indian case file: Noah Sand. For other examples, see the enrollment packets of Samuel Chuwee, Sam Sixkiller, and Ned Turtle.

27. Polly Brown, the eldest daughter of Eliza Brown, was not married. Neither was her younger sister Florence, who seemed to be sickly. Henry Crittenden, the son of Sam Crittenden, also remained unmarried. He was deaf and mute.

28. Cherokee census: 1880, 1890. U.S. census: 1900, 1910, 1920.

29. Thornton, *Cherokees*, 52–53.

30. Bureau of the Census, Report on Indians Taxed and Not Taxed, 255.

31. Thornton, *Cherokees*, 172–74.

32. No evidence points to intermarriage with people of African descent in this community.

33. George Welch Sr. married Margaret Jones, a white woman from Virginia. His son George Jr. married Nancy Jones, another Anglo-American woman. Another son of George Sr., Lemuel, married an Anglo-American woman, Mary. Lemuel's son George married a white woman, Louisa. U.S. census: 1860, 1870, 1900. Cherokee census: 1880, 1890. Eastern Cherokee application: Tom Welch, James Mack Welch, John Welch, Mack Welch.

34. McGinnis, "James Daniel Brown," 229. Love is the nickname of Narcissa. Eastern Cherokee application: Narcissa Thompson. Enrollment packet: John and Emily Brown, James and Eliza Brown, James and Ida Brown. Love, John, and Cap intermarried. Edwin, Wilson, Oscar, and Ophelia married non-Indians. Sarah and John married other Cherokees. Enrollment packet: Edwin and Lucinda Cannon, Oscar and Annie Cannon, John and Lee Cannon, Ophelia J. Harless, Wilson L. Cannon.

35. Her mother was Elizabeth Taylor. Her maternal grandmother was Jennie Bigby. Her great-grandparents, James and Catherine Foreman, were Cherokees with intermarried parents, presumably white fathers. Eastern Cherokee application: Mary Brown.

36. James and Martha Phillips were both Cherokees from families with histories of intermarriage. Martha's mother, Mahalia Parris, for example, was non-Indian. At least five of James and Martha's children married non-Indians: John, William, Maggie, James, and Jennie. Cherokee census: 1890. U.S. census: 1900. Eastern Cherokee application: Maggie Chance. Hagan and Ballenger, "James and Martha Phillips," 514–15. I was not able to determine whom Sarah Mary Lou, or Sallie, married except that his last name was Murphy.

37. Logan and Ousley, "Hypergamy, Quantum, and Reproductive Success."

38. Perdue, *Cherokee Women*, 81–83.

39. Mounce also claimed another field of about fifteen fenced acres and a small orchard. These were located a small distance from her homestead and may have been improvements she claimed on behalf of other family members who also picked land

nearby. Allotment jacket: Joe and Rosanna Mounce. Baker, "Joel and Nellie (Quinton) Kelley Family," 401–2.

40. Allotment jacket: Steve and Nannie Dog. Eastern Cherokee application: Nannie Dog. Cherokee census: 1890. Reese Mitchell, probate records, Goingsnake District, CNR.

41. Mihesuah, *Cultivating the Rosebuds*; Johnston, *Cherokee Women in Crisis*.

42. Ned Foreman died in 1892. Eastern Cherokee application: Nannie Dog, Fannie Turtle, Charlotte Swimmer, Betsy Suake (listed as Waker). Cherokee census: 1880, 1890. U.S. census: 1910.

43. Eastern Cherokee application: Birch Anderson, Cleo Welch, Fannie Mitchell. Cherokee census: 1880, 1890. In the 1890 census, Alice and May are listed on the orphan roll, although it appears that they, too, like Birch and Cleo, lived with their maternal aunt Nancy and her family. May is listed as attending the Moses Prairie School, which must be a typo. The Mosley's Prairie School was a Cherokee Nation school near the Arkansas border. Jack D. Baker, "Schools: Cherokee National Schools, Flint and Goingsnake Districts," *HAC*, 61–67. David Hampton, Descendants of Nancy Ward, genealogy chart in author's collection. Hampton is the president of the Association of the Descendants of Nancy Ward.

44. Enrollment packet: Oscar and Annie Cannon.

45. Enrollment packet: Mose and Minnie Crittenden.

46. Enrollment packet: Tom and Nancy Suake. Nancy was Tom's wife during the time period of enrollment.

47. Probate file: Ezekiel Suake.

48. IPP: James Brown. For examples, see the enrollment packet of Mose and Minnie Crittenden and Tom and Nancy Suake.

49. Enrollment packet: Joe and Rosanna Mounce. Probate file: Thomas Mounce. U.S. census: 1910. Nancy Suake provides a comparable example. She had several long-term relationships, and whether these were formal marriages is unclear. Enrollment packet: Tom and Nancy Suake.

50. Cherokee census: 1880, 1890. In the 1896 Cherokee census, Louella and Sam are listed under Tom's surname, Wolfe. The Dawes Commission cross-checked enrollment applications against the 1896 census, which was the last taken by the Cherokee government although it never validated the results. Snippets of the 1896 Cherokee census are thus available in enrollment packets. Enrollment packet: Tom and Nannie Wolfe. Probate file: Tom Wolfe.

51. Enrollment packet: Nelson and Jennie Crittenden.

52. Baker, "Joel and Nellie (Quinton) Kelley Family," 401–2. In the 1880 Cherokee census, the children still are listed in Goingsnake District, but they are in the Canadian District by the 1890 Cherokee census.

53. Cherokee census: 1880, 1890. Enrollment packet: Tom and Nannie Wolfe.

54. Enrollment packet: Sam Crittenden.

55. Enrollment packet: Edwin and Lucinda Cannon, John Welch. U.S. census: 1920.

56. Enrollment packet: Tom and Nannie Wolfe. Probate file: Tom Wolfe.

57. Eastern Cherokee application: Nelson Crittenden.

58. Enrollment packet: Noah Sand. Baker, "Daniel Downing Family," 303.

59. Cherokee census: 1890. Enrollment packet and allotment jacket: Bill and Annie Chewey. Eastern Cherokee application: Annie Suake. In the 1870 U.S. census, Eliza Brown's youngest, Rachel Raper, is listed with her parents along with a newborn son. She remained in North Carolina and did not remove to Indian Territory. She must have married because she does not remain on the census by the surname Raper.

60. Cherokee census: 1880, 1890.

61. Enrollment packet: Steve and Nannie Dog.

62. Cherokee census: 1880, 1890.

63. Eastern Cherokee application: Lewis Bird. The Bird family is listed in the Guion Miller roll by the surname Jesse.

64. Cherokee census: 1880, 1890. U.S. census: 1910, 1920. Eastern Cherokee application: Nelson Crittenden, Sam Crittenden. Jack D. Baker, genealogy chart for Nelson Crittenden, in author's collection.

65. Baker, "Joel and Nellie (Quinton) Kelley Family," 401–2.

66. Eastern Cherokee application: Margaret Sixkiller. Mose Crittenden's parents appear to be an Old Settler male and a Ross Party female. U.S. census: 1920.

67. Shadburn, *Cherokee Planters*, 172–73.

68. Tyner, *Those Who Cried*, 188. Reese Mitchell Sr. appears on the 1860 U.S. census for "Indian Lands West of Arkansas." He is listed in Goingsnake District.

69. Cherokee census: 1880, 1890. Enrollment packet and Eastern Cherokee application: Minnie Crittenden, Nannie Dog, Fannie Welch, Birch Anderson.

70. Enrollment packet: Tom and Fannie Welch.

71. Enrollment packet: Mose and Minnie Crittenden.

72. Enrollment packet: Nannie Palone.

73. Enrollment packet: Birch and Lizzie Anderson, Mack and Cleo Welch.

74. Sarah was a sister of Zeke, and although they are listed as full bloods in the 1835 census, Shadburn suggests that Will had a significant white ancestry, perhaps half. Dicey was a member of the Downing family, meaning a descendant of John Downing, a British officer who had married a Cherokee woman during the eighteenth century. See *Cherokee Planters*, 17, 108. Eastern Cherokee application: Nannie Dog. Enrollment packet: Steve and Nannie Dog.

75. Enrollment packet: James and Hattie Holland.

76. For example, the Quintons, Crittendens, and Kirks intermarried. These families had migrated west together and lived among each other in Arkansas for twenty years, and then some moved across the border into Goingsnake District after the Civil War. Two of Nellie's children, Wiley and Nancy, married Crittendens, her father's people, but this may have been a product of proximity as much as a nod to tradition because her other seven children did not marry into her father's family. Jack D. Baker, "Joel and Nellie (Quinton) Kelley Family," 401–2.

77. Enrollment packet: Tom and Nannie Wolfe. Eastern Cherokee application: Louella Sunday, Jennie Crittenden. Cherokee census: 1880.

78. A clerk working for the Dawes Commission noted on Tom Wolfe's allotment jacket that he had made improvements to this land and, thus, according to Cherokee law, owned this farm. Cherokee census: 1880, 1890. In 1880, Tom Wolfe is listed as numbers 1942 and 2164. Allotment jacket: Tom and Nannie Wolfe.

79. Carselowey commented that "it is almost like a list of Who's Who when thinking of the prominent men of the Cherokee Nation who went to the California Gold Strike of 1849–50." These lists also included future chief Joel Mayes. Carselowey, *Cherokee Pioneers*, 46. Carselowey, "Chief Dennis Wolf Bushyhead," *Early Settlers*, 25. Carselowey, *Cherokee Notes*, 28. All of Carselowey's works are located in the JMC.

80. Wahrhaftig's example is John Chewie in "Making Due with Dark Meat."

81. G. E. Condra, "Opening of the Indian Territory," 6–8, LH. DD: Richard Manus.

82. Bureau of the Census, Report on Indians Taxed and Not Taxed.

83. IPP: Wyly Beavers interview.

84. IPP: James Brown interview. Krause, *Environmental History*, 33–34.

85. IPP: Wyly Beavers, Oscar Cannon, James Brown. DD: Sam Chewey. Krause, *Environmental History*, 34.

86. DD: Nellie Smith Wolf.

87. DD: Edith Duncan Thomas, Richard Manus, Jess Wright. Several Cherokee families from Goingsnake District recorded their brands, including the Chances, Crittendens, and Hollands. See CNR, vol. 99.

88. DD: Nellie Smith Wolf, Edith Duncan Thomas, Richard Manus, Jess Wright. IPP: James Brown.

89. IPP: James Brown interview. DD: Edith Duncan Thomas, Richard Manus, Jess Wright interview.

90. DD: Jess Wright.

91. IPP: Wyly Beavers, Oscar Cannon, James Brown. DD: Sam Chewey. Although the Missouri, Kansas, and Texas Railroad laid tracks into the Cherokee Nation beginning in 1871 and other oral history evidence suggests that Cherokees used the railroads, I did not find evidence of this in interviews with individuals from the Chewey region. The nearest stop was Westville, a non-Indian town in which the primary store, run by Tuck and Ell Alberty, dealt mostly in lumber, specifically railroad ties. In other communities, Cherokees probably could have used the railroads, but in this area, they seem not to have done so with regularity. DD: Jake Whitmire.

92. DD: Jensie Dick.

93. Charlotte Bettylee Rhea Johns, "Wash Lee, Cherokee Lawman," article published by Goingsnake District Historical Association and sent to author by Gail Crittenden, in author's collection.

94. Others who attended the school at Baptist did learn to read Cherokee, however. Tom Suake, a generation older than Dennis and Kate Sixkiller, learned to read, write, and speak English there, but he also learned to read Cherokee, although not write it. It is unclear, however, whether he learned this skill at school or home. U.S. census: 1900, 1910, 1920. Application for Removal of Restrictions for 1908: Abraham Sixkiller, Dennis Sixkiller, Kate Sixkiller. The Suakes provide another example. Tom Suake's brother Lawyer attended school through the sixth grade, and his younger siblings also were literate in English. Application for Removal of Restrictions for 1908: Tom Suake, Lawyer Suake.

95. Indian case file: Sam Chewey. U.S. census: 1920. Nannie Wolfe also was listed as literate in the 1920 census.

96. Application for Removal of Restrictions for 1908: Jim Hogshooter, Oce Hogshooter. Oce must have been proficient in both Cherokee and English. He also served as the secretary for the Nighthawks, and their records were kept in Cherokee. Jack D. Baker, "Chewey," *HAC*, 54–55.

97. U.S. census: 1920. Enrollment of restrictions form for 1927: Dora Wolfe. Federal probate file: Steve and Nannie Dog, Tennessee (also known as Tinna) Dog. Indian case file: Tennessee Dog.

98. U.S. census: 1900, 1910.

99. U.S. census: 1860, 1900, 1910, 1920. Application for Removal of Restrictions for 1904: Samuel Kirk. The evidence regarding John Kelley is contradictory. He is listed as literate in the 1900 census and literate in the 1910 and 1920 censuses. All of John's children could read, but two could not write. Two of Laura's seven children were not educated. Their oldest son, Samuel, had vision problems and tried but did not learn how to read and write. Their youngest son, Isaac, born during the enrollment period, also was illiterate. Rosanna's youngest son, Ellis, six during enrollment, was unable to read and write, but his older brother Wyly, eighteen years older than him, could.

100. U.S. census: 1900. Baker, "Schools: Cherokee National Schools, Flint and Goingsnake Districts," 63. "Wilson Lumpkin Cannon Family," *HAC*, 686–87.

101. McLoughlin, *Champions of the Cherokees*. Jack D. Baker, "Baptist Mission," *HAC*, 87. For information about the satellite churches, see Marion G. Urich, "Flint-Antioch-Peavine Baptist Church," *HAC*, 90–91, and Reverend J. R. Stogsdill, "Echota Baptist Church," "Fairfield Baptist Church," and "Salem Baptist Church," *HAC*, 92.

102. "New Hope Missionary Baptist Church," *HAC*, 98–99. The book provides brief histories of the other churches in the area, and the institutionalization of Christian churches mostly postdated statehood, although a few churches date earlier.

103. These include George Welch (1839–90), who I think was the father of Tom Welch, and Mary and Jesse Raper, the mother and father of Eliza Brown and Martin Raper. Carselowey, *My Journal*, 67, JMC.

104. Carselowey, *My Journal*, 34. IPP: Moses Welch. DD: Maude Welch.

105. For example, Sixkiller's paternal uncle Peach Eater Sixkiller served in the National Council in 1879 along with James Crittenden, the father of Mose Crittenden, who himself served in public office. Carselowey, *My Journal*, 49. For a record of Abe Sixkiller's service, see CNR, vol. 284, p. 213.

106. Each district was divided into two precincts. Carselowey, *Cherokee Notes*, 21.

107. DD: Jake Whitmire interview. IPP: James Brown interview. Moses Welch remembered the move of the courthouse as taking place prior to the Proctor shooting. IPP: Moses Welch.

108. IPP: Wyly Beavers.

109. Estimating exact numbers of Keetoowahs at any time is difficult. Robert Thomas estimates membership at upwards of 6,000, but it is not clear whether he includes men and women in that number. During the allotment era, leader Redbird Smith believed himself to represent a pan-tribal movement of over 24,000 tradition-alists, and I think his total is gender inclusive. Thomas, "Origin and Development of the Redbird Smith Movement," 154. U.S. Senate, *Report of the Select Committee*, 97–100.

110. Thomas, "Origin and Development of the Redbird Smith Movement."
111. LL: Dora Wolfe.

CHAPTER THREE

1. Samuel H. Mayes et al., "Cherokee Delegates," January 30, 1896, box M-50, folder 37, SM. S. H. Mayes, C. J. Harris, G. W. Benge, Roach Young, and Joseph Smallwood signed this letter, written to the U.S. Congress in response to a report of the Dawes Commission that characterized the government of the Cherokee Nation as hopelessly corrupt and recommended the Indian republic's immediate dissolution.

2. Hoxie, *Final Promise*. Keller, *American Protestantism*. Prucha, *American Indian Policy in Crisis*. Prucha, *Great Father*, 618–23. Thompson, "Origins and Implementation."

3. Hoxie, *Final Promise*, and Pascoe, *Relations of Rescue*.

4. Theisen, "'With a View toward Their Civilization.'" Wanken, "'Women's Sphere' and Indian Reform."

5. Hagan, *Indian Rights Association*. Cartwright, "Board of Indian Commissioners." Faulkner, "U.S. Board of Indian Commissioners."

6. Burgess, "Lake Mohonk Conference."

7. Mark, *Four Anthropologists*.

8. For example, in "Tribal Life among the Omahas," Alice C. Fletcher rewrote the Omahas' recent history so that she was central to it. She asserted that she shared their suffering and worked only to protect them even though her work brought her pleasure, power, and material rewards unlike those normally available to women in that era.

9. Denson, *Demanding the Cherokee Nation*, 211–12.

10. Bureau of the Census, Report on Indians Taxed and Not Taxed, 257.

11. *Congressional Record*, 49th Cong., 1st sess., 1886: 1559.

12. Seven men served as principal chief during the period that allotment was debated and implemented: William Potter Ross (1872–75), Charles Thompson (1875–79), Dennis Wolf Bushyhead (1879–87), Joel Bryan Mayes (1887–91), C. J. Harris (1891–95), Samuel Houston Mayes (1895–99), and T. M. Buffington (1899–1903). William Charles Rogers (1903–17) is seen largely as a figurehead. Frank J. Boudinot, the elected chief of the Keetoowah Society, could more accurately be considered a representative of the Cherokee people, but the U.S. government did not recognize him as such. IPP: Frank J. Boudinot.

13. Take, for example, Dennis Wolf Bushyhead, who had lived part of his adult life in California participating in the gold rush, and William Potter Ross, who attended Princeton. Meserve, "Chief Dennis Wolf Bushyhead." Meserve, "Chief William Potter Ross."

14. Miner, *Corporation and the Indian*. Sober, *Intruders*.

15. For good examples of this correlation, see the Commissioner of Indian Affairs, annual report for 1877, 51, 114.

16. As William H. Lyon of the Board of Indian Commissioners remarked, "I believe in homes for the Indians. . . . There is no civilization without homes. The homes of the

Indians that I have seen are not such as would lead to civilization,—many of them at least." Lake Mohonk Conference of the Friends of the Indian, proceedings for 1885, 45, IC.

17. Congressmen also named them bills "to provide law for the Indians." Both seem to be equally used throughout the *Congressional Record*.

18. Ironically, many female reformers later came to recognize that Native women's labor gave them the economic independence and social status that non-Indian women, particularly those involved in the emerging women's rights movement, wanted. Late in her career, Alice C. Fletcher, who published several articles on American Indian women, observed that their status declined as they lost access to productive labor, and she theorized that social evolution extended from women's cooperative work, which, in her mind, sparked civilization. See Pascoe, *Relations of Rescue*, 59, and Mark, *Stranger in Her Native Land*, 53–64.

19. Reformers did not differentiate between those women who traditionally farmed and those whose societies were not agricultural. As anthropologist Alice B. Kehoe comments, "The traditional picture of the Plains Indian women is really that of an Irish housemaid of the late Victorian era clothed in a buckskin dress." See "Shackles of Tradition," 70.

20. Fletcher, *Indian Education and Civilization*, 13–19. Throughout the 1890s and perhaps as a result of her own struggle for recognition as an allotment agent and scholar, Fletcher came to an entirely different understanding of the role of women's labor in Indian societies. Newman, *White Women's Rights*.

21. For particularly good examples, see the Board of Indian Commissioners, annual report for 1887, 120–21; annual report for 1888, 22; annual report for 1891, 30, IC; and the Women's National Indian Association, annual report for 1884, 32–38.

22. Lake Mohonk Conference, proceedings for 1887, 52–53, IC. Pascoe, *Relations of Rescue*, 32–69.

23. Allen, *Sacred Hoop*, 27.

24. The WNIA, in particular, criticized the federal government for allowing Indian men to be robbed of their livelihood without giving them a viable alternative. Carabel Gilman, "The Religious Nature of the Indian," WNIA pamphlet, IC.

25. An agent to the Shawnees chided, "The most ignorant and uncivilized are content to live upon corn raised mostly by the female portions of their family." U.S. Congress, House Committee on Indian Affairs, *Lands to Indians in Severalty to Accompany Bill H.R. 5038* (hereafter referred to as H.R. Report No. 1576), 3.

26. Commissioner of Indian Affairs, annual report for 1882, 42.

27. The quote continues: "He will hunt or make war at an immense expenditure of strength, and in the prosecution of those pursuits he will exhibit great tenacity of purpose; but when he is talked to about the necessity of toil as a means to earn his bread legitimately, he turns a deaf ear and imposes upon his squaw the burden and drudgery of work." Commissioner of Indian Affairs, annual report for 1877, 4.

28. Bederman, *Manliness and Civilization*, 170–215. Berkhofer, *White Man's Indian*.

29. Board of Indian Commissioners, annual report for 1889, 151–52, IC. *Congressional Record*, 49th Cong., 1st sess., 1886: 189–92, 224–26, 772–73, 1558–59, 1630–35, 1762–64.

30. *Congressional Record*, 49th Cong., 1st sess., 1886: 189–92, 224–26, 772–73, 1558–59, 1630–35, and 1762–64. This debate over Indian men's ability to work culminated on January 20. U.S. Congress, House Committee on Indian Affairs, *Lands to Indians in Severalty to Accompany Bill H.R. 6268* (hereafter referred to as H.R. Report No. 165). H.R. Report No. 1576. Fletcher, "New Orleans Exhibition."

31. H.R. Report No. 165, 2.

32. Gans, "Deconstructing the Underclass," 80–86.

33. McClintock, *Imperial Leather*, 252–53.

34. Tengan, *Native Men Remade*, 33–64.

35. Trexler, *Sex and Conquest*, 12–37.

36. Bederman, *Manliness and Civilization*, 184–96.

37. For an example, an 1890 IRA report described the sale of Chilkat girls into sexual slavery by their families. Indian Rights Association, annual report for 1890, 64–65, IC. For late-nineteenth-century Americans, who were unaccustomed to reading sexually explicit material, these reports could be quite racy, and I have to question whether the allure of that taboo enhanced the appeal of the reform literature and its authors' agenda. Some titillating content seems intended to shock.

38. For good examples of the WNIA's vignettes, see Women's National Indian Association, "Missionary Work of the Women's National Indian Association and Letters of Missionaries," 1885, 16–17, IC; Board of Indian Commissioners, annual report for 1888, 117, IC; Women's National Indian Association, annual report for 1884, 34–38; and Women's National Indian Association, report of missionary work, November 1885–November 1886, 20–21. I do not doubt that many Indian women had real problems, but I question the authenticity of reformers' romanticized stories because they lack any hint of Indian women's agency, a main theme permeating the scholarship in American Indian women's history.

39. Green, "Pocahontas Perplex."

40. D'Emilio and Freedman, *Intimate Matters*, 56, 87–93, 134–38. Pascoe, *Relations of Rescue*, 56–59.

41. Perdue, "Columbus Meets Pocahontas."

42. Reformers commonly accused Native men of exploiting Native women's sexuality by selling their wives and daughters into prostitution or bartering them for economic favors or even alcohol; see Commissioner of Indian Affairs, annual report for 1883, 43, and Indian Rights Association, annual report for 1890, 61–67, IC. The Friends of the Indian did concede that white men sexually assaulted Indian women and joined agency doctors, agents, and Indian commissioners to point their fingers at the men staffing army posts, mining camps, and trapping bands—along with the liquor associated with them—to explain the high rate of sexually transmitted diseases in many American Indian communities. Fritz, "Humanitarian Background," 76–77, 263–66. Commissioner of Indian Affairs, annual report for 1883, 4–7.

43. DuBois and Dumenil, *Through Women's Eyes*, 295.

44. Shoemaker, *American Indian Population Recovery*, 41–54.

45. For several good examples, see the Women's National Indian Association, annual report for 1884. Pascoe, *Relations of Rescue*, 50–51.

46. Commissioner of Indian Affairs, annual report for 1877, 3.

47. Ibid., annual report for 1882, 34.

48. Ibid., 6–7, IC. Indian Rights Association, annual report for 1890, 4, IC. Lake Mohonk Conference, proceedings for 1887, 58, IC. Women's National Indian Association, annual report for 1884, 34–35.

49. Merrill E. Gates, "Land and Law as Agents in Educating Indians," Board of Indian Commissioners, annual report for 1878, 30–31, IC.

50. Ibid., 13–35.

51. Commissioner of Indian Affairs, annual report for 1877, 121.

52. During the debate over the Coke bill, which was a first draft of comprehensive legislation discussed extensively during the 3rd session of the 46th Congress, many congressmen did not understand why it excluded Indian Territory, which popular opinion held was ready to implode. The Dawes Act also excluded Indian Territory. This is because the tribal republics, unlike those Indians living on reservations, owned their land through a communal patent. This distinction necessitated separate legislation.

53. Commissioner of Indian Affairs, annual report for 1877, 75–76, 121. Burgess, "Lake Mohonk Conference," 38. Fletcher, "Crowning Act." Prucha, *Great Father*, 747–55.

54. Gates, "Land and Law as Agents in Educating Indians," 27.

55. Commissioner of Indian Affairs, annual report for 1878, 27–28.

56. During the debates over the Coke bill, senators repeatedly used the term "individualization" interchangeably with "allotment." Congressmen also used the term "absorption." Burgess, "Lake Mohonk Conference," 99.

57. *Congressional Record*, 46th Cong., 3rd sess., 1881: 906.

58. Hagan, "Private Property." The House Committee on Indian Affairs specifically believed that allotment caused Indians to cultivate more land, grow a greater variety of crops, use machines in their work, live in appropriate houses, drink less, speak English, buy necessary and luxury goods, adopt white customs, educate their children, express interest in American citizenship, and die less often. See H.R. Report No. 1576.

59. Women's National Indian Association, annual report for 1884, 53.

60. Lake Mohonk Conference, proceedings for 1887, 4, IC. Painter was on to something in noting this new trend in policy. Prior to this point, missionaries had focused assimilationist efforts on women and children, and this turn to men was a shift in Indian policy. See D'Emilio and Freedman, *Intimate Matters*, 93.

61. Reformers designed allotment policy to do this by denying land to married women. Although they knew that women generally owned dwellings and their contents and governed domestic affairs in Native societies, legislators wrote the Dawes Act to eliminate married Indian women's customary property rights, which made possible their economic independence from men. For a particularly dramatic example, see *Congressional Record*, 46th Cong., 3rd sess., 1881: 912.

62. During the 1885 Lake Mohonk conference, James Rhoades, the president of Bryn Mawr College, insisted that the policy create male-dominated families: "I must say I am opposed to giving the husband a certain quantity, and to the wife a certain quantity, and to the child another. I want for the Indians to be brought

together in families. There will never be any civilization without families." Lake Mohonk Conference, proceedings for 1885, 33, IC. Prior to the amendment of the Dawes Act, reformers never considered allotting land to female-headed Indian families and intentionally excluded polygamous wives from the policy. As initially passed, the Dawes Act granted 160 acres to heads-of-household, presumably men or, rarely, widowed women; 80 acres to single adults and orphans regardless of gender; and 40 acres to minor children. Within a few years, Congress equalized allotments and granted married women 80 acres retroactively in response to demand from allotment agents, Indian Service staff, and Indian people. Indian people believed that the policy unfairly excluded women, and reformers watched in horror as the policy seemed to encourage men to abandon their wives to take up with single women who had received allotments. See Board of Indian Commissioners, annual report for 1889, 8–9, IC; Indian Rights Association, annual report for 1890, 9–10, IC; Lake Mohonk Conference, proceedings for 1889, 76, and proceedings for 1890, 105, IC.

63. Reformers were willing to let Indians suffer during this transition. In the 1875 annual report of the Board of Indian Commissioners, the commissioners concurred that only the "pangs of hunger" would motivate Indian men to work. See pages 23–25, IC. Commissioner of Indian Affairs Hiram Price proposed relocating all Indians onto homesteads, giving them one year's worth of supplies, and letting them live or die according to their own efforts. Commissioner of Indian Affairs, annual report for 1881, v.

64. Commissioner of Indian Affairs, annual report for 1878, 74.

65. Ibid., annual report for 1876, 3–25. *Congressional Record*, 46th Cong., 3rd sess., 1881: 878–81. H.R. Report No. 165, 2–3.

66. Commissioner of Indian Affairs, annual report for 1879, 4–5.

67. Or as the Board of Indian Commissioners explained, "Naturally, when a man begins to toil for that which he receives, he beings to learn the value of personal-property rights, and thus takes the first step in separating from his tribe, and toward individual manhood." Board of Indian Commissioners, annual report for 1875, 23–25, IC. See also H.R. Report No. 1576.

68. Board of Indian Commissioners, annual report for 1883, 69–70, IC.

69. Commissioner of Indian Affairs, annual report for 1881, 3.

70. Gates, "Land and Law as Agents in Educating Indians," 27.

71. Commissioner Price confessed, "[The allotment system] teaches the Indians habits of industry and frugality, and stimulates them to look forward to a better and more useful life, and, in the end, it will relieve the government of large annual appropriations." Commissioner of Indian Affairs, annual report for 1881, 22. H.R. Report No. 165. U.S. Congress, House Committee on Indian Affairs, *Lands to Indians in Severalty to Accompany Bill S. 48*, 1–2.

72. *Congressional Record*, 46th Cong., 3rd sess., 1881: 907.

73. D'Emilio and Freedman note how white Americans combined sexual and racial ideology to justify their control of non-white people, particularly women. *Intimate Matters*, 86–87.

74. *Congressional Record*, 46th Cong., 3rd sess., 1881: 877.

75. Commissioner of Indian Affairs, annual report for 1878, 27.

76. Board of Indian Commissioners, annual report for 1881, 8, IC.

77. Lake Mohonk Conference, proceedings for 1889, 19, IC.

78. Indian Rights Association, annual report for 1888, 24–25, IC.

79. Lake Mohonk Conference, proceedings for 1887, 53–54, IC.

80. Other organizations, including the federal government and several Christian churches, supported female missionaries and matrons. See the Board of Indian Commissioners, annual report for 1887, 129; annual report for 1890, 42–44; annual report for 1891, 30, IC; Women's National Indian Association, annual report for 1886, 11; and Pascoe, *Relations of Rescue.*

81. Gates, "Land and Law as Agents in Educating Indians," 30–31.

82. As the IRA reported, "The children, in a home of their own, form industrious habits, which give promise of good citizenship." Indian Rights Association, annual report for 1888, 24–25, IC.

83. *Congressional Record*, 46th Cong., 3rd sess., 1881: 779.

84. Indian Emancipation Day Program for 1889, boxes 12 and 13: Dawes Bill/ Indian Citizenship Days records, IC.

85. H.R. Report No. 1576.

86. For an interesting example of these home education programs, see the Board of Indian Commissioners, annual report for 1884, 40–41, IC. For more on home loan programs, see Women's National Indian Association, annual report for 1886, 12, IC; and Lake Mohonk Conference, proceedings for 1887, 53–54, IC. Indian boarding schools, such as Hampton, ran home programs on their campuses.

87. H.R. Report No. 165.

88. Indian Rights Association, annual report for 1888, 24–25, IC.

89. Cartwright, "Board of Indian Commissioners," 101–2.

90. Fletcher, "Crowning Act."

91. Commissioner Hayt remarked in 1879 that within a few years, allotment would lead to Indians being "clothed with citizenship and left to their own resources to maintain themselves as citizens of the republic." H.R. Report No. 165.

92. Priest, *Uncle Sam's Stepchildren*, 198–216.

93. *Congressional Record*, 49th Cong., 1st sess., 1886: 189–92.

94. Ibid., 1634.

95. Indian Rights Association, annual report for 1887, 82, IC.

96. Burgess, "Lake Mohonk Conference," 47–50.

97. Board of Indian Commissioners, annual report for 1883, 5–6, IC.

98. Ibid., annual report for 1888, 4.

99. Indian Emancipation Day Program for 1892, boxes 12 and 13: Dawes Bill/ Indian Citizenship Days records, IC.

100. Indian Emancipation Day Flier for 1887, ibid.

101. *Congressional Record*, 49th Cong., 1st sess., 1886: 226, 1559. In 1893, Congress established the Dawes Commission to complete this unfinished business of allotment.

102. S. Mayes et al., "Cherokee Delegates."

103. The late nineteenth century was a particularly charged time in Cherokee party politics as coalitions collapsed and reorganized as the Downing, National, and Union Parties. Wardell, *Political History*, 255–349.

104. Denson, *Demanding the Cherokee Nation*, 214–15. The Cherokees had examples of other tribes, such as the nearby Quapaw, who had agreed to allotment under their own terms.

105. Harris, message of C. J. Harris to the Honorable National Council, November 11, 1893, box H-55, folder 24, CJH.

106. Joel B. Mayes, fourth annual message of Joel B. Mayes, November 4, 1890, box M-48, folder 71, JM.

107. Thomas, "Cherokee Values and Worldview," 1.

108. Gulick, *Cherokees at the Crossroads*, 88–94; quote on p. 91.

109. Thomas, "Cherokee Values and Worldview," 7.

110. DD: Richard Manus. This pattern of bringing food and eating together continues today at stomp grounds and rural churches.

111. On occasion, Cherokee statesmen sarcastically commented that, if nothing else, their grudging patience toward these intruders and reluctant acquiescence to land sales proved their benevolence and hospitality toward non-Indians. S. Mayes et al., "Cherokee Delegates." Editorial on R. B. Ross, 1899, box M-51, folder 16, SM.

112. Thomas, "Cherokee Values and Worldview," 1.

113. S. Mayes et al., "Cherokee Delegates." "Memorial Adopted by the International Convention of the Cherokee, Creek, Choctaw, Chickasaw, and Seminole Indians," June 27, 1895, box P-19, folder 13, ARP.

114. Denson, *Demanding the Cherokee Nation*, 228–30.

115. *Congressional Record*, 46th Cong., 3rd sess., 1881: 781.

116. S. Mayes et al., "Cherokee Delegates."

117. Bushyhead, first annual message of D. W. Bushyhead, November 26, 1879, box 4, folder 160, DWB.

118. S. Mayes et al., "Cherokee Delegates."

119. Harris, annual message of C. J. Harris, November 6, 1894, box 56, folder 19, CJH.

120. Bushyhead, Bushyhead's letter of acceptance, May 11, 1891, box 3, folder 156, DWB.

121. Cherokee statesmen repeatedly appeared to be referring to the language of their removal treaty, which referred to, as Ross paraphrased it, "a permanent home, and which shall, under the most solemn guarantee of the United States, be and remain theirs forever—a home that shall never in all future time be embarrassed by having extended around it the line or placed over it the jurisdiction of a State or Territory, nor be pressed upon by the extension in any way of any of the limits of any existing Territory or State." See Ross, speech of W. P. Ross, September 1874, box 1, folder 21, WPR.

122. William Potter Ross made this distinction in his public writings. Ross, speech of W. P. Ross, September 1874. For other examples, see D. W. Bushyhead, letter of D. W. Bushyhead to Dr. M. Frazee, 1891, box 3, folder 157, DWB; and Joel B. Mayes, third annual message, November 6, 1889, box M-48, folder 46, JM.

123. J. Mayes, fourth annual message of Joel B. Mayes. Joel B. Mayes, message of J. B. Mayes, January 4, 1888, box M-48, folder 4, JM. In an interesting comparison, Nancy Shoemaker argues that by adopting their constitution of 1848, the Seneca

Nation separated familial life from politics. Perhaps it is a matter of linguistics, but the Cherokees seem to have considered their government inseparable from their families. "Rise or Fall."

124. Harris, "An Appeal for Justice," February 27, 1895, box F-56, folder 33, CJH. J. Mayes, fourth annual message of Joel B. Mayes. Ross, speech of W. P. Ross, September 1874.

125. D. W. Bushyhead, fifth annual message of D. W. Bushyhead, November 16, 1883, box 4, folder 166, DWB. *Indian Journal,* "Meeting of Representatives of Five Civilized Tribes," February 22, 1894, box H-56, folder F-1, CJH.

126. Joel B. Mayes criticized the federal government for urging the National Council to sell the Cherokee Strip, the lands west of the Arkansas River, without putting the issue before the Cherokee people, as was customary: "The National Council has never assumed the sole right of disposing of lands belonging to the Cherokee people." Mayes warned the council that this sale would be unconstitutional and set an unfortunate precedent. J. Mayes, fourth annual message of Joel B. Mayes. The Cherokee people voted to accept both the sale of their outlet and the Cherokee Agreement of 1902, although many Cherokees boycotted that election, tipping the results in favor of allotment.

127. Harris, annual message for 1894. J. Mayes, third annual message.

128. For an interesting commentary on accountability, see Samuel H. Mayes, first annual message, 1896, box M-50, folder 26, SM.

129. Ibid.

130. Harris, memorial of C. J. Harris, January 3, 1894, box F-55, folder 37, CJH.

131. Bushyhead, first annual message. J. Mayes, third annual message.

132. Miner, *Corporation and the Indian,* 39–42.

133. Joel B. Mayes, letter of J. B. Mayes to Stephen Teehee, August 16, 1890, box M-48, folder 68, JM.

134. J. Mayes, fourth annual message of Joel B. Mayes.

135. Rogers, *Ani-Yun-Wiya,* 242–45.

136. J. Mayes, fourth annual message of Joel B. Mayes.

137. IPP: Moses Welch.

138. DD: Jack Whitmire.

139. For a good example, see S. Mayes et al., "Cherokee Delegates."

140. Like modern-day political leaders, Cherokee politicians made many campaign promises to balance the budget and run their government more efficiently. See D. W. Bushyhead, campaign speech of D. W. Bushyhead to friends and fellow citizens of the Cherokee Nation, July 31, 1879, box 4, folder 159, DWB; D. W. Bushyhead, message of D. W. Bushyhead, December 14, 1883, box 3, folder 115, DWB; J. Mayes, third annual message of Joel B. Mayes; J. Mayes, fourth annual message of Joel B. Mayes; S. Mayes, first annual message.

141. D. W. Bushyhead, fourth annual message of D. W. Bushyhead, November 10, 1882, folder 165, DWB.

142. J. Mayes, third annual message of Joel B. Mayes. W. C. Rogers, second annual message of W. C. Rogers, November 19, 1904, box R-34, folder 49, WCR.

143. Rogers, second annual message of W. C. Rogers.

144. Application for Removal of Restrictions for 1908: Oce Hogshooter.

145. In her study of the Cherokee Female Seminary, *Cultivating the Rosebuds*, Devon A. Mihesuah portrayed the school as both elitist and assimilationist, an interpretation that others such as Cherokee scholar Julia Coates have challenged.

146. From their early contact with whites, Cherokee parents sought out educational opportunities for their children—but on their terms. See McLoughlin, *Cherokees and Missionaries*. Cherokees remained involved in their children's education in Indian Territory. In 1874, Chief William Potter Ross secured their exemption from a bill that would have placed their independent school system under the supervision of the federal government; see "Letter of Native to the Editor," *Cherokee Advocate*, June 6, 1874.

147. S. Mayes et al., "Cherokee Delegates." Samuel H. Mayes, message of S. H. Mayes, 1896, Box M-50, Folder 43, SM.

148. D. W. Bushyhead, sixth annual message of Dennis Wolf Bushyhead, November 13, 1884, box 4, folder 16, DWB. S. Mayes et al., "Cherokee Delegates."

149. J. Mayes, third annual message of Joel B. Mayes. S. Mayes, et al., "Cherokee Delegates."

150. J. Mayes, third annual message of Joel B. Mayes. J. Mayes, fourth annual message of Joel B. Mayes.

151. Certainly, the Cherokees were not the only nation in Indian Territory who believed that they had a good thing. Mary Jane Warde has suggested that Creek nationalists held similar views of their own culture's superiority to Anglo-American culture, and they were fiercely devoted to the maintenance of their own nation. See *George Washington Grayson*.

152. Bushyhead, Bushyhead's letter of acceptance.

153. Ross, speech of W. P. Ross, September 1874.

154. First ratified in 1827 and modified in 1839 and again in 1866, the Cherokee constitution established legislative, executive, and judicial branches, and while statesmen tinkered with these throughout the century, the basic governing structure remained consistent. Elected by popular vote, the principal chief and assistant chief served for four-year terms, and the legislature, also popularly elected, appointed an executive council, including a treasurer, to advise the chief. Two houses made up the legislative branch, or National Council. Two members selected from each district served in the upper house, or National Committee, and three men selected from each district participated in the lower house, or Council. The National Council selected delegates to represent the nation in Washington, D.C., and to other Indian nations. It also appointed judges to a supreme court for four-year terms and created and disbanded lower courts as necessary. District officials were popularly elected. Ross, speech of W. P. Ross, February 21, 1874, box 1, folder 14, WPR. Joel B. Mayes, letter of J. B. Mayes, October 25, 1888, box M-48, folder 32, JM. Harris, memorial of C. J. Harris. Samuel H. Mayes, letter of S. H. Mayes, January 18, 1896, box M-50, folder 36, SM. Mayes et al., "Cherokee Delegates."

155. Harris, memorial of C. J. Harris.

156. Harris, message of C. J. Harris to the Honorable National Council, November 11, 1893. Harris, annual message of C. J. Harris, November 6, 1894, Box 56, Folder 19,

CJH. For another good example, see William Potter Ross et al., memorial of William Potter Ross, June 18, 1870, box R-36, folder 3, WPR.

157. Mayes et al., "Cherokee Delegates."

158. "Letter from Going Snake District," *Cherokee Advocate*, April 2, 1896.

159. Joel B. Mayes, letter of J. B. Mayes to President Harrison, March 6, 1890, box M-48, folder 62, JM.

160. J. Mayes, fourth annual message of Joel B. Mayes.

161. D. W. Bushyhead, third annual message of Dennis Wolf Bushyhead, November 6, 1881, box 4, folder 164, DWB.

162. Cherokee statesmen lobbied other Indian nations to resist allotment and form a united front against the Dawes Commission and the federal government. See Bushyhead, fifth annual message.

163. Ross, speech of W. P. Ross, September 1874.

164. This devotion to their nation was not a new development. As early as 1827, Thomas L. McKinney, then the director of the Office of Indian Affairs, commented regarding the Cherokees: "It is so much to be regretted that the idea of sovereignty should have taken such a deep hold of these people." As quoted in McLoughlin, *Cherokees and Missionaries*, 213. Ross, speech of W. P. Ross, September 1874.

165. D. W. Bushyhead et al., letter of D. W. Bushyhead and the Cherokee Delegation to H. M. Teller, August 9, 1882, box 1, folder 63, DWB. The delegation included the following men: D. W. Bushyhead, Daniel H. Ross, R. M. Wolf, and Wm. A. Philips.

166. Harris, "Appeal for Justice."

167. J. Mayes, third annual message.

168. Harris, message of C. J. Harris to the Honorable National Council, November 11, 1893. Harris, message of C. J. Harris, November 6, 1894.

169. Hagan, *Taking Indian Lands*. Savage, *Cherokee Strip Livestock Association*.

170. "The Five Tribes in Congress," *Claremore Progress*, February 19, 1898, and April 9, 1898, box M-50, folders 59 and 62, SM.

171. Prucha, *Great Father*, 747–55. In *And Still the Waters Run*, Debo debunks the research behind these reports. See pages 24–25. Likewise, in his study of the Jerome Commission, *Taking Indian Lands*, Hagan attributes American politicians' hostility toward Cherokees to the latter's resistance to federal assimilation laws.

172. "A Meeting of the Five Tribes in Congress," *Claremore Progress*, January 15, 1898, box M-50, folder 58, SM.

173. Carter, *Dawes Commission*.

174. Coates, "'None of Us Are Supposed to Be Here,'" 142.

CHAPTER FOUR

1. Hill, *Weaving New Worlds*, 2–7. Hudson, *Southeastern Indians*, 122–28.

2. The most famous example of collaboration might be Cherokee genealogist and historian Emmet Starr, who worked with the Dawes Commission and enrolled those he felt were being wrongly excluded. Sue Brown McGinnis, "James Daniel Brown," *HAC*, 229. For a useful comparison of Creeks who worked with the Dawes Commission, see Posey, "Journal of a Creek Enrollment and Field Party."

3. Carter, "Deciding Who Can be Cherokee," 180–86.

4. Enrollment packet: John and Jennie Oakball. John was less frequently called Dennis, but Jennie identified him in English as John. Eastern Cherokee application: Jennie Oakball. Walkingstick also repeatedly approached Annie Chewey at the home she shared with Bill and their two daughters. She also refused to enroll. Enrollment packet: Bill and Annie Chewey. Stories told today about allotment suggest that the disappearance of Cherokee men when the staff of the Dawes Commission was canvassing was not a coincidence but a strategy to avoid arrest for refusal to cooperate. Sexism protected Cherokee women; their inability to see women as politically informed and active meant that federal officials would not arrest them.

5. Scholars, particularly those whose interests lie in Oklahoma history rather than Indian history, have misrepresented enrollment as a simple, straightforward process. Perhaps the best example from the secondary literature comes from Muriel H. Wright, who wrote, "All members of the Cherokee Nation were now duly enrolled. Every man, woman, and child (41,693 reported in 1914)." See *Guide to the Indian Tribes of Oklahoma*, 73. This misrepresentation pervades the secondary literature on Oklahoma history. Other scholars have ignored the making of rolls altogether, implying that allotment entailed *only* the division of tribal resources. For example, in *The Great Father*, Prucha does not discuss enrollment, although he emphasizes that tribal attorneys challenged federal jurisdiction over their affairs throughout the 1890s. Such omissions obscure the impact of this loss of sovereignty on the Cherokee Nation. Recent scholarship has highlighted the final roll's imperfections, specifically errors in blood quantum and the exclusion of some Cherokees. In *The Indians of Oklahoma*, Rennard Strickland discusses the conditions under which some Cherokees avoided enrollment while others supposedly enrolled at a lower blood quantum then they may have possessed in an effort to avoid restrictions on their property. See pages 48–49. I did not find evidence of this, as commissioners generally did not ask Cherokees in this study to designate their own blood quantum. Other scholars have discussed the negative long-term impact of the language of blood quantum but do not explain the complicated process through which it was imposed upon and ultimately adopted by American Indian people. For example, in her otherwise outstanding study of race, culture, and identity among the Cherokees, *Blood Politics*, Circe Sturm does not problematize the creation of the Dawes roll and treats it as a representation of Cherokee racial construction. See pages 78–81 and 87–88.

6. The complicated series of events leading to enrollment was explained first by Brown in "The Dawes Commission" and more recently by Carter in *The Dawes Commission*.

7. Hoxie, *Final Promise*.

8. Elias Cornelius Boudinot and Robert L. Owen are the two best examples. Parins, *Elias Cornelius Boudinot*. Kilcup, *Cherokee Woman's America*.

9. Debo, *And Still the Waters Run*. The context in which Debo wrote her masterpiece and in which it was initially received by her contemporary Oklahomans speaks to the persistence of allotment-era exploitation well into the twentieth century. See the documentary *Indians, Outlaws, and Angie Debo*, directed by Martha Sandlin.

10. Stremlau, "'To Domesticate and Civilize Wild Indians.'"

11. Fletcher did this among the Omaha in 1883–84 and the Winnebago in 1887–88 to facilitate their assimilation. Her experience allotting the Nez Perce between 1889 and 1892 was more difficult, and she seems not to have been able to conduct such research. Mark, *Stranger in Her Native Land*.

12. The Census Bureau's definition of who and what constituted a family did vary, but significant changes to the described practice did not occur until the 1930 census. Seward, *American Family*, 71–74.

13. Carter, *Dawes Commission*, 105–24.

14. Carselowey, *Cherokee Old Timers*, 68, JMC.

15. According to the *Cherokee Advocate*, the tribe posted attorneys, stenographers, and sheriffs in the enrollment offices. *Cherokee Advocate*, August 4, 1900. I have not found this corroborated in other sources.

16. Using this information, the commission confirmed legitimate applicants, investigated doubtful cases, and published lists of rejected claimants in the *Cherokee Advocate*. For example, see the *Cherokee Advocate*, March 28, 1902.

17. Today, the term "Dawes number" refers to that given to individuals. Carter, *Dawes Commission*, 105–24.

18. *Cherokee Advocate*, July 21, 1900.

19. Ibid.

20. At least one family, the Sixkillers, recorded birth and marriage information in their Bible, which likely dated to the pre-allotment era. Copy of "Some Births and Marriages from the Sixkiller Bible," an article copied from the *Goingsnake Messenger*, March 1987, sent to author by Gail Crittenden. The Sixkillers, who attended Baptist Mission and were opposed to allotment, did not enroll themselves. If they had, would they have used the family Bible to authenticate the information shared with the commissioners? No other Cherokee families who enrolled did so.

21. Prior to removal, the Cherokee government authorized censuses in 1809 and 1825. After relocation, the National Council mandated the taking of censuses in 1880, 1883, 1890, 1893, and 1896. It did not authenticate or certify the results of any roll after 1880. The purpose of these censuses primarily was to facilitate the distribution of resources and discourage intrusion by non-Cherokees.

22. No family in this study has consistent ages or birthdates for all of its members throughout the documentary record.

23. According to the 1880 Cherokee census, Betsy would have been fifty-two in 1907, and the 1890 Cherokee census roll suggests she would have been a year older— fifty-three. A neighbor and informant estimated that Betsy was at least sixty-two years old. In 1906 or 1907, she said she was born in 1853 and therefore would have been fifty-three or fifty-four years old. In 1908, she suggested that she was then fifty-seven. Cherokee Nation census: 1880, 1890. Enrollment packet and Eastern Cherokee application: Betsy Suake. Probate file: William Palone.

24. Johnston, *Cherokee Women in Crisis*, 18–23. Perdue, *Cherokee Women*, 30–36.

25. Although she appears by the standardized version of her name, "Beulah," in subsequent records, on the enrollment cards, John Cannon's daughter is listed as her mother and midwife thought she should be: Bular. Enrollment packet: John and Lee Cannon.

26. Enrollment packet: John and Jennie Oakball.

27. Affidavits were requested of the following parents, who did not respond: Lewis and Betsy Bird, Jim and Mary Hogshooter, White and Susie Oakball. See their enrollment packets.

28. Enrollment packet: John and Lee Cannon. Another example is Mack Welch for his daughters Myrtle and Georgie. Enrollment packet: Mack and Emma Welch.

29. Enrollment packet: Ira and Lizzie Cannon.

30. Enrollment packet: Oscar and Annie Cannon. Other examples include Tilman Chance for his son William, and John Kelley for his daughter Maud. Enrollment packet: Tilman and Maggie Chance, John and Susan Kelley.

31. Enrollment packet: John and Lee Cannon, Oscar and Annie Cannon. For Harry Welch's information, see Edwin and Lucinda Cannon's enrollment packet. Birch Anderson also enrolled his first child, daughter Willie May, this way in June 1901. See Birch and Lizzie Anderson's enrollment packet. Mack Welch returned to enroll his daughter Ethel on May 22, 1902. See Mack and Emma Welch's enrollment packet.

32. For example, Henry Holland, the son of Hattie Holland (then Lewis), was enrolled along with his older siblings, listed on the 1896 census, and his younger brother, for whom an affidavit was provided. Enrollment packet: James and Hattie Holland. James Brown's daughter Artie was likewise enrolled without affidavit. Enrollment packet: James and Ida Brown. William and Laura Kirk's children Rosa, Floyd, and Isaac were enrolled without affidavit. Enrollment packet: William and Laura Kirk. In general, the young children of Nighthawks, including the Birds, Cheweys, Crittendens, Hogshooters, Oakballs, Palones, Sands, Sixkillers, and Suakes, were enrolled without affidavits.

33. Notably, women and men served as administrators. I found only two such statements by individuals in this study: Nannie Dog (then Mitchell) for her husband, Reese, and Bill Chewey for his father, Joe. Neither transacted any property. CNR, vol. 124, image #28.

34. When I learned that the Oklahoma Historical Society had a file entitled "Vital Statistics" in the Cherokee Nation Records, I was excited to see how the Cherokee government maintained such data. Reading this file confirmed that they did not; it comprises a handful of tributes to deceased persons of importance. This is box 149.

35. Enrollment packet: Martin and Martha Raper. Rosanna Mounce's son Jesse also died in the fall of 1901 and was stricken from the roll. Enrollment packet: Joseph and Rosanna Mounce. Bill Chewey died in June 1905, and his death is noted although no affidavit was provided. Allotment jacket: Bill and Annie Chewey.

36. James Brown died in December 1903. His family reported it in December 1904. Enrollment packet: James and Eliza Brown. Marsh Brown's daughter Eliza died, and he reported her death within two months in 1904. Enrollment packet: Marsh and Mary Brown. John Brown's daughter Mary died in January 1903, but John waited until October 1904 to produce an affidavit, which he submitted when he went to Tahlequah to file for land. Enrollment packet and allotment jacket: John and Emily Brown. Nighthawk Betsy Bird died in 1903, but the Dawes Commission had no record of it. Eastern Cherokee application: Lewis Bird. Allotment jacket: Lewis and Betsy Bird.

37. Enrollment packet: James and Hattie Holland.

38. Enrollment packet and allotment jacket: Mose and Minnie Crittenden.

39. Allotment jacket: Marsh and Mary Brown. For another example, see the enrollment packet and allotment jacket for John and Emily Brown. In the eighth chapter of *The Dawes Commission*, Carter describes in detail the fits and starts through which Cherokee land distribution took place. The pace suggested by the Browns' experiences was normal.

40. Enrollment packet: Moses Welch. U.S. census: 1910. I was not able to determine whether or not Lizzie's family cared for the children at any time. Notably, most of her family appears to have died prior to 1900, so there may not have been extended maternal family to step in when she passed away. Eastern Cherokee application: Mollie Welch.

41. *Cherokee Advocate*, November 1876. Cherokee census: 1880, 1890. Commissioners ultimately decided in James's favor because of the language of the Cherokees' 1866 Reconstruction treaty granting full citizenship rights to adopted citizens married to Native Cherokees. John and Emily Brown faced the same situation because they had married prior to relocating from North Carolina. Emily Brown was denied inclusion in the Dawes roll. Enrollment packet: John and Emily Brown.

42. Enrollment packet: Edwin Cannon, Ira Cannon. Cherokee census: 1890.

43. Enrollment packet: Sterling Cannon.

44. Ibid. The fact that many men left for work and returned home in part reflected the limited economic opportunities available within Indian Territory. Joe Mounce's testimony exemplified that men who practiced mechanical trades in the Cherokee Nation often had to work away from their homes—industrial jobs were rare there during the 1890s. Enrollment packet: Joe and Rosanna Mounce.

45. No restrictions applied to Cherokee men's relationships with white women. Enrollment packet: Tilman and Maggie Chance, Joe and Rosanna Mounce. In *Race and the Cherokee Nation*, Yarbrough argues that throughout the nineteenth century, the tribal government increasingly restricted interracial marriage. Unions with those of African descent was criminalized, and the National Council further regulated intermarriage with an 1855 law establishing a multistep process as the only means through which white non-Indian men could marry Cherokee women and gain access to tribal property. I found the license of Joe Mounce entitling him to marry Rosanna Kelley. CNR, vol. 123, images #108–9.

46. Yarbrough's study of marriages recorded with the tribal government includes some Cherokee couples, and so some Cherokees did register their marriages to other Cherokees. *Race and the Cherokee Nation*, 78–80. I was able to find only one for those in this study: Betsy Suake's son Jim recorded his marriage to Sallie Chewie in 1897. CNR, vol. 123, image #279. Because so few people registered their marriages, some did not know the date when they wed. Tom Swimmer did not remember exactly when he married Charlotte Turtle, but he knew that it was during July 1902. The particular moment was less important than that the couple had lived together since then. Federal probate file: Charlotte Turtle.

47. CNR, vol. 123, image #60.

48. Ibid., image #91.

49. Enrollment packet: Oscar and Annie Cannon. Albert Wayne Lacie, "The Lacie Family," *HAC*, 418–19. Reverend Lacie also married Mose and Minnie Crittenden (see their enrollment packet) and Tom and Charlotte Suake (see Tom and Nancy Suake's enrollment packet).

50. Enrollment packet: John and Lee Cannon.

51. Enrollment packet: Ira and Lizzie Cannon.

52. Enrollment packet: Edwin and Lucinda Cannon. Jack D. Baker has noted an increase in registration of marriages, even among those opposed to allotment, corresponding with the arrival of the Dawes Commission.

53. Reid, *Law of Blood*, 117–22.

54. Enrollment packet: Joe and Rosanna Mounce.

55. Enrollment packet: Nannie Palone.

56. Enrollment packet: Mose and Minnie Crittenden. For other examples, see the enrollment packets of James and Eliza Brown, Sterling Cannon, and James Mack and Cleo Welch.

57. Two informants spoke through translators: Rider Hammer and Isaac Youngbird. Simon Walkingstick and Sam Foreman served as translators.

58. Enrollment packet: Nannie Palone, Betsy Suake, Tom and Nancy Suake.

59. Lacie also provided information about Noah Sand. Enrollment packet: Betsy Suake, Nannie Palone, Tom and Nancy Suake. For information about Abe's involvement in Baptist Mission, see CNR, vol. 545, p. 58.

60. Enrollment packet: Sam Crittenden, John and Jennie Oakball. James Crittenden provided information about his neighbor, John's mother. Enrollment packet: Betsy Oakball. Zeke Proctor also commented that he had known Steve and Betty Sand their whole lives. See their enrollment packet.

61. Clerks noted the age and community of the informants before their testimony: Rider Hammer, 43; James Crittenden, 53; Reverend Lacie, 56; Isaac Youngbird, 58; Zeke Proctor, 70.

62. Zeke Proctor was a former sheriff. One or two unnamed women were midwives. Adam Lacie was a minister.

63. Enrollment packet: Nelson and Jennie Crittenden, Steve and Nannie Dog, Tom and Nannie Wolfe, Nelson and Jennie Crittenden.

64. Enrollment packet: Lewis and Betsy Bird, Samuel Chuwee, Nelson and Jennie Crittenden, Jim and Mary Hogshooter, Noah Sand, Steve and Betty Sand, Nannie Palone, Tom and Nancy Suake, Arch and Fannie Turtle.

65. Hammer shared information with less reticence than other witnesses and informants. This may reflect both his personality and circumstance. For example, he freely discussed the sexual histories of his neighbors. Enrollment packet: Mose and Minnie Crittenden, Joe and Rosanna Mounce, Tom and Nancy Suake, Nannie Palone.

66. He identified Lewis and Betsy Bird's youngest child, an infant, as Susan rather than Frank. Enrollment packet: Lewis and Betsy Bird. Indian case file: Susan/Frank Bird. He also said that all of Tom Wolfe's sons were dead. John was alive and lived a long life. Enrollment packet: Tom and Nannie Wolfe. Cherokee census: 1880, 1890.

U.S. census: 1920. Hammer did not think that Steve Dog was opposed to enrollment. They were Nighthawks. Enrollment packet: Steve and Nannie Dog. Eastern Cherokee application: Steve Dog.

CHAPTER FIVE

1. Enrollment packet: Joe and Rosanna Mounce.

2. For early examples of pleas for regulatory legislation, see the Commissioner of Indian Affairs, annual report for 1878, 27–28; annual report for 1879, 13; and annual report for 1881, 69. For an example of how this item on reformers' agenda evolved, see Lake Mohonk Conference, proceedings for 1889, 39, IC. Burgess, "Lake Mohonk Conference," 184.

3. For an account of early partisan politics in the twin territories that became the state of Oklahoma, see Baird and Goble's *Oklahoma*. Although civil service reform criteria expanded to include positions in the Indian Service beginning in 1891, the Dawes Commission was exempted from such protections against patronage until 1908. Carter, *Dawes Commission*, 224. Prucha, *Great Father*, 723–33.

4. Thomas, "Cherokee Values and World View."

5. *Cherokee Advocate*, May 26, 1900.

6. Enrollment packet: Joe and Rosanna Mounce. These interviews occurred during enrollment or, less often, in the field. The commissioners questioned family members and neighbors about each other, sometimes summoning them for this purpose, and they sent field parties out to investigate cases and interview Indians in their homes and communities.

7. Cherokee census: 1880, 1890. Enrollment packet: Joe and Rosanna Mounce, Wyly Beavers. Probate file: Thomas Mounce. U.S. census: 1910.

8. Ibid. (all citations in n. 7).

9. As adults, William was called Johnnie Proctor, and Andrew also was called William or Willie Palone.

10. U.S. census: 1900 (note that the family is listed under Betsie Wickey), 1920. Enrollment packet: Nannie Palone (note that the family is listed under Betsy Swake). Probate file: Betsy Suake.

11. Enrollment packet: Nannie Palone.

12. U.S. census: 1900, 1920. Enrollment packet: Nannie Palone. Probate file: Betsy Suake. In *And Still the Waters Run*, Debo explains that Adair was one of the few Oklahoma counties in which robbing Indian wards was frowned upon and made difficult, but she notes an example from Craig County in which the guardian profited from mismanaging the property of children who lived several counties away. See pages 227–29 and 308–9. For another example, see Steve and Nannie Dog's enrollment packet.

13. Enrollment packet: Tom and Nancy Suake, Bill and Annie Chewey. Application for Removal of Restrictions for 1908: Tom Suake. U.S. census (under Thomas Swake): 1920.

14. Brady, "New Middle-Class Family," 83–123. Coontz, *Way We Never Were*, 97. Coontz, "Working Class Families."

15. Cole, *The Journey of Life*, 141 and chapter 8. Coontz, *Way We Never Were*, 190. Mintz and Kellogg, *Domestic Revolutions*, 108. Seward, *American Family*, 132.

16. Enrollment packet: Eliza and James Brown, John and Emily Brown, Marsh and Mary Brown, Birch and Lizzie Anderson, Martin Raper. Allotment jacket: Eliza and James Brown, John and Emily Brown, Marsh and Mary Brown, Birch and Lizzie Anderson. Eastern Cherokee application: Eliza and James Brown. Dawes Commission to the Five Civilized Tribes, allotment plat maps. For other examples, see Betsy Oakball's enrollment packet. She probably shared a home with her son White and his family. Enrollment packet and allotment jacket: Betsy Oakball, White and Susie Oakball.

17. Enrollment packet and allotment jacket: Betsy Suake. U.S. census: 1900, 1910, 1920. Probate file: Andrew Palone, William Proctor, Ezekiel Suake.

18. Enrollment packet: Eliza and James Brown. Cherokee census: 1880, 1890.

19. Enrollment packet: Mack Welch. Nancy is listed as "adopted white" on both the 1880 and 1890 Cherokee censuses.

20. Enrollment packet: Noah Sand, Steve Sand, Will Sand, John Sand. Indian case file: Noah Sand. Cherokee census: 1880, 1890. U.S. census: 1920. For another example, see Samuel Chuwee's enrollment packet.

21. Federal probate file: Charlotte Turtle.

22. Enrollment packet: William and Laura Kirk. U.S. census: 1920. Although he married, Sam continued to live with his parents and some of his siblings at least until 1920. Other examples of young men segregated from their families are Jesse Bird, Baskum Brown, Charley Kelley, John Sand, Will Sand, and Ned Turtle.

23. Perdue, *Cherokee Women*, 131.

24. Enrollment packet and allotment jacket: James and Eliza Brown, John and Emily Brown.

25. For example, see the enrollment packets of Nannie Dog, Rosanna Mounce, and Nannie Wolfe.

26. Enrollment packet and allotment jacket: Bill and Annie Chewey, Tom and Nancy Suake. Eastern Cherokee application: Annie Suake. Probate file: Ezekiel Suake. I assume but do not know definitively that Annie took her daughters with her into her marriage to Tom Suake.

27. Enrollment packet: Lewis and Betsy Bird. Commissioners also relied on their interpreters to translate names into English even when an individual went by a Cherokee name. When Isaac Youngbird enrolled his son-in-law and grandchildren in May 1902, he spoke Cherokee names that Sam Foreman then translated into English when he knew them. Dah-lo-des-kee became Henry. War-dee became Watt. Coo-tah-ye remained by her Cherokee name rather than her English name, Carrie. Enrollment packet: Sam Crittenden. Eastern Cherokee application: Henry, Watt, Carrie Crittenden.

28. Enrollment packet: Tom and Nannie Wolfe. Rider knew Etarkust Turtle. The Dawes Commission, however, enrolled him as William. Enrollment packet: Arch and Fannie Turtle. Reverend Lacie also identified individuals by Cherokee names. He knew the youngest son of Noah Sand as Oo-do-la-ner, but the Dawes Commission asked if the young man's English name was John. Lacie replied that he did not know someone named John Sand. Oo-do-la-ner appears on the Dawes roll as John anyway.

Enrollment packet: John Sand. This scenario also played out during the enrollment of Redbird Smith's children. See Carter, *Dawes Commission*, 116.

29. Several scholars have ably documented that Cherokees engaged in their own discourse about race. See Perdue, *"Mixed Blood" Indians*; Yarbrough, *Race and the Cherokee Nation*; and Sturm, *Blood Politics*.

30. Prucha, *Great Father*, 882–83. Mirroring the correlation between the Dawes Act and the Curtis Act, the Burke Act was passed first and applied to all reservation-based communities that had been allotted. Congress extended similar provisions to reduce federal control in the Five Tribes Bill, passed later that year. Carter, *Dawes Commission*, 173.

31. In a letter to Congress, Principal Chief Samuel Mayes defined full bloods as "those who speak practically only the Cherokee language." Mayes et al., "Cherokee Delegates."

32. Enrollment packet: Lewis and Betsy Bird, Bill and Annie Chewey, Sam Crittenden, Steve and Nannie Dog, Jim and Mary Hogshooter, Abe and Margaret Sixkiller, Arch and Fannie Turtle. ·

33. Enrollment packet: Abe and Margaret Sixkiller.

34. Thornton, *Cherokees*, 118.

35. Enrollment packet: William and Laura Kirk.

36. Enrollment packet: James and Hattie Holland.

37. This is also common knowledge among those descendants of the allotted who have an interest in their family's history. See LL: Mavis Doering.

38. Enrollment packet: Edwin and Lucinda Cannon, John and Lee Cannon, Oscar and Annie Cannon, Sterling Cannon, Ophelia Harless.

39. Enrollment packet: John and Susan Kelley, William and Laura Kirk, Joe and Rosanna Mounce.

40. Bureau of the Census, Report on Indians Taxed and Not Taxed. U.S. census: 1900.

41. Thomas, "Origin and Development of the Redbird Smith Movement," 146–47. Hendrix, *Redbird Smith*, 68.

42. Carter, *Dawes Commission*, 149.

43. Enrollment packet: John and Emily Brown.

44. Thomas, "Origin and Development of the Redbird Smith Movement," 147. Hendrix, *Redbird Smith*, 68.

45. Thomas, "Origin and Development of the Redbird Smith Movement," 111–203.

46. Carter, *Dawes Commission*, 114–17.

47. *Cherokee Advocate*, March 22, 1902. Carselowey noted that Cherokee men began wearing their hair short and growing facial hair only in the 1880s. *Cherokee Notes*, 51, JMC.

48. Sturm, *Blood Politics*.

CHAPTER SIX

1. Enrollment packet and allotment jacket: Birch and Lizzie Anderson. Eastern Cherokee application: Lizzie Anderson, Birch Anderson. U.S. Geological Survey,

Cherokee township maps, township 19 North, Range 24 East, November 3, 1898, map case 1, drawer 1, folders 6,7, and 9, Oklahoma Historical Society (hereafter cited as plat map 19N, 24E).

2. Cherokee census: 1880, 1890. Enrollment packet and allotment jacket: Steve and Nannie Dog. Eastern Cherokee application: Nannie Dog, Steve Dog. Plat map 19N, 24E.

3. Debo, *And Still the Waters Run*, 31–158.

4. Carter, *Dawes Commission*, 125–53.

5. Miner uses that phrase as the title of chapter 10 in his *Corporation and the Indian*.

6. Strickland, *Indians in Oklahoma*, 48. For an earlier version of this story, see Wright, *Guide to the Indian Tribes of Oklahoma*, 221.

7. Lynn-Sherow, *Red Earth*. In *The Cheyenne and Arapaho Ordeal*, 148–81, Berthrong suggests that bands selected their allotments together or refused to participate in the program collectively. Likewise, in *United States–Comanche Relations*, Hagan explains that Comanches also tended to select allotments according to existing residential patterns. See page 225.

8. There were over half a dozen land runs on territory that now is included in Oklahoma. These pictures are commonly reprinted and part of the public domain. Several films, including the 1992 motion picture *Far and Away*, have included a dramatization of the 1893 land run on the Cherokee Strip.

9. The Oklahoma Historical Society has several hundred images of allotment and the Dawes Commission; see <http://www.okhistory.org/research/collections/photos.html>.

10. Joe Lemaster Collection, #21186.3.3 and #21186.3.6, Oklahoma Historical Society. Neither of these photos identifies the tribe, but the Indians are of the Five Tribes and could be Cherokee.

11. B. Smith, "Keetoowah Society," 16. Thomas, "Origin and Development of the Redbird Smith Movement," 117–82.

12. Curtis was a complicated man whose life testifies to the hard, sometimes contradictory choices made by American Indians during the late nineteenth and early twentieth centuries. Although Kaw, he gave his political allegiance to the U.S. government, and his opposition to tribal sovereignty deepened over the course of his own political career. Ultimately, he served as vice president under Herbert Hoover. Unrau, *Mixed-Bloods and Tribal Dissolution*.

13. Henry Dawes, for example, opposed the bill because he believed this particular version of allotment policy was too cumbersome and unenforceable. See Carter, *Dawes Commission*, 34–35.

14. "The Five Tribes in Congress," February 19, 1898. "The Five Tribes in Congress," *Claremore Progress*, April 23, 1898, box M-50, folder 63, SM. S. Mayes, special message of S. H. Mayes, box M-50, folder 6, SM.

15. Wardell, *Political History*, 321.

16. Cherokee leaders first challenged the law's constitutionality, but the Supreme Court refused to hear the case. Cherokee attorneys then initiated a complaint in the lower courts that challenged the Dawes Commission's power to interfere with their property rights. On appeal, the Supreme Court decided against them.

17. Carter, *Dawes Commission*, 33–38. Wardell, *Political History*, 320–26.

18. In this agreement, Cherokee statesmen sought to exclude all allotments from taxation for thirty-five years; to limit freed persons (the former African American slaves of Cherokees) to forty-acre allotments; and to arrange for conservative tribal members to take adjoining allotments, incorporate them, and hold them communally. The Dawes Commission rejected this last proposal but acceded to the other demands of Cherokee leaders, and the agreement went to Cherokee voters, who approved it.

19. They resolved to start allotments at eighty acres, to supplement those who received inferior land with additional acreage or cash, to designate a portion of each allotment as an inalienable homestead, and to protect those Cherokees who statesmen worried would fall prey to speculators and grafters. In 1901, President Theodore Roosevelt approved the amendments negotiated the previous spring, and Cherokee citizens again voted on the plan. By this time, the Dawes Commission had completed its preliminary enrollment of Cherokee citizens, however, and their total proved lower than anticipated. For this reason, some Cherokee citizens sought to increase allotments to 120 acres.

20. Of the 6,716 votes cast, 4,340 of them approved. I have been unable to find out how many Cherokee men were eligible to vote on the Cherokee agreement, although historians agree that the turnout was light. Carter, *Dawes Commission*, 117. The census of 1890 lists 10,308 male heads of households, and since young men over eighteen were also entitled to vote, the number of eligible voters would have been greater. In 1890, there were 15,161 men over the age of eighteen. In other words, probably only half of Cherokee voters participated in this referendum, and only a quarter, at the most, voted for it. Bureau of the Census, Report on Indians Taxed and Not Taxed. For more on the politics of this era, see Wardell, *Political History*, 347–49, and Duvall, *Oral History*, 40.

21. IPP: Wyly Beavers.

22. IPP: Oscar Cannon.

23. Debo, *And Still the Waters Run*, 33–35. Wardell, *Political History*, 320–26. W. C. Rogers, first annual message (1903), box R-34, folder 29, WCR.

24. Maps for 19N, 24–26E, box 12, folder 10, LH. Classification list, box 12, folder 7, LH. In 1898 and again in 1901, the Dawes Commission surveyed towns in the Indian Territory.

25. In 1902, Commissioner Tams Bixby sent into the Cherokee Nation a team of five surveyors charged with determining which Cherokees occupied "excess holdings," or more than their allotment entitled them to have, and to appraise their improvements. Carter, *Dawes Commission*, 125–53. Carselowey, *Cherokee Old Timers*, 16, 23, JMC. Condra, "Opening of the Indian Territory," LH.

26. Carter, "Deciding Who Can Be Cherokee," 121, quote on p. 125. Enrollment packet and allotment jacket: John and Emily Brown.

27. Carter, *Dawes Commission*, 141–44.

28. Carter, *Dawes Commission*, 127.

29. Allotment jacket: James and Eliza Brown, John and Emily Brown, Marsh and Mary Brown, Birch and Lizzie Anderson. John Brown's adult daughters included Ollie Hart, whose husband ran the mill. Sue Brown McGinnis, "James Daniel Brown."

30. For example, Polly and Florence Brown and Nancy Suake selected their own allotments. None had enrolled herself. Allotment jacket: James and Eliza Brown, Tom and Nancy Suake.

31. Bonaparte criticized the way that the commissioners handled their work, but his suggestions for improvement also were impractical. Debo, *And Still the Waters Run*, 99.

32. Allotment jacket: Mack and Emma Welch.

33. Allotment jacket: Ira Cannon.

34. While the other members of the Kelley family were likely illiterate, or at least marked rather than signed their allotment jackets, Tinsie's letter is in perfect English, suggesting someone else wrote it for her because she doesn't exhibit that level of literacy in any other record. She claimed land near her family. Allotment jacket: John and Laura Kelley.

35. In cases like Hattie's, where a woman was widowed and remarried, the Dawes Commission seems not to have updated surnames. Even though James Holland died eighteen months before the Dawes roll closed and Hattie remarried a month before that deadline, the Dawes Commission enrolled and allotted her as Hattie Holland under her late husband's name. Allotment jacket: James and Hattie Holland.

36. Allotment jackets: James and Eliza Brown, Martin Raper.

37. Allotment jacket: Tom and Fannie Welch, James Mack and Cleo Welch.

38. Allotment jacket: John and Laura Kelley, Joe and Rosanna Mounce.

39. Allotment jacket: Birch and Lizzie Anderson. Other young married couples made similar decisions regarding their allotments, but their kin lived beyond the scope of my study. Mose and Minnie Crittenden divided their claims and those of their children between township 19 North, 24 East, and township 20 North, 18 East. The family claimed farms at both locations. Allotment jacket: Mose and Minnie Crittenden. John and Lee Cannon also divided their allotments and those of their children between their farm in township 23 North, 19 East, and timberland near John's kin in Chance. Allotment jacket: John and Lee Cannon.

40. Some Cherokees claimed only their small farms and asked the Dawes Commission to arbitrarily allot the remainder of their land. See Mack and Emma Welch's allotment jacket.

41. John Welch's selection of allotments is a notable exception to this generalization in this study. He selected land in Chance, which appeared to be his farm, but selected land in the public domain in township 21 North, 18 East, for his children and his nieces and nephews, who were his wards following the death of their parents. Allotment jacket: John and Dovie Welch, Moses Welch and siblings.

42. Allotment jacket: Mack and Emma Welch.

43. Lynn-Sherow, *Red Earth*, 26–28.

44. Allotment jacket: James and Eliza Brown, John and Emily Brown, Marsh and Mary Brown.

45. Allotment jacket: John and Dovie Welch, John and Emily Brown, Marsh and Mary Brown.

46. For an example, see James Mack and Emma Welch's allotment jacket.

47. Allotment jacket: James and Eliza Brown.

48. Allotment jacket: Tom and Fannie Welch, Marsh and Mary Brown, John and Susan Kelley, Joe and Rosanna Mounce, James and Hattie Holland.

49. Allotment jacket: Joe and Rosanna Mounce.

50. Allotment jacket: Tom and Fannie Welch, John and Emily Brown, Marsh and Mary Brown, Birch and Lizzie Anderson. USGS surveyors noted Mitchell as the owner of the improvements on their map. Plat map 19N, 25E.

51. During the early nineteenth century, some Cherokees abandoned customs associated with their matrilineal clan system, particularly relating to property ownership. Some elites, for example, willed property to their sons in contrast to Cherokee custom. Cherokee women retained their rights to property, however. Perdue, *Cherokee Women*, 139–41, 152–54. Using wills, Johnston argues that Cherokee women gave special attention to the economic well-being of their daughters well into the nineteenth century. See *Cherokee Women in Crisis*, 137–38.

52. Allotment jacket: James and Hattie Holland.

53. Allotment jacket: William and Laura Kirk.

54. Allotment jacket: Edwin and Lucinda Cannon, Oscar and Annie Cannon, John and Lee Cannon, Sterling Cannon, Ira and Lizzie Cannon.

55. For examples, see William and Laura Kirk and Tom and Nancy Suake's allotment jackets. The Dawes Commission appears to have accepted the verbal contracts but only when Cherokees purchased improvements from neighbors. See Betsy Suake's allotment jacket, for example.

56. Although such interactions were possible, there is no note of them in the Dawes records, nor have I found this to be a common theme in oral histories of the area. Corruption, however, is *the* dominant theme in some histories of the era, particularly Debo's *And Still the Waters Run*. It is possible that in areas where land was of greater value, corruption proved more widespread and could have included Indians and non-Indians.

57. Chance selected land in the northern part of 18 North, 25 East, for his and Maggie's homesteads. Allotment jacket: Tilman and Maggie Chance. For information about mineral deposits, see maps 70 and 71 in the *Historical Atlas of Oklahoma*, compiled by Morris, Goins, and McReynolds.

58. Tams Bixby assumed this position. Carter, *Dawes Commission*, 125–53.

59. Hendrix, *Redbird Smith*, 54–55. Thomas, "Origin and Development of the Redbird Smith Movement," 115–19.

60. See McIntosh, "Chitto Harjo."

61. Thomas, "Origin and Development of the Redbird Smith Movement," 140–42, 161–67, quote on p. 164. The Cherokee revival does not correspond to the model set forth by Anthony F. C. Wallace in his *Death and Rebirth of the Seneca*, which predominates in the literature on religious revitalization. For a comparison, see Thomas, "Redbird Smith Movement," from *Symposium Cherokee and Iroquois Culture*.

62. Thomas, "Origin and Development of the Redbird Smith Movement," 156. Perdue, "Cherokee Relations with the Iroquois," 141.

63. Hendrix, *Redbird Smith*, 54–55.

64. Thomas, "Origin and Development of the Redbird Smith Movement," chapter 3.

65. Hendrix, *Redbird Smith*, 50. Citing the differing recollections of two of Smith's sons, John and George, Thomas offers two possible reasons for the withdrawal of the Nighthawks from the Four Mothers Society. John Smith suggested that his father generally disagreed with Creek conservatives, but George Smith maintained that the break occurred for a very specific reason: the Creeks hired an African American attorney to represent the Four Mothers Society in Washington, D.C. Although many Creeks considered African Americans as equals, some conservative Cherokees did not. Thomas, "Origins and Development of the Redbird Smith Movement," 147–59. McIntosh, "Chitto Harjo."

66. Thomas, "Origin and Development of the Redbird Smith Movement," 157–75. Thomas, "Redbird Smith Movement," 165.

67. Thomas, "Origin and Development of the Redbird Smith Movement," 157–75.

68. Carter, *Dawes Commission*, 114–17.

69. Thomas, "Origin and Development of the Redbird Smith Movement," 180–82.

70. Ibid., 200.

71. The USGS maps did not identify the owners of improvements, except in rare circumstances (perhaps two names in an entire township), and I have not been able to locate the maps of the Dawes Commission that did, if they even existed. The commissioners noted the errors on these maps, which reflected surveyors' failure to study fully isolated areas or those where conservatives lived. As a result, those least likely to have taken an allotment were also those about whom accurate information was most difficult to obtain.

72. Carter lists the number as 775 Cherokees, but since the commission expected to deal with heads-of-households, I think this means that 775 families, as grouped onto one enrollment card, had yet to pick their allotments. *Dawes Commission*, 144.

73. Carter, *Dawes Commission*, 143–45.

74. Smith's testimony confirmed Eufala Harjo's. U.S. Senate, *Report of the Select Committee*, 89–93, 97–100.

75. Carter cited Tams Bixby as asserting that it proved impossible to determine who owned many of the improvements in the Cherokee Nation, which led to many contests. Although this could suggest that some Cherokees took advantage of those who had not selected allotments, it also suggests that Cherokees may have shared some resources, such as pastures, orchards, and the like. *Dawes Commission*, 143.

76. U.S. Senate, *Report of the Select Committee*, 89–93.

77. Allotment jacket: Bill and Annie Chewey, Betsy Suake.

78. Miles, "'Circular Reasoning.'" Enrollment packet: Betsy Suake, White and Susie Oakball, John and Jennie Oakball. Supplemental information to allotment jacket: White and Susie Oakball. Interestingly, in his 1906 Eastern Cherokee application, White claims that he enrolled with the Dawes Commission. In her application submitted the following year, Susie Oakball states that she did not enroll. Although White's actual answer may have been lost in translation, this evidence might suggest that he was willing to acknowledge the Dawes roll's existence when Susie would not do so. Eastern Cherokee application: White Oakball, Susie Oakball. For other examples, see the enrollment packets of Tom and Nannie Wolfe and Lewis and Betsy Bird.

79. Enrollment packet, Eastern Cherokee application, and probate file: Betsy Oakball. Allotment jacket: White and Susie Oakball, Betsy Oakball. Cherokee census: 1880.

80. Ibid.

81. Allotment jacket: Tom and Nannie Wolfe.

82. They also separated Martin Foreman, Jennie's son from a previous marriage, from the rest of the family. Allotment jacket: Nelson and Jennie Crittenden. Although Sam Crittenden's two youngest children received the majority of his farm, the family did not retain all of it. Allotment jacket: Sam Crittenden. Allotment jacket: Samuel Chuwee. For other examples, see the allotment jackets of White and Susie Oakball and Abe and Margaret Sixkiller.

83. Allotment jacket: Bill and Annie Chewey.

84. Allotment jacket: Lewis and Betsy Bird. The Wolfes are the only family who received their allotments in Chewey and in a distant township. A clerk allotted Tom Wolfe a portion of his farm in Chewey while another farm that the family supposedly owned in Buffalo Prairie was assigned to Nannie, Tom's wife, and her son Sam Chewey. Allotment jacket: Tom and Nannie Wolfe.

85. Allotment jacket: Jim and Mary Hogshooter.

86. Allotment jacket: Jim and Mary Hogshooter, Will Sand, John Sand, Noah Sand.

87. Allotment jacket: Tom and Nanny Suake. Carter, *Dawes Commission*, 155–79.

88. Allotment jacket: Nannie Palone.

89. U.S. Senate, *Report of the Select Committee*, 89–93. Carter, *Dawes Commission*, 147.

90. This was not the only incident of violence against Indian people. Rumors of such attacks permeated Indian communities and may have served to discourage resistance to allotment. Richard Manus remembered bodies of Indian men showing up along the tracks of the Kansas City Southern railroad. DD: Richard Manus. See also Littlefield, *Seminole Burning*.

91. Debo, *And Still the Waters Run*, 163.

92. At the same time that they were envisioning an Indian state, tribal leaders were taking apart their own republic. According to the Cherokee Agreement, the Cherokee Nation ceased to exist on March 4, 1906, and as the date approached, Cherokee leaders sought to conclude the affairs of their nation rather than leave matters for the secretary of the interior to resolve. W. C. Rogers, second annual message (1904), box R-34, folder 49, WCR. Debo, *And Still the Waters Run*, 162–64.

93. Many leaders of the Sequoyah movement attended and profoundly influenced the Oklahoma state constitutional convention. Early Oklahoma's political allegiance was largely Democratic. The president was a Republican, and his party opposed admitting two Democratic states whose senators, representative, and delegates to the Electoral College would undermine their control. Baird and Goble, *Oklahoma*, 163–76.

94. Wright, "Wedding of Oklahoma."

95. Dale, "Two Mississippi Valley Frontiers."

CHAPTER SEVEN

1. Application for Removal of Restrictions for 1908: Dennis Sixkiller. Reading through these records, one cannot help but wonder at the psychological issues manifesting themselves in the white clerks' deep-seated mistrust of whiteness and those with white ancestry. This trend is such an ironic theme in these records.

2. Debo, *And Still the Waters Run*, 253–55.

3. In 1914, another field clerk called Abe "a pronounced 'Night Hawk,'" but I think he may actually have been affiliated with the Keetoowah Society. The Sixkillers belonged to the Baptist Mission, and they seem to have selected their allotments, although their file is unclear. Cherokee census: 1890. U.S. census: 1900. Enrollment packet: Stan Gibson. Application for Removal of Restrictions for 1908: Dennis Sixkiller, Abe Sixkiller (source of above quotation).

4. Indian case file: Tinna Dog. Probate file: Nannie Dog.

5. Federal probate file: Tinna Dog.

6. Ibid.

7. Ibid. Indian case file: Tinna Dog. Probate file: Nannie Dog.

8. This clock started ticking on the date each individual allotment certificate was issued. Most Cherokee allotment certificates dated from 1904 and 1905, but the process stretched between 1902 and 1910. It is worth noting that restrictions were placed on the individual and not on his or her land. See Carter, *Dawes Commission*, 125–53.

9. Debo, *And Still the Waters Run*, 89.

10. This bill was an effort to tidy up the loose ends of the Dawes Commission and move it toward completing the allotment of the Five Tribes. See Carter, *Dawes Commission*, 172–73, 205–15.

11. Carter, *Dawes Commission*, 176.

12. Debo wrote the most thorough account of this entire process in *And Still the Waters Run*, and Carter notes these developments throughout his book, *The Dawes Commission*. Prucha provides an abbreviated description in *Great Father*, 900–903.

13. In 1904, some members of the National Council appealed to Congress for the removal of restrictions. Although the National Council had functioned as a representative body, by 1904, critics of allotment, including Keetoowahs and Nighthawks, had withdrawn, and the men serving thus did not reflect the sentiments of the whole Cherokee population. "News Item of W. C. Rogers," box R-34, folder 52, WCR.

14. Dozens of Cherokees testified about this concern before the Senate Select Committee to Investigate Matters Connected with Affairs in the Indian Territory. See in the *Report of the Select Committee* the testimony of Joseph Fox, 101–04; Richard Glory, 113–25; Spencer Stevens, 292–307, and W. H. Walker, 337–39.

15. In particular, they resented the interference of guardians. U.S. Senate, *Report of the Select Committee*. See John Corntassel's testimony, 107–13. Regarding restrictions, see also Frank J. Boudinot, 282–93; S. H. Colson, 199–201; and J. A. Wood, 321–37.

16. Secretary of the Interior Ethan Allen Hitchcock appointed Tams Bixby in spite of controversy and accusations of corruption.

17. Carter, *Dawes Commission*, 207–29. Debo, *And Still the Waters Run*, 159–254. Prucha, *Great Father*, 759–60, 897–900.

18. U.S. Senate, *Report of the Select Committee*, Levi Gritts testimony, 318–21.

19. For an example from this area, see the ad announcing the sale of Annie Suake's (now Gritts) land in the local newspaper published out of Stilwell, Oklahoma: *Standard-Sentinel*, April 8, 1915: 2.

20. For an example from this area, see the *Adair County Republican*, October 23, 1914: 4–9.

21. For an example from this area, see the *Adair County Republican*, November 13, 1913: 1; *Standard-Sentinel*, January 7, 1915: 1, and April 8, 1915: 2.

22. Probate file: Andrew Palone.

23. U.S. Senate, *Report of the Select Committee*, Joseph Fox testimony, 101–4, and David Muskrat testimony, 273–76.

24. U.S. Senate, *Report of the Select Committee*, J. Henry Dick testimony, 276–78.

25. Bushyhead's name appears throughout local papers involved in a variety of cases, usually related to allotment and land, especially that of Cherokee minors.

26. Thorne, *World's Richest Indian*.

27. Indian case file: Steve Sand. Jessie B. Scott Kaiser, "Proctor," *HAC*, 59–60. Eula Fullerton, "Joseph Augustus Lawrence," 122–23.

28. Application for Removal of Restrictions for 1908: Charley Turtle. The buyer, William Banowitz of Iowa, notified the superintendent for the Five Civilized Tribes that he had been billed incorrectly and actually owed $100 more than he had been requested to pay.

29. Indian case file: Jesse Bird.

30. Application for Removal of Restrictions for 1908 (second of two): Lucy Chewey.

31. Ibid.: Tom Suake. Because Tom spelled his surname "Suake" in other records, and because his mother and siblings used this spelling as well, I also used it for the whole family throughout this book so as to not confuse readers. In reality, surnames and given names often varied in spelling.

32. Indian case file: Sam Chewey.

33. Debo explains this initiative as a means to increase land available for taxation and for sale to non-Indians for development. *And Still the Waters Run*, 281–87.

34. Application for Removal of Restrictions for 1908: Oce Hogshooter, Jim Hogshooter.

35. Sam Chewey's appeal for the removal of restrictions echoes the same theme. In 1914, Chewey, then twenty-seven, was married. He and his wife, Annie, lived with his mother, Nannie Wolfe, on her allotment. Chewey sought to sell forty acres of his surplus in order to buy his own land for a farm and the supplies and tools he would need to build it. The field clerk granted his request. Chewey, however, never left his mother's household. Indian case file: Sam Chewey. U.S. census: 1920.

36. Application for Removal of Restrictions for 1904: Sam Kirk. Sam's father was one of the Cherokees who had speculated rather unsuccessfully to obtain allotments in oil- and gas-rich areas.

37. Debo, *And Still the Waters Run*, 159–350. Prucha, *Great Father*, 903–9. It is telling that guardianship records remain restricted.

38. Probate file: Andrew Palone, William Proctor.

39. Probate file: Linnie Scott, James Crittenden, Lizzie Lacie.

40. *Adair County Republican*, December 12, 1913: 1.

41. Debo, *And Still the Waters Run*, 159–350. Prucha, *Great Father*, 903–9.

42. Debo, *And Still the Waters Run*, 228.

43. Probate file: Emma Welch, Myrtle Welch, Esther Welch, Georgia Welch, Ethel Welch, and Cecil Welch. For another example of a parent legally establishing his guardianship of his child in order to sign an oil and gas lease, see Artie Brown's probate file.

44. Probate file: Henry Crittenden. John Chandler had been appointed to be Henry's guardian in 1926. I was not able to determine what happened in this year or why Sam then sought to be his guardian.

45. Probate file: William Bird, Frank Bird, Myrtle Welch, Esther Welch, Georgie Welch, Ethel Welch, Floyd Kirk, Isaac Kirk.

46. Probate file: Wirt Cannon.

47. Indian case file: Charlotte Turtle.

48. Application for Removal of Restrictions for 1908: Jennie Oakball.

49. Indian case file: Fallingpot Oakball (Walter was known as Fallingpot as a child).

50. Ibid. U.S. census: 1920.

51. Indian case file: Charlotte Turtle. The extended Bird family also experienced a similar situation.

52. For an explanation of specific policies, see Prucha, *Great Father*, 760–83.

53. Application for Removal of Restrictions for 1908: Jim Hogshooter.

54. Ibid.: Oce Hogshooter. Hendrix, *Redbird Smith*, 74–75.

55. Application for Removal of Restrictions for 1908: Retta Sixkiller.

56. Ibid.: Lucy Chewey (two separate files).

57. Ibid.: Lincoln Sixkiller, Abe Sixkiller.

58. Ibid.: Lawyer Suake. U.S. census: 1920.

59. Probate file: Jennie Crittenden. Rosanna Mounce's sexual history confused the court as well. Probate file: Thomas Mounce. Such exchanges were equally awkward when parents were asked to discuss the sexual relationships of their dead children. See John Sand's probate file.

60. Application for Removal of Restrictions for 1908: Dora Mitchell.

61. LL: Dora Wolfe interview.

62. This included Will Sand, Louis Bird, Sam Crittenden, Nelson Crittenden, White Oakball, and Tom Wolfe. U.S. census: 1910.

63. U.S. census: 1910.

64. Ibid. In contrast, David Sapsucker, a Cherokee, was the enumerator in John and Jennie Oakball's community to the north, and he generally obtained information from families.

65. Her grandmother Eliza was listed as one-eighth Cherokee and her mother, Love, had married a white man, so Hattie should have been enrolled as one-thirty-second Cherokee, according to the math of blood quantum. Enrollment packet: Lizzie Anderson, Marsh Brown, James Brown, Hattie Holland. U.S. census: 1910, 1920.

66. U.S. census: 1900, 1910, 1920.

67. Ibid.: 1920.

68. Enrollment packet: John and Susan Kelley family. The extended Welch family was also white by the 1920 census, as was the Brown family and the Cannon family. U.S. census: 1900, 1910, 1920.

69. U.S. census: 1910.

70. Carselowey, *Cherokee Pioneers*, 64, JMC.

71. See *Standard-Sentinel*, February 18, 1915: 13.

72. For Tom Welch's service to the Cherokee Nation, see CNR, vol. 618, p. 3, and vol. 315-A, p. 115. U.S. census: 1920. "Elected County Officials of Adair County," *HAC*, 124–25. Tom Wolfe's dad, Young Wolfe, had been a member of the National Council in the 1870s. See CNR, vol. 274, front cover; vol. 270, p. 47; and vol. 269, p. 69. Both Abe and his father, Soldier Sixkiller, had been members of the National Council. See CNR, vol. 284, p. 213; vol. 263, p. 1; and vol. 258, p. 97.

73. Francis Pathkiller and Ben Bailey signed the form. A Cherokee family by that name also lived in the area in which the Pathkillers lived. Indian case file: Frank Bird. U.S. census: 1920. I did not find evidence that Frank was charged, but many other Cherokees were. Newspapers regularly listed those whom the state was prosecuting for this crime. For example, see the *Adair County Republican*, December 25, 1914: 1, and *Standard-Sentinel*, January 7, 1915: 1. I noted this because it involved a man named John Wolfe, who I subsequently realized was not the man included in this study.

74. Carselowey, *My Journal*, 18, JMC. The couple filed for the license in Whitmire on April 22, 1907, when the region was still Indian Territory.

75. Probate file: Steve Dog.

76. Ibid.: Betsy Suake.

77. Ibid.: Thomas Mounce.

78. Ibid.: Jennie Crittenden, Nelson Crittenden.

79. Ibid.: Lewis Bird.

80. Debo, *And Still the Waters Run*, 66–75, 276–78.

81. The *Cherokee Advocate* was an early critic of proposed school closings. See the April 29, 1905, edition.

82. U.S. Senate, *Report of the Select Committee*, Eufala Harjo testimony, 89–93.

83. *Adair County Republican*, November 13, 1914: 1.

84. Wahrhaftig, "In the Aftermath of Civilization," 24.

85. DD: Lena Cary.

86. Narrative and Statistical Reports of the Supervisor of Education to the Commissioner of Indian Affairs, Annual Report of the Supervisor of Indian Education for 1930, 3, 7.

87. This includes the children of Lizzie Anderson, John Brown, Marsh Brown, James Brown, and Hattie Lewis. U.S. census: 1910, 1920.

88. U.S. census: 1910, 1920. Nelson Crittenden sent his children to school, but his son Sam did not send his children to school. U.S. census: 1920.

89. U.S. census: 1920. Application for Removal of Restrictions for 1908: Susie Oakball.

90. U.S. census: 1920.

91. U.S. census: 1910, 1920.

92. U.S. census: 1910. Allotment jacket: John and Jennie Oakball.

93. "Reconnaissance Erosion Survey of the State of Oklahoma," 1922, 39–341, LH.

94. DD: Amos Christie, Saugee Grigsby, Richard Manus, Jefferson Tindall, Jack Whitmire, Wiley Wolf, Dora Wolfe. Wahrhaftig, "In the Aftermath of Civilization," 29–31, 107–9.

95. Krause, *Environmental History*, 56.

96. DD: Amos Christie, Saugee Grigsby, Richard Manus, Jefferson Tindall, Jack Whitmire, Wiley Wolf, Dora Wolfe. Wahrhaftig aptly describes this process in "In the Aftermath of Civilization," 29–31, 107–9. Krause, *Environmental History*, 65–67.

97. Application for Removal of Restrictions for 1908: Steve Sand.

98. Probate file: Ezekiel Suake.

99. Application for Removal of Restrictions for 1908: Steve Sand.

100. DD: Lena Cary, Jess Mayes, Arch Ray, Ross Rector, Isaac Rogers, Jack Whitmire, Jess Wright. Duvall, *Oral History*, 127.

101. Tortorelli, "Floods and Droughts."

102. Baird and Goble, *Oklahoma*, 221–22.

103. Ibid. Krause, *Environmental History*, 56–57.

104. DD: Van Bly, Amos Christie, Saugee Grigsby, George Hummingbird, Ross Rector, George Young.

105. Eastern Cherokee application: Tinsie Kelley.

106. U.S. census: 1910, 1920.

107. Coates, "Family of Families."

108. Bohaker, "Nindoodemag."

109. Other regions of the former Cherokee Nation averaged a 10 percent retention rate. Historical geographer Leslie Hewes theorized that the rate of loss was lower in this region because more Cherokees remained restricted and, therefore, could not sell, or lose, their land. Restricted Indians then made up 12 percent of the population, and they owned approximately 6 percent of the region's real estate. "Indian Land in the Cherokee Country of Oklahoma," LH.

110. IPP: Oscar Cannon, Tom Welch, James Brown.

111. Debo describes the Red Cross campaign in Oklahoma in *And Still the Waters Run*, 375–76. Red Cross, "Red Cross Drought Relief Work," 8. Red Cross, "Approaching the Apex," 131. Red Cross, "Steady Flowing Stream," 519–21.

112. Few scholars have paid attention to this organization, which warrants a monograph-length study of its own. See Wright, *Guide to the Indian Tribes of Oklahoma*, 76, and B. Smith, "Keetoowah Society," 27.

CHAPTER EIGHT

1. DD: Sam Chewey. Other Cherokees from that region echoed Chewey's perspective. See DD: Van Bly, Jefferson Tindall, Ross Rector, Jess Mayes, Isaac Rogers, Jack Whitmire, and Rufus Lacie.

2. Ironically, Angie Debo did much to popularize the idea that Indians were incapable of adapting to allotment in *And Still the Waters Run* even though she spent

little time exploring actual Indian responses to the policy. Her intent, however, was to prove that Indians were being abused, not to demonstrate their ability to mitigate an abusive system.

3. U.S. census: 1920. Eastern Cherokee application: Carrie Crittenden.

4. It is not clear who raised Jim and Charlotte, the oldest two children born to Steve and Lizzie. In 1910, they were not living with Steve and Maria, but in 1920, Jim, then twenty-four, again lived with his father. The extended Turtle family lived in Cherokee County, not Adair County. U.S. census: 1910, 1920.

5. Probate file: Martin Raper.

6. U.S. census: 1910.

7. Eastern Cherokee application: Jennie Oakball. U.S. census: 1920.

8. Eastern Cherokee application: Frank Bird. U.S. census: 1920.

9. U.S. census: 1910, 1920.

10. Ibid.: 1920.

11. Ibid.

12. Ibid.: 1910, 1920.

13. Ibid.: 1910. Similarly, Wyly Beavers also is listed as a "boarder" in the 1920 census. Along with his wife and child, he lived with his maternal first cousin Lace and his family. Elderly women, such as Polly Brown, were not listed as boarders, suggesting that census takers did not consider them to be contributing to the family's subsistence.

14. Ibid.

15. Ibid.: 1900, 1910. Probate file: Charley Turtle.

16. U.S. census: 1920.

17. Ibid. Allotment jacket: Nelson and Jennie Crittenden.

18. U.S. census: 1910.

19. In 1920, John's sister Laura Kirk also shared her household with a newly inter-married son and his wife and another son who was a widower with a young son. Eastern Cherokee application: Charley Kelley. U.S. census: 1910, 1920.

20. U.S. census: 1910.

21. Ibid.: 1920. See Nelson and Jennie Crittenden's family in the 1920 census for another good example.

22. Ibid.: 1900, 1910, 1920. Eastern Cherokee application: Lawyer Suake.

23. U.S. census: 1910, 1920.

24. Ibid.: 1920.

25. Ibid.: 1910, 1920.

26. Ibid.: 1920.

27. Ibid.

28. Ibid. Application for Removal of Restrictions for 1908: Susan Crittenden.

29. U.S. census: 1910.

30. Ibid.: 1920.

31. Ibid.: 1910, 1920.

32. Ibid.: 1920. Application for Removal of Restrictions for 1908: Sam Chewey.

33. U.S. census: 1910.

34. Application for Removal of Restrictions for 1908: Nannie Dog.

35. U.S. census: 1910.

36. Ibid.: 1920.

37. Jack D. Baker, "The John P. Mounce Family," *HAC*, 492–94.

38. U.S. census: 1910. Like his parents, Jesse Bird also divorced and remarried and provides another good example. His son was raised by his mother, who also remarried. In 1920, Jesse was married to Betsy, and they had a three-year-old son, Ketcher. In 1920, he was married to Sissa. I think Ketcher is listed in 1920 as Andy Bird, living with his mother and her husband, John Glass, in Bunch, a nearby community. U.S. census: 1920.

39. Ibid.: 1920. Frank Bird, who had a son with Jeanette Pathkiller in 1932, provides another example. Indian case file: Frank Bird.

40. U.S. census: 1920.

41. Baker, "The Daniel Downing Family," 303–4, and "The John P. Mounce Family," 493–94.

42. U.S. census: 1910.

43. DD: Richard Manus.

44. *New Era*, June 23, 1906.

45. Application for Removal of Restrictions for 1904: John Brown. Abe Sixkiller provides another good example. See his three Applications for Removal of Restrictions for 1908. In particular, in the second one, dated 1914, the field clerk noted that Sixkiller wanted to sell his land to improve his daughter's homestead, where he lived, during his lifetime.

46. There was a third heir, which may have been a child. I was not able to determine the nature of their relationship. Probate file: John Sand. For other examples, see Susie Oakball's Application for Removal of Restrictions for 1908.

47. Application for Removal of Restrictions for 1908: Dora Mitchell.

48. Ibid.: Abe Sixkiller, Lincoln Sixkiller, Retta Sixkiller.

49. Annie may have had four children from her previous relationship. I was not able to determine whether infant Nancy was Annie's daughter or granddaughter through Annie's sixteen-year-old daughter, Rachel. Application for Removal of Restrictions for 1908: Tom Suake.

50. Probate file: Maud Kelly.

51. Ibid.: Myrtle Welch, Esther Welch, Georgie Welch, Ethel Welch. U.S. census: 1920.

52. Probate file: Eliza Brown. For other examples of women's decision making about their allotments, see the Application for Removal of Restrictions for 1908 for Susie Oakball, Dora Mitchell, Katie Sixkiller, and Retta Sixkiller. In her oral history collection, Duvall included stories emphasizing women's continued leadership in their families and communities. See the story of Salley Toney Davis starting on page 42 for a particularly good example.

53. Probate file: Charlotte Turtle.

54. Ibid.: Ira C. Welch, Harry Welch, Roy Welch.

55. Ibid.: Maud Kelley. For additional examples, see Floyd Kirk and Isaac Kirk's probate files.

56. Ibid.: Robert H. F. Holland.

57. Ibid.: Arthur G. Lewis. Lewis may not have been the best financial manager, but he clearly developed a relationship with his stepsons. When he passed away in

1949, he divided his assets equally among his sons and stepsons. Probate file: F. M. Lewis.

58. Ibid.: Ned Harlin.

59. Ibid.: Noah Sand.

60. Krause, *Environmental History*, 54–58.

61. Wahrhaftig suggests that some isolated Cherokee communities did not incorporate cash into their daily economy until the 1960s. He does not specify whether Chewey was one of these communities. Wahrhaftig, "Community and the Caretakers," 67; "In the Aftermath of Civilization," 105–7.

62. DD: Rufus Lacie, Richard Manus, Edith Thomas.

63. Ibid.: Ross Rector, Jack Whitmire.

64. Application for Removal of Restrictions for 1908: Steve Sand. Krause, *Environmental History*, 57.

65. Application for Removal of Restrictions for 1908: Oce Hogshooter.

66. Brown listed a thresher among his possessions. His family owned the only one in this study. Application for Removal of Restrictions for 1904: John Brown.

67. Krause, *Environmental History*, 54–58. The *Adair County Republican* repeatedly covered the strawberry crop in 1914 and 1915 as though this was a great economic boon to the region.

68. This number was compiled from the number of cultivated acres reported in all Applications for Removal of Restrictions for 1908 in this study.

69. U.S. census: 1920. Educational census of restricted families for 1930: Adam and Nellie Turtle Family.

70. DD: Walter O. Hale, Arch Ray, Edith Thomas, Jefferson Tindell.

71. Ibid.: Rufus Lacie, Edith Thomas.

72. Application for Removal of Restrictions for 1904: John Brown, Sam Kirk. Application for Removal of Restrictions for 1908: Susan Crittenden, Oce Hogshooter, Jim Hogshooter, Dennis Sixkiller, Charley Turtle. A 1930 survey conducted by the Department of the Interior that included restricted families with school-age children shows that few families owned any livestock, in contrast to the claims made in removal of restrictions applications. Two things could explain this discrepancy. First, the drought may have forced families to eat their livestock if they could not water it. Second, families may not have cooperated with the agent taking the survey. Educational census for restricted families for 1930.

73. Application for Removal of Restrictions for 1904: John Wesley Brown.

74. DD: Sam Chewey, Jensie Dick, Richard Manus, Wilson Terapin, Jack Whitmire.

75. Ibid.: Walter O. Hale.

76. Application for Removal of Restrictions for 1908: Charley Turtle, Susie Oakball, Annie Chewey (second of two).

77. U.S. census: 1920.

78. Probate file: Betsy Oakball, Andrew Palone.

79. Ibid.: Andrew Palone.

80. Application for Removal of Restrictions for 1908: Susie Oakball.

81. DD: Jess Mayes, Wilson Terrapin, Tohnee Turtle, Jack Whitmire.

82. Hendrix, *Redbird Smith*, 70. DD: Jess Mayes, Richard Manus, Arch Ray.

83. U.S. census: 1920. Indian case file: Steve Sand.

84. DD: Arch Ray, Ross Rector.

85. Probate file: Lucy Bird.

86. Ibid.: William Bird, Frank Bird.

87. Application for Removal of Restrictions for 1908: Susie Oakball.

88. Supplemental information to allotment jacket: White and Susie Oakball.

89. IPP: James Brown. Of course, there were exceptions to this. Others used the banking system, and families who earned money through leases loaned it to others. For example, Dennis Wolf Bushyhead loaned $200 of Betsy Suake's grandsons' money at 10 percent interest, and the investment paid off nicely for the boys. Probate file: Andrew Palone.

90. IPP: Moses Welch.

91. Probate file: Marsh Brown, Mary Brown.

92. U.S. census: 1910, 1920. Sue Brown McGinnis, "James Daniel Brown," *HAC*, 229.

93. McGinnis, "James Daniel Brown," 229.

94. U.S. census: 1920.

95. U.S. census: 1910. Application for Removal of Restrictions for 1908: Susie Oakball.

96. DD: Sam Chewey, Maud Hess, Richard Manus, Jess Mayes, Arch Ray, Ross Rector, Isaac Rogers, Edith Thomas, Jake Whitmire, Jess Wright.

97. Ibid.: Maud Hess.

98. DD: Richard Manus.

99. The Meriam Report was formally titled *The Problem of Indian Administration*. Debo, *And Still the Waters Run*, 351–78. Prucha, *Great Father*, 806–13. Strickland, *Indians in Oklahoma*, 72.

100. As quoted in Prucha, *Great Father*, 962.

101. Ibid., 969–73.

102. Enrollment of restrictions form for 1927: Dora Wolfe.

103. Allotment jacket: Lucy Bird, White and Susie Oakball.

CONCLUSION

1. DD: Jay Beech, Lena Cary. Wahrhaftig, "Tribal Cherokee Population."

2. Wahrhaftig, "Institution Building among Oklahoma's Traditional Cherokees," 138.

3. Ibid., 139–40.

4. Kilpatrick and Kilpatrick, *Friends of Thunder*, 129–34.

5. Ibid.

6. Mankiller, *Mankiller*, 231–25.

Bibliography

MANUSCRIPT COLLECTIONS

Indian Collection, Hampton University Archives, Hampton University, Hampton, Va.
   Board of Indian Commissioners, annual reports
   Dawes Bill/Indian Citizenship Days records
   Indian Rights Association, annual reports
   Lake Mohonk Conference of the Friends of the Indian, proceedings
   Women's National Indian Association, miscellaneous pamphlets and publications
North Carolina Collection, Wilson Library, University of North Carolina,
Chapel Hill, N.C.
   Thomas, Robert K. "Cherokee Values and Worldview."
Oklahoma Historical Society, Oklahoma City, Okla.
   James Mansford Carselowey Collection
   Indian-Pioneer History Collection
   Joe Lemaster Collection
   Living Legends Oral History Collection
Western History Collection, University of Oklahoma, Norman, Okla.
   Dennis Wolf Bushyhead Collection
   James M. Carselowey Collection
   Doris Duke Oral History Collection
   C. J. Harris Collection
   Leslie Hewes Collection
   Joel B. Mayes Collection
   Samuel H. Mayes Collection
   Anne Ross Piburn Collection
   W. C. Rogers Collection
   William Potter Ross Collection

*Records of the Bureau of Indian Affairs, Record Group 75, National Archives
and Records Administration—Southwest Region, Fort Worth, Tex.*

Applications for Removal of Restrictions for 1904
Applications for Removal of Restrictions for 1908
Commission to the Five Civilized Tribes, Applications for Allotment (referred to as allotment jackets)
Commission to the Five Civilized Tribes, Applications for Enrollment (referred to as enrollment packets)
Commission to the Five Civilized Tribes, Enrollment Cards
Educational Census of Restricted Families for 1930
Enrollment of Restrictions Form for 1927
Individual Indian case files
Guion Miller roll (referred to as Eastern Cherokee applications)
Narrative and Statistical Reports of the Supervisor of Education to the Commissioner of Indian Affairs, Annual Report of the Supervisor of Indian Education for 1930
Records of probate attorneys, case files of individual Indians

Oklahoma Historical Society, Oklahoma City, Okla.

1883 Cherokee census
1893 Cherokee census
Cherokee National Records
Dawes Commission to the Five Civilized Tribes, allotment plat maps (Indian Territory Map Company, 1896–1906)
U.S. Geological Survey, Cherokee township maps (Washington, D.C.: 1898)

Published Government Documents

Bureau of the Census. Censuses of the United States for 1820, 1830, 1840, 1860, 1870, 1880, 1890, 1900, 1910, and 1920. Washington, D.C.
———. Report on Indians Taxed and Not Taxed as the Eleventh Census: 1890. Washington, D.C.: Government Printing Office, 1894.
Commissioner of Indian Affairs. Annual Reports. Washington, D.C.: Government Printing Office, 1877–92.
Fletcher, Alice C. *Indian Education and Civilization.* Senate Executive Document no. 95. 48th Cong., 2d sess., ser. 2264. Washington, D.C.: Government Printing Office, 1888.
Riggs, Brett H. *Removal Period Cherokee Households and Communities in Southwestern North Carolina (1835–1838).* Raleigh, N.C.: North Carolina State Historic Preservation Office, 1996.
U.S. Congress. *Congressional Record.* Washington, D.C.: Government Printing Office, 1881–1902.

————. House Committee on Indian Affairs. *Lands to Indians in Severalty to Accompany Bill H.R. 6268*. 45th Cong., 3rd sess., 1879. H.R. Report No. 165.

————. House Committee on Indian Affairs. *Lands to Indians in Severalty to Accompany Bill H.R. 5038*. 46th Cong., 2nd sess., 1879. H.R. Report No. 1576.

————. House Committee on Indian Affairs. *Lands to Indians in Severalty to Accompany Bill S. 48*. 48th Cong., 2nd sess., 1884. H.R. Report No. 2247.

U.S. Senate. *Report of the Select Committee to Investigate Matters Connected with Affairs in the Indian Territory*. Washington, D.C.: Government Printing Office, 1907.

NEWSPAPERS

Adair County Republican (Bunch, Okla.)
Cherokee Advocate (Tahlequah, Okla.)
Daily Chieftain (Vinita, Okla.)
Daily Oklahoman (Oklahoma City, Okla.)
New Era (Stilwell, Okla.)
Standard-Sentinel (Stilwell, Okla.)

PUBLISHED PRIMARY SOURCES

Benge, Barbara L., comp. *The 1880 Cherokee National Census (Oklahoma)*. Bowie, Md.: Heritage Books, 2000.

————. *The 1890 Cherokee National Census (Oklahoma)*. Bowie, Md.: Heritage Books, 2007.

Cherokee History and Genealogy Research. Adair County Probates, 1901 to 1964, Including Westville Division. Stilwell, Okla.: Lepricon Software, a Division of JR Enterprises.

Duvall, Deborah L. *An Oral History of Tahlequah and the Cherokee Nation*. Chicago: Arcadia, 2000.

Fletcher, Alice C. "The Crowning Act." *Morning Star* 7 (March 1887): 1.

————. "The New Orleans Exhibition." *Southern Workman* 14 (1885): 79.

————. "Tribal Life among the Omahas." *Century Magazine* 51 (January 1896): 451–53.

Kilcup, Karen L., ed. *A Cherokee Woman's America: The Memoirs of Narcissa Owen, 1831–1907*. Gainesville: University of Florida Press, 2005.

Kilpatrick, Jack F., and Anna G. Kilpatrick. *Friends of Thunder: Folktales of the Oklahoma Cherokee*. 1964. Norman: University of Oklahoma Press, 1995.

Mankiller, Wilma, with Michael Wallis. *Mankiller: A Chief and Her People*. New York: St. Martin's Press, 1993.

Meriam, Lewis. *The Problem of Indian Administration*. Baltimore: Johns Hopkins University Press, 1928.

Mooney, James. *History, Myths, and Sacred Formulas of the Cherokees*. Ashville, N.C.: Historical Images, 1992.

Perdue, Theda, and Michael D. Green, eds. *The Cherokee Removal: A Brief History with Documents.* Boston: Bedford/St. Martin's, 1995.

Posey, Alexander. "Journal of a Creek Enrollment and Field Party, 1905." *Chronicles of Oklahoma* 46 (1968): 2–19.

Red Cross. "Approaching the Apex of Drought Relief." *Red Cross Courier,* March 2, 1931: 131.

———. "Red Cross Drought Relief Work in Seven States: Seed Distribution and Planting Goes Forward Rapidly." *Red Cross Courier,* October 15, 1930: 8.

———. "The Steady Flowing Stream of a Nation's Beneficence: An Index of the Sublimity of Selflessness." *Red Cross Courier,* March 2, 1931: 519–21.

Tyner, James W. *Those Who Cried: The 16,000.* N.p.: Thomason Company, 1992.

Women's National Indian Association. Annual Reports of the Women's National Indian Association. Philadelphia: n.p., 1884–87. N.p.: Clearwater Publishing Company, 1981; microfiche.

PUBLISHED SECONDARY SOURCES

Adair County History Committee. *The History of Adair County, Including Flint and Goingsnake Districts.* Cane Hill, Ark.: ARC Press of Cane Hill, 1991.

Allen, Paula Gunn. *The Sacred Hoop: Recovering the Feminine in American Indian Traditions.* 1986. Boston: Beacon Press, 1992.

Amnesty International. "Maze of Injustice: The Failure to Protect Indigenous Women from Violence." April 24, 2007. <http://www.amnestyusa.org/women/maze/report.pdf>.

Axtell, James. "Ethnohistory: A Historian's Viewpoint." *Ethnohistory* 26.1 (Winter 1979): 1–13.

———. *Natives and Newcomers: The Cultural Origins of North America.* Oxford: Oxford University Press, 2001.

Baird, W. David. "Are There Real Indians in Oklahoma? Historical Perspectives on the Five Civilized Tribes." *Chronicles of Oklahoma* 68.1 (1990): 4–23.

Baird, W. David, and Danney Goble. *Oklahoma: A History.* Norman: University of Oklahoma Press, 2008.

Bederman, Gail. *Manliness and Civilization: A Cultural History of Gender and Race in the United States, 1880–1917.* Chicago: University of Chicago Press, 1995.

Berkhofer, Robert F., Jr. *The White Man's Indian: Images of the American Indian from Columbus to the Present.* 1978. New York: Random House, 1979.

Berthrong, Donald J. *The Cheyenne and Arapaho Ordeal: Reservation and Agency Life in the Indian Territory, 1875–1907.* Norman: University of Oklahoma Press, 1976.

Biolsi, Thomas, and Larry J. Zimmerman, eds. *Indians and Anthropologists: Vine Deloria, Jr., and the Critique of Anthropology.* Tucson: University of Arizona Press, 1997.

Bohaker, Heidi. "Nindoodemag: The Significance of Algonquian Kinship Networks in the Eastern Great Lakes Region, 1600–1701." *William and Mary Quarterly* 63 (January 2006): 23–52.

Brady, Marilyn Dell. "The New Middle-Class Family (1815–1930)." In *American Families: A Research Guide and Historical Handbook*, edited by Joseph M. Hawes and Elizabeth I. Nybakken. New York: Greenwood Press, 1991. 82–123.

Brown, Loren N. "The Dawes Commission." *Chronicles of Oklahoma* 9 (1931): 71–105.

Carter, Kent. *The Dawes Commission and the Allotment of the Five Civilized Tribes.* Orem, Utah: Ancentry.com, 1999.

———. "Deciding Who Can Be Cherokee: Enrollment Records of the Dawes Commission." *Chronicles of Oklahoma* 69 (1991): 174–205.

Cole, Thomas. *The Journey of Life: A Cultural History of Aging in America.* Cambridge: Cambridge University Press, 1992.

Confer, Clarissa. *The Cherokee Nation in the Civil War.* Norman: University of Oklahoma Press, 2007.

Conley, Robert J. *The Cherokee Nation: A History.* Albuquerque: University of New Mexico Press, 2005.

Coontz, Stephanie. *The Way We Never Were: American Families and the Nostalgia Trap.* New York: Basic Books, 1992.

———. "Working Class Families, 1870–1890." In *American Families: A Multicultural Reader*, edited by Maya Parson Coontz and Gabrielle Raley. New York: Routledge, 1999. 94–127.

Dale, Edward Everett. "Two Mississippi Valley Frontiers." *Chronicles of Oklahoma* 26 (Winter 1948–49): 367–84.

Debo, Angie. *And Still the Waters Run: The Betrayal of the Five Civilized Tribes.* 1940. Princeton: Princeton University Press, 1972.

D'Emilio, John, and Estelle B. Freedman. *Intimate Matters: A History of Sexuality in America.* New York: Harper and Row, 1988.

Denson, Andrew. *Demanding the Cherokee Nation: Indian Autonomy and American Culture, 1830–1900.* Lincoln: University of Nebraska Press, 2004.

DuBois, Ellen Carol, and Lynn Dumenil. *Through Women's Eyes: An American History.* Boston: Bedford/St. Martin's, 2005.

Finger, John R. *The Eastern Band of Cherokees, 1819–1900.* Knoxville: University of Tennessee Press, 1984.

Foreman, Grant. *Indian Removal: The Emigration of the Five Civilized Tribes of Indians.* Norman: University of Oklahoma Press, 1974.

Fullerton, Eula. "Joseph Augustus Lawrence: 1856–1938." *Chronicles of Oklahoma* 17 (1939): 122–23.

Galloway, Patricia. *Practicing Ethnohistory: Mining Archives, Hearing Testimony, Constructing Narratives.* Lincoln: University of Nebraska Press, 2006.

Gans, Herbert. "Deconstructing the Underclass." In *Race, Class, and Gender in the United States: An Integrated Study*, edited by Paula S. Rothenberg. New York: Worth, 2001. 80–86.

Geertz, Clifford. "Thick Description: Toward an Interpretive Theory of Culture." In *The Interpretation of Cultures: Selected Essays.* New York: Basic Books, 1973. 3–30.

Gibson, Arrell Morgan. "The Centennial Legacy of the General Allotment Act." *Chronicles of Oklahoma* 65 (3): 228–51.

Green, Rayna. "The Pocahontas Perplex: The Image of Indian Women in American Culture." *Massachusetts Review* 16 (1975): 698–714.

Gulick, John. *Cherokees at the Crossroads*. Chapel Hill: Institute for Research in Social Science, University of North Carolina, 1960.

Hagan, William T. *The Indian Rights Association: The Herbert Welsch Years, 1882–1904*. Tucson: University of Arizona Press, 1985.

———. "Private Property, the Indian's Door to Civilization." *Ethnohistory* 3 (1956): 126–37.

———. *Taking Indian Lands: The Cherokee (Jerome) Commission*. Norman: University of Oklahoma Press, 2003.

———. *United States–Comanche Relations: The Reservation Years*. 2nd ed. Norman: University of Oklahoma Press, 1990.

Hatley, Tom. "Cherokee Women Farmers Hold Their Ground." In *Appalachian Frontiers: Settlement, Society, and Development in the Preindustrial Era*, edited by Robert D. Mitchell. Lexington: University of Kentucky Press, 1991. 37–51.

———. *The Dividing Paths: Cherokees and South Carolinians through the Era of the Revolution*. Oxford: Oxford University Press, 1993.

Hendrix, Janey B. *Redbird Smith and the Nighthawk Keetoowahs*. Park Hill, Okla.: Cross-Cultural Education Center, 1983.

Hill, Sarah H. *Weaving New Worlds: Southeastern Cherokee Women and Their Basketry*. Chapel Hill: University of North Carolina Press, 1997.

Hoxie, Frederick E. "Ethnohistory for a Tribal World." *Ethnohistory* 44.4 (Fall 1997): 595–615.

———. *A Final Promise: The Campaign to Assimilate the Indians, 1880–1920*. Lincoln: University of Nebraska Press, 1984. Reprint, Cambridge: Cambridge University Press, 1989.

———. *Parading through History: The Making of the Crow Nation in North America, 1805–1935*. 2nd ed. Cambridge: Cambridge University Press, 2008.

Hudson, Charles. "Cherokee Concept of Natural Balance." *Indian Historian* 3 (1970): 51–54.

———. *Knights of Spain, Warriors of the Sun: Hernando de Soto and the South's Ancient Chiefdoms*. Athens: University of Georgia Press, 1997.

———. *The Southeastern Indians*. Knoxville: University of Tennessee Press, 1976.

Jaimes, M. Annette, and Theresa Halsey. "American Indian Women: At the Center of Indigenous Resistance in Contemporary North America." In *The State of Native America: Genocide, Colonization, and Resistance*, edited by M. Annette James. Boston: South End Press, 1992. 310–44.

Johnston, Carolyn Ross. *Cherokee Women in Crisis: Trail of Tears, Civil War, and Allotment, 1838–1907*. Tuscaloosa: University of Alabama Press, 2003.

Justice, Daniel Heath. *Our Fires Survive the Storm: A Cherokee Literary History*. Minneapolis: University of Minnesota Press, 2006.

Kauanui, J. Kehaulani. *Hawaiian Blood: Colonialism and the Politics of Sovereignty and Indigeneity*. Durham: Duke University Press, 2008.

Kehoe, Alice B. "The Shackles of Tradition." In *The Hidden Half: Studies of Plains Indian Women*, edited by Patricia Albers and Beatrice Medicine. Washington, D.C.: University Press of America, 1983. 53–70.

Keller, Robert H. *American Protestantism and United States Indian Policy, 1869–1882*. Lincoln: University of Nebraska Press, 1983.

Krause, Robert. *An Environmental History of the Illinois River: Agriculture, Urban Development, and Recreation in Northeastern Oklahoma, 1818–2005*. Saarbrücken, Germany: VDM Verlag, 2008.

Littlefield, Daniel F. *Seminole Burning: A Story of Racial Vengeance*. Jackson: University Press of Mississippi, 1996.

Logan, Michael H., and Stephen D. Ousley. "Hypergamy, Quantum, and Reproductive Success: The Lost Indian Ancestor Reconsidered." In *Anthropologists and Indians in the New South*, edited by Rachel A. Bonney and J. Anthony Paredes. Tuscaloosa: University of Alabama Press, 2001. 184–202.

Lomawaima, K. Tsianina. *They Called It Prairie Light: The Story of Chilocco Indian School*. Lincoln: University of Nebraska Press, 1994.

Lynn-Sherow, Bonnie. *Red Earth: Race and Agriculture in Oklahoma Territory*. Lawrence: University Press of Kansas, 2004.

Mark, Joan. *Four Anthropologists: An American Science in Its Early Years*. New York: Science History Publications, 1980.

———. *A Stranger in Her Native Land: Alice Fletcher and the American Indians*. Lincoln: University of Nebraska Press, 1988.

McClintock, Anne. *Imperial Leather: Race, Gender, and Sexuality in the Colonial Contest*. New York: Routledge, 1995.

McIntosh, Kenneth W. "Chitto Harjo." In *Encyclopedia of North American Indians: Native American History, Culture, and Life from Paleo-Indians to the Present*, edited by Frederick E. Hoxie. Boston: Houghton Mifflin, 1996. 231–34.

McLoughlin, William. *Champions of the Cherokees: Evan and John B. Jones*. Princeton: Princeton University Press, 1990.

———. *Cherokee Renascence in the New Republic*. Princeton: Princeton University Press, 1990.

———. *Cherokees and Missionaries, 1789–1839*. New Haven: Yale University Press, 1984.

Meserve, John Bartlett. "Chief Dennis Wolf Bushyhead." *Chronicles of Oklahoma* 14 (1936): 349–59.

———. "Chief William Potter Ross." *Chronicles of Oklahoma* 15 (1937): 21–29.

Mihesuah, Devon A. *Cultivating the Rosebuds: The Education of Women at the Cherokee Female Seminary, 1851–1909*. Urbana: University of Illinois Press, 1997.

Mihesuah, Devon A., and Angela Cavender Wilson. *Natives and Academics: Research and Writing about American Indians*. Lincoln: University of Nebraska Press, 1998.

Miles, Tiya. "'Circular Reasoning': Recentering Cherokee Women in the Antiremoval Campaigns." *American Quarterly* 61.2 (June 2009): 221–43.

Miner, H. Craig. *The Corporation and the Indian: Tribal Sovereignty and Industrial Civilization in Indian Territory, 1865–1907*. Columbia: University of Missouri Press, 1976.

Mintz, Stephen, and Susan Kellogg. *Domestic Revolutions: A Social History of American Family Life.* New York: Free Press, 1988.

Morris, John W., Charles R. Goins, and Edwin C. McReynolds. *Historical Atlas of Oklahoma.* 3rd ed. Norman: University of Oklahoma, 1986.

Newman, Louise M. *White Women's Rights: The Racial Origins of Feminism in the United States.* New York: Oxford University Press, 1999.

O'Neill, Coleen. *Working the Navajo Way: Labor and Culture in the Twentieth Century.* Lawrence: University Press of Kansas, 2005.

Osburn, Katherine M. B. *Southern Ute Women: Autonomy and Assimilation on the Reservation, 1887–1934.* Albuquerque: University of New Mexico Press, 1998.

Otis, D. S. *The Dawes Act and the Allotment of Indian Lands.* Edited by Francis Paul Prucha. 1934. Norman: University of Oklahoma Press, 1973.

Parins, James W. *Elias Cornelius Boudinot: A Life on the Cherokee Frontier.* Lincoln: University of Nebraska Press, 2006.

Pascoe, Peggy. *Relations of Rescue: The Search for Female Moral Authority in the American West, 1874–1939.* New York: Oxford University Press, 1991.

————. *What Comes Naturally: Miscegenation Law and the Making of Race in America.* Oxford: Oxford University Press, 2009.

Perdue, Theda. "Cherokee Relations with the Iroquois in the Eighteenth Century." In *Beyond the Covenant Chain: The Iroquois and Their Neighbors in Indian North America, 1600–1800,* edited by Daniel K. Richter and James H. Merrell. Syracuse, N.Y.: Syracuse University Press, 1987. 135–49.

————. *Cherokee Women: Gender and Culture Change, 1700–1835.* Lincoln: University of Nebraska Press, 1998.

————. "Columbus Meets Pocahontas in the American South." *Southern Cultures* 3 (1997): 4–21.

————. *"Mixed Blood" Indians: Racial Construction in the Early South.* Athens: University of Georgia Press, 2003.

Piker, Joshua. *Okfuskee: A Creek Indian Town in Colonial America.* Cambridge: Harvard University Press, 2004.

Priest, Loring Benson. *Uncle Sam's Stepchildren: The Reformation of United States Indian Policy, 1865–1887.* 1942. Lincoln: University of Nebraska Press, 1969.

Prucha, Francis Paul. *American Indian Policy in Crisis: Christian Reformers and the Indian, 1865–1900.* Norman: University of Oklahoma Press, 1975.

————. *The Great Father: The United States Government and the Indians.* Unabridged ed. Vols. 1 and 2. Lincoln: University of Nebraska Press, 1984.

Reid, John Phillip. *A Law of Blood: The Primitive Law of the Cherokee Nation.* New York: New York University Press, 1970.

Richter, Daniel K. *The Ordeal of the Longhouse: The Peoples of the Iroquois League in the Era of European Colonization.* Chapel Hill: University of North Carolina Press, 1992.

Rogers, Mary Evelyn. *Ani-Yun-Wiya: A Brief History of the Cherokee Nation, 1540–1906.* Baltimore: Gateway Press, 1986.

Sattler, Richard. "Women's Status among the Muskogee and Cherokee." In *Women and Power in Native North America*, edited by Laura F. Klein and Lillian Ackerman. Norman: University of Oklahoma Press, 1995. 214–29.

Saunt, Claudio. *Black, White, and Indian: Race and the Unmaking of an American Family.* Oxford: Oxford University Press, 2005.

Savage, William W. *The Cherokee Strip Livestock Association.* Columbia: University of Missouri Press, 1973.

Schultz, Jack M. *The Seminole Baptist Churches of Oklahoma: Maintaining a Traditional Community.* Norman: University of Oklahoma Press, 1999.

Seward, Rudy Ray. *The American Family: A Demographic History.* Beverly Hills: Sage, 1978.

Shadburn, Don L. *Cherokee Planters in Georgia, 1832–1838: Historical Essays on Eleven Counties in the Cherokee Nation of Georgia.* Roswell, Ga.: W. H. Wolfe Associates, 1900.

Shoemaker, Nancy. *American Indian Population Recovery in the Twentieth Century.* Albuquerque: University of New Mexico Press, 1999.

———. "The Rise or Fall of Iroquois Women." *Journal of Women's History* 2 (1991): 39–57.

Smith, Linda Tuhiwai. *Decolonizing Methodologies: Research and Indigenous Peoples.* Dunedin, New Zealand: University of Otago Press, 1999.

Sober, Nancy Hope. *The Intruders: The Illegal Residents of the Cherokee Nation, 1866–1907.* Ponca City, Okla.: Cherokee Books, 1991.

Stremlau, Rose. "'To Domesticate and Civilize Wild Indians': Allotment and the Campaign to Reform Indian Families, 1875–1887." *Journal of Family History* 30.3 (July 2005): 265–86.

Strickland, Rennard. *Fire and the Spirits: Cherokee Law from Clan to Court.* Norman: University of Oklahoma Press, 1982.

———. *The Indians in Oklahoma.* Norman: University of Oklahoma Press, 1990.

Sturm, Circe. *Blood Politics: Race, Culture, and Identity in the Cherokee Nation of Oklahoma.* Berkeley: University of California Press, 2002.

Tengan, Ty P. Kāwika. *Native Men Remade: Gender and Nation in Contemporary Hawai'i.* Durham: Duke University Press, 2008.

Thomas, Robert K. "The Redbird Smith Movement." *Symposium Cherokee and Iroquois Culture.* Edited by William N. Fenton and John Gulick. Smithsonian Institution Bureau of Ethnology, Bulletin 180. Washington, D.C.: Government Printing Office, 1961. 161–66.

Thorne, Tanis C. *The World's Richest Indian: The Scandal over Jackson Barnett's Oil Fortune.* Oxford: Oxford University Press, 2005.

Thornton, Russell. *The Cherokees: A Population History.* Lincoln: University of Nebraska Press, 1992.

Tortorelli, R. L. "Floods and Droughts: Oklahoma." Water Supply Paper 2375. U.S. Geologic Survey, National Water Summary, 1899–89.

Trexler, Richard C. *Sex and Conquest: Gendered Violence, Political Order, and the European Conquest of the Americas.* Ithaca: Cornell University Press, 1995.

Unrau, William E. *Mixed-Bloods and Tribal Dissolution: Charles Curtis and the Quest for Indian Identity.* Lawrence: University Press of Kansas, 1989.

Wahrhaftig, Albert L. "Community and the Caretakers." *New University Thought* 4 (1966): 54–76.

———. "Institution Building among Oklahoma's Traditional Cherokees." In *Four Centuries of Southern Indians*, edited by Charles Hudson. Athens: University of Georgia Press, 1975. 132–49.

———. "Making Due with Dark Meat: A Report on the Cherokee Indians in Oklahoma." In *American Indian Economic Development*, edited by Sam Stanley. The Hague: Mouton, 1978. 409–510.

———. "The Tribal Cherokee Population of Eastern Oklahoma." *Current Anthropology* 9 (1968): 510–18.

Wallace, Anthony F. C. *The Death and Rebirth of the Seneca.* New York: Vintage, 1972.

Warde, Mary Jane. *George Washington Grayson and the Creek Nation, 1843–1920.* Norman: University of Oklahoma Press, 1999.

Wardell, Morris L. *A Political History of the Cherokee Nation, 1838–1907.* Norman: University of Oklahoma Press, 1980.

Washburn, Wilcomb E. *The Assault on Indian Tribalism: The General Allotment Law (Dawes Act) of 1887.* Philadelphia: J. B. Lippincott, 1975.

Wishart, David J. *An Unspeakable Sadness: The Dispossession of the Nebraska Indians.* Lincoln: University of Nebraska Press, 1994.

Wright, Muriel H. *A Guide to the Indian Tribes of Oklahoma.* Norman: University of Oklahoma Press, 1951.

———. "The Wedding of Oklahoma and Miss Indian Territory." *Chronicles of Oklahoma* 35 (Fall 1957): 255–64.

Yarbrough, Fay A. *Race and the Cherokee Nation: Sovereignty in the Nineteenth Century.* Philadelphia: University of Pennsylvania Press, 2008.

UNPUBLISHED SECONDARY SOURCES

Burgess, Larry E. "The Lake Mohonk Conference on the Indians, 1883–1916." Ph.D. diss., Claremont University, 1972.

Cartwright, Charles Edward. "The Board of Indian Commissioners: Hope, Failure, and Abandonment, 1869–1887." M.A. thesis, University of Arizona, 1980.

Coates, Julia. "A Family of Families: Community and Identity among the Cherokee Nation's Diasporic Citizens." Talk given to the Native American and Indigenous Studies Association. May 22, 2010.

———. "'None of Us Are Supposed to Be Here': Ethnicity, Nationality, and the Production of Cherokee Histories." Ph.D. diss., University of New Mexico, 2002.

Faulkner, Sandra McDermott. "U.S. Board of Indian Commissioners, 1869–1887." M.A. thesis, University of Oregon, 1984.

Fritz, Henry. "The Humanitarian Background of Indian Reform, 1860–1890." Ph.D. diss., University of Minnesota, 1956.

Goodwin, Gary. "Cherokees in Transition: A Study of Changing Culture and Environment Prior to 1775." Ph.D. diss., University of Chicago, 1977.

Odell, Marcia Larson. "Divide and Conquer: Allotment among the Cherokee." Ph.D. diss., Cornell University, 1975.

Smith, Benny. "The Keetoowah Society of Cherokee Indians." M.A. thesis, Northwestern State College, 1967.

————. "A Perspective of the Clans." Author's collection.

Theisen, Terri Christian. "'With a View toward Their Civilization': Women and the Work of Indian Reform." M.A. thesis, Portland State University, 1996.

Thomas, Robert K. "The Origin and Development of the Redbird Smith Movement." Ph.D. diss., University of Arizona, 1953.

Thompson, Gregory Coyne. "The Origins and Implementation of the American Indian Reform Movement, 1867–1912." Ph.D. diss., University of Utah, 1981.

Wahrhaftig, Albert L. "In the Aftermath of Civilization." Ph.D. diss., University of Chicago, 1975.

Wanken, Helen M. "'Women's Sphere' and Indian Reform: The Women's National Indian Association, 1879–1901." Ph.D. diss., Marquette University, 1981.

White, Max. "An Ethnoarchaeological Approach to Cherokee Subsistence and Settlement Patterns." Ph.D. diss., Indiana University, 1980.

DOCUMENTARIES

Indians, Outlaws, and Angie Debo. Directed by Martha Sandlin. PBS, *The American Experience*, 1988.

Index

~✷✶~

Cobell settlement, 6–7, 244
Coke bill, 103, 270 (nn. 52, 56)
Collier, John, 238
Commissioner of Indian Affairs. *See* Office
 of Indian Affairs
Commissioner to the Five Civilized Tribes,
 187
Competency, 192–94
Corn, 24–25, 63, 232, 242–44
Corruption, 150–51, 163–64, 170–71, 175–76,
 188, 261 (n. 9). *See also* Guardians
Craig County, 133, 195
Crazy Snake Rebellion, 169
Creeks, 36, 72, 146, 157, 166–69, 171, 177, 190
Crittenden, family of Annie and Sam, 55,
 124, 196–97, 218. *See also* Crittenden,
 family of Jennie and Nelson; Youngbird,
 family of Nancy and Isaac
Crittenden, family of Catherine and Aaron,
 57
Crittenden, family of Jennie and Nelson,
 26, 54–55, 57, 165, 174, 202–3, 207, 218,
 220–21, 223, 225. *See also* Batt, William;
 Huckleberry family; Wolfe, family of
 Nannie and Tom
Crittenden, family of Minnie and Mose,
 53, 97–98, 117, 123, 205. *See also* Proctor,
 family of Rebecca and Zeke
Cult of true womanhood, 52, 71, 81, 87
Curtis, Charles, 153
Curtis Act, 5, 104, 106–7, 153–57, 177–78, 187

Dale, Edward Everett, 179
Daniel Redbird v. United States, 146
Dawes, Henry L., 73, 85, 89–90, 155, 238
Dawes Act, 4, 89–90, 103–4, 110
Dawes Commission, 5, 246–47; records
 of, 10–11, 15–16, 249–50; enrollment of
 Cherokees, 54, 103–26, 127–48, 203–4;
 allotment of land, 149–76, 192; manage-
 ment of allotments, 185–87, 222–23
Dawes roll, 105–26, 156, 249; compilation
 of, 112–13, 127–48; purpose of, 110–12,
 127–28, 135
Debo, Angie, 16–17, 111, 150, 180, 185, 195–96,
 295 (n. 2)
Deloria, Vine, Jr., 255 (n. 21)
Denson, Andrew, 94
Department of the Interior, 5–7, 71, 73, 111,
 154–55, 187, 194, 198, 228, 237. *See also*
 Office of Indian Affairs

Dick, Jensie, 62
Dick, J. Henry, 188
Disease, 25–26, 191
Division of Survey and Appraisement,
 155–56
Divorce, 54–55, 122–23, 131–33
Documentation: of marriage and divorce,
 53, 119–23, 206–7; of birth, 113–16; of
 death, 116–18, 206–7, 236; of allotment
 and land ownership, 161, 176–77, 180; of
 paternity, 206; of military service, 259
 (n. 68)
Dog, family of Nannie and Steve, 12, 16, 27,
 51–52, 58–59, 61, 64, 149–50, 165, 206,
 225. *See also* Proctor, Sarah
Doris Duke Collection, 11, 215, 251
Dougherty, family of Mary Dean and
 James, Jr., 34
Downing, Dan, 43, 56, 138–39, 175, 226. *See
 also* Sand, family of Noah
Downing, Joe, 199
Drought, 211, 213

Eastern Band of Cherokees, 21, 33, 92, 119,
 119
Eastern Cherokee roll. *See* Guion Million
 Commission
Education: Cherokee Nation schools, 63–65,
 98–100, 263 (n. 43); after statehood,
 207–10
Elders, 6, 24, 46–47, 55, 134, 159, 218–19,
 221–22; marginalization of by Dawes
 Commission, 136–38, 173–74
Ellijay River, 26
Enrollment, 105–26; cards, 112–13
Erosion, 210–11, 213
Ethnohistorical methodology, 9
Etowah River, 26, 28, 31
Exendine, A. A., 184
Extended family households, 45–49, 220

Fields family, 45, 219
Five Tribes, 72–73, 90, 93, 102–3, 151–52,
 166, 187
Five Tribes Bill, 142, 165, 185
Fletcher, Alice C., 76, 111, 245, 268 (n. 18)
Folsom, Melvina, 45, 51, 245. *See also*
 Kelley, family of Nellie and Joel
Foltz, W. E., 196
Foreman, family of James and Catherine,
 262 (n. 35)

INDEX 315

Indian Territory, 32–39, 135, 153, 155, 166, 178, 237, 250
Intermarriage, 13–15, 27–35, 40–42, 44–46, 48–51, 119–22, 137–38, 143–46, 164, 225–26
Intruders, 33, 40, 101–2

Jeh-si, 26, 28
Jerome Commission, 103
Joe Chewey School, 64
Johnson, Caty, 34. *See also* Raper, family of Mary and Jesse
Johnston, Carolyn Ross, 17, 52, 260 (n. 72)
Jones, Evan, 65, 67, 189
Justice, Daniel Heath, 256 (n. 28)

Kansas, 37
Kauanui, J. Kehaulani, 18
Keetoowah Society, 13, 63, 66–67, 107, 145–47, 154–55, 165, 168, 186–87
Kehoe, Alice Beck, 268 (n. 19)
Kelley, family of Nellie and Joel, 31, 45, 54–55, 64. *See also* Quinton, family of Lydia and Samuel, Jr.
Kelley, family of Susan and John, 144, 159, 162, 196, 204–5, 209, 212, 219, 221, 223, 230, 296 (n. 13). *See also* Kelley, family of Nellie and Joel
Kilpatrick, Jack and Anna, 242–44
Kingfisher, Catherine, 12
Kinney, J. F., 88
Kinship, 4, 17–18, 22–24, 27, 50–51, 75–90, 169–70, 182–83, 217–19; persistence of behaviors associated with, 39, 43, 67, 212, 214, 216, 230; and selection of allotments, 149, 157–61
Kirk, family of Laura and William, 45, 143, 144, 196, 204, 209, 225, 233, 234; Sam, 139, 193–94, 219. *See also* Kelley, family of Nellie and Joel
Krause, Robert, 232

Lacie, Adam, 53, 122–25, 143, 173, 283 (n. 28)
Lake Mohonk Conference, 71–72
Land, 83–92; sale of, 2, 193, 199, 207, 211, 227–32, 235; probate of, 2, 199–200, 202–3, 207, 216, 250; communal owner-ship of, 92–103; categorization of, 156; renting or lease of (including mineral resources), 183, 184, 193, 197–98, 218–23, 233, 255 (n. 13)
Lee, Wash, 62–63

Lewis, family of Hattie Holland, 35–36, 59, 117, 143, 150, 159, 162, 165, 204, 231–32
Literacy, 29–30, 63–64, 99, 113–14, 187–88, 203–5, 207–10
Logan, Michael H., 50
Lomawaima, K. Tsianina, 17
Lowery, George, 37
Luna Branch, 175
Lynn-Sherow, Bonnie, 151, 160

Mankiller, Wilma, 18, 244
Manning, Johnson, 233
Manus, Richard, 93, 227, 237
Marriage, 53–59, 121–22, 131–35, 178–79, 197–98, 201–2, 226
Marrs, David, 188, 194–95
Matrilineality, 24, 43–47, 54–56, 59, 218–21, 231–32
Matrilocality, 44–46, 59, 220–21
Mayes, Joel B., 92, 94, 96, 100–101, 103
Mayes, Samuel H., 69, 94, 96, 101, 154
McClintock, Anne, 79
McDaniel family, 27, 30, 40–42
McKinley, William, 153
McLoughlin, William, 39, 260 (n. 72)
Men, Cherokee, 55–56, 60, 69, 120–21, 227, 237; labor, 29, 55–56, 60, 120–21, 225; bachelorhood, 48–49, 158–59, 223–24; critique of traditional roles, 77–82, 84–89
Meriam, Lewis, 237
Meriam Report, 237, 239
Midwives, 108, 114–15, 124
Migration, 60, 119–21, 212, 219–21. *See also* Removal
Mihesuah, Devon, 52, 155 (n. 26)
Miles, Tiya, 172
Miner, H. Craig, 150
Mitchell, family of Rachel and Reese, Sr., 44, 46, 51–52, 53, 58–59, 149, 161; John, 149, 162, 218
Mixed bloods. *See* Blood quantum
Mooney, James, 21
Morgan, Thomas Jefferson, 86–87
Morris, John B., 123
Mounce, family of Rosanna and Joe, 51, 55, 61, 122, 127–28, 131–32, 144, 159, 162–63, 204, 209; Ellis, 207, 223. *See also* Kelley, family of Nellie and Joel
Mounce, family of Susie and George, 218, 223, 225. *See also* Crittenden, family of Jennie and Nelson

Sam, Creek, 166
Sand, family of Noah, 44, 48–49, 124,
    138–39, 165, 175, 221–22, 228, 232; Will,
    56, 209, 234
Sand, family of Steve, 48, 125, 190, 209,
    210–11, 218, 232, 234. *See also* Sand, fam-
    ily of Noah
Saunt, Claudio, 255 (n. 26)
Schultz, Jack M., 10, 15
Scott, Charlie, 166
Second Indian Home Guard, 37–38
Secretary of the Interior. *See* Department of
    the Interior
Sells, Cato, 196
Selu and Kana'ti, 21–22, 41, 242–43
Seminoles, 72, 167
Sequoyah (state), 178
Seven Clan Rule. *See* Traditional Cherokee
    spirituality
Seven Clans Society, 214, 232, 241–42
Sexuality, 52–53, 56–59, 80–81, 111–12,
    128–35, 205–6, 225–26
Shadburn, Don L., 257 (n. 24)
Shannon, D. H., 180–84
Shoemaker, Nancy, 81, 273 (n. 123)
Siblings, relationships among, 43, 48, 121,
    159, 222–23, 229, 233
Siquanid, 242–43
Sixkiller, Bluford, 64
Sixkiller, family of Kate and Soldier, 47,
    49, 63
Sixkiller, family of Margaret and Abe, 47, 57,
    65–66, 123–24, 143, 165, 174, 201–2, 205,
    209, 222, 228–29, 233, 278 (n. 20); Dennis,
    180–84, 225–26. *See also* Crittenden,
    family of Catherine and Aaron; Sixkiller,
    family of Kate and Soldier
Skinner, Thomas, 89
Slavery, 29, 77
Smallwood, Joseph, 267 (n. 1)
Smiley, Albert K., 71
Smith, Bill, 54, 132
Smith, Chadwick, 5–6, 244
Smith, George, 167, 170
Smith, J. E., 195
Smith, Jesse, 54, 132
Smith, John, 167
Smith, Redbird, 145, 166–70, 177, 200
Snell, Maria, 218
Sourjohn, Joe, 254 (n. 2)
Sourjohn, Lewis, 1

South Carolina, 23
Sovereignty, 110, 247, 276 (n. 164)
Squatters, 171, 191
Starr, Belle, 97
Stephens v. Cherokee Nation, 154
Stilwell, 173, 187, 197, 199, 205, 213
Stilwell Standard Sentinel, 11
Stomp grounds. *See* Traditional Cherokee
    spirituality
Strickland, Rennard, 151
Sturm, Circe, 148, 277 (n. 5)
Suake, family of Betsy and Yellowhammer,
    12, 38, 47, 52–53, 114, 123, 137, 141, 165,
    172–73, 204, 206–7, 209, 222, 226, 299
    (n. 89); Nannie Palone and sons, 58,
    132–33, 176, 188, 194–95, 234; Lawyer,
    202, 225. *See also* Proctor, Sarah
Suake, family of Tom, 53, 56, 63, 123,
    134–35, 141, 175, 191–92, 209, 222, 226,
    230. *See also* Suake, family of Betsy and
    Yellowhammer
Sulleteskee, Crust, 218
Sulphur Springs, 166–67
Sunday, Jesse, 54, 59
Superintendence for the Five Civilized
    Tribes, 180, 187, 190, 197–99, 211, 239, 250
Suwagee, family of Nakey, 261 (n. 10)
Swimmer, Thomas, 197–98

Tahlequah, 74, 112, 157–58, 187, 190, 199, 247
Tarepin, Catherine, 63
Taylor, Elizabeth, 262 (n. 35)
Taylor, family of Jennie and Andrew, 27,
    28, 30, 32
Taylor, family of Mary Ann and David, 27, 32
Teehee, Stephen, 96
Teller, Henry, 102–4
Tengan, Ty P. Kawika, 79
Tennessee, 23, 27, 32–33
Texas, 33, 37
Thomas, Robert K., 92–93, 167, 169
Thomas-Rogers Act, 238
Thompson, Charles, 119
Thornton, Russell, 30, 50, 143
Towns: in Old Nation, 23–26, 257 (n. 9); in
    Indian Territory, 169–70
Trade and commerce, 2, 62, 183–84, 190, 234;
    and extension of credit, 190–91, 234–37
Traditional Cherokee spirituality, 145, 152,
    165–70, 177, 246–47
Trail of Tears. *See* Removal

Treaties, 108, 273 (n. 121); Treaty of
Hopewell, 26, 67; Treaty of New Echota,
31; Treaty of Washington, 32
Tulsa, 211
Turtle, family of Fannie and Arch, 27,
49, 52, 124, 184, 218, 220, 224, 231, 233;
Charlotte, 53, 197, 199–200, 280 (n. 46);
Charley, 190–91, 209, 220. *See also*
Proctor, Sarah
Tyner, J. W., 215–16

Union Agency, 176, 187, 191
United Keetoowah Band, 10
U.S. census, 111, 144, 203–4, 216, 220, 222,
226, 249–50
U.S. Congress, 69, 74, 90, 94, 102–4, 107,
110–11, 153, 178, 194, 237–38
U.S. courts, 146, 147, 154, 156, 164, 177, 250
U.S. Geological Survey, 155–56, 250
U.S. marshals, 147, 177

Valley River, 27
Vann, family of Nancy and Joe, 220
Vann, "Rich" Joe, 31
Vian, 177
Vice, 80–81
Vinita, 157, 188, 195
Vinita Indian Chieftain, 11, 188

Wahrhaftig, Albert L., 60, 208, 232, 241
Walkingstick, Simon, 105–9, 125, 143, 172
Wampum belts, 167–68
War, 25–26, 36, 60, 192, 184, 215, 257 (n. 21).
See also Civil War
Ward, family of Nancy and Bryan, 12, 53
Washington, Elizabeth and John, 45
Water, 23, 26, 237 (n. 22)
Watie, Stand, 31, 38, 67
Watts (town), 202
Welch, family of Cleo and James Mack, 46,
58, 138, 159, 213, 221, 223. *See also* Welch,
family of Nancy and George, Jr.
Welch, family of Dovie and John, 116, 118,
122, 219, 221, 223, 231, 234. *See also* Welch,
family of Lizzie and George
Welch, family of Emma and Mack, 118, 158,
160, 196, 213, 219, 221, 230–31. *See also*
Welch, family of Lizzie and George

Welch, family of Fannie and Tom, 44, 46,
57–58, 66, 131–32, 144, 159, 162, 184, 205,
213, 220–21, 223; Maud Hess, 236. *See also*
Welch, family of Nancy and George, Jr.
Welch, family of Lizzie and George, 50, 97,
118, 219. *See also* Welch, family of Mary
and Less
Welch, family of Margaret and George, Sr.,
28, 29, 30, 34–35, 57
Welch, family of Mary and Less (Lemuel),
35. *See also* Welch, family of Margaret
and George, Sr.
Welch, family of Nancy and George, Jr.,
34–35, 46, 50, 58, 138, 221. *See also* Welch,
family of Margaret and George, Sr.
Welch, Moses, 97, 118, 213, 221, 236. *See also*
Welch, family of Lizzie and George
Welch, Sam, 184–85
Westville, 112, 122, 201, 205, 235–36
Wheeler-Howard Act, 238
White Path. *See* Traditional Cherokee
spirituality
Whitmire, White, 98
Wilson, family of Bettie and Jim, 3, 219
Wolf, Nellie and Jack, 61–62
Wolf, Richard, 146
Wolfe, family of Dora and John, 1–2, 55,
58–60, 64, 67–68, 149–50, 203–4, 220,
222–23, 225, 239. *See also* Dog, family
of Nannie and Steve; Wolfe, family of
Nannie and Tom
Wolfe, family of Nannie and Tom, 1–3,
54–55, 59–60, 142, 165, 174, 205, 215, 220,
222–25, 281 (n. 66)
Women, Cherokee, 18, 47, 52–59, 140–41,
182–83, 233–34; and property ownership,
51–52, 171–74, 228–29, 231; critique of
traditional roles of, 76–82
Women's National Indian Association
(WNIA), 71–72, 80, 87–88, 129
Work, Hubert, 237
Wright, Jess, 62
Wright, Muriel H., 277 (n. 5)

Yarbrough, Fay A., 255 (n. 26), 280 (n. 45)
Young, Roach, 267 (n. 1)
Youngbird, family of Nancy and Isaac, 55,
124, 218